Magritte A to Z

Edited by Christoph Grunenberg and
Darren Pih with contributions from:

Patricia Allmer
Manchester Metropolitan University

Xavier Canonne
Musée de la Photographie, Charleroi

Krzysztof Fijalkowski
Norwich University College of the Arts

Gisela Fischer
Albertina, Vienna

Christoph Grunenberg
Tate Liverpool

Neil Matheson
University of Westminster

Darren Pih
Tate Liverpool

Ian Walker
University of Wales, Newport

John C. Welchman
University of California, San Diego

MAGRITTE

A to Z

Tate Publishing

6 Absence
6 Abstraction
8 *Alice in Wonderland*
9 Anonymity
9 Apple
10 Appropriation
12 Artifice
12 Automatism and Automatic Writing

14 Banality
14 Georges Bataille
16 Charles Baudelaire
17 Belgium
18 *Bilboquet*
21 Book Illustration
21 André Bosmans
22 Bottles
22 Victor and Pierre Bourgeois
24 Bowler Hat
28 André Breton
28 Marcel Broodthaers
29 *Bulletin international du surréalisme*

30 Cabinet of Curiosities
31 Le Centaure
32 Chance
32 Giorgio de Chirico
32 Clouds
35 Paul Colinet
36 Collage
36 Colour
40 Commercial Art
43 Communism
45 *Correspondance*
45 Cubism
45 Curtain

46 Dada
46 Salvador Dalí
46 Paul Delvaux
46 Jacques Derrida
46 Detective Stories
49 *Distances*
49 *The Dominion of Light*
51 Double
53 Drawing
54 Dreams
54 Marcel Duchamp

56 Elective Affinities
57 Paul Éluard
57 England
59 James Ensor
59 Max Ernst
59 Eroticism
64 Ersatz
65 Eye

66 Fantômas
69 Female Form
69 Fetish
70 *The Fidelity of Images*
73 Film
74 Fire
74 Forgery
77 Michel Foucault
77 Frame
85 Sigmund Freud
85 Futurism

86 Camille Goemans

86 Martin Heidegger

87 Alexandre Iolas

88 Edward James
88 Juxtaposition

90 Kitsch
91 Knokke Casino Mural

92 Language
94 Marcel Lecomte
95 Legacy
98 Letters
98 London Gallery
98 *The Lost Jockey*

100 Georgette Magritte
100 Léopold and Régina Magritte
101 Paul Magritte
101 Mannequin
103 Marcel Mariën
104 *Marie: Journal bimensuel pour la belle jeunesse*
104 Mask and Masquerade
105 Meaning
108 George Melly
113 John and Dominique de Menil
113 E.L.T. Mesens
113 Metamorphosis
114 Joan Miró
114 Mirror
114 Moon
116 Music scores
117 Mystery

118 Jacqueline Nonkels
118 Paul Nougé

120 **Object**
122 *Objet trouvé*
122 *Œsophage*

123 **Paris**
123 **Parody and Pastiche**
124 **Pattern**
125 **Roland Penrose**
128 *Période*
128 **The Petrified Image**
132 **Philosophy**
134 **Photography**
136 **Francis Picabia**
136 **Pipe**
140 **Pleasure**
140 **Edgar Allan Poe**
141 **Poetry**
141 **Portraiture**
149 **Postcards**
151 **Psychoanalysis**

152 **Renoir Period**
152 **Repetition and the Encounter**
158 **Representation and Resemblance**
160 *La Révolution surréaliste*
161 *Rhétorique*
161 **Alain Robbe-Grillet**

162 **Scale**
162 **Sculpture**
162 **Louis Scutenaire and Irène Hamoir**
164 **Self-Reference and Self-Portraiture**
165 **Victor Servranckx**
166 *7 Arts*
166 **Shock**
166 **Shop Window Display**
168 **Surrealism and Surrealists**
169 **David Sylvester**

170 **Yves Tanguy**
170 **Theatrical Display**
170 **Titles**
175 **Harry Torczyner**
175 *The Treachery of Images*
177 **Trompe l'oeil**

178 **Vache Period**
178 **Geert Van Bruaene**
178 **Paul-Gustave Van Hecke**
179 *Variétés*
183 **Violence**
183 **Visual Fracture**

184 **Wallpaper**
184 **Jacques Wergifosse**
184 **Window**
186 **World War II**

188 **Zwanzeur**

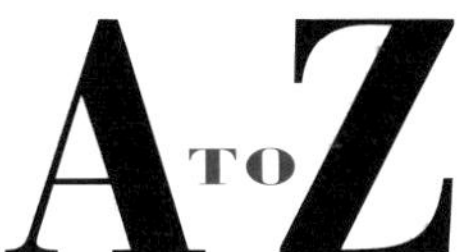

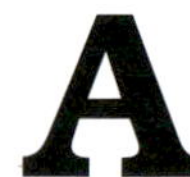

A

Absence, or rather making absence present, is a persistent concern in Magritte's oeuvre. Magritte uses absence/presence to query conventional perceptions of word and image. This is evident in paintings such as *Man with a Newspaper* 1928, where the only difference in four otherwise identical images is the presence of a man with a newspaper in one of the scenes. Magritte here queries the relationship between word and image, since the 'man with a newspaper' might be absent from three of the four pictorial images, but is present in the title of the work. Magritte also explores absence to challenge conventional perceptions of representation. In *Blood-Letting* 1938–9, he represents a frame which seemingly contains the bare brick wall beyond. Magritte states: 'Behind the colours in the pictures is the canvas. Behind the canvas there is a wall, behind the wall there is … etc. Visible things always hide other visible things. But a visible image hides nothing.'[1] When asked the reason for painting a brick wall, Magritte replied: 'I was wondering at the time what would be absolutely forbidden to show in a picture.'[2] What is absolutely forbidden is to show the absence of reality 'behind the painting', behind **representation**. As Jean Baudrillard comments, it is 'dangerous to unmask images, since they dissimulate the fact that there is nothing behind them'.[3]

Magritte unmasks the conventional and traditional role of art as asserting presence and permanence, revealing the truth of art as an assertion of absence and impermanence. This is evident in *Perspective: David's Madame Récamier* 1951. Here David's sitter is replaced with a coffin, a symbolic assertion of absence from the image. What is revealed is that far from painting being able to assert presence and timelessness, it is the very medium which reveals absence and impermanence. **(PA)**

See also: **Anonymity**

Abstraction: Magritte was an abstract painter in the style of **Cubism** and Fauvism up until his encounter with the work of **Giorgio de Chirico** in the mid-1920s. He subsequently came to find the idea of creating an image abstracted or separated from a real object abhorrent, writing of the 'age-old stupidity … when the art of painting was replaced by so-called abstract, non-figurative, or formless art – which consists in depositing the "material" on a surface with varying degrees of fantasy and conviction'.[4] For Magritte an exclusive concern with aesthetics would put distance between the viewer and the poetic thought he hoped to express in his work. In the late 1920s, however, Magritte can be seen to engage with strategies of abstraction, particularly in his

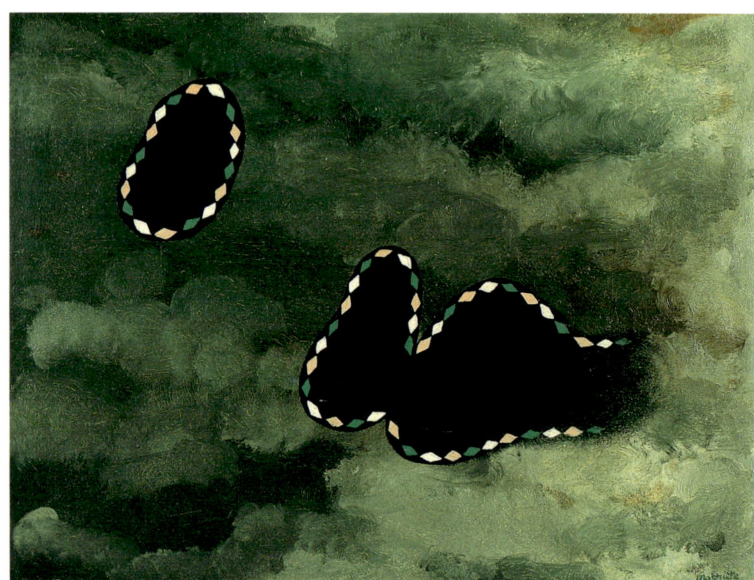

The Apparition
L'Apparition 1928,
oil on canvas, 54 × 73 cm.
Foundation Challenges,
Netherlands, CR 264

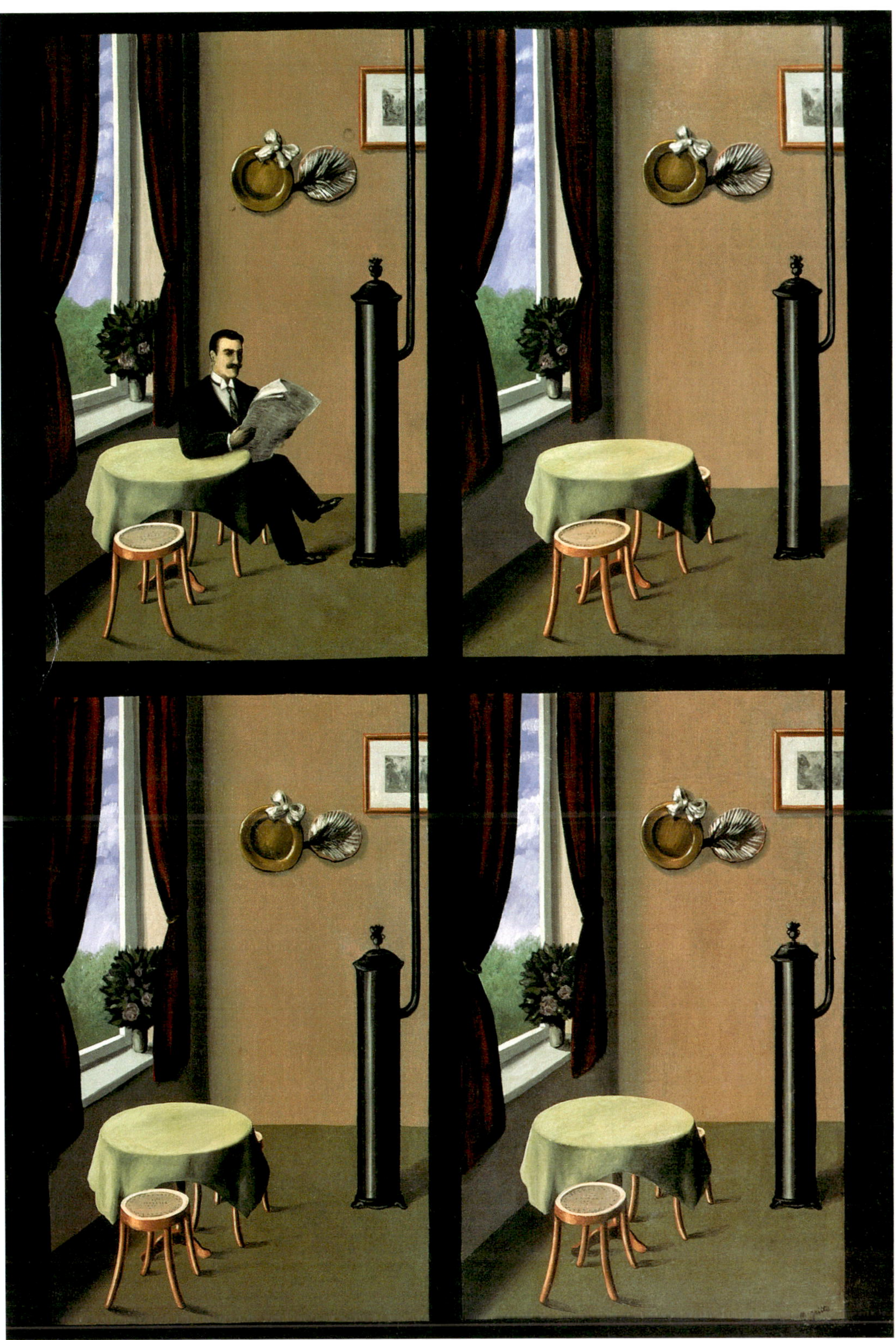

Man with a Newspaper
L'Homme au journal 1928, oil on canvas, 116 × 81 cm.
Tate. Presented by the Friends of the Tate 1964, CR 270

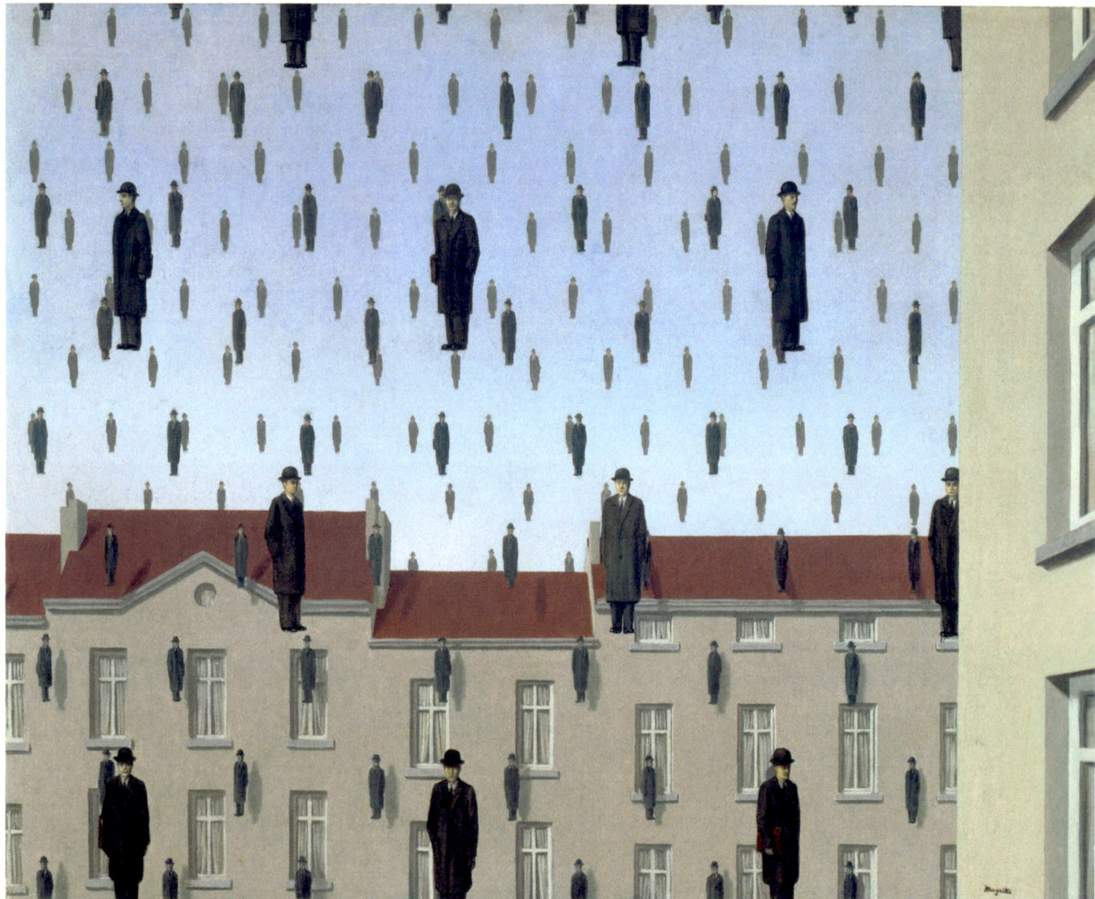

Golconda
Golconde 1953, oil on canvas, 80.7 × 100.6 cm.
The Menil Collection, Houston, CR 787

paintings informed by the biomorph works of **Joan Miró**. *The Apparition* 1928 situates two entirely non-representational forms floating in a state of tension to one another, with one blending into the brooding clouded background through a process of **metamorphosis**. Here the biomorph is fused with the artist's postulation that an object can be represented by any abstract shape, a theoretical position that necessarily results in his most abstract paintings. Similarly *A Taste for the Invisible* 1927 presents seemingly torn abstract forms as an element laid flat on the picture surface together with entirely non-representational improvised painterly mark making. **(DP)**

See also: **Pattern**

Alice in Wonderland: The fantastic world conjured by Lewis Carroll's *Alice's Adventures in Wonderland* (1865, translated into French 1869) and its play

with logic, nonsense and language exerted a great fascination on the **Surrealists**, with **Max Ernst** and **Salvador Dalí** referencing the novel in their work. In 1946–47, Magritte created four paintings with the title *Alice in Wonderland*. As Magritte himself described, he animated the tree and sky by giving them anthropomorphic features, the clouds appearing in the shape of a pear with a face, taken from Daumier's famous caricature of King Louis-Philippe.[5] The motif of doors opening on a tree trunk which first appeared in *The Learned Tree* 1935, and subsequently in various versions of *The Voice of Blood* 1959, has also been connected to *Alice*. In 1957 Magritte also adopted the story in one of his short home movies, featuring **Georgette** and one of his *Alice* paintings, creating a typically playful scenario around the theme of reading and dreaming. **(CG)**

See also: **Appropriation; Scale**

Anonymity is an insistent trope in Magritte's work. On one level it manifests itself in the recurrent image of bowler-hatted men, such as in *Golconda* 1953. Magritte's bowler-hatted men constitute endless reproductions of each other, their identity and individuality lost. For Magritte the bowler-hatted man is the man of the crowd, the bourgeois *par excellence*. Ben Stoltzfus argues 'Magritte has painted man's anonymity, his void, his emptiness, because, in essence, every bourgeois has the same face […]'[6] As well as critiquing the bourgeoisie by representing the anonymity of the everyman, Magritte adopted the uniform of the everyman as his wardrobe, recognising the subversive potential of anonymity. He further embraced an anonymous painting style, deliberately refraining from any personal expression and mimicking the cold detachment of photography and commercial illustration. This concern with anonymity as subversion belongs to a wider belief of the Brussels Surrealists. For Magritte's hero **Fantômas**, anonymity is a disguise which allows the working of the 'enemy from within'.

The representation of the anonymous men in bowler hats connects with Magritte's wider exploration of 'rendering anonymous', as in *The Lovers* 1928 and its variations, whose faces are obscured by white cloths; in *Not to be Reproduced* 1937, where a mirror no longer reflects, but reproduces, doubling the view of a man's back; or in *The Pleasure Principle* 1937, where a man's head has been replaced by a ray of light. **Paul Colinet** described this strategy of literal effacement *portraits manqués*, failed portraits, referring to 'a new potential in Magritte's images that had been constantly recurring in his work of a decade: the back view, the missing face, the mirror image'.[7] (PA)

See also: **Appropriation; Bowler Hat; Mirror; Portraiture; Representation and Resemblance**

Apple: Magritte created his first version of *The Listening Room* in 1952, creating three additional variations over the course of the decade. The image depicts a box room within which we see a monumentally scaled apple, which dominates the space. Where it had once been laden with symbolic meaning, the apple is transformed into a non-referential sign, challenging the viewer's ingrained responses. 'My paintings,' stated Magritte, 'portray such

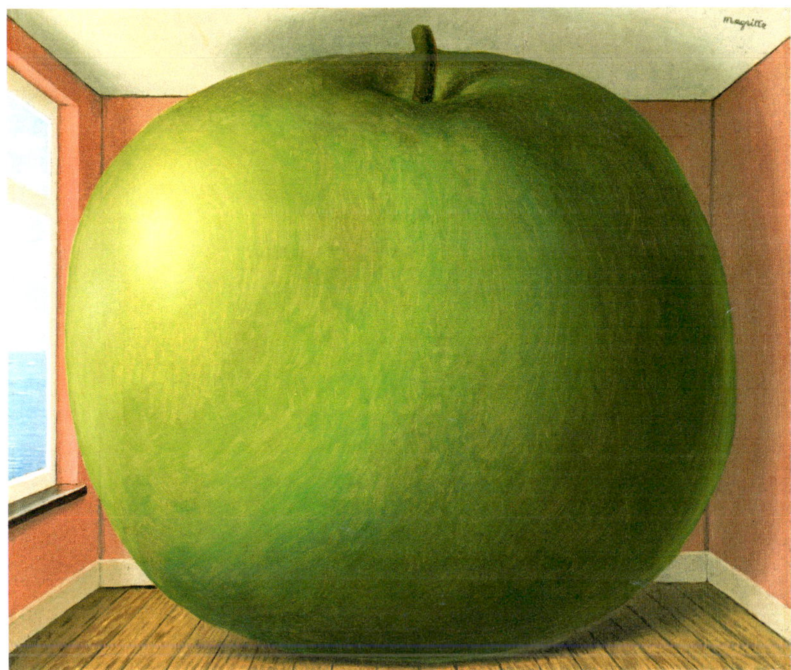

The Listening Room
La Chambre d'écoute
1958, oil on canvas,
38 × 46 cm.
Kunsthaus Zurich,
Walter Haefner
Donation, CR 878

familiar things: an apple, for instance, makes us ask questions. We don't understand any more when we see an apple: all that is mysterious about it has been evoked.'[8] (**GF**)

👁 **See also: Object; Scale**

Appropriation: In the context of the visual arts, appropriation describes an artist's conscious and intentional use of material that derives from a source outside of the work, and the incorporation of such material into their own work. Magritte's practice is organised around a troubling paradox: as much as it constitutes a pure product of the mind, as both the result of thought and an invitation to reflection, it is also absolutely anchored in our experience of reality. Indeed, it aims to colonise and annex that reality, in order to carry it back by stealth to the dimensions of a picture frame. Magritte's paintings, in short, appropriate rather than depict the real, but by the same manoeuvre drain the real of all certainty, substituting themselves for it. Crucial components of this ruse include his staged philosophical dramas in environments that are immediately apprehensible yet curiously anonymous, the artist frequently borrowing real locations for his pictorial settings, but tending to select precisely those least remarkable places and characteristics. Furthermore his images feature objects notable for their generic yet entirely believable appearance. As he noted in 1938, 'into my pictures I introduced elements with all of the details they present to us in reality and I immediately saw that these elements, represented in this way, directly challenged their equivalents in the real world'.[9] The extensive use of photographic sources, staged by the painter using his friends, and above all his wife **Georgette**, are a reminder that however tempting it might be to read Magritte's world as a realm of fantasy, it is in fact always rooted in actuality rather than invention.

While many works thus appear as standing as a kind of universal value for external reality, others, in contrast, borrow images or details from existing art and media sources, part of a wider set of intertextual references that situate Magritte's work as a critical practice aimed at questioning the active relationship between looking, showing and knowing. The most direct of these, perhaps, is *The Flame Rekindled* 1943, in which a colossal gentleman in evening suit, top hat and masked eyes towers over the city of Paris. Chin in one hand, rose in the other, the piercing gaze questions us impudently when it is the viewer who might have challenged him: lover or assassin? Both, of course, for this is the legendary arch-criminal **Fantômas**. Apart from replacing a dagger with a flower and adding painterly touches in line with his style of the moment, Magritte has done little to adapt the painting's original source, the cover of the 1911 pulp novel by Marcel Allain and Pierre Souvestre that launched the series of exploits in book and film beloved by many Surrealists. An appropriation that would have been instantly apparent to anyone of the painter's generation, choosing 1943 as the year in which to paint an anarchic spectre looming over Paris, and the substitution of a weapon with a blossom, cement an ambiguous but provocative act.

'The art of painting is an art of thinking,' Magritte claimed.[10] Despite remaining committed to the gestures of painting, **drawing** and **collage** (a few forays into three-dimensional work notwithstanding), his practice can be viewed as fundamentally conceptual, playful yet profoundly challenging to our basic understandings. In this sense, and despite his radically different choice of media, the artist closest to Magritte might be seen as **Marcel Duchamp**, whose provocative appropriation of equally generic commodities, chosen with 'disinterest', in the formation

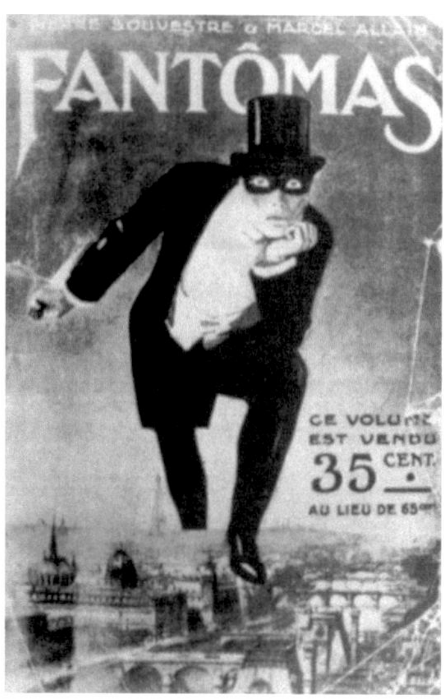

Fantômas
Pierre Souvestre and Marcel Allain, book cover, 1911

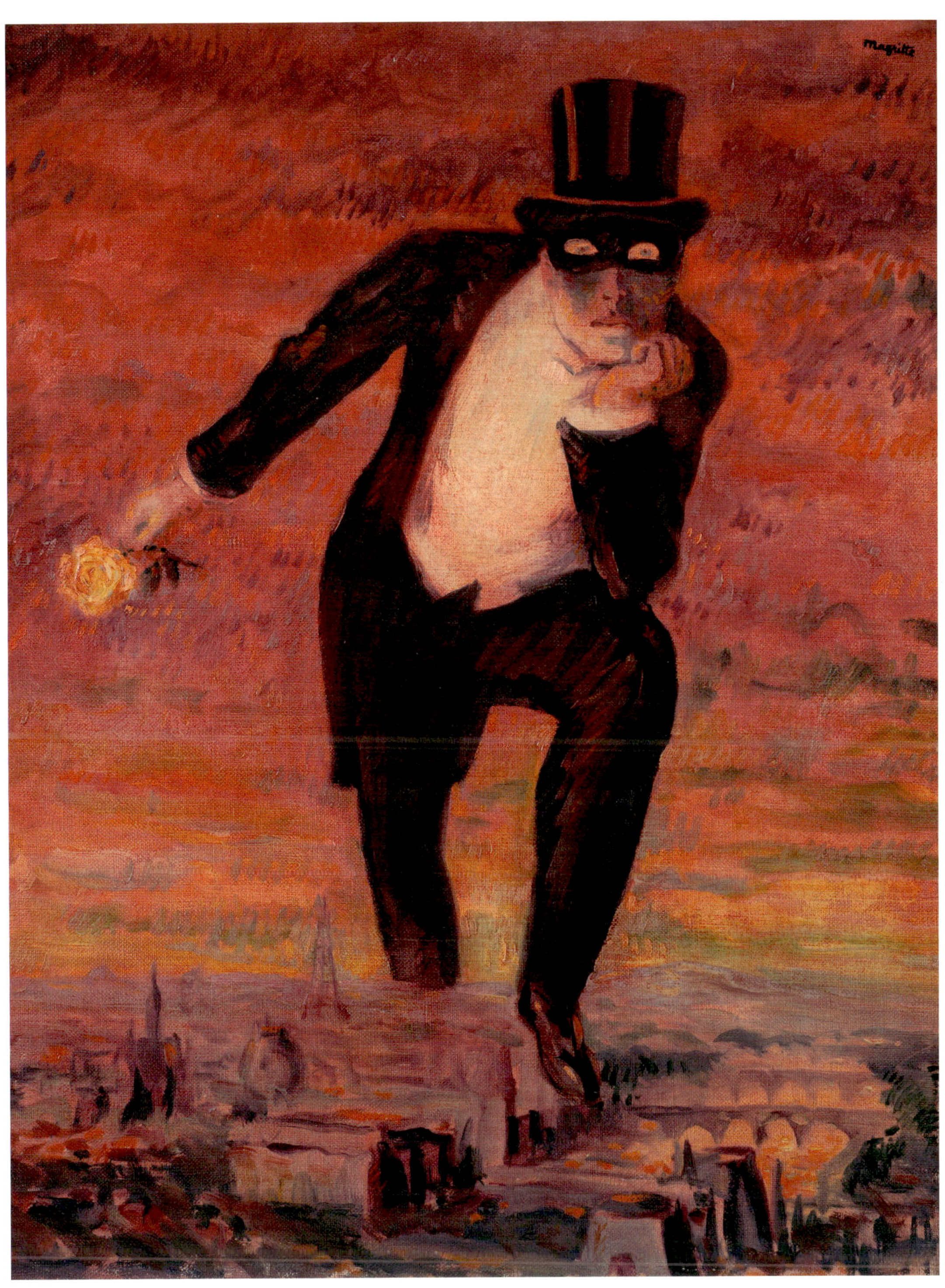

The Flame Rekindled
Le Retour de flamme 1943, oil on canvas, 65 × 50 cm.
Private Collection, CR 535

of the readymades offers a natural family relationship with Magritte's puzzling objects and jarring recontextualisations. Magritte may well have approved of Duchamp's observation that since painters used ready-made paint, all paintings are effectively 'readymades aided' and assemblages.

Appropriated in turn by the fields of mass media, design and advertising that gleefully borrowed his trademark imagery, reinserting them back into the world of popular culture, it might be observed that Magritte himself, in repeating and developing his own themes, was interested in effectively using his own work as a reservoir of source material. If aside from the strong tradition of Belgian Surrealist painters, Magritte has no apparent 'school' of followers, this is in part because it is in the trajectory of European and North American Conceptual art from the 1960s onwards, starting with **Marcel Broodthaers**, that we find Magritte's **legacy** sustained. (**KF**)

See also: **Commercial Art**; **Detective Stories**; **Film**; **Forgery**

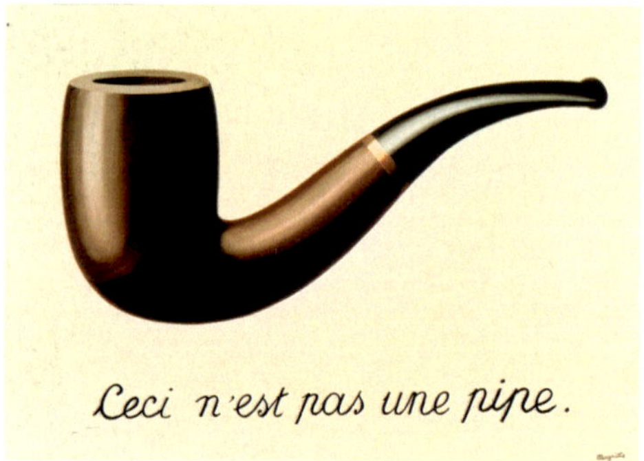

The Treachery of Images (This is not a Pipe)
La Trahison des images (Ceci n'est pas une pipe) 1929, oil on canvas, 60 × 81 cm. Los Angeles County Museum of Art, CR303

Artifice: Magritte's paintings repeatedly insist on what they are not, revealing the artifice of representation and treachery of the words and images we use to mediate and communicate reality. The revelation of artifice also manifests itself in his **repetitions** and reproductions of artworks and within artworks. These insist on the absence of an original – a copy here is always a copy of another copy, a model always a model of another model. In Magritte's universe there is no outside of representation, only

reference to another representation, just like in a dictionary where the reader, searching for meaning, is eternally referred – or rather deferred – to another term. Magritte's stage-like compositions question our notions of reality and representation. They incorporate aesthetic conventions of **trompe l'oeil**, evident in his staple imagery of curtain folds, tears in paper, wood grain – all are there not to deceive the eye, but to reveal the deception of conventional representations. 'Who would dare pretend that the REPRESENTATION of a pipe IS a pipe?' asks Magritte. 'Who could smoke the pipe in my picture? Nobody. Therefore it IS NOT A PIPE.'[11] (**PA**)

See also: **Ersatz**; **Forgery**; **Pattern**; **Representation and Resemblance**; **Theatrical Display**; *The Treachery of Images*; **Wallpaper**

Automatism and Automatic Writing: **André Breton** defined **Surrealism** in terms of 'psychic automatism in its pure state', a concept rooted in a Freudian model of the subject as divided between conscious and unconscious elements, where the essential 'inner' subject could be accessed by techniques such as free association or the analysis of the subject's dream life.[12] Surrealism developed various forms of 'automatism' as a means of accessing that inner world and deploying it to produce writings and artworks, as for example with 'automatic writing', where the writer simply spontaneously wrote whatever came to mind, as quickly as possible. With visual artwork this assumed a variety of techniques, including drawing or painting freely, making rubbings (*frottage*), or using smoke (*fumage*). Magritte, though, as he made clear to Suzi Gablik, although a strong advocate of **chance**, had no interest in automatic drawing, viewing it as 'too mechanical and mediumistic a process'.[13] We do, however, see a kind of displacement whereby Magritte incorporates **collage** techniques and a highly theatrical, painterly simulation of *frottage* into many of his works of around 1926 and 1927. David Sylvester notes how these works echo the wood textures of *frottage*, as developed by **Max Ernst**, and Patricia Allmer argues that Magritte engages in a dialogue with Ernst that can be read as a kind of 'meta-surrealism, analysing and arguing with Surrealist positions'.[14] (**NM**)

See also: **Dreams**; **Sigmund Freud**; **Metamorphosis**

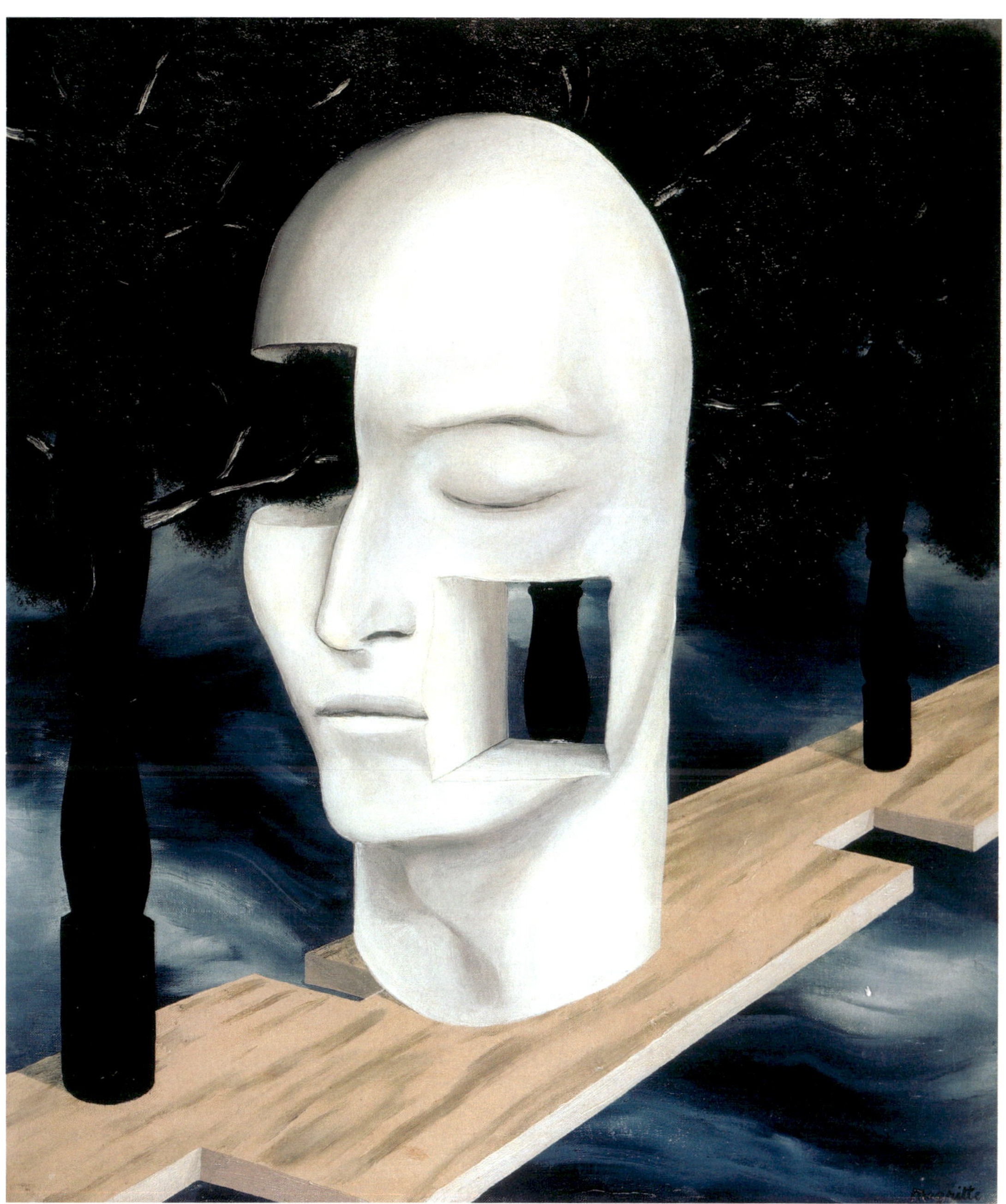

The Face of Genius
Le Visage du génie 1926, oil on canvas, 75 × 65 cm.
Musée d'Ixelles, Brussels, ancienne collection Max Janlet, CR 110

B

Banality: The notion of banality is a persistent element of Magritte's work and life. His desire to live an anonymous routine existence was apparent in 1921 when he confided his intent to 'make Georgette as happy as possible … in the calm of a nice steady bourgeois life'.[15] Even in later life when he was well off, Magritte continued to live a life of routine bourgeois conformism in which every aspect of his life was ordered, arranged by the watch.[16] Banality can also be understood to be the basis of his artistic practice, his repertoire of standard manufactured **objects** – **pipes**, umbrellas and the like – chosen and repeatedly depicted in painting, emphasising their status as inauspicious everyday objects. He even declared that the act of 'painting *bores* me like everything else … it is bound up in the series of activities – that seems to change almost nothing in life, the same habits are always recurring'.[17] Banality extended to his appearance. Whilst in London in 1938, for example, rather than purchasing a distinguished Lock & Co. **bowler hat**, he chose an ordinary bowler which came to be a vital element of the image he presented to the media. For him, the mass-produced bowler hat symbolised the unindividuated Everyman. His ordinary suits and sober hairstyle were regarded in subversive terms, selected as a means to comment on the absurdity of everyday life. (**DP**)

See also: **Anonymity; Georgette Magritte**

Georges Bataille (1897–1962) French philosopher who played a prominent role in **Surrealism**, in particular as editor of the journal *Documents* 1929–30. Bataille was fascinated by the extremes of human behaviour and excess in any form, such as the expression of uninhibited sexual desire, death, crime, cannibalism, human sacrifice and blasphemy, pushing mankind to the realisation of the ultimate truths of existence.

Magritte would have felt an affinity with Bataille's provocative vision, himself employing at times in his art and writing lewd sexual allusions and puns, vulgarity and profanity. They also shared a fascination with crime as a means to break through the façade of bourgeois normality, the fictional criminal **Fantômas** featuring prominently in *Documents*. Both played with the tension between the orderly appearance of objects and their hidden meanings,

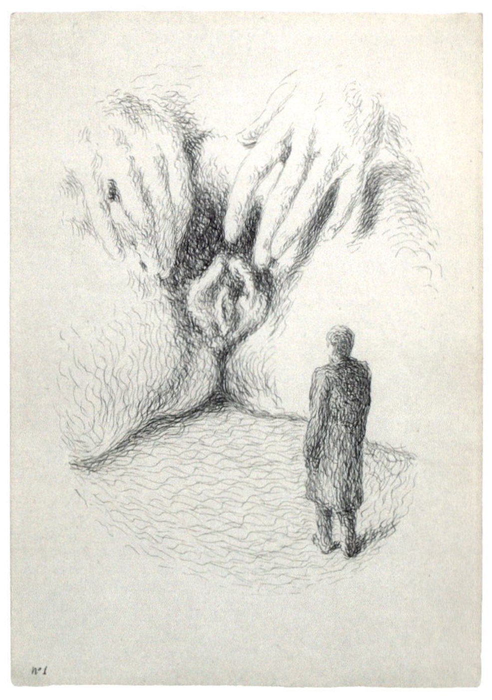

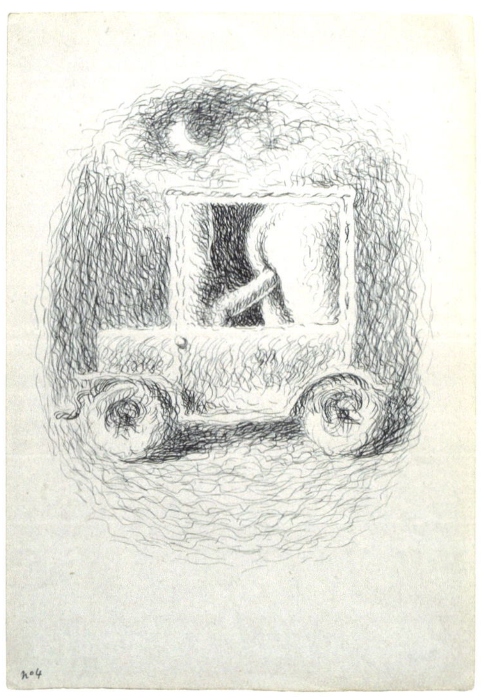

Illustrations for Georges Bataille, *Madame Edwarda* 1946, ink on paper, set of six drawings, each 40 × 30 cm. Private Collection, courtesy Keitelman Gallery

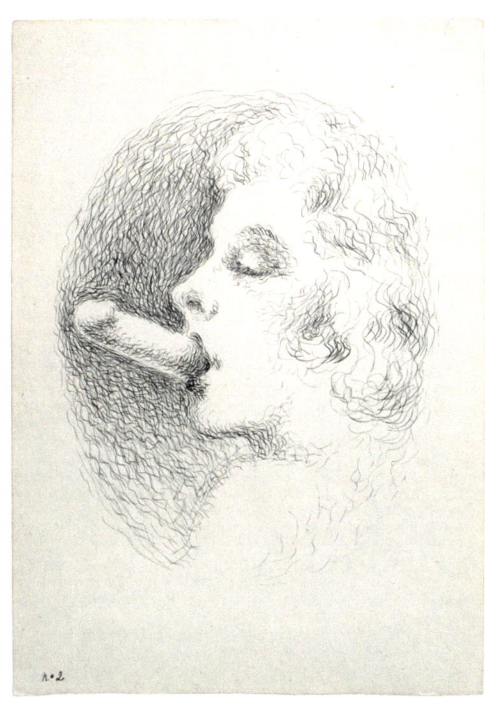

n.2

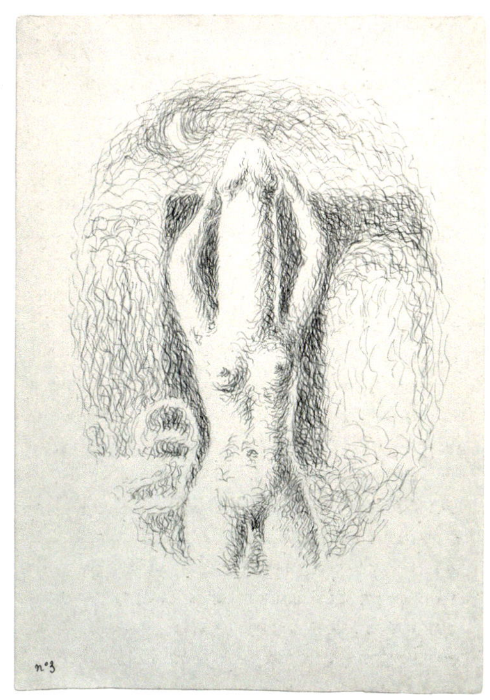

n.3

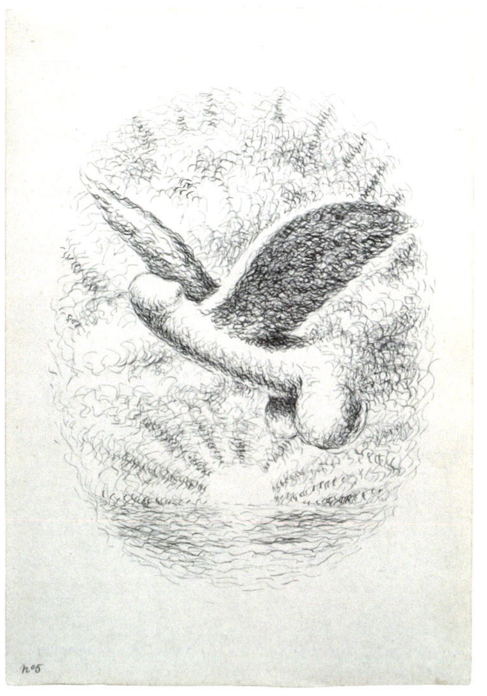

n.5

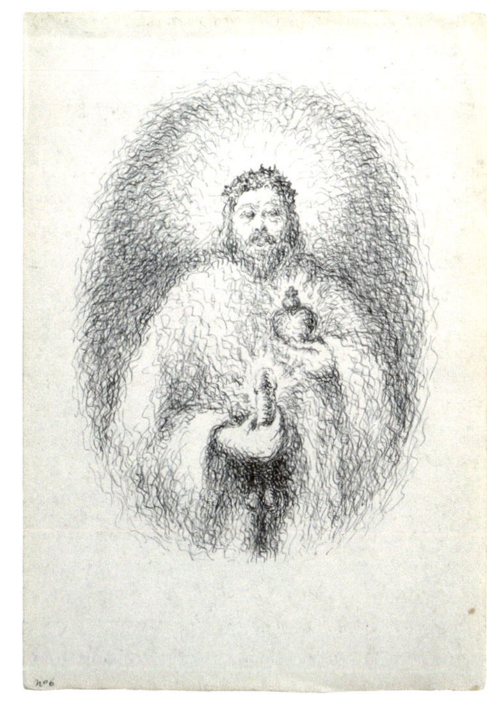

n.6

Bataille suggesting in the entry on 'Formless' in his 'Dictionary' that 'A dictionary would begin as of the moment when it no longer provided the meanings of words but their tasks.' He defines as the task of the 'informe' (formless) 'to declassify,' to question the need for everything to have a fixed form, meaning or definition.[18] Magritte's whole work can be understood as a process of destabilisation of received **meanings**, associations and conventions. Magritte also explored the 'formless' formally in a number of early works created in an unusually painterly manner and with heavy impasto, dissolving familiar **objects** into amorphous daubs of paint (for example, *Biomorphs with Words (The Pipe)* of 1928). The so-called **Vache Period** (1948) displays a similar divergence from stylistic cohesion with the formal integrity of objects, figures and patterns collapsing in painterly expressiveness. The deliberately sloppy application of paint might be interpreted as a defiant act of anarchic laughter, challenging expectations of taste and convention.

In 1946 Magritte created a number of illustrations for Bataille's *Madame Edwarda*. Published in 1941 under the pseudonym of Pierre Angélique, the short story is a typically transgressive fantasy of sex, brutality, scatology, blasphemy and death. The protagonist's hallucinatory journey through the nightly Paris and encounter with a prostitute in a brothel climaxes in an ecstatic orgy in a taxi. Magritte's delicate ink drawings evoke six dreamlike scenes from the text without directly illustrating specific events. They are unusually explicit, the artist abandoning his usual distancing technique of impersonal representation. Instead, he applies his transformative powers to the human anatomy, depicting a male member with wings, a naked female torso morphing into a penis and a masturbating priest. Magritte captures the exaggerated and trance-like quality of the plot with its liberal exploration of the extremes of **pleasure** and pain as a means to induce an existential crisis of belief that Bataille, as he explains in the foreword to the story, considers requisite for the unmasking of bourgeois hypocrisy and the brutal revelation of reality.[19] (**CG**)

👁 See also: **Book Illustration; Eroticism; Metamorphosis; Philosophy; Shock; Violence**

Charles Baudelaire (1821–1867) French poet, art critic and essayist. The sense of striving for freedom at the same time as searching for refuge in the certain knowledge of the foundations of one's own being were fundamental creative motivations

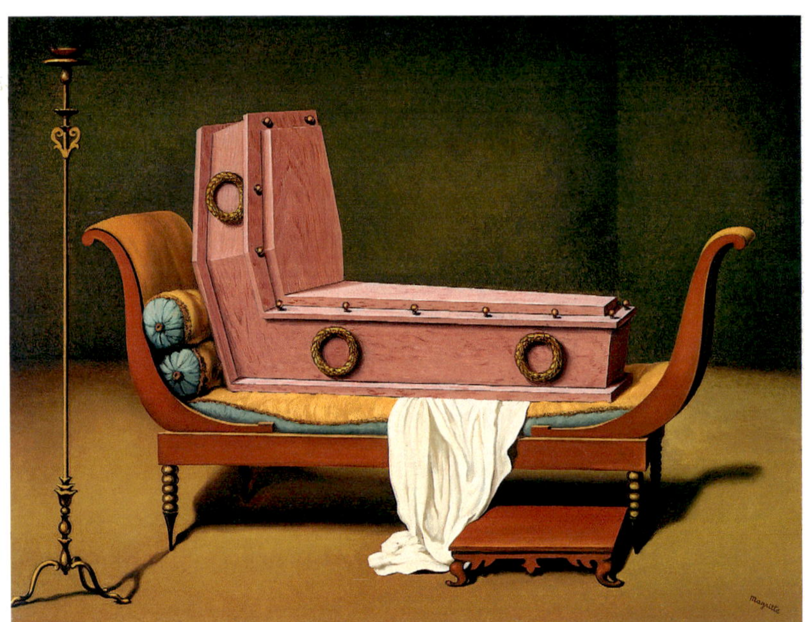

Perspective: David's Madame Récamier
Perspective: Madame Récamier de David
1951, oil on canvas, 60 × 80 cm. National Gallery of Canada, Ottawa. Purchased 1997, CR 757

for both Magritte and Baudelaire. Magritte's painting *The Giantess* 1931 incorporates the text of a poem, signed 'Baudelaire' but actually written by **Paul Nougé** – one of five variations on poems by Baudelaire he composed between 1931 and 1934. The image of a giantess indicates that mystery may be revealed through an artist's ability to defy the existing order of constrained, bourgeois civilisation and to conceive of an artificial *Über*-nature. Magritte made the connection with the work of the French poet in a number of other paintings, such as *Lola de Valence* 1948, and *Les Fleurs du mal* 1946. (**GF**)

See also: **Mystery; Poetry; Scale**

Belgium: René Magritte was born in 1898 in Belgium at Lessines, a small town just outside of Charleroi, in the province of Hainaut. He spent most of his life in Brussels, living in the suburbs. His only extended sojourn was a move, together with his wife **Georgette**, to the Parisian suburb of Le Perreux-sur-Marne in August 1927. In 1930 they returned to Brussels. Although Magritte rejected notions of national identity, his artworks can be seen to emerge out of and closely tie in with 'national' Belgian Surrealist activities. In particular, most of Magritte's thoughts and artworks are a 'collective invention' in which the Brussels Surrealist group played a significant role. Magritte's position on national identity is made clear in his interview with Claude Vial in 1966. 'I'm often asked,' he stated, 'whether I feel myself as an inheritor of the great Belgian artists. Why exactly the Belgian? For me Belgian painting is one amongst a number of episodes in the general history of art. And people cite Bosch … Hieronymus Bosch lived in a world of folklore, of phantasy. I live in the real world.'[20]

Magritte was part of the Brussels Surrealist group which came into being in 1926. It was the first, but certainly not the only Surrealist group in Belgium. The Brussels group would go through a number of re-arrangements, groupings and regroupings. Belgian Surrealist groupings were complex, a complexity which has a lot to do with Belgium's novelty as a country, which formed in 1830 and consists of a Flemish and a Francophone part. Magritte's artworks often reference Belgian art historic traditions – a number of his paintings allude to the Flemish artist **James Ensor**, for example his **Vache Period** painting

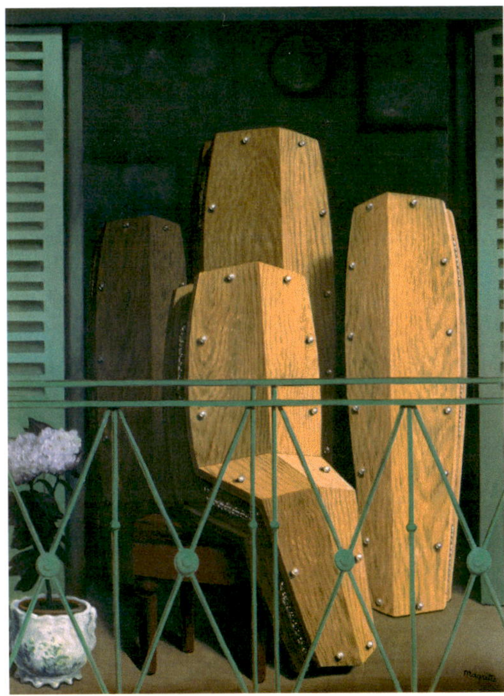

Perspective: Manet's Balcony II
Perspective: Le Balcon de Manet II 1950, oil on canvas, 80 × 60 cm. Museum voor Schone Kunsten, Ghent, CR 710

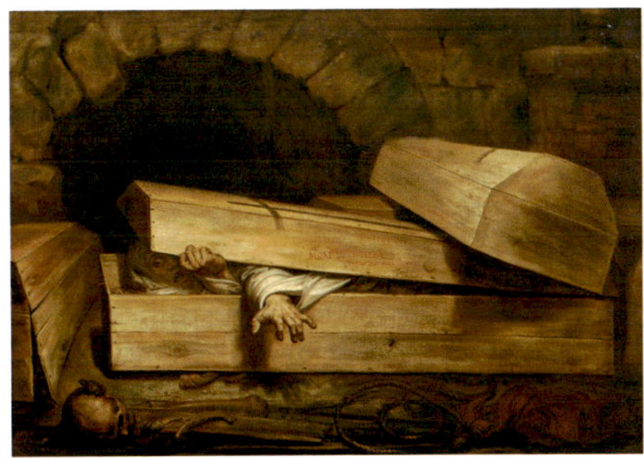

Antoine Wiertz (1806–1865): *The Premature Burial (L'Inhumation précipitée)* 1854, oil on canvas, 160 × 235 cm. Royal Museums of Fine Arts of Belgium, Brussels

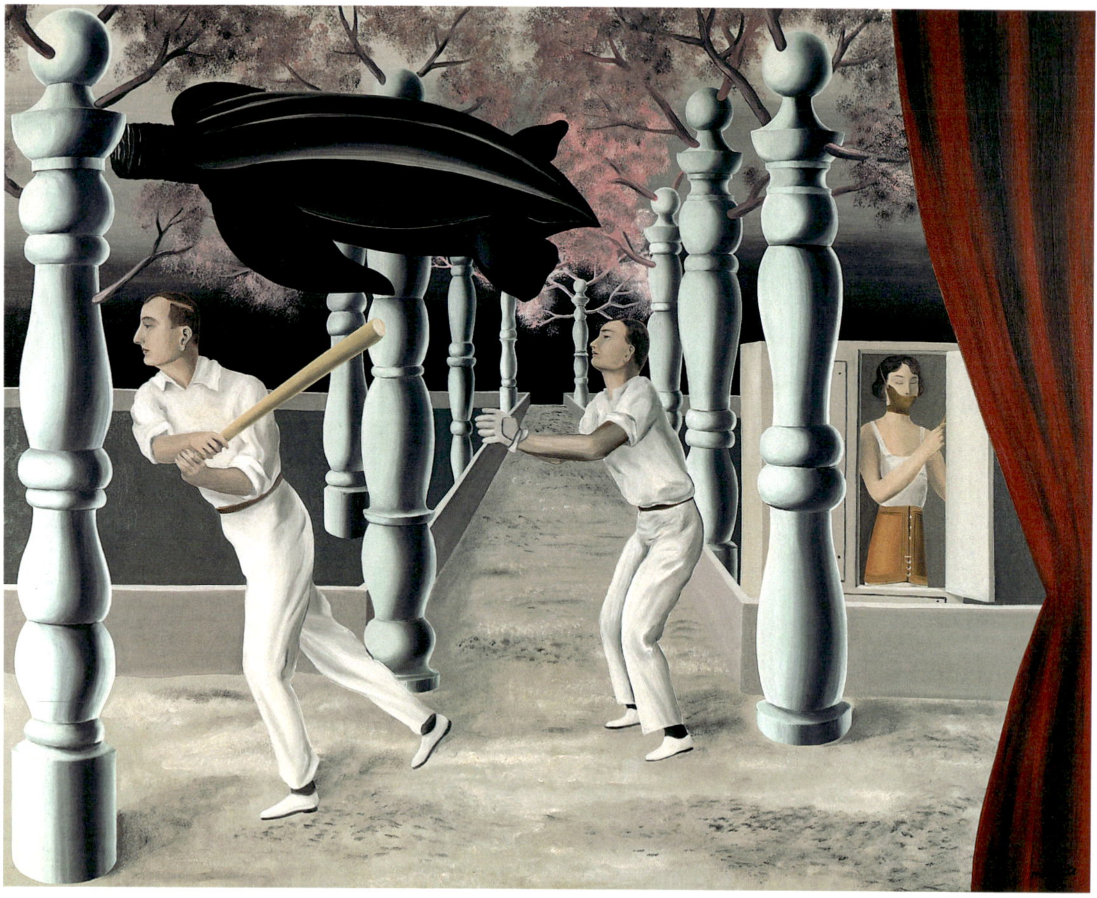

The Secret Player
Le Joueur secret 1927, oil on canvas, 152 × 195 cm.
Royal Museums of Fine Arts of Belgium, Brussels, CR 138

Famine 1948, which alludes to Ensor's *Skeletons Fighting over a Pickled Herring* 1891. In Magritte's *Perspective* series of the early 1950s sitters from famous paintings such as David's *Madame Récamier* are replaced by coffins, the coffins being a direct allusion to the Belgian artist Antoine Wiertz's painting *The Premature Burial* 1854 showing a cholera victim awakening after being placed in a coffin. Magritte's *grisaille* paintings, also from the 1950s, deployed **trompe l'oeil** representation of sculpted form and bas-relief, a device frequently practised in the art of Flanders and Holland to produce highly deceptive imitations of marble statuary. Flemish painters used *grisaille* to decorate the backs of their polyptych wings, as seen in Jan Van Eyck's *Annunciation* c.1436.

Belgian land and cityscapes are present in the iconography of Magritte's artworks. Belgian lace pattern, architecture and the bowler-hatted man – a stereotype of the Belgian bourgeois – are recurring motifs. These derive from his everyday environment, be it in the form of a magazine, a pictorial encyclopaedia or dictionary entry, or the immediate environment of his home, most prominently the interior and exterior of his house in Jette, an outskirt of Brussels, in 135 Rue Esseghem, now home to the René Magritte Museum, where Magritte and his wife lived from 1930 to 1954. (**PA**)

See also: **Anonymity; Banality; Bowler Hat; Paris; Surrealism and Surrealists**

Bilboquet: Like **Giorgio de Chirico**, Magritte had a defined set of visual motifs which he deployed extensively in his own compositions. Resembling a kind of decorative wood turned baluster or

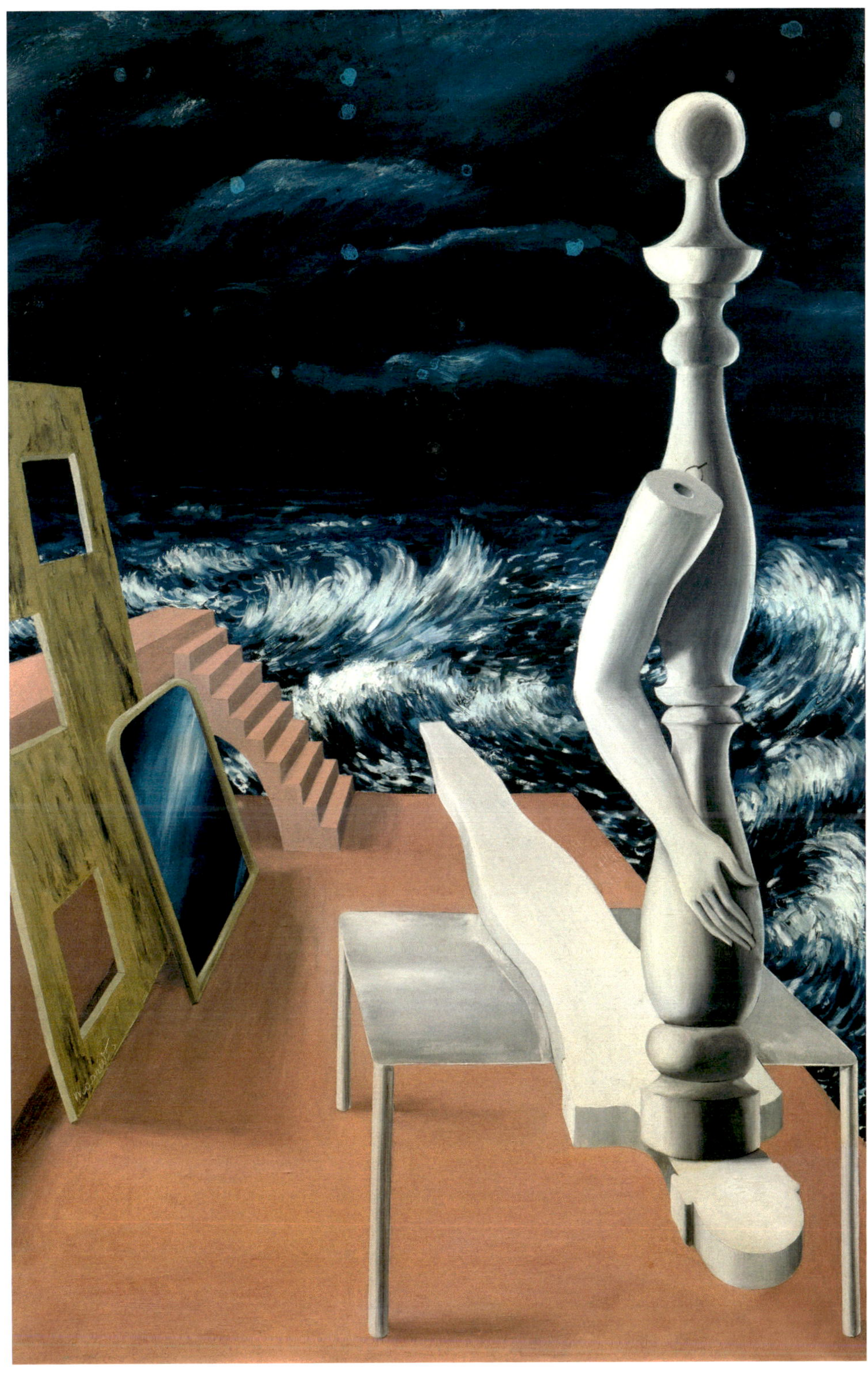

The Birth of the Idol
La Naissance de l'idole 1926, oil on canvas, 120 × 80 cm.
Private Collection, courtesy Hauser & Wirth, CR 89

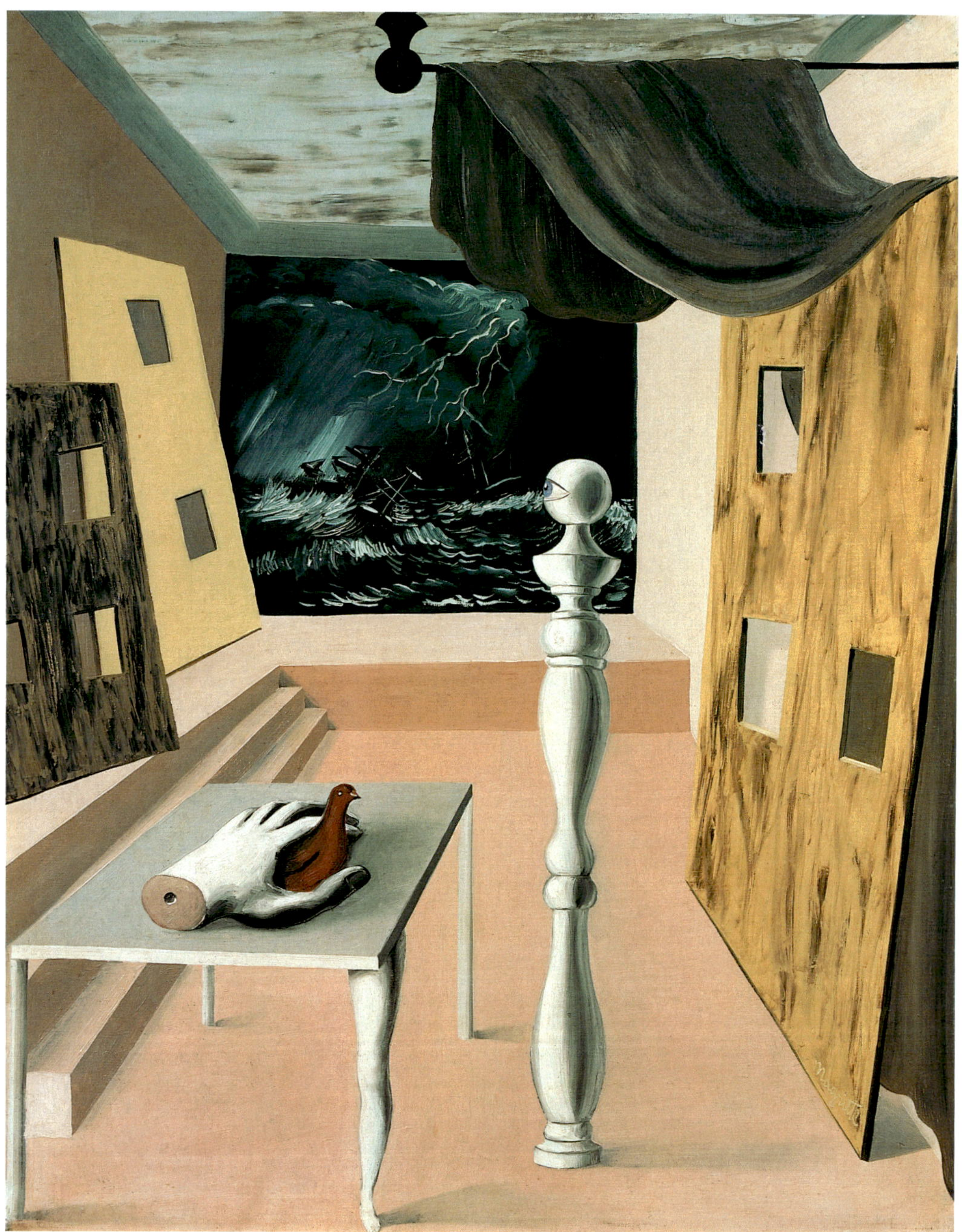

The Difficult Crossing
La Traversée difficile 1926, oil on canvas, 80 × 65 cm.
Kunstkring Vanthournout, Belgium, CR 84

chess piece, the *bilboquet*, as Magritte called it, constituted one of the artist's most enduring visual elements, and it appeared in his commercial design works and in paintings throughout his career. In *The Annunciation* 1930, the *bilboquet* appears as part of a staged ensemble of objects in a rock-strewn landscape, whilst in *The Difficult Crossing* 1926, the form adopts an anthropomorphic presence by being depicted with an **eye**. Magritte returned to this theme in *The Difficult Crossing* 1963. In it he presents two *bilboquets*, their equivalency to the human form emphasised through one being depicted wearing an everyman suit, its 'head' transformed into an all-seeing eye. In certain compositions the *bilboquet* holds distinctly phallic connotations, for example *The Invention of Fire* 1946. Magritte's *bilboquet* plays a similar role to that of de Chirico's **mannequin**, which was inspired by Alberto Savinio's *The Songs of Half-Death* 1914, a dramatic poem whose protagonist was a 'man without voice, without eyes or face'.[21] A potent motif for **Dada** and **Surrealist** artists, Magritte's version of the mannequin can be seen to play on disturbing notions of the inanimate animated. The *bilboquet* later evolved in the humanised form seen in images such as *Sentimental Conversation* 1945, in which the form adopts an explicitly figurative presence. **(DP)**

See also: **Double; Repetition and the Encounter**

Book Illustration: Magritte was first commissioned to produce illustrations for books in 1944: a set of twelve drawings for an edition of William Beckford's *Vathek*, which was never published. In his book illustrations, the artist aimed for both the interconnection and independent identity of text and image. His images are autonomous, valid in their own right with no need for any extraneous or symbolic interpretation. He took the view that the 'coming together' of an existing text and an image selected from existing images constituted the happiest encounter between pictures and words. 'Another meaning of illustration is acceptable,' he stated, 'if it is intended in the sense of "making illustrious".'[22] It was in this spirit that Magritte created illustrations for **Georges Bataille**, *Madame Edwarda* 1946; **Paul Éluard**, *Exemples* 1946; and Comte de Lautréamont, *Les Chants de Maldoror* 1948. **(GF)**

See also: **Juxtaposition; Language; Poetry**

André Bosmans (born 1938) In 1958, having finished his military service, Bosmans, a young poet, future teacher and librarian, began an exchange of **letters** with Magritte. Meetings soon followed and these led to the journal ***Rhétorique*** with thirteen issues appearing between 1961 and 1966. Bosmans, whose first published poetry collections were illustrated by Magritte, became the last of the painter's young

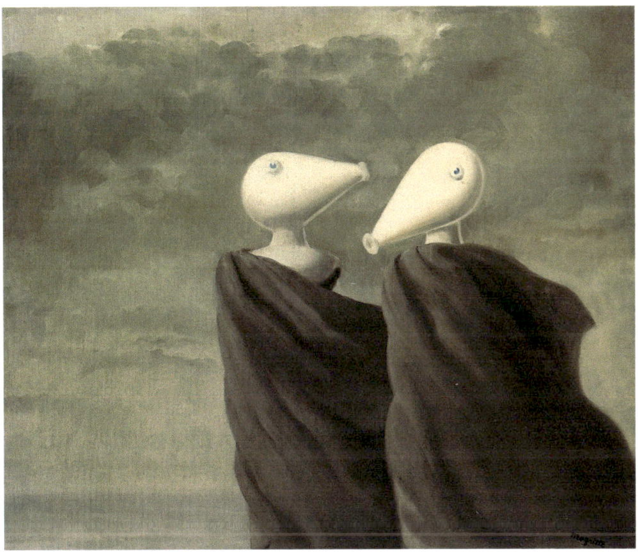

Sentimental Conversation
Le Colloque sentimental 1945,
oil on canvas, 54 × 65 cm.
Private Collection, cr vol.II,
app. no.80

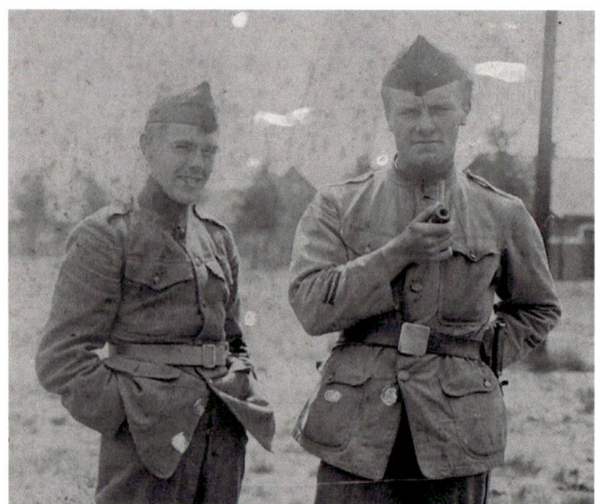

René Magritte and Pierre Bourgeois, Beverlo, 14 June 1921

fans, followed along the way throughout his career by **Marcel Mariën** and **Jacques Wergifosse** who organised Magritte's retrospective in Liège in October 1960. Bosmans' correspondence with Magritte was published in 1990, shedding light on the painter's thinking, distancing him from the activity of the Brussels group and its agents.[23] (**XC**)

Bottles: Magritte started to paint bottles in the 1940s. As well as being a banal everyday object, the bottle also provided a solution to the shortage of canvas during **World War II**.[24] Magritte's use of found, mass-produced objects corresponded with Surrealist aims, in this case the artist's creative engagement with reality as freely available material. **Edward James** found eager buyers for these innovative objects in the United States – 'It's New York taste exactly, and Hollywood's too.'[25] Magritte created between twenty and thirty painted bottles, decorated with female figures, **clouds** and other motifs, alluding to works by Pablo Picasso or his own paintings. Either as a petrified object or, as in *The Explanation* 1952, mutating into a carrot, the bottle served as a means for Magritte to explore the nature of **metamorphosis**. (**GF**)

See also: **Object; Sculpture**

Victor and Pierre Bourgeois (1897–1962; 1898–1976) Pierre Bourgeois was a poet and art critic who became a close friend of Magritte. In 1919–20 the two were stationed together during their military service, at which time Magritte painted a number of portraits of his friend. In 1919 he co-founded

Centre d'Art, a Brussels gallery which staged Magritte's first exhibition, a presentation of his poster designs. With his architect brother Victor, they were important promoters of modern art and architecture in Brussels. They also collaborated on various avant-garde journals, including *Au Volant*, of which four issues appeared in 1919, all featuring Magritte illustrations, and **7 Arts**, which was published from 1922 to 1929. While Pierre allied himself primarily with literature with social and political overtones, Victor became a renowned architect, his diverse projects including the Cité Moderne at Berchem-Sainte-Agathe, Brussels, and working in 1927 with Walter Gropius and Le Corbusier on the Weissenhofsiedlung in Stuttgart. (**XC**)

See also: **Poetry**

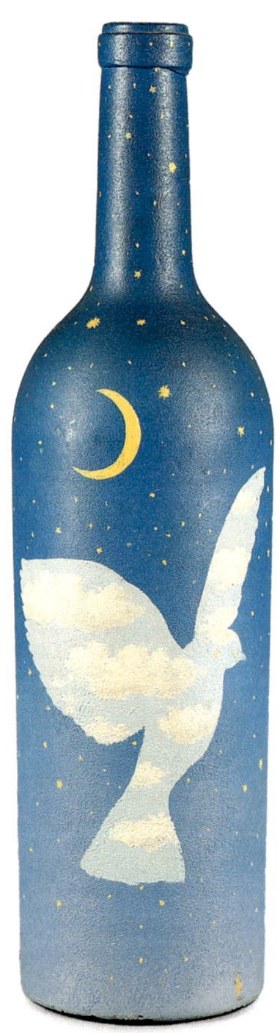

Night Sky with Bird
c.1945, oil on glass bottle, h. 30.7 cm. Private Collection, courtesy Keitelman Gallery, CR 706

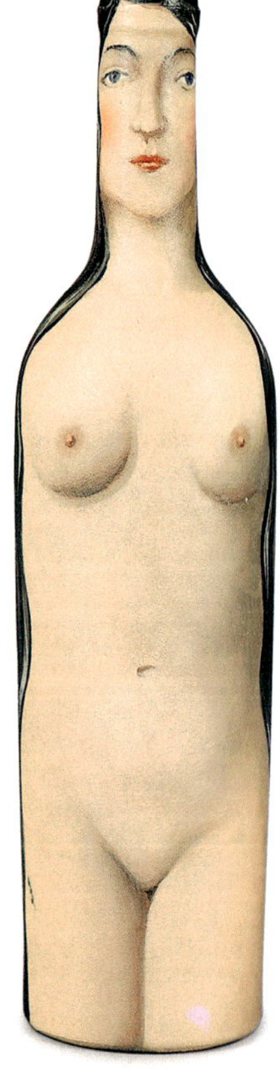

Bottle-Woman
Femme-bouteille c.1945, oil on glass bottle, h. 30 cm. Private Collection, courtesy Keitelman Gallery, CR 705

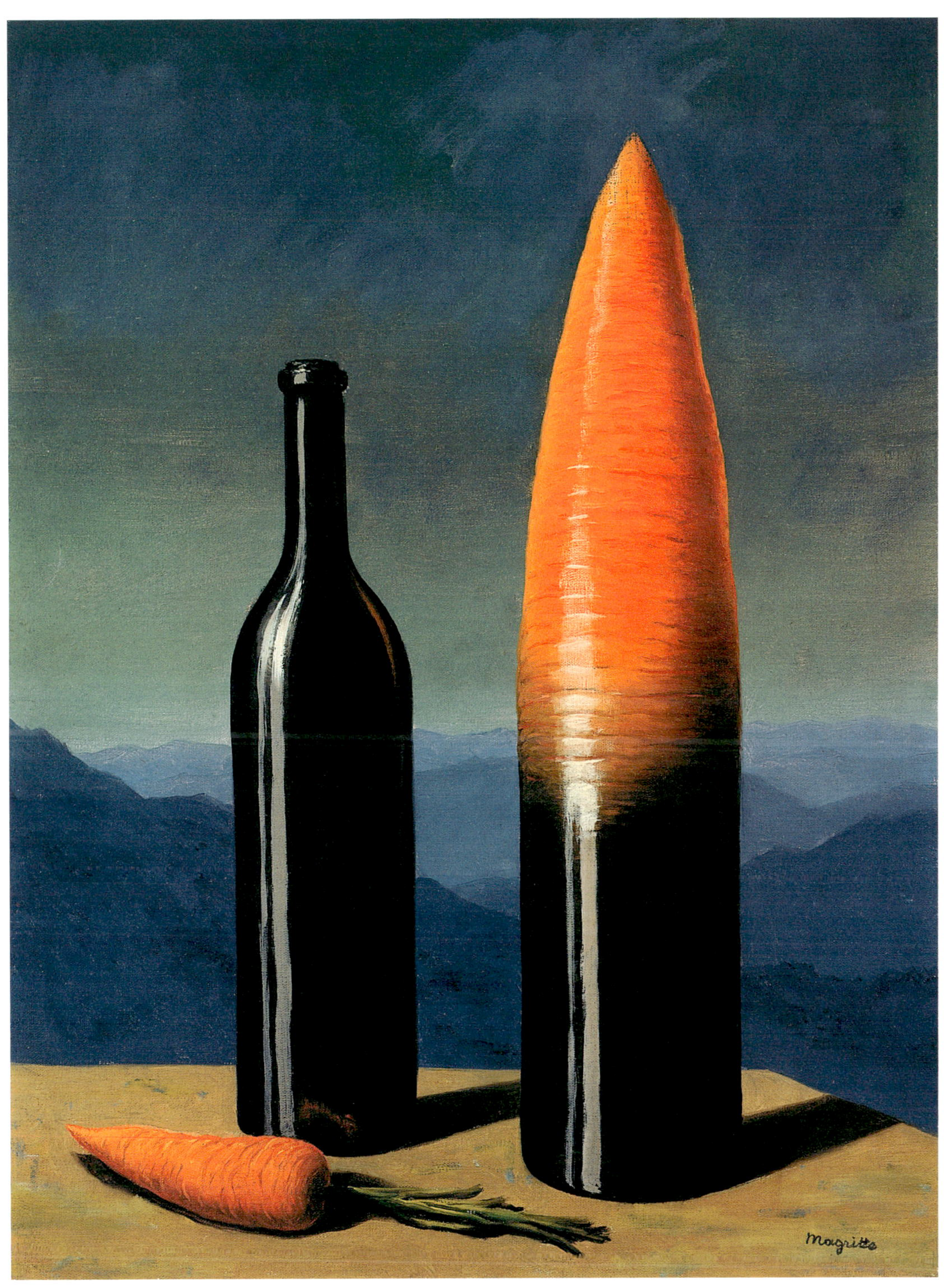

The Explanation
L'Explication 1952, oil on canvas, 46 × 35 cm. Private Collection,
courtesy Guggenheim, Asher Associates, Inc., CR 784

Towards Pleasure
A la Rencontre du plaisir 1962, oil on canvas, 46 × 55 cm.
Private Collection, CR 946

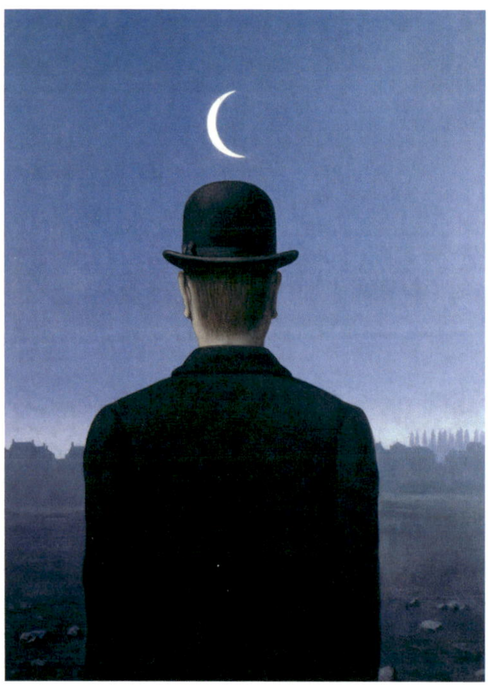

The Schoolmaster
Le Maître d'école 1955, oil on canvas, 80 × 60 cm.
Private Collection, CR 818

Bowler Hat: All his life Magritte was torn between his inner life and his external persona. On one hand there was his desire to be in the limelight – looking back at the death of his mother, he recalled feeling 'intense pride at the thought of being the pitiable centre of attention in a drama'.[26] It was precisely this kind of attention that he was striving for as an artist by destabilising the usual order of things. On the other hand, there was the unremarkable, conformist – even uniformed – figure that he cut in public.

The hat is one of those banal objects which Magritte integrated into his art without changing it. In paintings such as *The Key to Dreams* 1930 and in his writings and lectures Magritte frequently made reference to the hat, as an everyday object, in order to illuminate his thinking on the relations between concepts and objects. In 1966 he turned the bowler hat into a readymade (*The Horrendous Stopper*), withdrawing even further from artistic decision-making by using a store-bought commodity. His Bowler Hat portraits in which we encounter a figure seen from behind (*The Intimate Friend* 1960) or with his face obscured behind a banal object, such as an apple (*The Son of Man* 1964), or a pipe (*Good Faith* 1964–5), thrive on the ambiguity between being lost

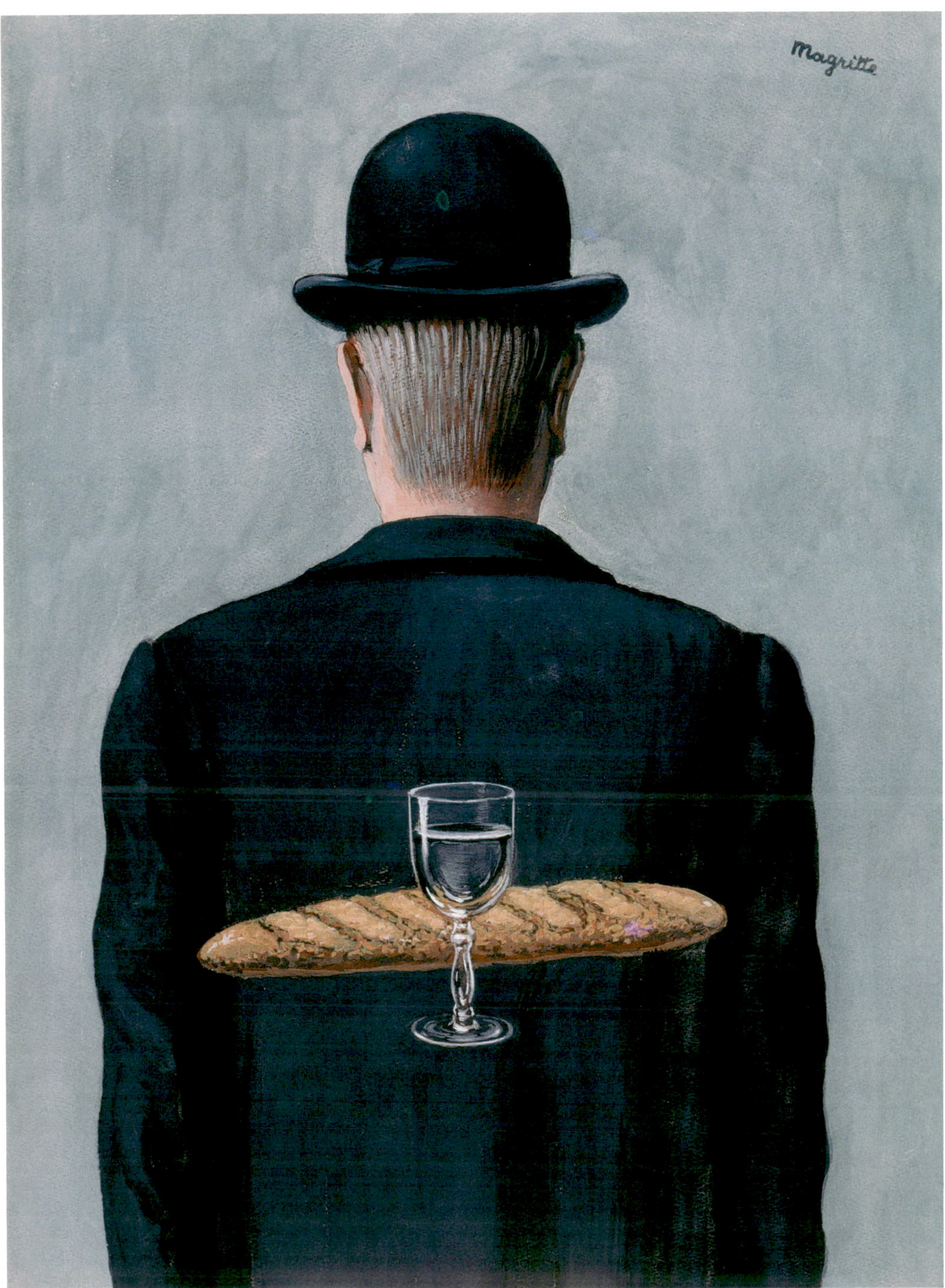

The Intimate Friend
L'Ami intime 1960, gouache on paper, 34.5 x 26 cm.
Private Collection, courtesy Guggenheim, Asher
Associates, Inc., CR 1474

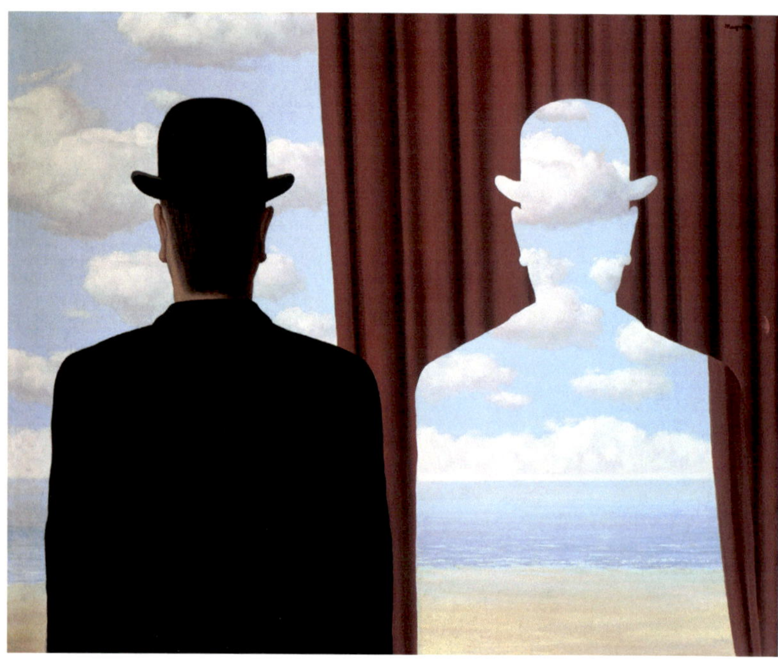

Decalcomania
La Décalcomanie 1966,
oil on canvas,
81 × 100 cm.
Collection Dr Noémi
Perelman Mattis and
Dr Daniel C. Mattis,
CR1054

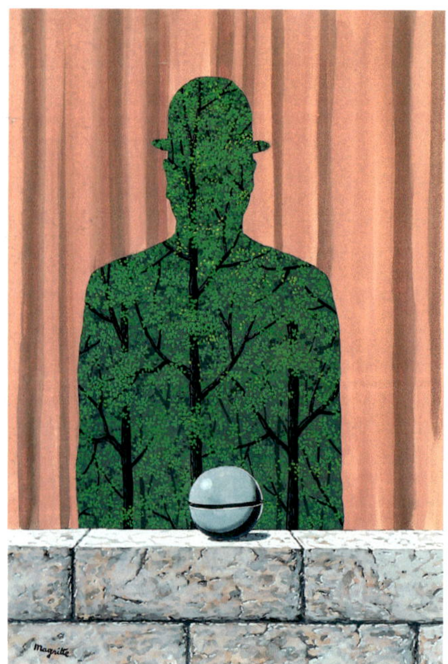

Man and the Forest
L'Homme et la forêt 1965, gouache on card,
49 × 29 cm. Private Collection, courtesy Keitelman
Gallery, CR1582

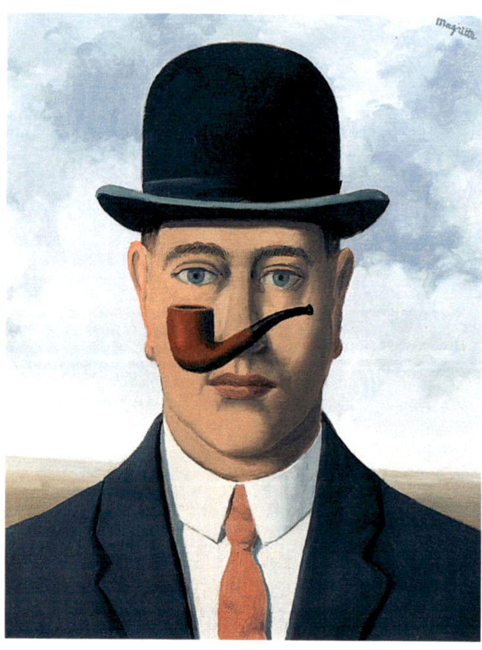

Good Faith
La Bonne Foi 1964–5, oil on canvas, 41 × 33 cm.
Private Collection, Brussels, CR1007

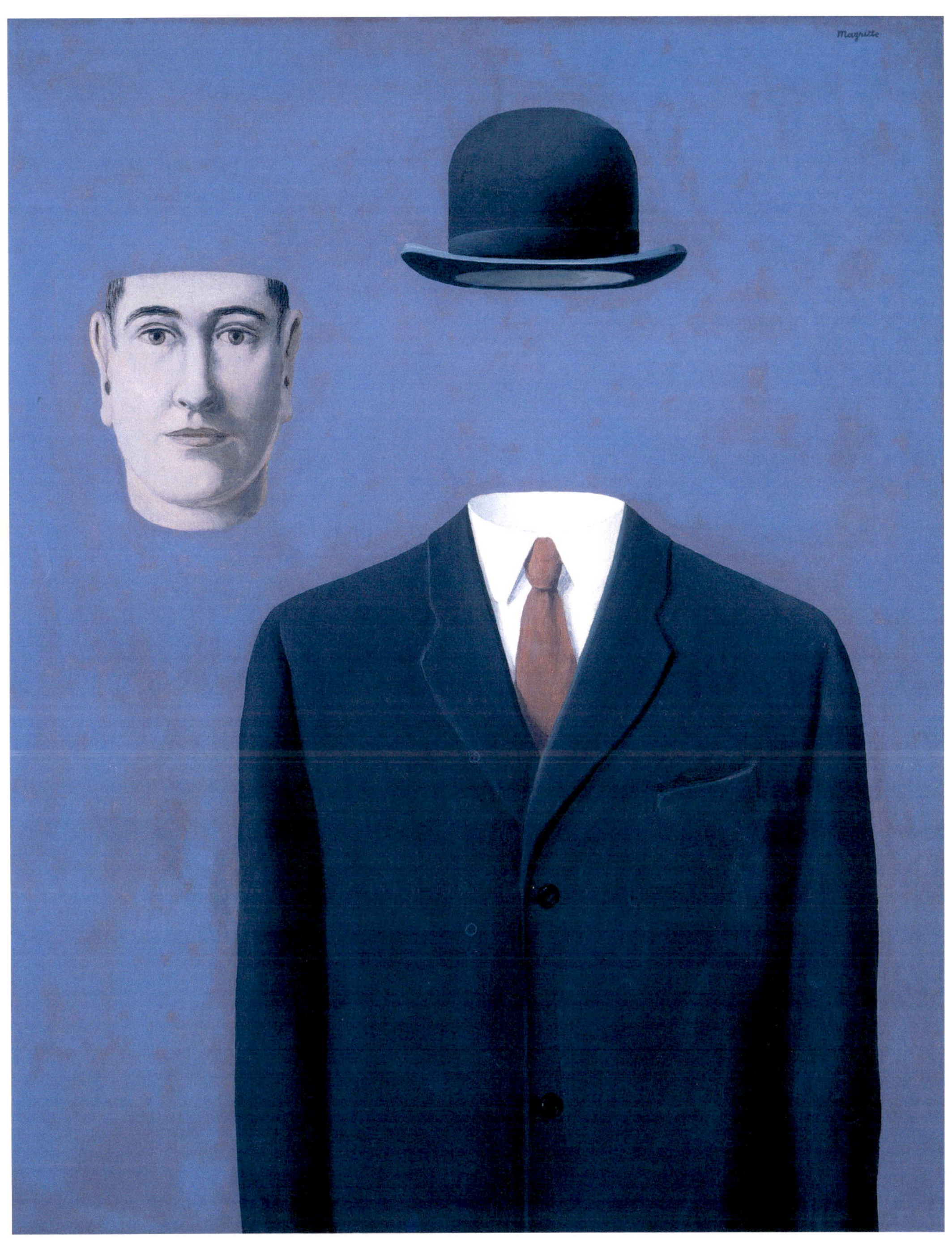

The Pilgrim
Le Pèlerin 1966, oil on canvas, 81 × 65 cm.
Private Collection, CR 1043

in the existence of reality and dissolving in being-ness – wishing to be subsumed in the absolute. With depersonalised motifs that are no more than signs, these 'portraits' can be read as reflections on the human condition and as projection surfaces for the individual unable to escape his or her own metaphysical loneliness. Bearing in mind his own tendency to dress in a suit and bowler hat, these pictures can also be read as 'anonymous self portraits', depictions of 'someone much of whose life was a performance of seeming not to be there'.[27] The fact that his mother was a milliner may also have had a bearing on his choice of the hat as a motif. (**GF**)

See also: **Absence; Anonymity; Banality; Object; Portraiture**

André Breton (1896–1966) Principal theoretician of **Surrealism** in **Paris**, his personality become identified from 1924, the year of publication of the 'First Surrealist Manifesto', with a movement of which he became the unchallengeable but frequently disputed leader. Whoever the group comprised, and whatever the frequently impassioned relations between its members, it cannot be denied that over forty years of Surrealism, Breton acted as a magnet and uncompromising judge among those who related to him. More than a new school of literature, Breton announced the principles of a veritable emancipation of man by **poetry**, by the imagination and by the unconscious which would not hesitate to link itself to revolutionary ideas, even if it would not submit to the discipline of the Communist Party. Advocating first and foremost a return to automatic writing, he detached himself progressively in order to privilege incantatory texts such as *The Night of the Sunflower* 1934 and *Free Union* 1931, or against romanticised form, a way of life such as that found in *Nadja* 1928 and *Mad Love* 1937. Even if they became stretched from time to time, the relations with the Brussels Surrealists were always marked by mutual respect, **Paul Nougé** and **Camille Goemans** signing the 1925 tract *Revolution First and Forever!* In 1929 Breton stated his intention to buy Magritte's painting *The Hidden Woman* 1929, which he would reproduce in the review **La Révolution surréaliste** along with photographs of members of the group, including the aforementioned Belgians. (**XC**)

See also: **Communism; Vache Period**

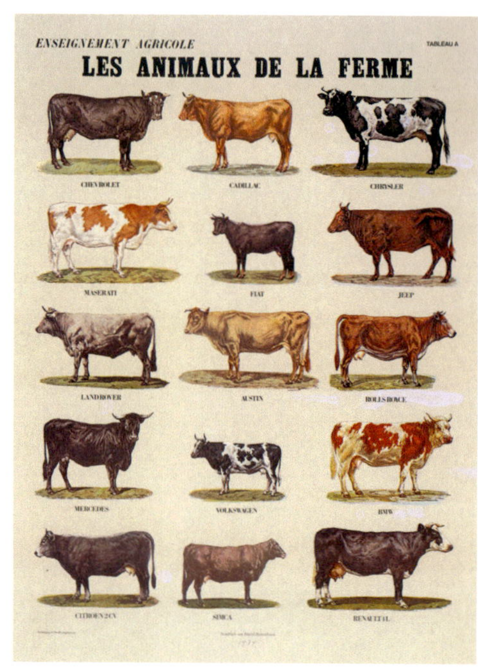

Marcel Broodthaers (1924–1976): *The Farm Animals* (*Les Animaux de la ferme*) 1974, lithograph on paper, 81.9 × 60.3 cm. Tate. Purchased 1980

Marcel Broodthaers (1924–1976) Belgian artist, film-maker and poet. Before being considered a representative of Conceptual Art in the line of **Marcel Duchamp**, Marcel Broodthaers had a long companionship with the Surrealists. A poet first and foremost, he frequented the Brussels group from 1945 onwards and took part in meetings aimed at gathering Surrealist forces in **Belgium**; he co-signed many tracts such as *No Quarter in the Revolution* 1947, and published four poetry collections between 1957 and 1964. A friend of **Paul Nougé** who corrected many of his texts and with whom he eventually fell out, it was at this time, around 1964, that Broodthaers turned towards the work of Magritte, symbolically abandoning his literary oeuvre for a plastic aesthetic on the occasion of his first solo exhibition at Galerie Saint-Laurent in Brussels. Broodthaers created a series of objects influenced by Surrealist assemblages, such as *Femur de l'homme belge* 1964–5 and *Pelle de salon* 1965, moving between the influences of Pop Art discovered in 1963 at the Palais des Beaux-Arts in Brussels, the artistic temperament of Piero

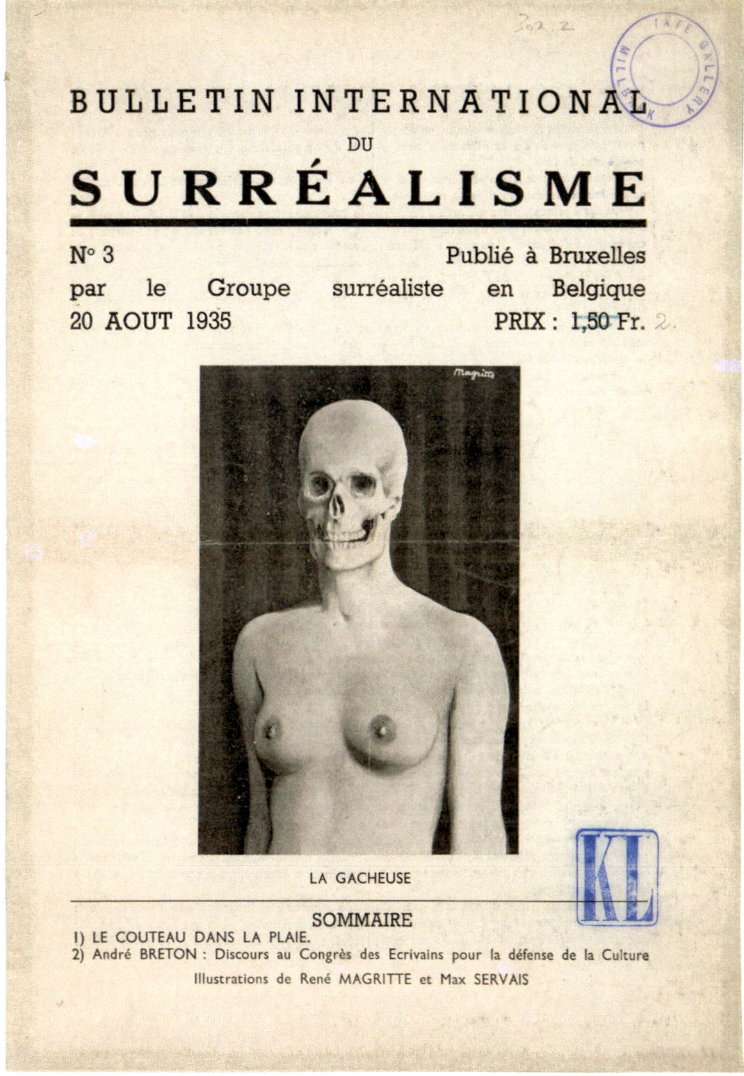

Bulletin international du surréalisme no.3, August 1935, published Brussels. Magritte's *The Bungler* (*La Gacheuse*) reproduced on front cover. Tate Library and Archive

Manzoni, and the example of Magritte from which he retained only the part connected to the relationship of words and images. (**XC**)

👁 See also: **Legacy**

Bulletin international du surréalisme: The third edition was published in Brussels on 20 August 1935, having previously been published in Prague in April 1935, then Tenerife. The fourth and final edition was published in London in September 1936 on the occasion of the *International Surrealist Exhibition*, staged at the New Burlington Galleries. Bringing together for the first time the Brussels group and the Hainaut group under the name *Groupe surréaliste de Belgique*, it reproduced the manifesto *The Cut in the Wound*, denouncing the Franco-Soviet pact, and the text of André Breton's lecture *The Defence of Culture*, which had been delivered that June by **Paul Éluard** to the Writers' Congress for the Defence of Culture. Its cover featured an image of Magritte's gouache *The Bungler* 1935. (**XC**)

👁 See also: **England; Edward James**

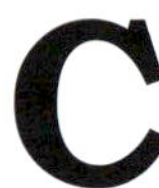

C

Cabinet of Curiosities, or *Wunderkammer*, was a recurrent model for Magritte. In the sixteenth and seventeenth century, cabinets of curiosities were early modern collections assembled by kings, scholars, medics and other educated and wealthy men. Objects in these collections were organised by the pursuit of polyhistoric knowledge. In these cabinets works of art, scientific and mystical objects were assembled with curiosities and rarities, without any generic separations or discriminations, allowing objects to enter into strange, unexpected and new relations with each other. Many Surrealists were attracted to the poetic potential of the cabinet of curiosities and adopted their structure in their artworks and for displaying their own collections.

In Magritte's paintings, the cabinet of curiosities provides the form to represent and summarise his themes in *On the Threshold of Freedom* 1937, and is the template for his use of compartmentalisation in *One-Night Museum* 1927 and *The Obsession* 1928. It is linked to other key areas in Magritte's art such as his use of **trompe l'oeil** (which originally was both an object to be collected in cabinets of curiosities as well as a genre representing those cabinets) and his use of framing devices. The structure of the cabinet of curiosities can also be traced in paintings such as Magritte's *The Human Condition* 1933, which constitutes a complex engagement with questions of reality and representation, or rather the constant framing of reality by representation. The structure of this painting resembles the system of a cabinet of curiosities which Patrick Mauriès described as 'nothing more nor less than a sequence of containers holding within them yet more containers in diminishing order or size […]'.[28]

While French **Surrealists** use the structure of the cabinet of curiosities to unearth unconscious links and relations between different objects, and

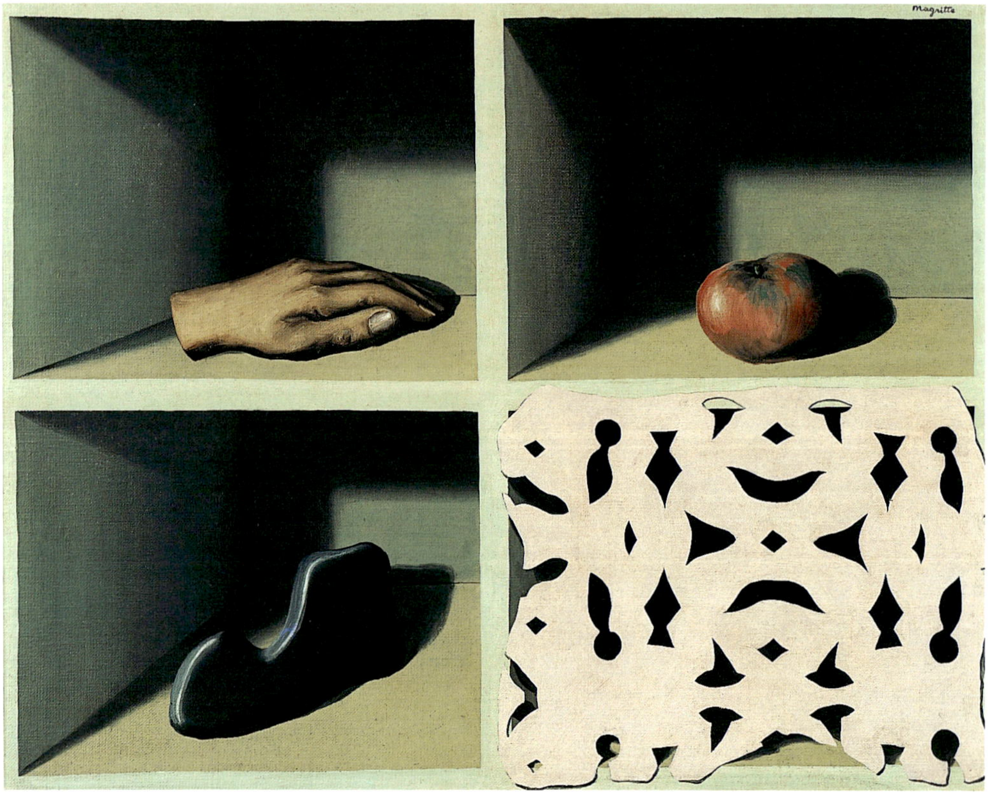

One-Night Museum
Le Musée d'une nuit 1927, oil on canvas, 50 × 65 cm.
Private Collection, London, CR 171

between the natural and the artificial, Magritte uses it to reveal conventionally understood 'natural links' such as those between word and image, and representation and that which is represented, to demonstrate that these links are arbitrary and constructed. **(PA)**

See also: **Object; Representation and Resemblance; Shop Window Display; Theatrical Display**

Le Centaure: Founded in 1921 in Brussels by Walter Schwarzenberg, La Galerie du Centaure championed mainly Flemish Expressionism and the French school, notably organising in 1923 the first exhibition of Raoul Dufy in Belgium. It was similar to **Paul-Gustave Van Hecke's** journal and gallery 'Sélection', to which Schwarzenberg was close, his gallery becoming one of the most attentive supporters of Belgian modern art, welcoming Magritte's oeuvre alongside Expressionist artists. In 1926 the gallery, renamed 'Le Centaure' after its move from Rue du Musée to Avenue Louise, signed a contract with Magritte before organising his first solo exhibition in April 1927. Jean Milo was entrusted with looking after the artistic direction of the gallery. Its journal *Le Centaure*, which first appeared in October 1926 and was edited by Georges Marlier, carried a number of Magritte's commercial advertisements, notably for the fashion house Norine, named after Van Hecke's wife. In 1929, after the close of the Galerie L'Époque founded by Van Hecke and directed by **E.L.T. Mesens**, Le Centaure bought back its entire stock of works by Magritte and other artists. Hit by the financial crisis, Le Centaure closed in 1931, its stock liquidated in October 1932. With the corresponding collapse in value, E.L.T. Mesens acquired, among others, the complete works of Magritte, totalling 150 works, for the equivalent of 5,000 Belgian francs. **(XC)**

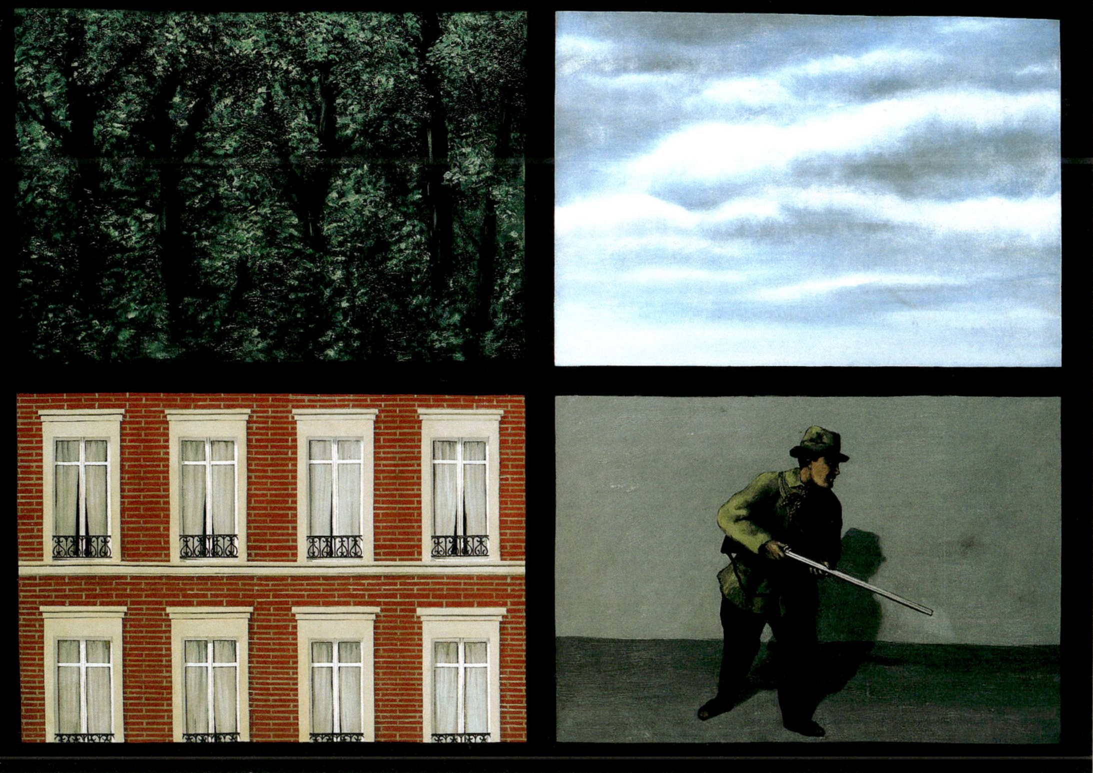

The Obsession
L'Idée fixe 1928, oil on canvas, 81 × 116 cm.
Neue Nationalgalerie, Staatliche Museen, Berlin, CR 269

Chance was a key Surrealist technique in conjuring a world of wonder and revealing the mechanics of the subconscious. The concept was most famously evoked by Comte de Lautréamont (pseudonym of Isidore Ducasse) in his statement 'beautiful as the chance meeting on a dissecting table of a sewing machine and an umbrella'.[29] For Magritte, the unlikely combination of everyday objects, body parts and locations is a key method of evoking a mysterious world: for example, floating giant turtles in the sky, situating oversized objects in an interior and placing a moon sickle in front of a tree. However, chance as such plays a limited role in the artist's arsenal of alienating techniques. For Magritte it was less the chance encounter than the suspension of the laws of logic and physics, the metamorphic transformation of objects and the skilful confusion of elements that were used to subvert expectations of reality. Most importantly, Magritte challenged the notion of a logical and ordered world by disrupting the semiotic relationship between the signifier and the signified – objects and their designations in language. In a process of apparently pure coincidental **juxtaposition**, in *The Interpretation of Dreams* 1930, ordinary everyday objects were combined with incongruous legends: a woman's shoe is described as 'The Moon', a glass as 'The Thunderstorm', a candle as 'The Ceiling' and an egg as 'The Acacia'. Similarly, he used the seemingly random and incongruous combination of image and title to create a productive poetic friction. (CG)

See also: **Automatism and Automatic Writing; Dreams; Elective Affinities; Metamorphosis; Poetry; Titles**

Giorgio de Chirico (1888–1978) Italian painter, sculptor, theatrical designer and writer. Giorgio de Chirico was Magritte's most important artistic influence. The exact date of Magritte's first encounter with de Chirico's painting *The Love Song* 1914 is unclear, though **David Sylvester** suggests that the artist first saw a reproduced image of the painting in the second half of 1923. Prior to this encounter Magritte had become increasingly disenchanted with creating art informed by the ideas of Purism. The juxtaposition in *The Love Song* of a series of unrelated objects – a rubber glove, a plaster antique head and a mysterious orb – revealed to Magritte for the first time the liberating power of the poetic image. The revelation that a painting could speak of something other than its image henceforth sustained his artistic practice. Describing de Chirico's influence during his lecture 'La Ligne de vie' in Antwerp in September 1938, Magritte declared: 'It was a new vision through which the spectator might recognise his own isolation and hear the silence of the world.'[30] De Chirico's influence was ubiquitous from late 1925 until early 1927, exemplified in works such as *Dawn at Cayenne* 1926. (DP)

See also: **Juxtaposition**

Clouds: The blue sky with regular cloud pattern is a recurrent motif which Magritte employed in a variety of forms throughout his oeuvre: as isolated surface pattern, superimposed onto unlikely objects (such as flags or faces) and as part of paradoxical landscapes. In the 1931 painting *The Curse*, Magritte for the first time liberates the sky completely from the horizon and creates his first skyscape, a convincing if strangely unnatural pattern of white and grey clouds floating on a bright blue sky. The careful study and representation of clouds in the sky goes back to at least the eighteenth century

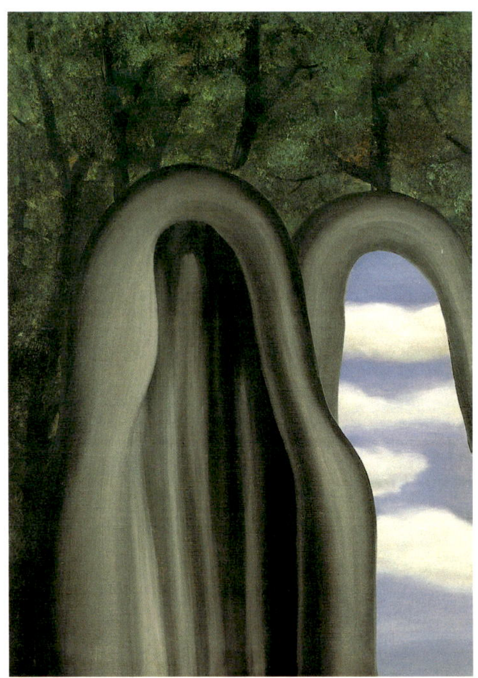

The Palace of Curtains
Le Palais de rideaux 1928, oil on canvas, 73 × 54 cm.
Safflane Holdings Limited, CR 267

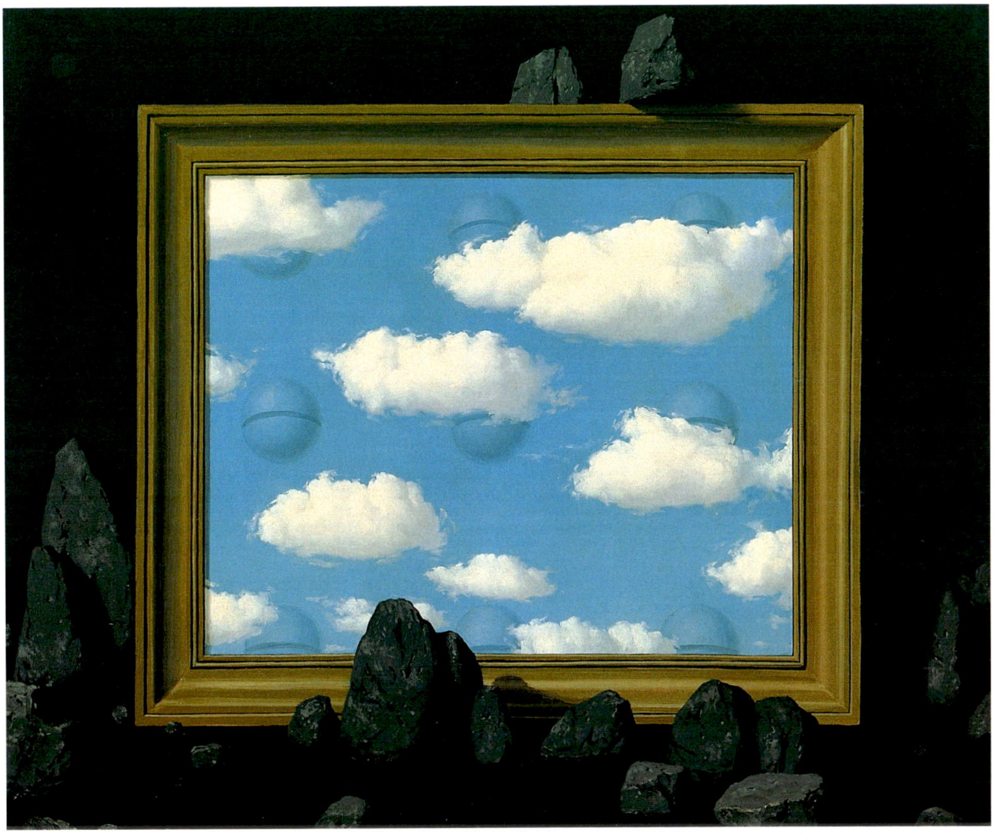

The Spring Tide
La Grande Marée 1951,
oil on canvas, 65 × 80 cm.
Private Collection, Brussels,
CR 767

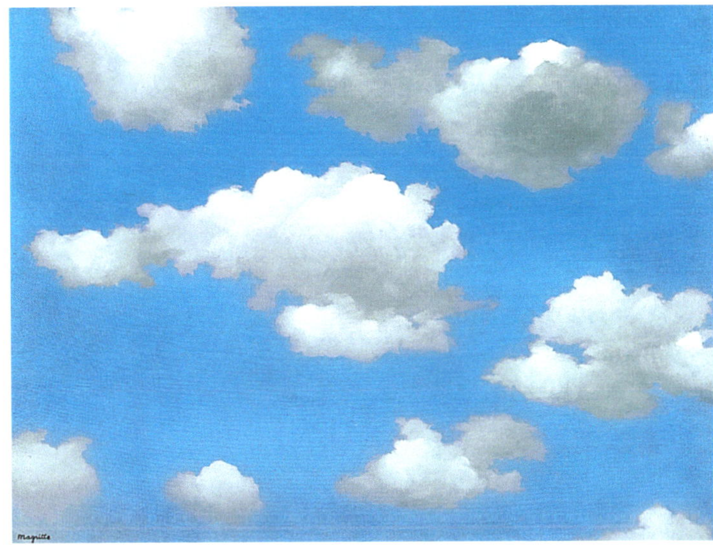

The Curse
La Malédiction 1931, oil on canvas,
54 × 73 cm. Caldic Collection,
Rotterdam, courtesy Galerie
Vedovi, Brussels, CR 337

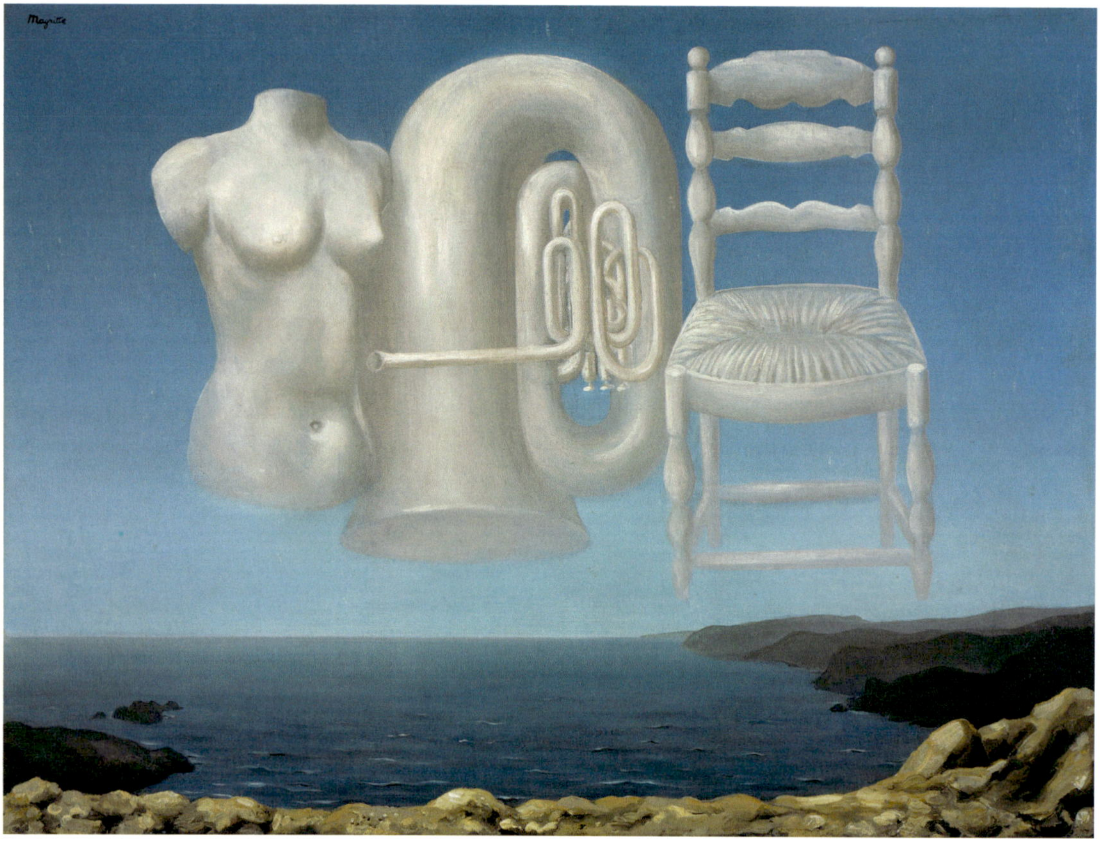

Threatening Weather
Le Temps menaçant 1929, oil on canvas,
54 × 73 cm. Scottish National Gallery of
Modern Art, Edinburgh. Purchased with
the support of the Heritage Lottery Fund
and the Art Fund 1995, CR 313

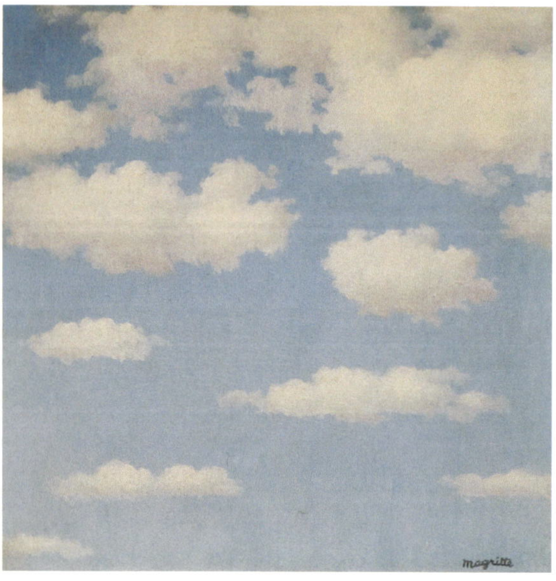

The Curse
La Malédiction 1937, oil on canvas,
12.8 × 12.8 cm. The Edward James Trust,
West Dean, CR 433

with Alexander Cozens and John Constable producing detailed studies of cloudy skies. Magritte uses clouds as a product of **artifice** rather than a truthful representation of nature, stripping the motif of any metaphysical meaning it previously might have possessed. In *Threatening Weather* 1929, clouds organise themselves into three familiar objects, giving visible form to the Surrealist game of identifying motifs in irregular shaped stains or blots. In ***The Dominion of Light*** series of the 1940s–60s, the **juxtaposition** of a night landscape with bright blue sky with clouds creates one of the artist's most intriguingly paradoxical inventions. (**CG**)

 See also: **Colour; Drawing; Pattern**

Paul Colinet (1898–1957) Belgian poet and writer. It was around 1933 that **Marcel Lecomte** introduced Colinet to the Brussels Surrealist group. Publishing little, he assisted Magritte in the search for **titles** for a number of his works. Refusing to give his signature to tracts or collective declarations, he found himself at a distance from Surrealist activities. His role was

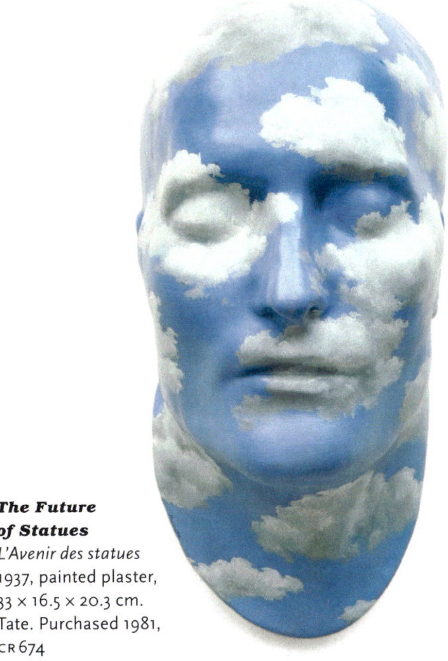

The Future of Statues
L'Avenir des statues 1937, painted plaster, 33 × 16.5 × 20.3 cm. Tate. Purchased 1981, CR 674

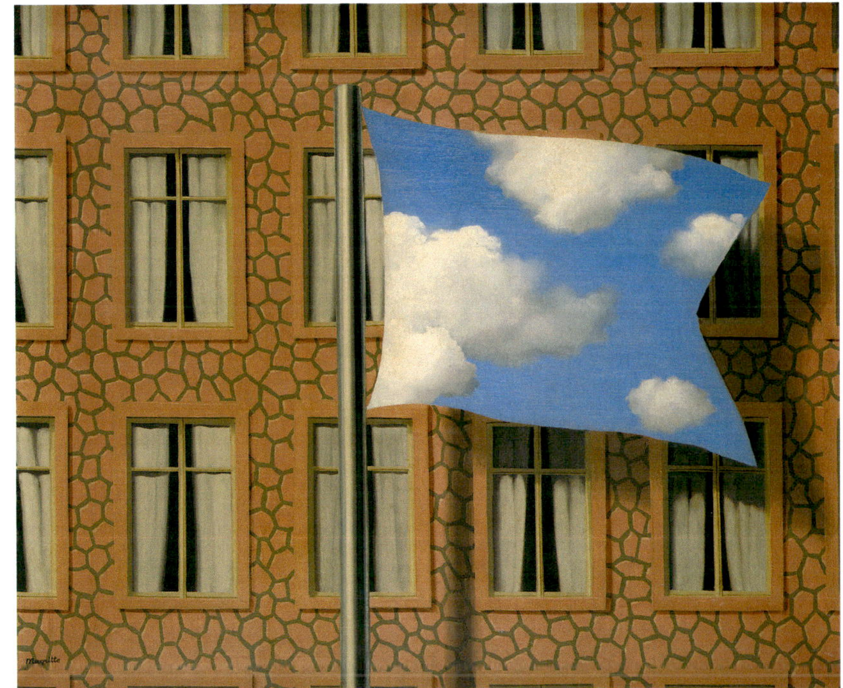

Summer
L'Été 1931, oil on canvas, 60 × 73 cm. Musée d'Ixelles, Brussels. Gift of Max Janlet, CR 338

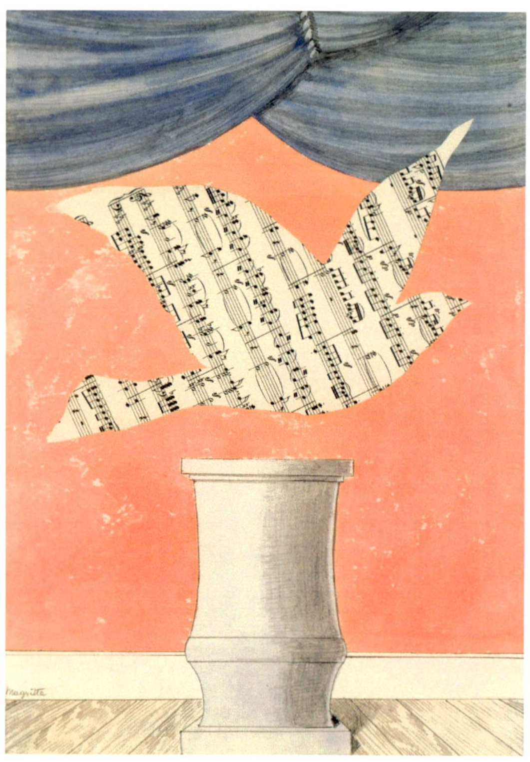

Dove
Colombe 1961–2, Printed paper, watercolour and pencil on
paper, 41.7 × 30.3 cm. Collection Mr and Mrs Wilbur Ross,
CR1653

affirmed after the war, above all alongside Magritte
when the influence of **Paul Nougé** receded, but
equally in being behind a range of journals and publications where he exercised his poetic and draughts-
man's talent. Among others he contributed to the
printed reviews *La Carte d'après nature* 1952–54
and *Le Ciel bleu* 1945 but above all a strange journal
manuscript of which the only example is *Vendredi*,
devised in 1949, under the direction of his nephew,
the illustrator Robert Willems from the Belgian
Congo. Shortly before his death he sponsored the
creation of the Surrealist journals *Phantômas* and
the *Daily-Bûl*. (**xc**)

Collage: Magritte began creating works in paper
collage (or *papier collé*) in late 1925, around the
same time as his earliest Surrealist paintings. His
interest in the medium was likely catalysed by his

admiration for the collages of **Max Ernst**. In his
1938 lecture 'La Ligne de vie', Magritte described
how Ernst's collage illustrations for **Paul Éluard's**
Répétitions led him to realise 'that everything that
gave traditional painting its prestige could easily be
dispensed with. Scissors, paste, images and genius
in effect superseded brushes, paints, models, style,
sensibility and that famous sincerity demanded of
artists'.[31] Magritte created around thirty works in
collage between 1925 and 1927, taking the medium
up again in 1959, creating another twenty-seven before his death in 1967. His early collages in particular
deploy pictorial elements that correspond closely
with his painted compositions. Indeed, Ernst once
described Magritte as a painter 'whose pictures
are collages entirely painted by hand'.[32] The use of
shapes cut from real sheet-music manuscript can be
seen to continue Magritte's concern with creating
imagery that explores the slippage between the real
and **representation**. (**DP**)
See also: **Colour; Cubism; Pattern**

Colour: Magritte's attitude to colour corresponded
with his apparent ambivalence towards aesthetic
considerations. 'I used light blue where sky had to
be represented', he wrote, 'but never represented the
sky … to have an excuse for showing one of my favourite colours next to one of my favourite greys.'[33]
For him, the expression of pure poetic thought
took priority. During his **Renoir Period** (1943–47),
however, Magritte engaged explicitly with colour by
adopting the 'sunlit' palette of Pierre-Auguste Renoir
and Jean-Auguste-Dominique Ingres. *Lightning* 1944
deploys a shift in palette to engage with ideas of
invisibility. The bouquet, portrayed as a mass of dull
grey that was anathema to the Impressionist artists,
reads as a kind of **absence** or disappearance in the
image. In this painting this notion of invisibility
chimes with Magritte's description of painting as
the 'art of juxtaposing colours in space in such a way
that the effective aspect of the colour disappears to
allow for the description of an inspired thought'.[34]
His subversive attitude to the application of colour
can also be seen in *The Harvest* 1943, an image of
a reclining nude whose limbs, torso and head are
each depicted in different and disparate harlequin
colours. (**DP**)

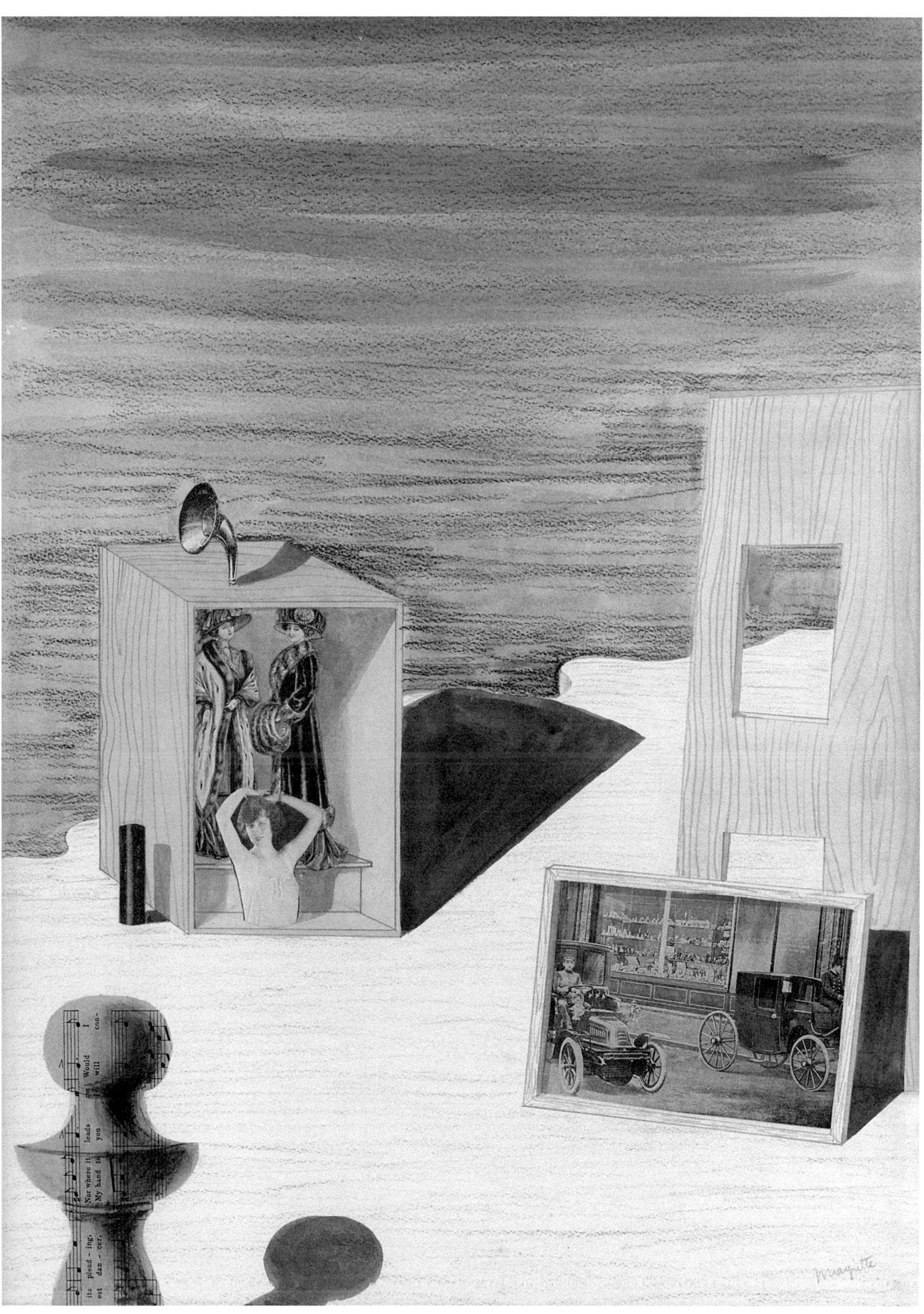

Untitled
1925, collage, printed paper, gouache, pencil and crayon on
paper, 53.7 × 39 cm. Musée d'Ixelles, Brussels, CR 1609

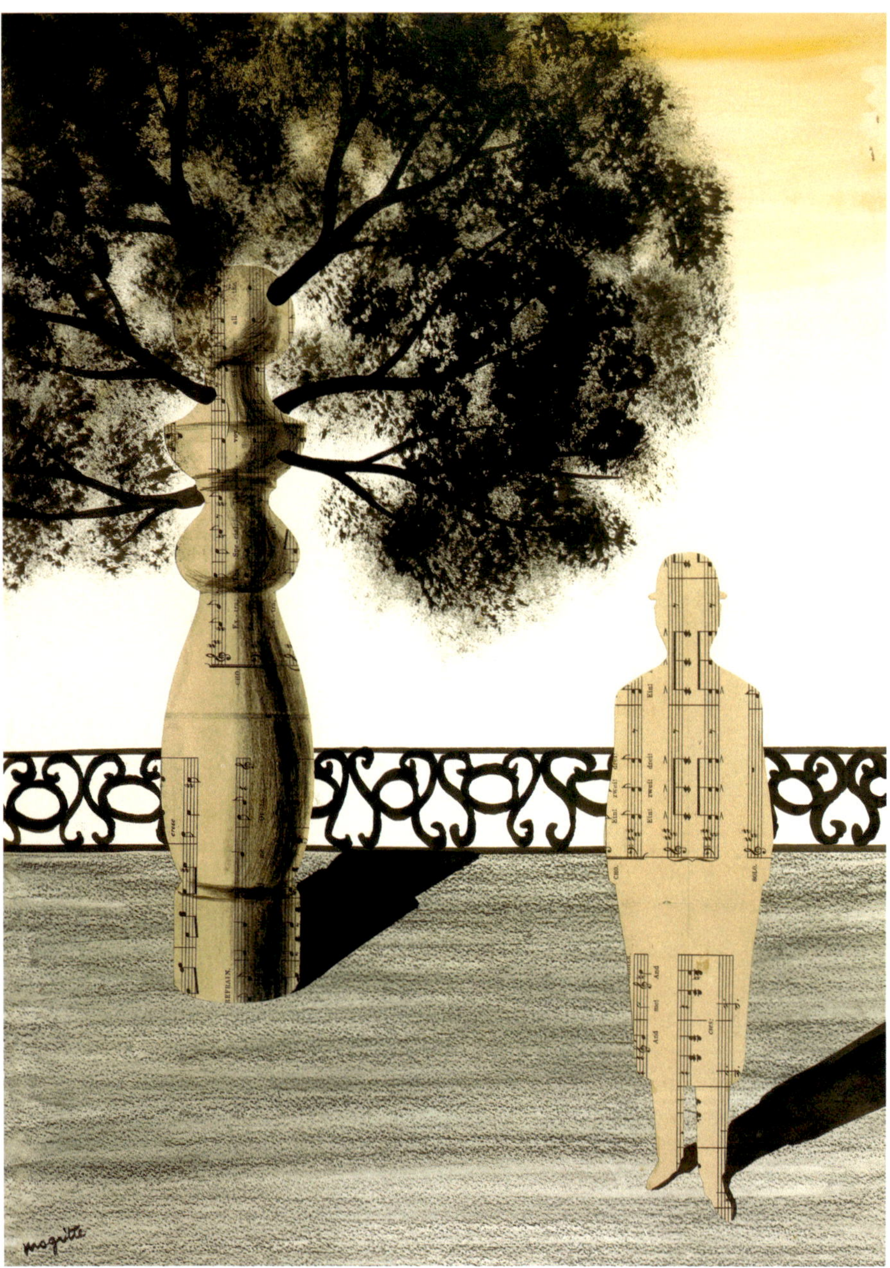

Untitled
1926, printed paper, gouache and watercolour on paper,
55 × 40 cm. Private Collection, CR 1616

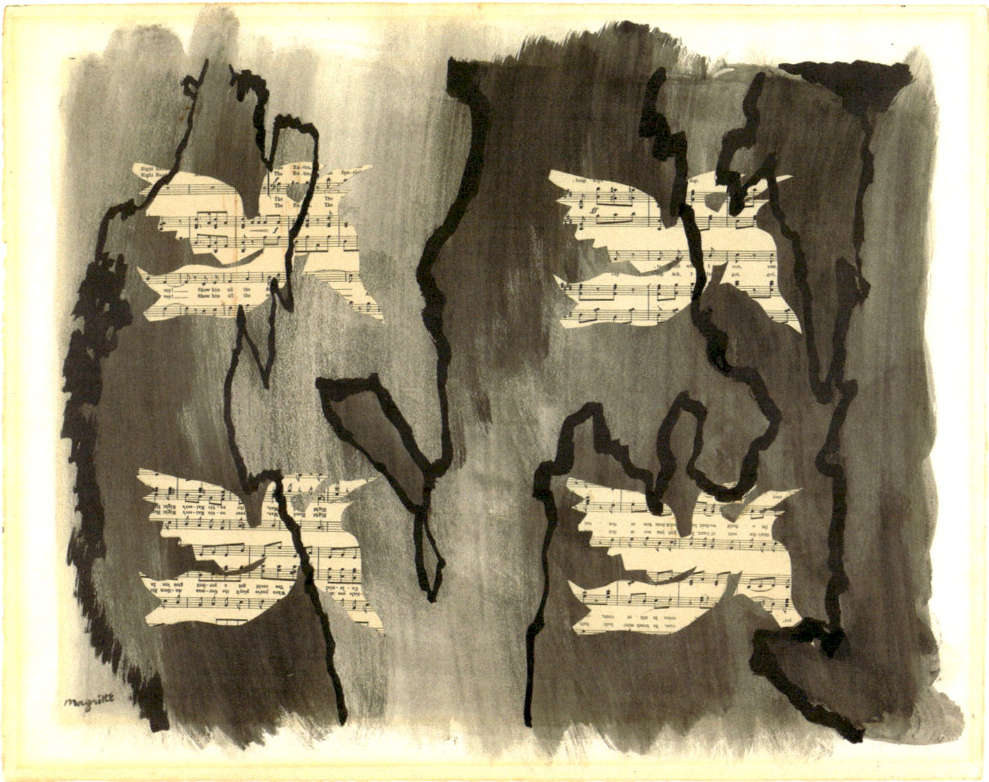

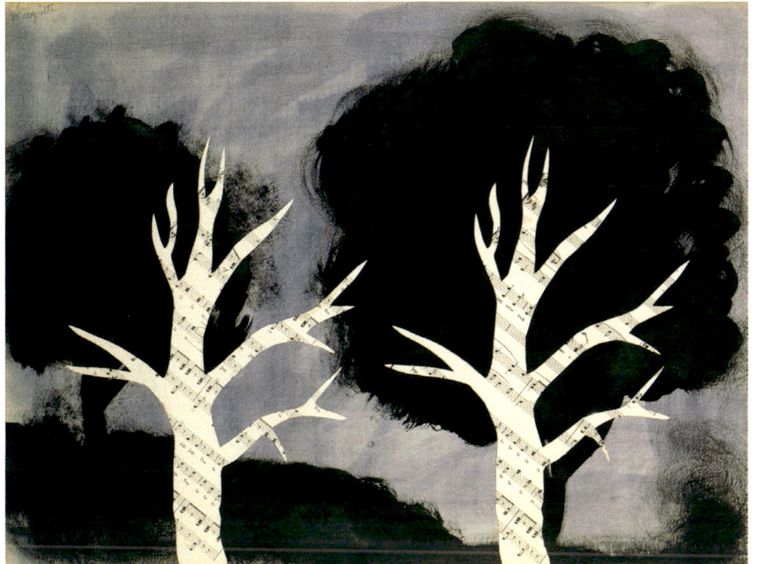

The Murderous Sky
Le Ciel meurtrier 1927,
printed paper, watercolour,
ink and pencil on paper,
50.3 × 65.2 cm. National
Gallery of Art, Washington,
DC, Collection Mr and Mrs
Paul Mellon, 1995, CR 1625

Nocturne
1927, printed paper and
gouache on paper, 42 × 56 cm.
Private Collection, courtesy
Galerie 1900–2000, Paris,
CR 1623

Commercial Art: When asked in 1946 what things he hated the most, amongst other things Magritte replied: 'I hate my past and that of others … I also hate the decorative arts [and] advertising.'[35] If Magritte detested the applied and commercial arts – indeed his first recorded text was a manifesto defending 'pure art' against such degradations – it is nonetheless true both that they had a tangible impact on his painting, and that over extended periods he found himself obliged to undertake 'travaux imbéciles' – the 'idiotic work' of advertising, publicity and commerce.[36] For the most part strictly a money-making exercise, not all of it is without interest, while the wider issues of the **appropriation** of commercial imagery within his own practice raise interesting questions about a relationship he was keen to play down.

Over his life, predominantly before 1936 and sometimes under a pseudonym, Magritte worked on a range of posters, leaflets, corporate identities, covers for sheet music and advertising brochures. Later in his career he would also provide images for high-profile publicity campaigns, drawing on his status as an established artist, at a time when his work was already being extensively borrowed or pastiched by the advertising industries. Magritte's very first contribution to an exhibition, in 1918, was a poster, and in early years he explored several opportunities in commercial art. In order to support himself and his bride-to-be **Georgette**, Magritte started work in 1921 at the Peters-Lacroix **wallpaper** factory in Haren, where for a year or so he produced wallpaper designs.

There was a tangible relationship between his commercial work and painting in the early to mid-1920s, during which he tested out the stylistic characteristics of **Futurism** and Fauvism traceable in both outcomes. Surprisingly, the final breakthrough into **Surrealism** in 1926 was also accompanied by a range of advertising work in which elements from his paintings – unexpected **juxtapositions**, the theatrical staging of objects and his trademark **bilboquets** – lent publicity images some of the enigmatic air of his 'serious' practice. The most interesting of these were the two trade catalogues produced for the Maison Samuel in Brussels in 1926 and 1927, featuring watercolour and collage illustrations of **mannequins** wearing fur coats, with accompanying texts by **Camille Goemans** and **Paul Nougé** respectively. The second of these in particular, in which Nougé's suggestive texts produced an effect quite distinct from the usual advertising copy, features artworks which, but for their context, might sit close enough to Magritte's paintings of the period

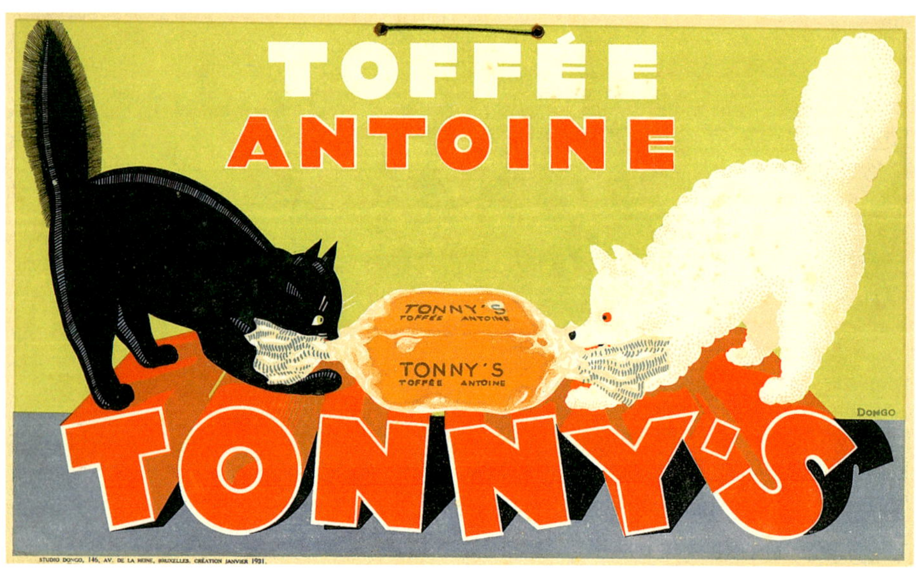

Toffée Antoine Tonny's
1931, lithograph, 26.7 × 45.4 cm. Agency: Studio Dongo, Brussels. Private Collection, courtesy Keitelman Gallery

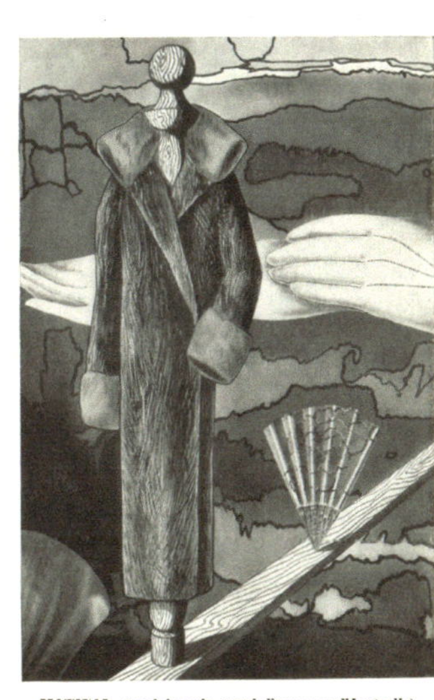

MATINAL (poulain noir garni d'opossum d'Australie)

Pour l'année 1928 la maison Samuel vous présente quelques manteaux
1927, illustrated leaflet, 22 × 15.5 cm. Maison Ch. Muller,
S. Samuel et Cie, successeurs, Brussels. Collection Isy Brachot

to suggest his interest in the possibilities of a hybrid practice – poetic interchanges between text, image and object – that might not exclude a commercial audience for his work.

Rather different was the work Magritte undertook with his brother **Paul** in the years 1931–36 under the umbrella of Studio Dongo, a commercial practice based in a shed at the bottom of his garden. Established on his return from a frustrating three years spent in Paris, the company promoted itself as specialising in 'Stands – Displays – Publicity Objects – Posters – Drawings – Photomontages – Advertising Copy'.[37] While Paul looked after commissions, René produced the artwork, signed with a pseudonym and, in contrast to his earlier work but in tune with the commercial styles of the 1930s, largely anonymous in appearance. Indeed, he would complain of clients' unwillingness to accept more distinctive ideas. During and after **World War II**,

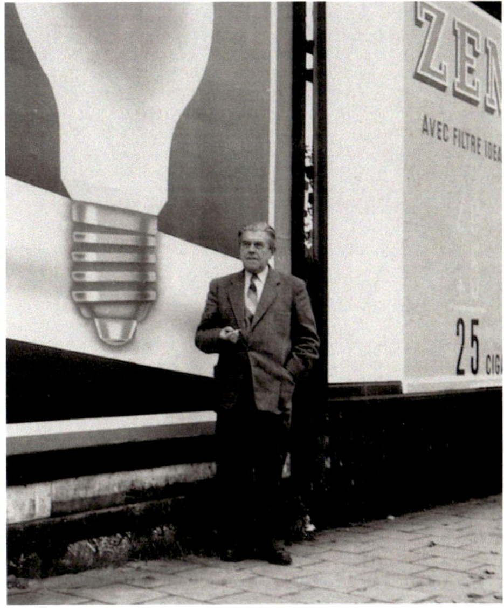

Georges Thiry (1904–1994): René Magritte standing in front of advertising billboard c.1955

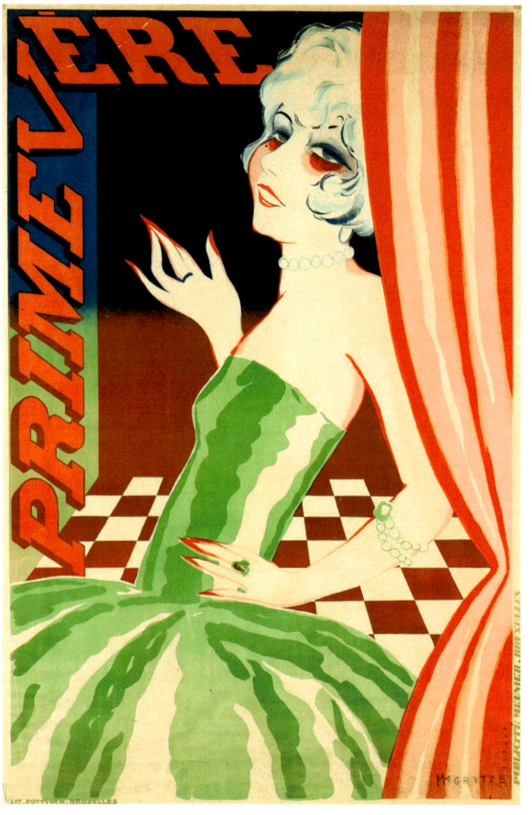

Primevère
1926, lithograph on paper, 124.5 × 85.2 cm. Agency: Publicité Meunier, Brussels. Private Collection, courtesy Keitelman Gallery

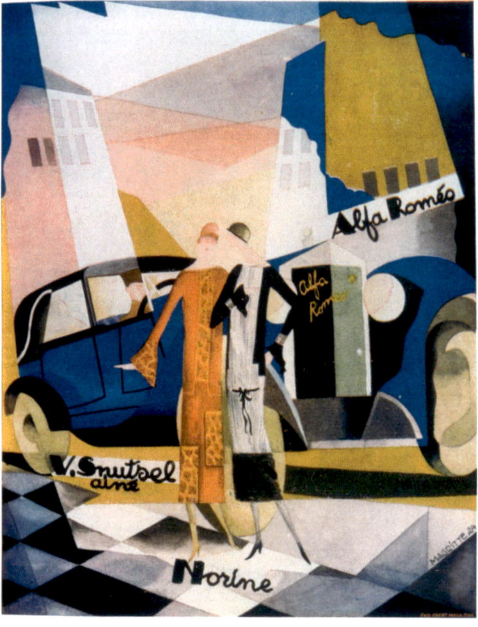

Alfa Romeo – V. Snutsel aîné – Norine
1924, group advertisement, 20 × 28 cm, *Englebert Magazine*, Liège, no.59–60, January–February 1925. Collection R.C.

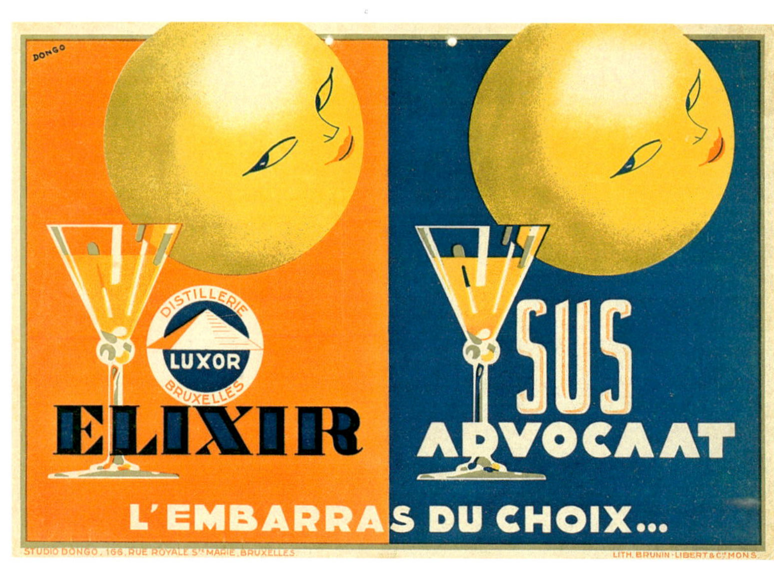

Distillerie Luxor Bruxelles Elixir Sus Advocaat
1935, lithograph, 27.7 × 40.7 cm. Agency: Studio Dongo, Brussels. Private Collection, courtesy Keitelman Gallery

Magritte would continue to propose and complete occasional poster and advertising projects, but increasingly on his own terms and featuring ideas rooted in his painting. There exists, for example, a clear relationship between Magritte's posters advertising French perfume of the mid-1940s and painted compositions such as *Forethought* 1943.

The period of Magritte's emergence as an artist was also a heyday of advertising and design, and French and Belgian Surrealists alike were intrigued by their presence in the urban environment, popular culture and the materiality of the everyday. If they were echoed surreptitiously in his paintings, one might note that Magritte's art centres on strategies of communication and language – especially the relationship between words and images and their codes of representation – in ways that appear universal yet deeply personal. These are also central concerns of design and advertising, even if their aim is the polar opposite of Magritte's unsettling, profoundly philosophical enquiry, and it is little wonder that commerce, in principle anathema to Surrealism, should find itself irresistibly drawn to the artist's mysterious yet instantly persuasive images. (**KF**)

👁 See also: **Anonymity; Kitsch; Legacy; Pattern; Shop Window Display**

Communism: Like many artists of his generation, and as a Surrealist activist, Magritte's political sympathies lay on the Left. His intellectual context in Brussels and **Paris** included the debates informing the radical political positions adopted by **Surrealism** and those close to it. While there is some difference of opinion about how many times Magritte committed himself directly to Communism (it has been claimed he joined twice during the 1930s, in 1932 and 1936)[38] on 8 September 1945 the Party's newspaper *Le Drapeau rouge* announced that the painter had joined the Belgian Communist Party (PCB) with a front-page article and photograph.[39] While most commentators have emphasised the short-lived nature of this commitment – by Magritte's own admission he stopped participating in Party activities after a few months, though he continued to support Party-sponsored events for some time longer – what seems more important to grasp is his explicit and life-long adherence to the principles and ethics of intellectual and social liberty.

OUVRIERS ET OUVRIERES TEXTILES
FÊTEZ LE
18 SEPT^RE
le
40^e
ANNIVERSAIRE
DE LA
CENTRALE DES OUVRIERS
TEXTILES DE BELGIQUE

Fêtez le 18 septembre
1938, gouache and pencil on paper, 24.3 × 16.3 cm.
Royal Museums of Fine Arts of Belgium, Brussels.
Bequest of Irène Scutenaire-Hamoir, 1996, CR X31

In the second half of the 1920s the Surrealist group in Brussels (which included **Paul Nougé**, a founder member of the PCB) contributed to the heated debates within international Surrealism around the need to commit to Communism, part of a wider defence of the values of freedom in the face of an oppressive bourgeois order, debates that led to acrimonious divisions in the Parisian group. While a number of the French Surrealists joined the Party, their hopes that it would find a role for Surrealism were soon quashed, and during the early 1930s the relationship between Surrealism and Communism soured to the point where by 1935, in the face of the rise of Stalinist authoritarianism, French and Belgian Surrealists signed the declaration 'On the Time the Surrealists were Right' confirming a definitive rupture.

This frustrated attempt to find a place within Party orthodoxy, and to challenge it with

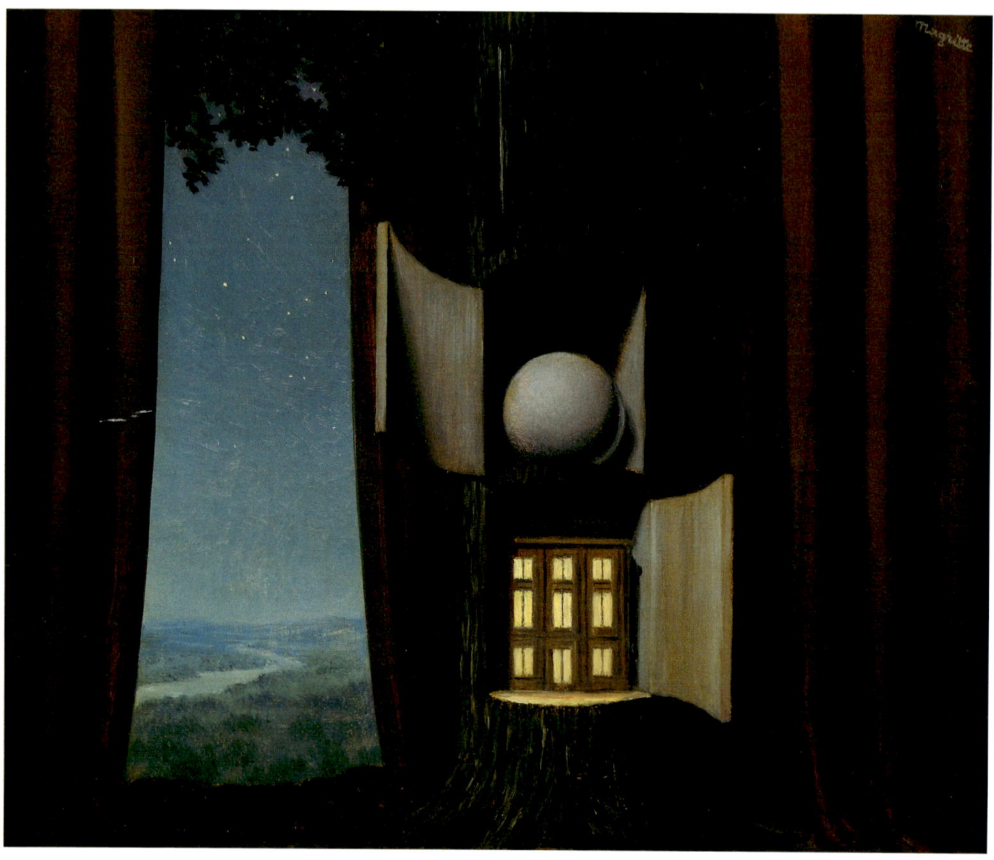

Blood Will Tell
La Voix du sang 1948, oil on canvas, 50 × 60 cm.
Private Collection, CR 660

Surrealist notions that lay well outside the bounds of Communists' espousal of a realist 'proletarian' art and literature, was mirrored by Magritte's experience of 1945. Like many at the end of the war, Magritte had felt that the only adequate response to the traumatic events and alienating politics of the preceding years lay with Communism, and as he explained to Patrick Waldberg, he hoped 'that we would be able, from the inside, to influence the Party's cultural orientation, to bend it more in the direction of our deeper aspirations'.[40] Unsurprisingly, this aspiration proved unfounded, and even his attempts to supply the Party with poster designs met with rejection. In the meantime he also maintained his distance from the short-lived but vocal Revolutionary Surrealism group in Belgium that attempted a more explicit combination of the two positions.

Magritte continued nevertheless to confirm that he saw the artist to be a worker like any other, and that his task lay in providing works capable of enriching the consciousness of others. While his paintings may not be overtly militant – unless we read the ubiquitous bowler-hatted functionaries of *Golconda* 1953, or *The Month of the Grape Harvest* 1959, as armies of the enemy – they remain profoundly ethical. The conventions and knowledge his paintings work so effectively to undo are those of the dominant order, to be demolished before a society of clarity can be built. (**KF**)

See also: **André Breton; World War II**

Correspondance: Published between November 1924 and June 1925, *Correspondance* was a series of twenty-two tracts issued at ten-day intervals which constituted the first manifestation of the future Brussels Surrealist group. Written by **Paul Nougé**, **Camille Goemans** and **Marcel Lecomte**, they were printed on coloured paper and distributed freely, in particular to poets and writers – **André Breton**, Louis Aragon, **Paul Éluard** or André Gide – to put them on guard against stylistic habits or lapses resulting from their literary practice. *Correspondance* made a great impression on the **Surrealists** in Paris. The tracts are characterised by a mimetic depersonalised style of writing, which was intended to give the reader a taste of the secret, of the anonymous and the mysterious which characterised the ideas of Nougé and his companions. (**xc**)

See also: **Anonymity**

Cubism: Before aligning with **Surrealism**, Cubism was a key artistic influence for Magritte. Works created between 1920 and 1924 express the dynamic visual fragmentation characteristic of the movement. Magritte admired the Cubist works of Georges Braque and Pablo Picasso, and their use of newspaper **collage** elements informed Magritte's works. For him Cubist art expressed its own legitimate reality that emphasised the disparity between the painted image and the actual object depicted. (**DP**)

See also: **Futurism**

Curtain: The motif of a curtain, with its contradictory capacity to both reveal and conceal, first appears in Magritte's early **Surrealist** paintings of 1925–26, where it is used to **frame** the image, creating a stage-like effect. Later on it reappears as an isolated **object** in space, almost like a scissor-cut silhouette, for example in *The Court of Love* 1960. When Magritte commented that 'we are surrounded by curtains' he was talking of our awareness that we see the world subjectively, as if through a veil of semblances.[41] His use of the curtain was similar to its use in traditional painting, where it served as a *repoussoir*, creating perspective and spatial contrast in the image. At the same time, its use reflected his conviction that an object needs in some sense to be veiled in order for it to be fully recognised. (**GT**)

See also: **Absence; Mask and Masquerade**

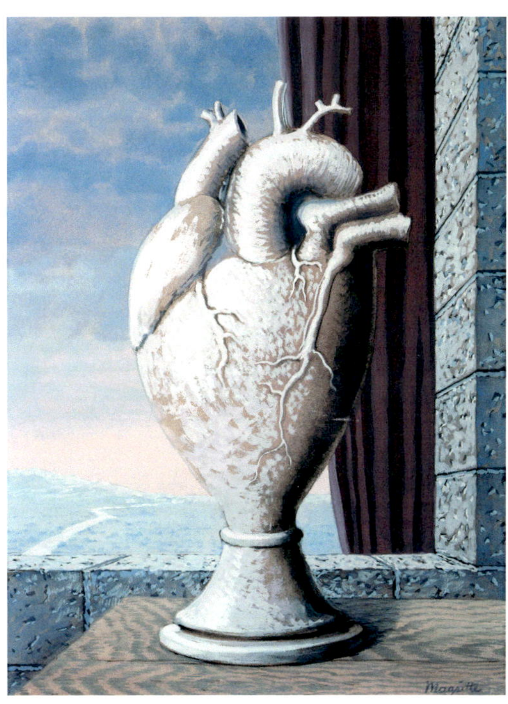

The Bag of Tricks
Le Sac à malice 1960, gouache on cardboard, 34.5 × 26 cm. Collection Triton Foundation, The Netherlands, CR 1477

D

Dada: Avant-garde movement which emerged in 1916 in Europe as a reaction by artists to what they saw as the horror and folly of World War I, which Dadaists believed was caused by the logic and rationality of bourgeois capitalist ideology. Magritte's brief engagement with Dada was steered by **E.L.T. Mesens**, who whilst in Paris became acquainted with Tristan Tzara. In 1924 Magritte and Mesens contributed to **Francis Picabia's** review *391*, which inspired them to launch the Dadaist review *Œsophage* in March 1925. Revolutionary in intent, Dada became an international movement, eventually forming the basis of **Surrealism** in Paris. (DP)

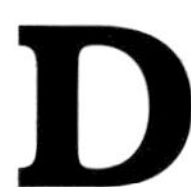 See also: **Marcel Duchamp; Object**

Salvador Dalí (1904–1989) Together, Magritte and Dalí were the foremost artists responsible for the reorientation of Surrealist art away from its initial emphasis on automatic techniques, towards works that privileged the image. Magritte joined the delegation invited to stay with Dalí in Cadaqués in the summer of 1929, cementing the latter's reception into the movement. While their outlook and intentions stand in sharp contrast – Dalí's extravagant persona and elaborations of unconscious dramas are far from Magritte's concerns – a shared interest in apparently outmoded academic technique, and an ability to provoke and fascinate their audiences, make them for many the definitive Surrealist artists of the 1930s. (KF)

See also: **Automatism and Automatic Writing; Edward James**

Paul Delvaux (1898–1994) Although he was a fellow student of René Magritte in 1920 at the Académie royale des Beaux-Arts, Delvaux's works did not immediately reveal the influence of **Surrealism**. It was not really until 1934, having met **E.L.T. Mesens** and discovered the oeuvre of **Giorgio de Chirico**, that his painting developed from Expressionism to Surrealism. While he was appreciated by **Paul Éluard** and **André Breton**, he situated himself prudently on the margins of the Brussels group, refusing the polemical and political aspects of Surrealism. (XC)

Jacques Derrida (1930–2004) French writer and philosopher. The theoretical basis of Derrida's deconstructivist philosophy of art and **language** corresponds with Magritte's engagement with the non-binding relationship between linguistic or pictorial signs and real objects. The question as to the 'presence' of the work of art ultimately amounts to a critique of mimesis. With his own notion of 'différance', the spatial and temporal disjuncture between what is perceived and the visual reproduction of the same, Derrida in effect denied the possibility of immediately grasping and communicating an event. The extent to which our ability to see is dependent on context means that this can only be done in retrospect, although what was perceived has already become something else and it is not feasible to repeat one and the same event. Derrida's conclusion is that it is impossible to distinguish between a copy and an original and that meaning only ever arises from endless sequences of 'references' – like pictures that refer to other pictures. The phenomenon of aesthetic ambiguity and reduced reality within a picture pave the way for the untangling of rigidified concepts and for a changed approach to perception. This corresponds to Magritte's disregard for the potential meaning of objects and the interpretative nature of his seeing: invisibility becomes the precondition for visibility. (GF)

See also: **Meaning; Philosophy; Representation and Resemblance**

Detective Stories: Magritte was very fond of detective stories, from cheap thrillers to the more sophisticated novels of Dashiell Hammett, Rex Stout and his countryman Georges Simenon. In 1953, Magritte published a short story entitled *Nat Pinkerton*, featuring a private detective who had originally appeared in weekly serials when Magritte was a boy.[42] In succinct, factual language, Magritte recounts the events of one day when, with little apparent effort, Pinkerton solves a mysterious crime. The story veers between the banal and the melodramatic, a quintessentially Magrittean mix. If, in *Nat Pinkerton*, Magritte seems to identify with the detective, his more natural sympathy lay with the criminal. As for all the Surrealists, this primarily meant **Fantômas**, the notorious anti-hero of novels by Marcel Allain and Pierre Souvestre and silent films by Louis Feuillade. In *The Menaced Assassin* 1927, Magritte adapted an image from a Fantômas film. A naked woman lies dead on a couch

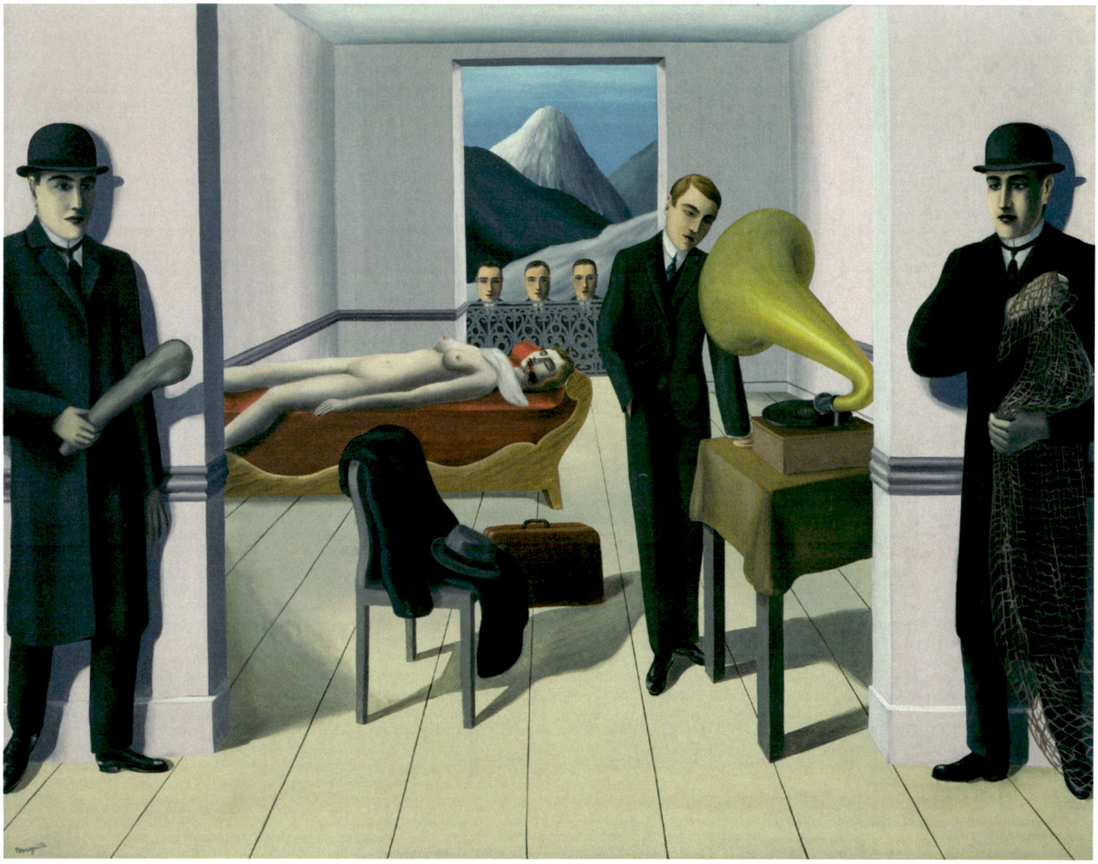

The Menaced Assassin
L'Assassin menacé 1927,
oil on canvas, 152 × 195 cm.
The Museum of Modern Art,
New York. Kay Sage Tanguy Fund,
CR 137

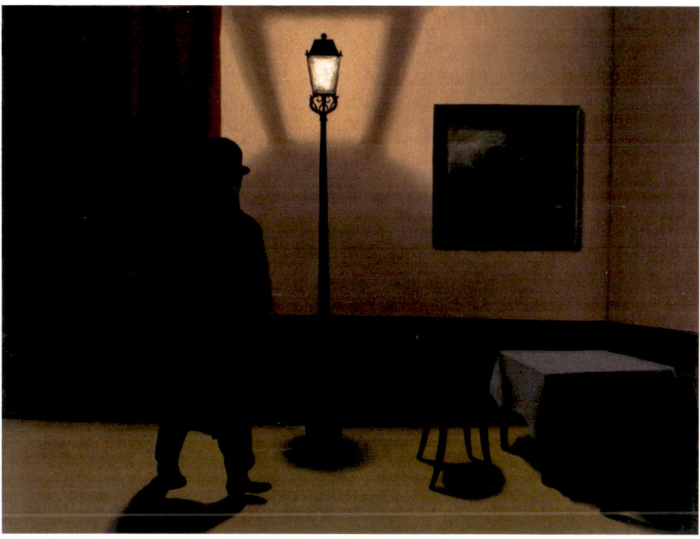

The Night Owl
Le Noctambule 1928,
oil on canvas, 54 × 73 cm.
Museum Folkwang, Essen, CR 271

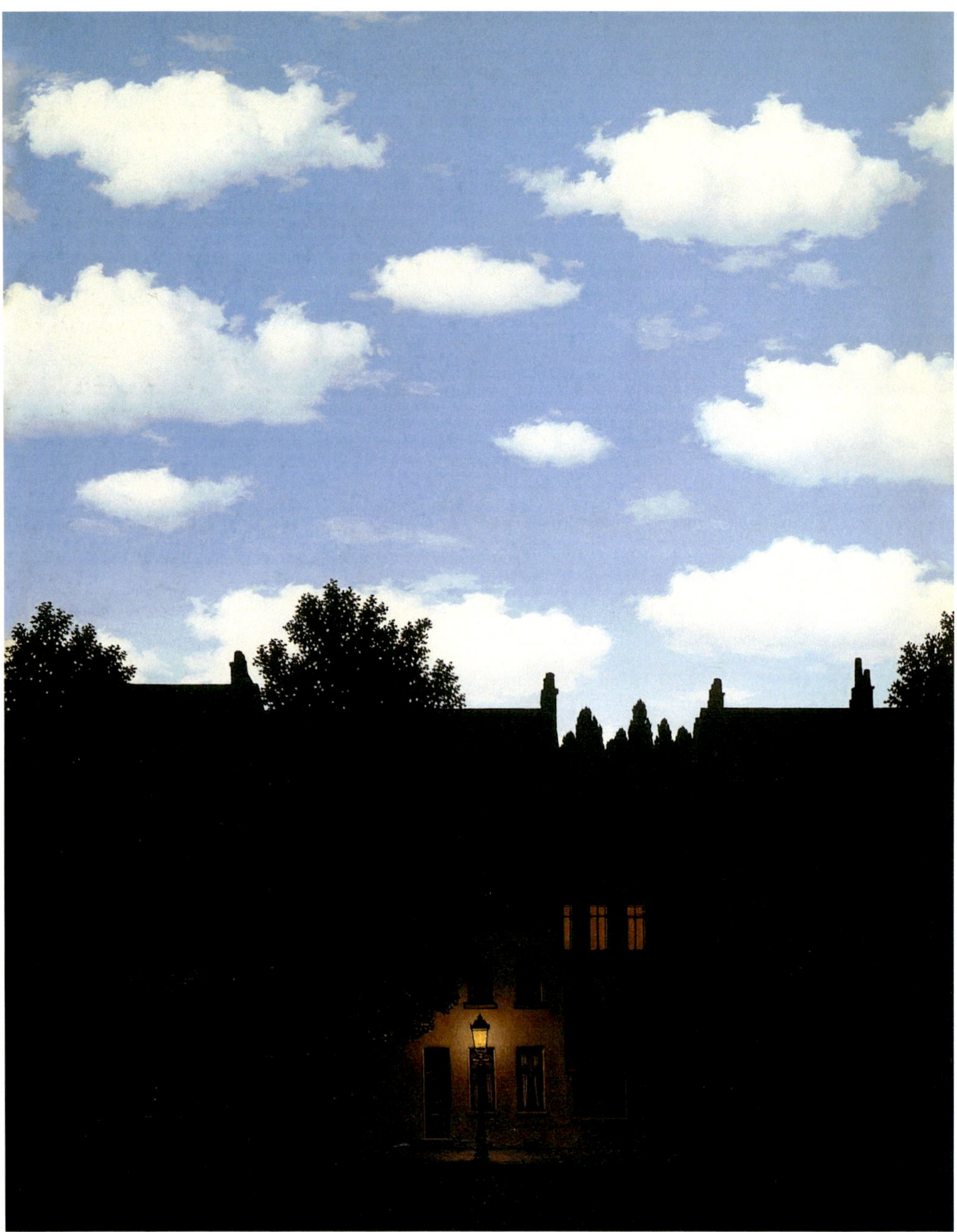

The Dominion of Light
L'Empire des lumières 1952, oil on canvas, 100 × 80 cm.
Private Collection, Seoul, CR 781

with her assassin paused in his flight, listening to a phonograph record. Outside the door stand two policemen, ready with club and net to catch him. But, if he is Fantômas, we know he will escape. (IW)

See also: **Appropriation; Film**

Distances: Surrealist review which appeared in three instalments, in January, February and April 1928, on the initiative of Magritte, **Camille Goemans** and **Paul Nougé**. Based in Paris at Goemans' home where he had opened an art gallery while Magritte based himself in the Parisian suburbs, it was printed in Brussels, most likely with the assistance of **E.L.T. Mesens**. As Nougé indicated, the journal's title was intended to express the 'distance' between their methods of action and artistic activity and those of **André Breton**. *Distances* opened with a tribute to the musician André Souris and developed in the manner of *Correspondance*, with contributions from Magritte and **Louis Scutenaire** (making his first appearance) alongside several others. (XC)

See also: **Paris; Surrealism and Surrealists**

The Dominion of Light: Magritte produced the series of *The Dominion of Light* paintings between the late 1940s and the early 1960s, consisting of seventeen oil paintings and ten gouaches. While there are differences between the versions of this painting, ranging from differences in size and format of the artworks to differing landscape motifs, the theme always remains the same: a bright blue daytime sky with soft white **clouds** overarches a 'typically' lantern-lit house-front. Discussing *The Dominion of Light* in April 1956, Magritte stated:

> what is represented in the picture *The Dominion of Light* are the things I thought of, to be precise, a nocturnal landscape and a skyscape such as can be seen in broad daylight. The landscape suggests night and the skyscape day. This evocation of night and day seems to me to have the power to surprise and delight us. I call this power 'poetry.' The reason why I believe the evocation to have this poetic power is, amongst other things, because I have always felt the greatest interest in night and day, without however having any preference for one or the other.[43]

The paintings' strategy of reconciling opposites was a method hailed by **Surrealists**. The combination in *The Dominion of Light* is intriguing, nostalgic and poetic. The **repetition** of this particular theme, and its slight variations from painting to painting in the series, expands the poetic patterning, creating rhythms and rhymes amongst them. The series, however, also demonstrates that Magritte held an ambivalent position towards repetitions of paintings. Such repetitions were not solely based on poetic considerations, but also on the pressures of the art market and his art dealer **Alexandre Iolas** to paint 'Magritte-like'. A number of versions of *The Dominion of Light* were commissioned by Iolas, and by other collectors such as the **de Menils**, **Harry Torczyner** and Pierre Crowet. Despite the restrictions in style, content and form imposed on Magritte by the art market, he remained concerned with 'achieving real poetic density, of finding a certain mental substance necessary for present-day living man […] I have had to find a way of justifying the replica in my own mind. I managed to enrich the first idea […]'[44]

The series is not only Surrealist in its reconciliation of night and day, but also a rich intertextual weaving, and through its reference to other Surrealist artists and writers. The title was found, as was the case with many other artworks, by Paul Nougé, while the simultaneity of night and day evokes **Max Ernst's** *Day and Night* 1941–2. Most prominently, the series refers to **André Breton**. Magritte's 1937 lecture in London conceptualised the relations between words, images and real objects, using poetic lines

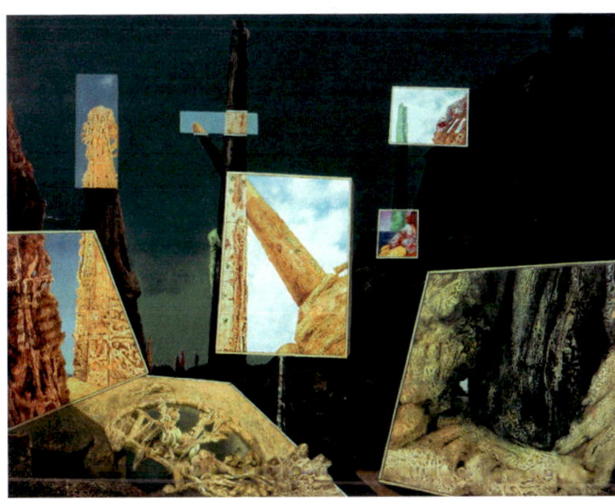

Max Ernst (1891–1976): *Day and Night* 1941–2, oil on canvas, 112 × 146 cm. The Menil Collection, Houston

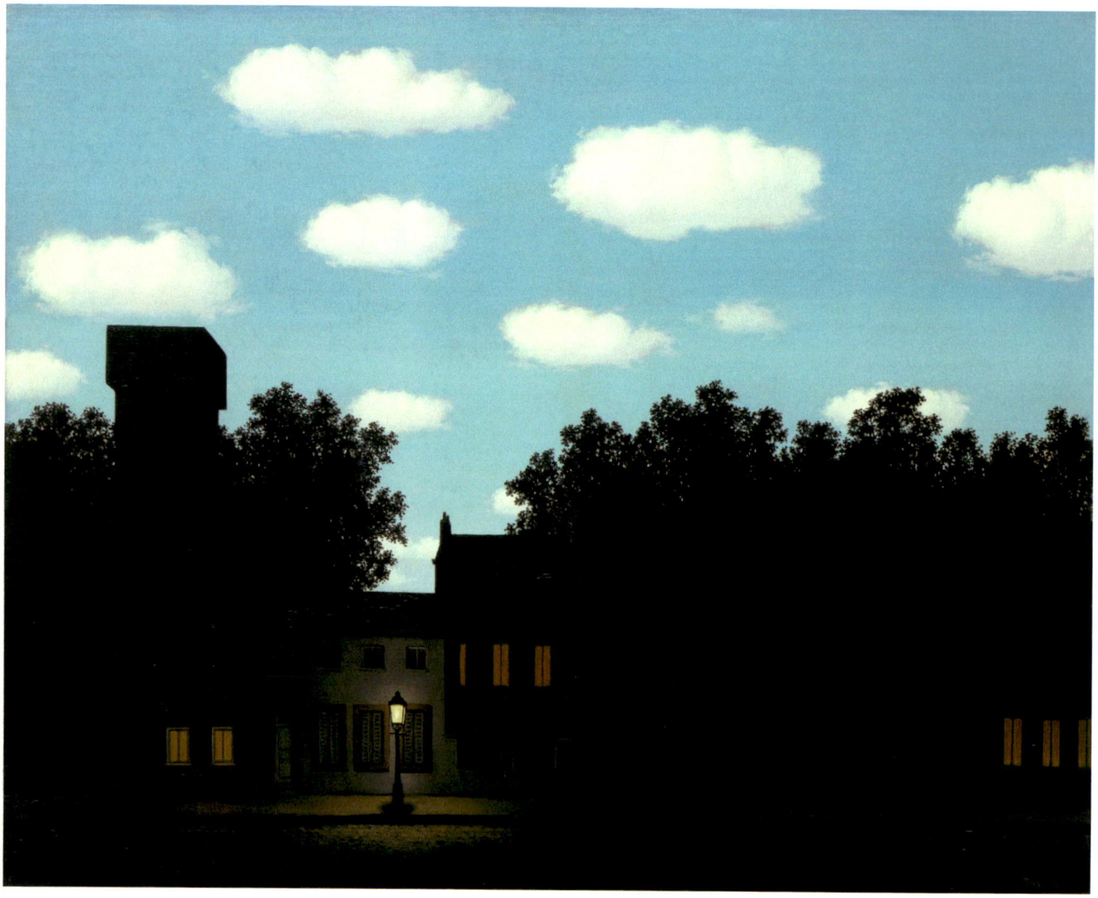

The Dominion of Light
L'Empire des lumières 1950,
oil on canvas, 78.8 × 99.1 cm.
The Museum of Modern Art,
New York. Gift of D. and
J. de Menil, CR 723

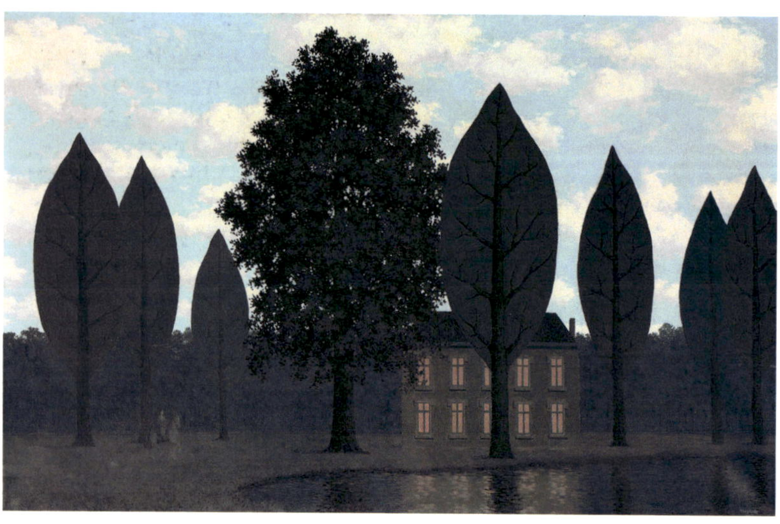

The Mysterious Barricades
Les Barricades mystérieuses
1961, oil on canvas, 81 × 128 cm.
Collection Mr and Mrs Wilbur
Ross, CR 932

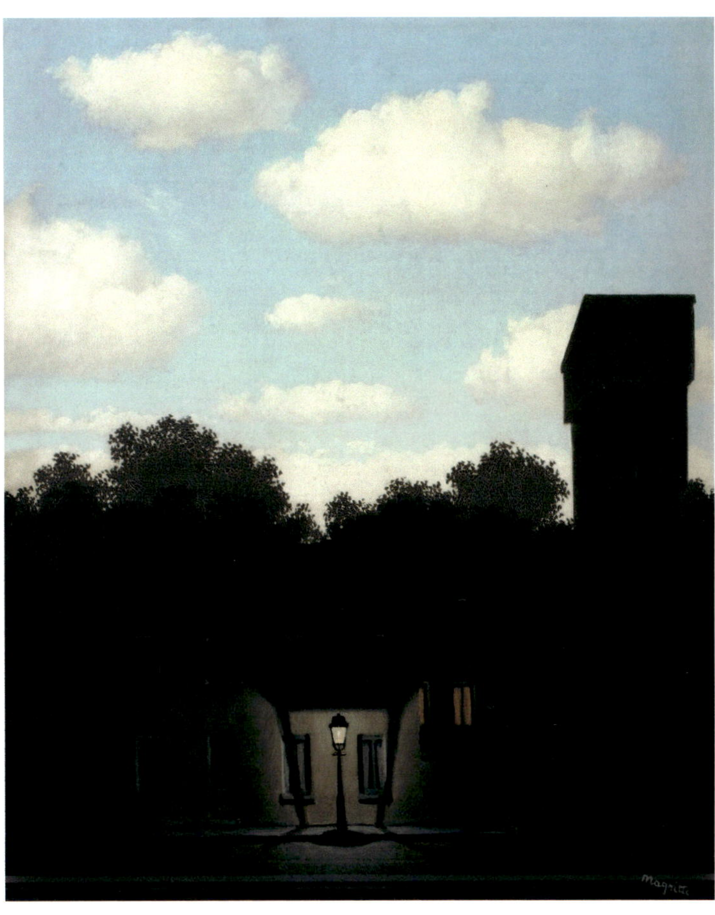

The Dominion of Light
L'Empire des lumières 1953,
oil on canvas, 46 × 38 cm.
Private Collection, courtesy
Guggenheim, Asher Associates,
Inc., CR 797

from a range of writers. The second example used in this lecture, 'Si seulement … IF ONLY THE <u>SUN</u> WOULD SHINE TONIGHT', derives from the first line of Breton's poem 'L'aigrette' in *Claire de terre* 1923. That this line remained relevant for Magritte is clear by his comment in a letter in 1946 to Breton, written at a time when they were in dispute about Magritte's new painting style. 'I recognise you more by this voice,' he wrote, '"If only the sun would shine tonight."' Breton's longing for the union between day and night finds a resolution in Magritte's *The Dominion of Light* paintings. (**PA**)

Double: The figure of the double plays a key role in the Freudian theory of the uncanny.[45] It is a source of horror as it evokes a disintegration of identity and indicates the return of repressed traumatic experiences and a foreshadowing of death. The double appears as a motif in various configurations throughout Magritte's oeuvre – from his early fascination with shop window **mannequins** and disembodied human limbs to the **bilboquets** – stand-ins for the human figure. Magritte shares this fascination with the **Surrealists** who were particularly attracted by the ambiguous status of wax figures, mannequins, dolls and automatons between life and death, the organic and inorganic and their function as fetishistic substitutes.

The double makes a powerful early appearance in Magritte's important portrait of his poet friend **Paul Nougé** of 1927, simply repeating the three-quarter figure. The painting is given additional psychological dimension through the left figure's action of opening an amorphous door through which the second figure passes, the fantastic nature of the scene enhanced by an abstract background pattern with cell-like formations. *The Secret Double* 1927 hints at the tension between outer appearance and inner consciousness by peeling away the face of a mannequin-like bust and revealing an animated metallic grey surface structure with strong suggestions of the technological abject. The encounter with two identical figures – or even worse one's own double – is a key element in the evocation of uncanny horror. *Not to be Reproduced* 1937 is one of the most successful evocations of the uncanny double, using the reflective properties of a mirror to paradoxically obscure the sitter's face, resulting in what **Paul Colinet** called *portraits manqué*.

The act of **repetition** – whether through doubling, the obsessive repetition of actions or the accumulation of objects through the collector – also functions as a defence against the inevitability of death. Magritte's own repetition of certain motifs and figures and his return to familiar compositions, particularly late in his life, can be seen as a form of doubling which he shared with his hero **Giorgio de Chirico**. *The Dominion of Light* series is the prime example for this, comprising over twenty-seven paintings and gouaches which repeat the motif of night landscape with bright blue sky with scattered **clouds** in slightly different variations. One of the most prominent series in his late work

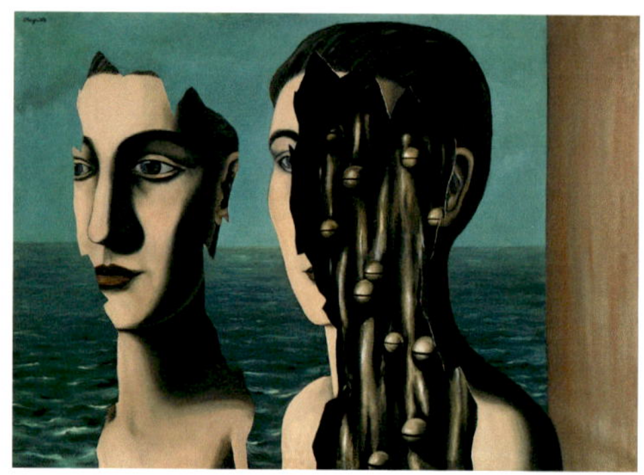

The Secret Double
Le Double Secret 1927, oil on canvas, 114 × 162 cm.
Centre Georges Pompidou / Musée national d'Art moderne /
Centre de Création industrielle, Paris, CR 164

reintroduces the figure of the man in **bowler hat**, dark coat and with blank demeanour – familiar from early paintings such as the programmatic *The Menaced Assassin* 1927. In the silhouetted figure (frequently facing away from us or with the face obscured by incongruous **objects** such as an **apple**, dove or **pipe**), we witness the endless multiplication of the double into an anonymous everyman or contemporary corporate 'Organisation Man'. (**CG**)

👁 See also: **Fetish; Sigmund Freud**

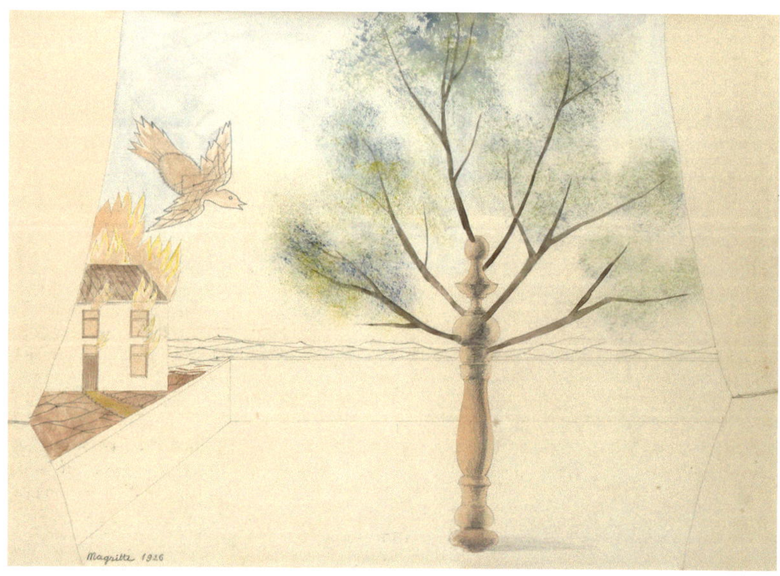

The Burning House
La Maison en feu 1926,
watercolour and pencil
on paper, 39.5 × 55.1 cm.
Musée d'Ixelles,
Brussels, CR 1106

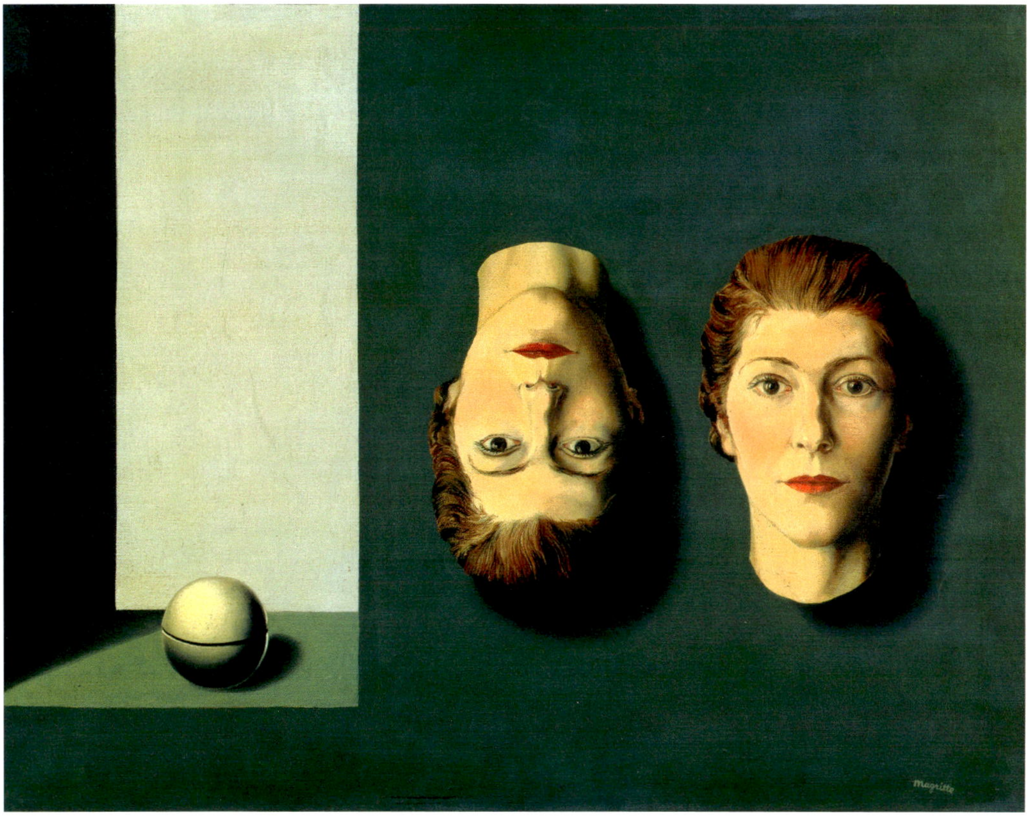

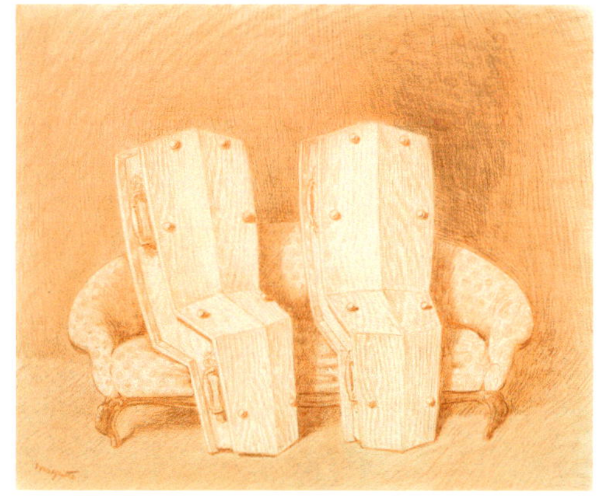

The Double Reality
La Double Réalité 1936, oil on canvas, 50 × 65 cm.
Private Collection, CR 398

Drawing: For Magritte drawing was the indispensable
foundation of visual art. He rejected the Surrealist
concept of drawing as an automatic, involuntary act
in which the artist's consciousness had no part. He
felt that an alert and engaged mind was crucial to his
own artistic production. His paintings are carefully
considered compositions that arise from a spontaneous thought process, which he called 'inspiration' –
the outcome of a 'necessary chance'. He stated: 'I
cannot paint until I have the complete picture in my
mind. It forms slowly. I have a sketch pad to hand.
Inspiration gives me an image: I am filled with the
desire to paint a cloud. So I draw **clouds**, a hundred,
maybe. And each time I surround them with shapes
whose meaning I do not understand until the moment when inspiration returns and I know what
should go beneath the cloud.'[46] **(GF)**

👁 See also: **Automatism and Automatic Writing;
Chance**

Madame Récamier
1950, sanguine on paper, 49 × 56 cm.
Private Collection, courtesy Keitelman Gallery

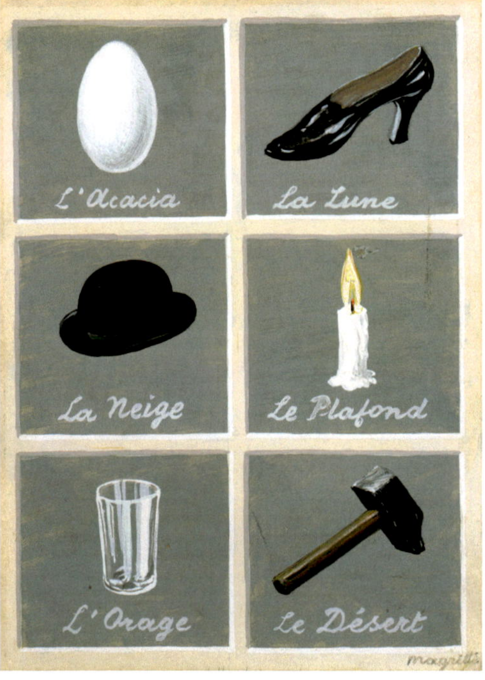

The Interpretation of Dreams
La Clef des songes 1952, gouache on paper, 18.8 × 14 cm.
Collection Timothy Baum, New York, CR 1326

Dreams: Whereas **André Breton** encountered **Sigmund Freud's** thought as early as World War I and made the dream a central element of **Surrealism** – 'Man, that inveterate dreamer' declares Breton at the start of the first *Manifesto of Surrealism* of 1924 – Magritte resolutely opposed such interpretations of his work, stating that: 'my paintings are the opposite of dreams, since the dream does not have the significance we ascribe to it. I can work only in lucidity.'[47] While respecting the world of dreams, Magritte insisted that his works are 'not oneiric'. '*On the contrary*,' he declared, 'if "dreams" are concerned … they are very different from those we have while sleeping. It is a question rather of *self-willed* dreams … "Dreams" which are not intended to make you sleep but to wake you up.'[48]

Nonetheless, Magritte's *The Interpretation of Dreams* 1927 and its variations refer to the title of Freud's *Traumdeutung* 1900 and develop a complex dialogue with its discussion of dream symbolism. Freud insisted on interpreting dream elements according to the meanings they hold for the individual, yet simultaneously offers a taxonomy of the symbols of 'typical dreams'. Magritte plays on this contradiction, the labels assigned in the painting confounding any search for fixed meaning. 'No object,' writes Magritte, 'is so closely linked with its name that one could not give it another name that suits it better.'[49] These dream-like objects, displayed like clues from a crime scene, combine classic Freudian sexual symbols – a knife and a bag, for instance – with items specific to Magritte, for instance a leaf and a **bowler hat**. The objects presented in the 1927 painting also feature in Magritte's short text that appeared in the February 1928 issue of **Distances**:

Now the princess runs, a fearless amazon, through limitless fields in search of mysterious proofs. She exhausts the thoughts and actions of a multitude of people. She surmounts poetic obstacles: the suitcase, the sky; the penknife, the leaf; the sponge, the sponge.[50]

Alain Robbe-Grillet in turn weaves Magritte's objects within an oneiric tale of ritualistic murder: 'also the pink crucifixion, with the sponge already spoken of … already spoken of '.[51] (**NM**)

See also: **Representation and Resemblance; Titles**

Marcel Duchamp (1887–1968) French painter, sculptor and writer, Duchamp was both a key figure of **Dada's** anti-art strategies and revered by the **Surrealists**, who enlisted him as artistic director for exhibitions from 1938 onwards. Duchamp's career posed an ironic challenge to the traditional roles of the artist, in particular painting, modes to which Magritte remained doggedly committed, yet there is much to connect their outlook. Like Duchamp, Magritte's work can be regarded as a deadpan intellectual proposition, leading unexpectedly away from the image and back towards a fundamental reappraisal of knowledge and representation, and restoring to the realm of the object a profound mystery and complexity. (**KF**)

See also: **Fetish; Object;** *Objet trouvé*

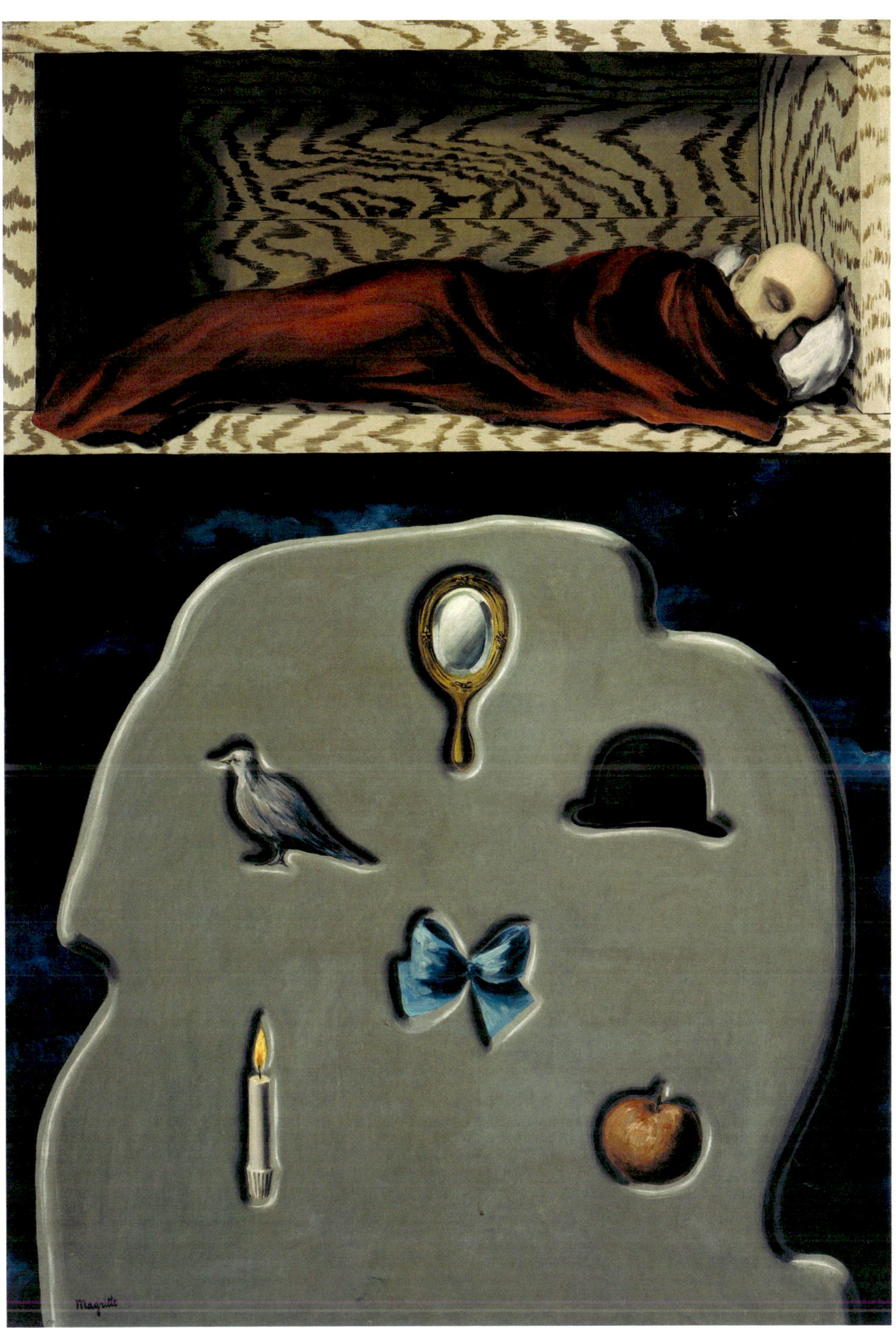

The Reckless Sleeper
Le Dormeur téméraire 1928, oil on canvas, 116 × 81 × 20 cm.
Tate. Purchased 1969, CR 217

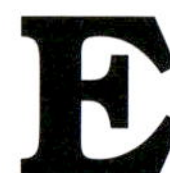

E

Elective Affinities: One of **Surrealism**'s fundamental discoveries, found in the writing of Comte de Lautréamont, was that of the aesthetic **shock** produced by the surprise **juxtaposition** of incompatible objects, on the model of the 'chance encounter, on a dissecting table, of a sewing machine and an umbrella'.[52] Magritte claimed a similar epiphany on waking from a **dream**, but where, in place of disjuncture, the **objects** now harbour some obscure affinity:

> One night in 1936, I awoke in a room in which a cage and the bird sleeping in it had been placed. A magnificent error caused me to see an egg in the cage instead of the bird. I then grasped a new and astonishing poetic secret, because the shock I experienced had been provoked precisely by the affinity of the two objects, the cage and the egg, *whereas previously I used to provoke this shock by bringing together objects that were unrelated.*[53]

Thereafter, Magritte sought other combinations of objects that would produce the same poetic effect, posed in terms of a 'problem' to be resolved – for example the 'problem of the door' which 'called for an opening through which one could pass' resolved by the irregular cut-out of the door in *The Unexpected Answer* 1933. This recalls **Marcel Duchamp's** paradoxical *rue Larrey door* 1927, which swung between two doorways – a door that, like Magritte's, was simultaneously 'open' and 'closed'. Magritte's birdcage similarly recalls the precedent of Duchamp's *Why Not Sneeze Rose Sélavy?* 1921, replica 1964, a birdcage filled with white blocks resembling sugar-cubes, but which when lifted, said Duchamp, 'weighs a ton' as the blocks are actually white marble. Magritte exhibited with Duchamp at the Galerie **Goemans** in 1930 and when he painted *Elective Affinities* in the spring of 1933 would have been aware of the *Exposition surréaliste* scheduled for June at the Galerie Pierre Colle in Paris, which focused on surreal objects, suggesting he may well have been aware of Duchamp's cage and that the influence of **Dada** on his work has been underestimated. (**NM**)

See also: **Chance; Representation and Resemblance**

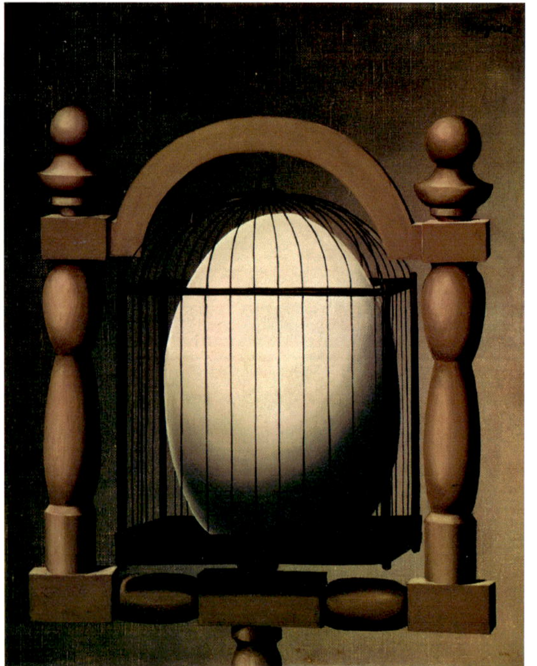

Elective Affinities
Les Affinités électives 1933, oil on canvas, 41 × 33 cm. Private Collection, CR 349

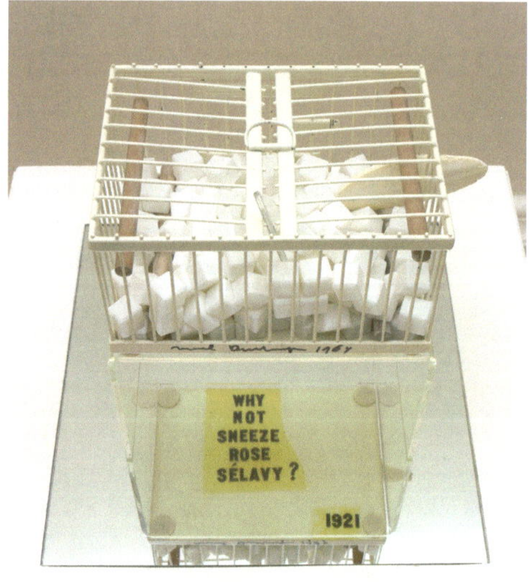

Marcel Duchamp (1887–1968): *Why Not Sneeze Rose Sélavy?* 1921, replica 1964, mixed media, 11.4 × 22 × 16 cm. Tate. Purchased 1999

Paul Éluard (1895–1952) Pseudonym of Eugène Grindel. Éluard was one of the founding members of **Surrealism**, in 1919 contributing to the **Dada** periodical *Littérature*, alongside **André Breton**, Philippe Soupault and Louis Aragon.

Éluard was a strong supporter of the Brussels Surrealists, and became Magritte's closest friend while he lived in Paris (1927–30), their friendship evident in a number of artistic collaborations. In 1935, Éluard wrote a poem entitled *René Magritte* which first appeared in *Les Cahiers d'art*, and was subsequently translated by Man Ray, with a version published in the *London Bulletin*, no.1, 15 April 1938:

Stairs of the eye
Through the bars of forms

A perpetual stairway
Repose which does not exist
One of the steps is hidden by a cloud
Another by a big knife
Another by a tree which unrolls
Like a carpet
Without gestures

All of the steps are hidden

Green leaves have been sown
Immense fields' forests deducted
Level with the clearing
In the thin milk of the morning

The sand quenches with rays
The silhouettes of mirrors
Their shoulders pale and cold
Their decorative smiles

The tree is tinted with invulnerable fruits

Magritte's painterly allusions to Éluard's **poetry** include two portraits of 1936, one entitled *White Magic* and one on the cover of a hand-made book produced by the Brussels Surrealist group in honour of Éluard. Magritte also illustrated two of Éluard's poetry editions, *La moralité du sommeil* 1941 and the 1946 re-issue of Éluard's *Les nécessités de la vie et les conséquences des rêves*, originally published in 1921. Notably, Éluard was the only French Surrealist poet Magritte illustrated. (PA)

See also: **Book Illustration**

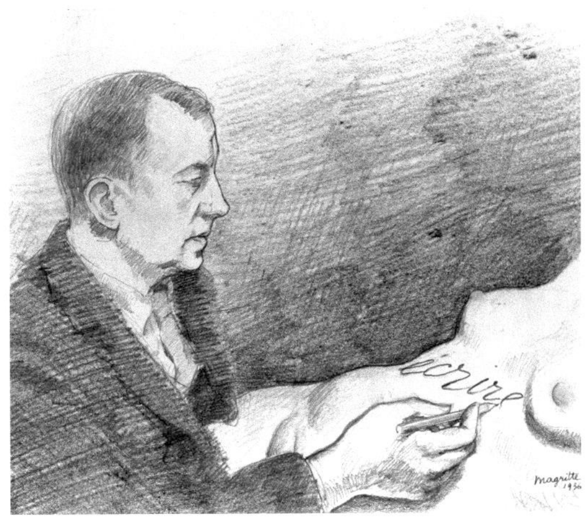

White Magic, Portrait of Paul Éluard
Magie blanche, Portrait de Paul Éluard 1936,
pencil on paper

England: The 1936 *International Surrealist Exhibition*, staged at the New Burlington Galleries in London during an uncharacteristically hot summer, created a sensation socially and in its impact upon a rather moribund English art scene. The Belgian contribution was entrusted by **André Breton** to **E.L.T. Mesens**, who deployed his considerable talents as a curator by entirely re-hanging the show, transforming the exhibition into a major event. Magritte was represented in the exhibition by eight oil paintings dating from 1925 onwards – including major works such as *The Annunciation* 1930 and *The Red Model* 1935 – as well as four gouaches and two **collages**.

The 1936 exhibition was mauled by an uncomprehending British press, with the critic of the *Scotsman* declaring that it 'almost persuaded [him] to be a Nazi'.[54] *The Sketch*, which reproduced Magritte's *The Interpretation of Dreams* 1930, below an image of André Breton examining Salvador Dalí's *Aphrodisiac Jacket* 1936, was equally baffled by Surrealism. The English artist **Roland Penrose**, though, had acquired a large collection of modern art, followed by his acquisition of **Paul Éluard's** collection of Surrealism, and went on in 1938 to take over the **London Gallery**, with Mesens as its Director, thus providing a base for **Surrealism** in Britain. Their opening show was devoted to Magritte and presented some forty-six works, most from Mesens' own extensive collection.

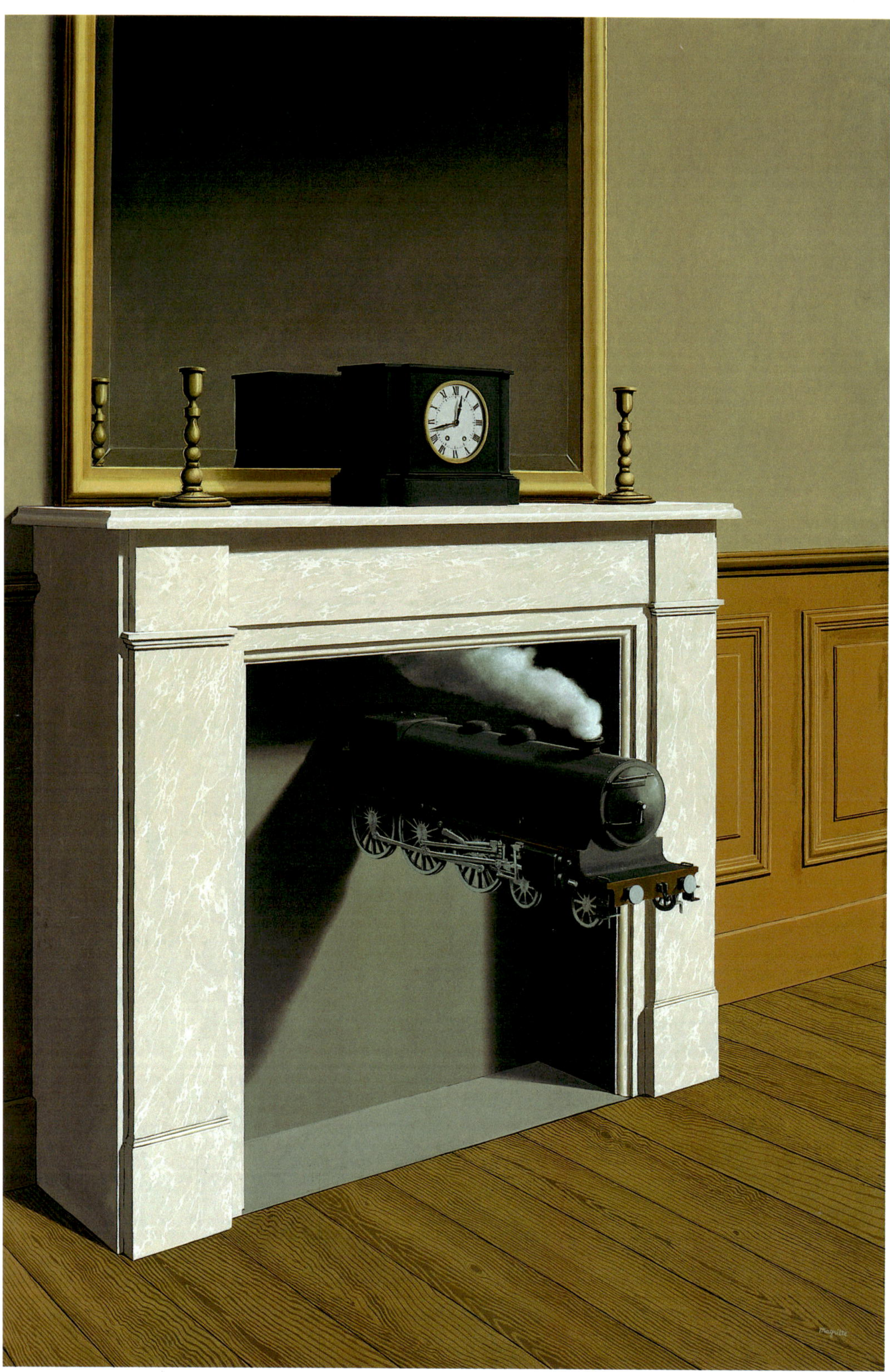

Time Transfixed
La Durée poignardée 1938, oil on canvas, 147 × 99 cm. The Art
Institute of Chicago, Joseph Winterbotham Collection, CR 460

Edward James, an aristocratic English collector and poet, visited the 1936 exhibition and became one of the rare patrons of Surrealist art in Britain, commissioning work from Dalí, Magritte and others. In the decoration both of Monkton, the home he created next to his property at West Dean in Sussex, as well as of his London home at 35 Wimpole Street, James demonstrated a theatricality and love of **trompe l'oeil** effects that made Magritte a perfect collaborator. In 1937, through Mesens, James commissioned Magritte to create three large canvases for the Robert Adam-designed ballroom of his Wimpole Street home and Magritte travelled over to paint them on site. Two of the images, *The Red Model* 1937 and *On the Threshold of Freedom* 1937, were variants of existing images included in the 1936 exhibition, while the third, *Youth Illustrated* 1937, was a variant on a recently completed image. Installed behind two-way mirrors and only visible when lights were turned on, the images constituted a 'looking-glass' world. James wrote afterwards to Magritte that the works had prompted a lot of discussion of Surrealism at his ball and that the 'human boots' of *The Red Model* in particular 'had touched the young dancing couples in capitalist heels'.[55]

The same year, Magritte produced a portrait of James, *Not to be Reproduced* 1937, in which the patron is seen from behind, staring into a mirror. This image was based on a photograph of James standing in front of *On the Threshold of Freedom* – a painting itself concealed behind a mirror – and in the portrait it is as though the lights behind the mirror had been turned off, causing the painting to disappear and leaving James staring into his own reflection – but a reflection of himself paradoxically seen from behind in this looking-glass world. This same mirror appears again in *Time Transfixed* 1938, acquired by James in 1939, in which a miniature locomotive under full steam erupts from a domestic fireplace based on that at 35 Wimpole Street.

Magritte and James maintained regular correspondence and when Magritte fled to Paris on the German invasion of Belgium in May 1940, while **Georgette** – said to have been involved in a relationship with **Paul Colinet** – refused to leave, it was James who acted as intermediary. James wrote, somewhat ironically, from the Waldorf Astoria Hotel in New York, sending news that Magritte was safe and staying with the poet Joë Bousquet at Carcassonne – a letter stamped with Nazi insignia of the Wehrmacht.[56] Later that year James wrote from Beverly Hills to Magritte, by now back in Brussels, explaining how he had tried to send money and to buy an air ticket to enable Magritte to somehow escape via Lisbon.[57] (**NM**)

James Ensor (1860–1949) Belgian artist whose work influenced Expressionism and **Surrealism**. Early works depicted realistic scenes in a sombre style. By 1885 he developed a highly personal fantastic style with grotesque mask-like figures and skeletons as a means to satirise the stupidities of human existence. In 1945 Magritte described the 'unenlightened euphoria and childish humour' of Ensor's portraiture as constituting a universal satire of the bourgeoisie that was applicable for both Ensor's time and for Magritte's.[58] Ensor's influence is especially evident in Magritte's **Vache Period** works, for instance the grotesque portraiture of *The Cripple* 1948 and *Famine* 1948, the latter having an affinity with his 1891 painting *Skeletons Fighting over a Pickled Herring*. (**DP**)

👁 See also: **Belgium**

Max Ernst (1891–1976) German-born Surrealist artist. Ernst, like Magritte, was influenced by **Giorgio de Chirico**. Ernst's collages of the early 1920s constitute some of the earliest manifestations of visual **Surrealism**. On encountering these works, Magritte came to the realisation that painted compositions could be pieced together from disparate elements and realities, describing Ernst's work as possessing 'the "reality" that is able to awaken … our trust in the marvellous, which cannot be isolated from the real-life situation in which it appears'.[59] The torn, cut-out and fragmented surfaces and shapes characteristic of collage recur as elements in Magritte's painted compositions, Ernst himself describing such works as 'hand-painted collage'. (**DP**)

👁 See also: **Collage**

Eroticism: In his 1938 lecture 'La Ligne de vie' Magritte looked back at the early days of his artistic life. He stated: 'It was a pure, strong feeling: eroticism. The little girl I met at the old cemetery was the object of my dreams … Thanks to that magic

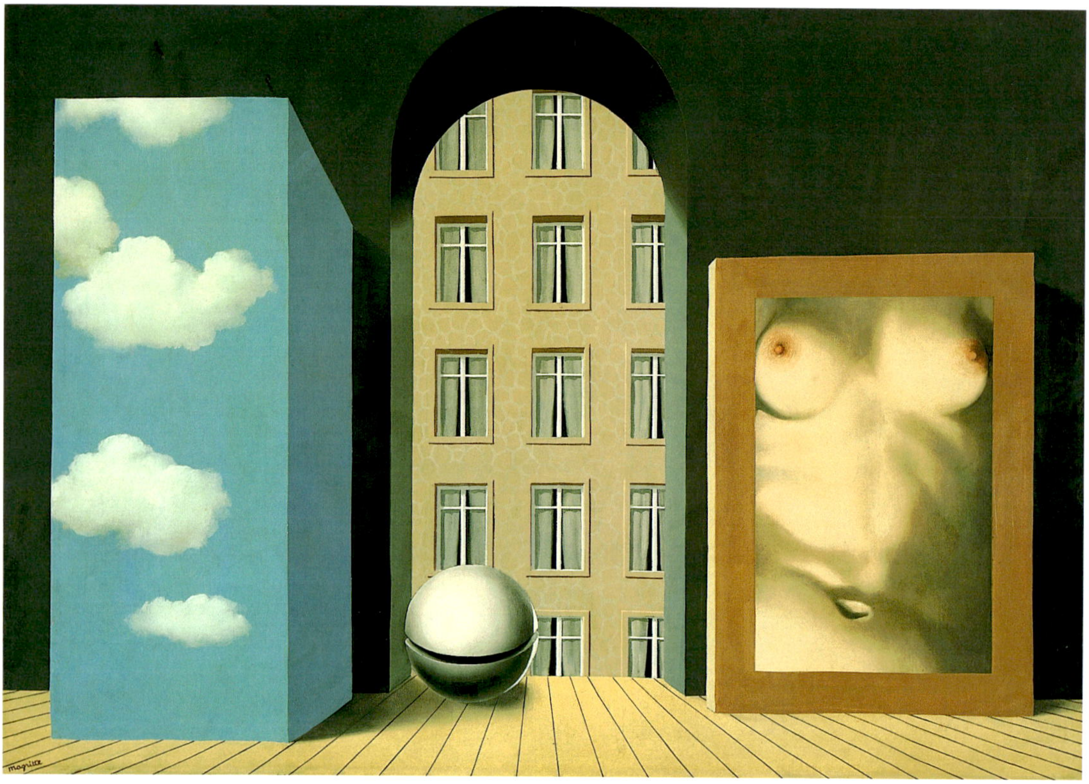

Act of Violence
L'Attentat 1932, oil on canvas, 70 × 100 cm.
Groeningemuseum, Bruges, CR345

painting I rediscovered the same feelings I had had during my childhood.'[60] In a revised version of the same talk, he added: 'Without doubt, a pure and strong feeling – eroticism – saved me, at the time, of falling prey to the traditional pursuit of formal perfection. All I wanted to do was to induce an emotional **shock**.'[61] Magritte associated eroticism with a positive attitude to life encapsulated in an intense response to physical **pleasure**, which was to become the driving force behind his creative output. Eroticism, as a psychological-mental attraction, implies a readiness for dissolution and destruction, the annihilation of the self in the hope of a yearning for harmony and – in Magritte's case – of nurturing his sense of a mystical experience. This yearning for harmony is expressed in the *Black Magic* series which Magritte started in 1934. The gradual morphing of

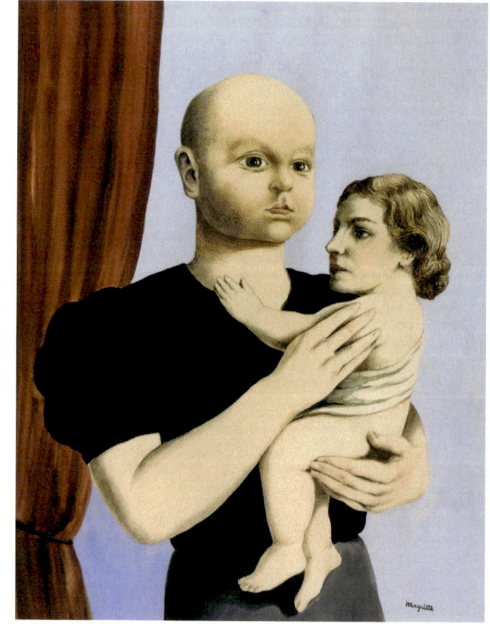

The Spirit of Geometry
L'Esprit de géométrie 1936 or 1937, gouache on paper, 37.5 × 29.4 cm. Tate. Presented by the Hon. Ivor Montagu, CR1123

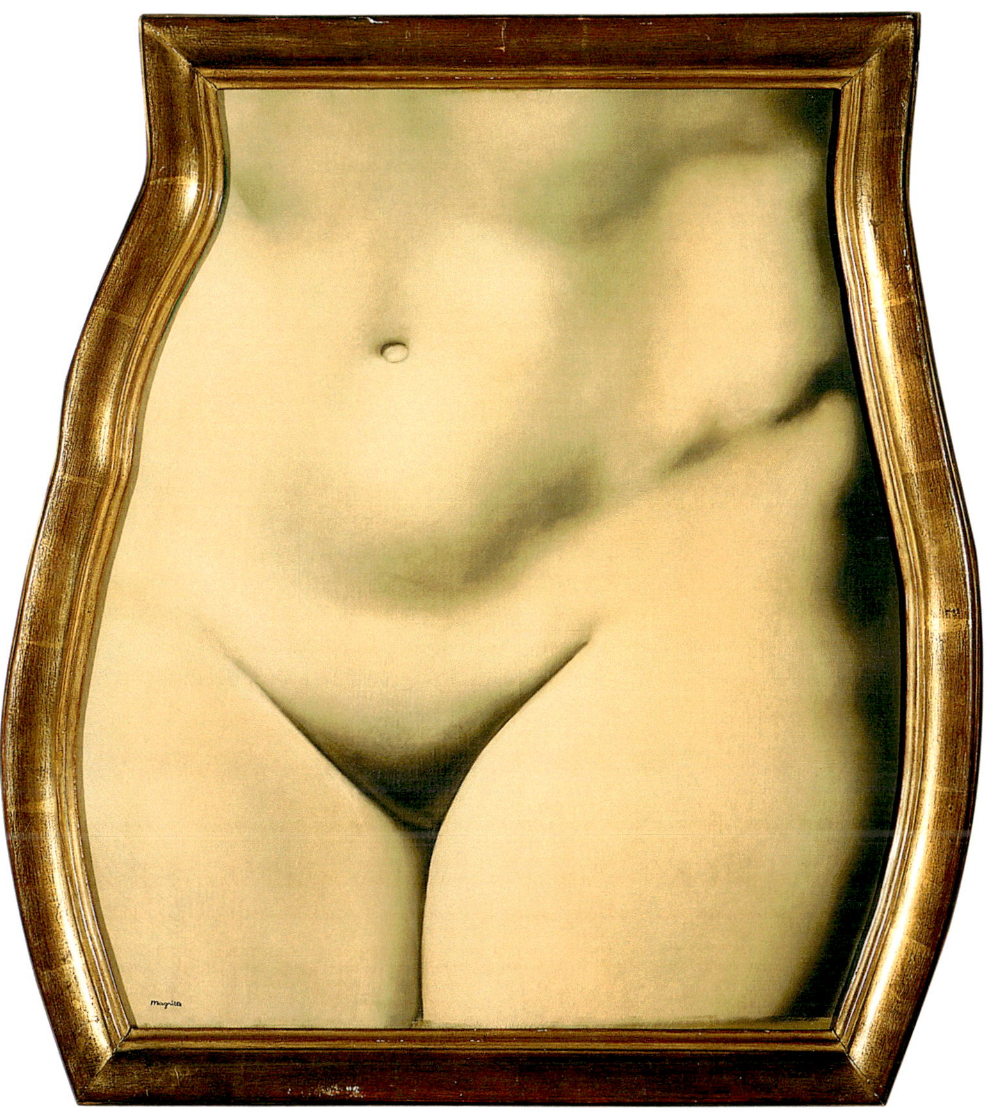

Representation
La Représentation 1937, oil on canvas, 48.5 × 44 cm.
Scottish National Gallery of Modern Art, Edinburgh.
Purchased 1990, CR 434

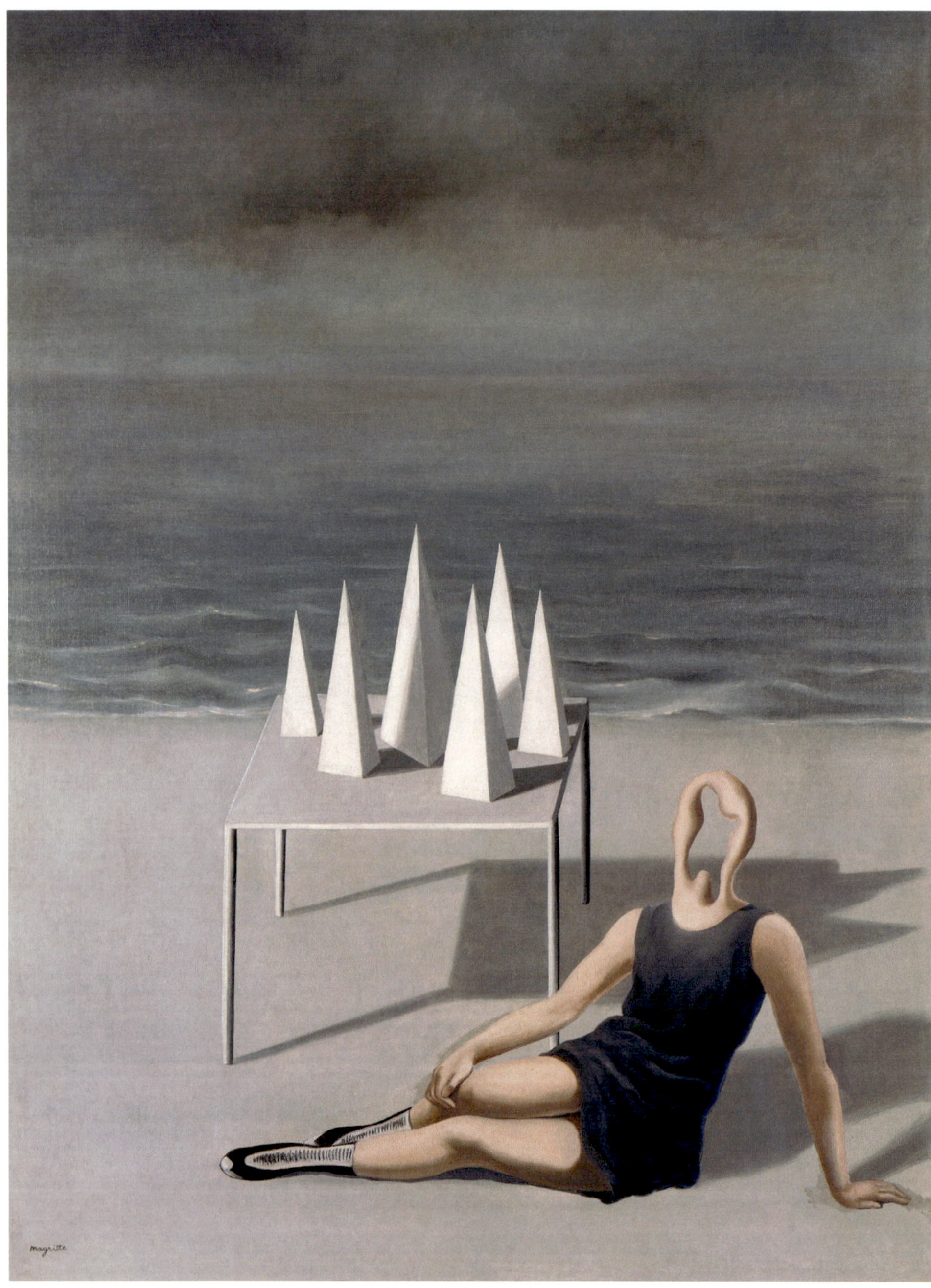

Surprises by the Sea
Les Surprises et l'océan 1927, oil on canvas, 98 × 74 cm.
Private Collection, courtesy Hauser & Wirth, CR 144

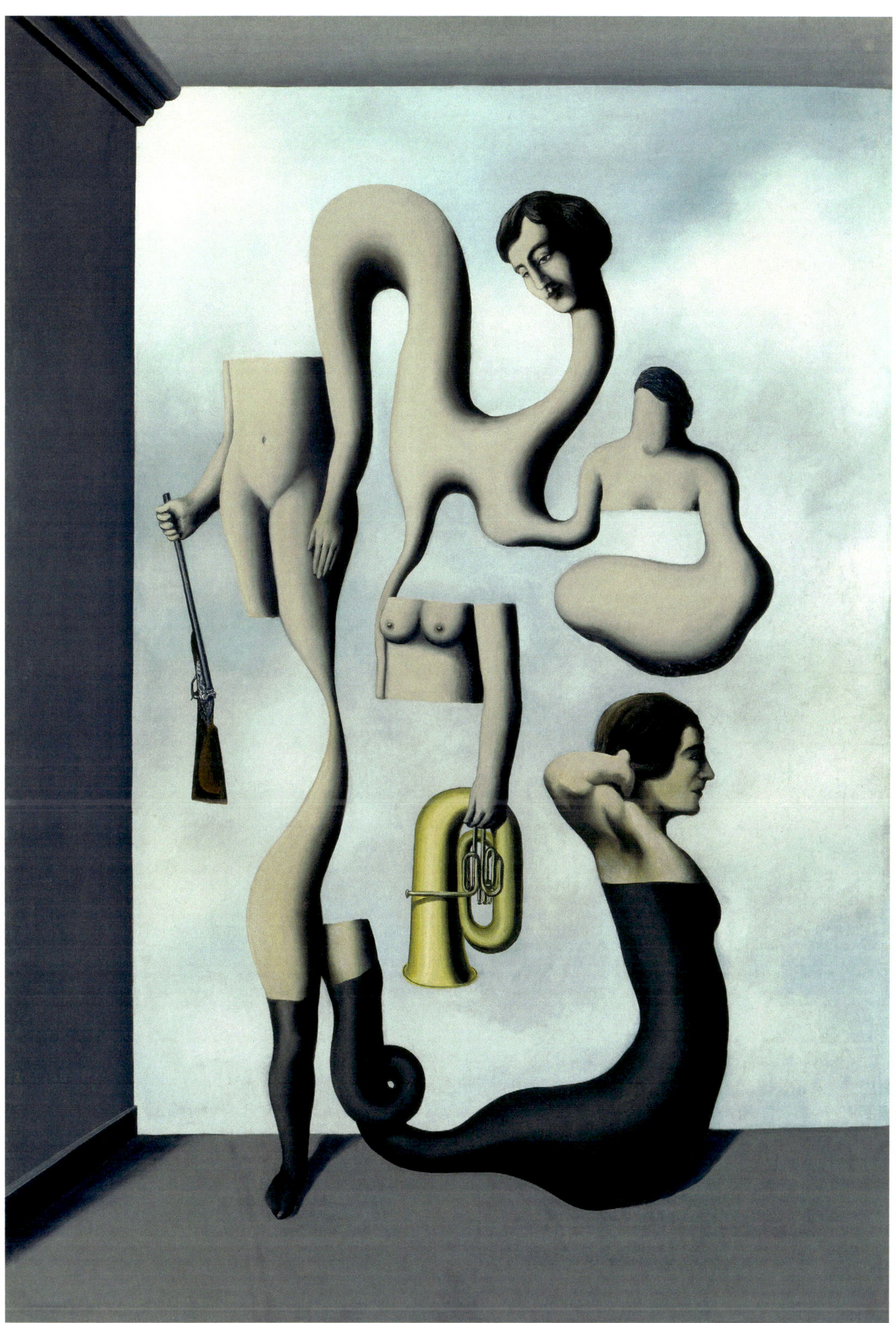

Acrobatic Ideas
Les Idées de l'acrobate 1928, oil on canvas, 116 × 80.8 cm.
Bayerische Staatsgemäldesammlungen München –
Pinakothek der Moderne, CR 224

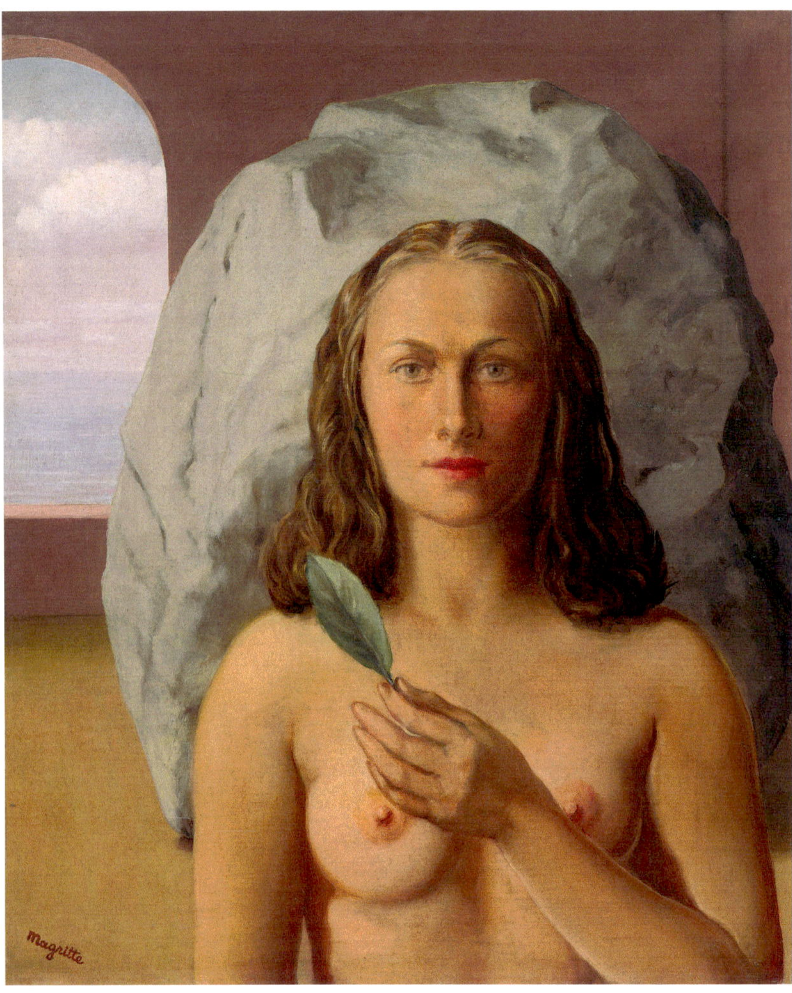

Perfect Harmony
L'Accord parfait 1947
or 1948, oil on canvas,
60 × 50 cm.
Private Collection,
New York, CR 637

the female nude into the blue sky transforms the body into a de-individualised object in harmony with the universe. **(GF)**

See also: **Georges Bataille; Female Form; Fetish; Metamorphosis; Object; Visual Fracture**

Ersatz (from the German; replacement or substitution) is a concept which is significant on a number of levels in Magritte's oeuvre. It is present in his theorisations of relations between words, images and real objects, evident in his 1937 lecture in London where he states: '(1) A word can replace an image. […]' and '(2) An image can replace a word.' A number of Magritte's paintings are based on this investigation. Here word and image can replace each other – there is no intrinsic link between them. Magritte also uses concepts of replacement to query our understanding of reality. In *The Human Condition* 1933, a painted canvas seemingly obscures, but also replaces, the view out of a **window**. The revelation of this painting lies not in questioning what this painted canvas hides, but in revealing that the substitute is the very thing which creates the scene. Replacement and substitution were also welcome strategies for Magritte in relation to the art market, as André Souris recalls: 'when **André Breton** returned from America with the cover of the second edition of *Surrealism and Painting* on which the famous shoes of Magritte were pictured, this picture at once gained an enormous market value. Magritte welcomed a lady at his home, who asked him whether this picture was on sale. He answered her politely: it is already sold, but I can make you a copy of it. In this rests the whole of Magritte.'[62] (**PA**)

See also: **Absence; Artifice; Forgery; Kitsch; Parody and Pastiche; Representation and Resemblance**

Eye: In *The False Mirror* 1935, Magritte explored the interplay between our external and internal worlds. For him, the eye marked the boundary between the visible and what he himself called the 'hidden visible'. Around ten years later, in the draft for the *Manifeste de l'amentalisme*, co-written with the poet **Jacques Wergifosse**, Magritte once again turned to the question of our perception of reality. As a counter-reaction to **Surrealism** – the 'praxis of an ineffective magic'[63] – they came up with the notion of the 'extramental' (shortly afterwards referred to as 'a-mental'), as a description of that which is distinct from our mental universe, from all that we perceive, think and feel.[64] 'Our sense that we cannot flee our mental universe gives us … the feeling that the extramental encircles us with an existence of which we can know nothing other than that it is there to act on us and to be modified by us in return.'[65] With this phenomenological approach, Magritte exhorted his fellow human beings to respond to life with relish and creativity. His paintings are intended to heighten our awareness, to alert us to the world of phenomena, to reinforce our sense of the hidden.[66] For Magritte, seeing was a form of thinking without ideas or explanations. 'My painting is a thought that *sees* without naming what it sees,' he stated, 'what it sees on an object, is another, hidden object.'[67] (**GF**)

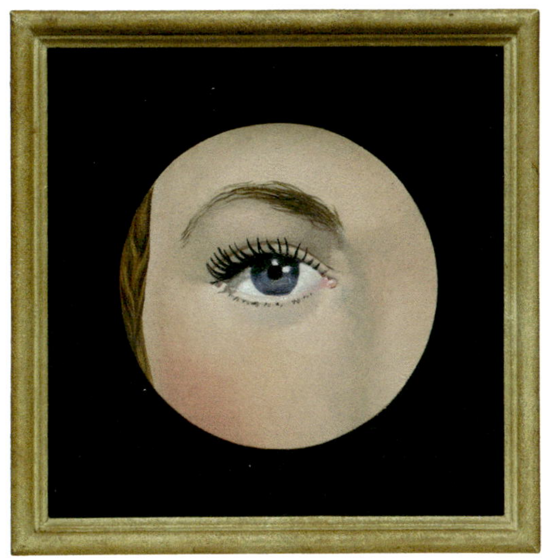

The Eye
L'Œil 1932–5, oil on canvas, 27 × 24.8 × 14.4 cm.
The Art Institute of Chicago, through prior gift of
Arthur Keating, CR 686

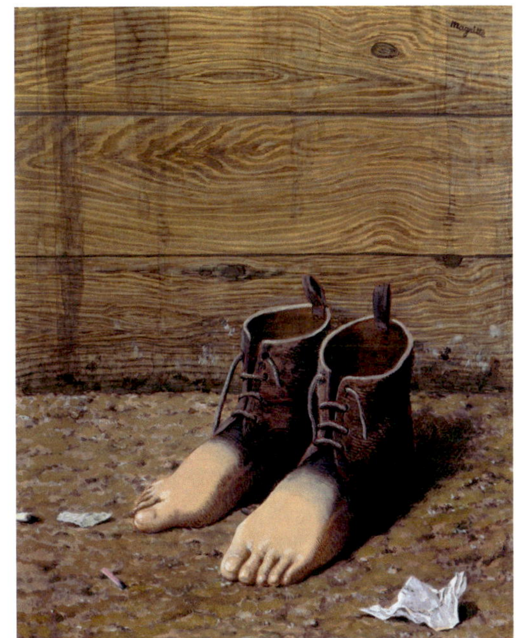

The Red Model
Le Modèle rouge 1947, gouache on paper, 45 × 36 cm.
Private Collection, CR 1249

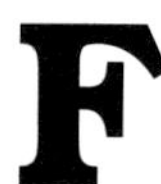

F

Fantômas: Magritte's tastes were eclectic. As well as engaging with the philosophical writings of **Michel Foucault** and **Martin Heidegger**, he also revelled in the products of pulp and popular culture. Slapstick **film**, with its unbridled visual expression, irrational or unexpectedly alarming scenarios and parodic depictions of reality, was a particular favourite, evidenced by his collection of silent films by Laurel and Hardy, Charlie Chaplin and Max Linder. These films fired the imaginations of many Surrealists, **André Breton** himself declaring that the poetic enchantment of such film was derived from it being 'condemned to extreme solutions' in their 'explorations of the deepest mental grottoes'.[68]

For Magritte, it was Fantômas who provided the most overt and pervasive influence. The thirty-two Fantômas crime novels of Marcel Allain and Pierre Souvestre, published between 1911 and 1913, five adapted into films by Louis Feuillade, were wildly popular in their time. Fantômas was an elusive 'Batman'-type figure, part lover and part criminal anti-hero, able to reinvent himself through strategies of evasion and disguise. The Feuillade adaptations in particular deploy suspense and scenes of charged inaction, creating a mode of poetic mystery that appealed to Magritte's sensibilities. Famously, a Fantômas film-still from 1913 would become the compositional basis for Magritte's 1927 painting *The Menaced Assassin*, and a number of other works allude to the character (*The Torturing of the Vestal Virgin* 1927; *The Man from the Sea* 1927). Most explicitly, Magritte would directly appropriate the book cover from an Allain and Souvestre Fantômas novel of 1911 for his 1943 painting *The Flame Rekindled*. The artist's own identification with Fantômas as a kind of agent of subversion is perhaps best expressed in the photograph taken at the **London Gallery** of *The Barbarian* 1927, which presents the visage of Fantômas, alongside Magritte himself, bowler-hatted and adopting a pose identical to that of his hero. It is a portrait that reveals much about the image of himself that Magritte wished to present to the world. (**DP**)

See also: **Appropriation; Commercial Art; Detective Stories; Film; Mask and Masquerade; Violence; Window**

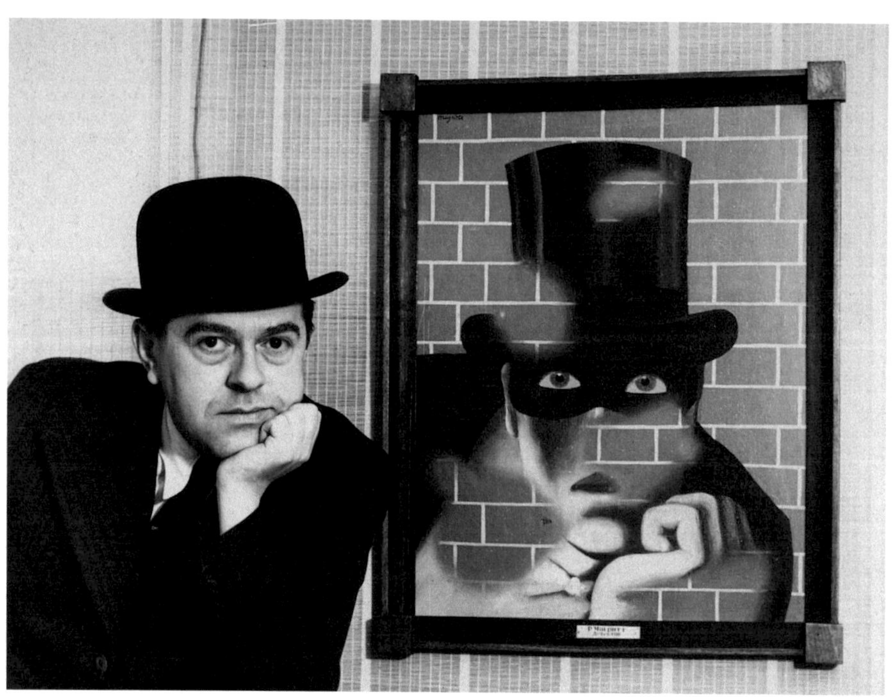

René Magritte and *The Barbarian*, London Gallery, 1938, photograph, gelatin silver print, 13.7 × 19.1 cm. Private Collection

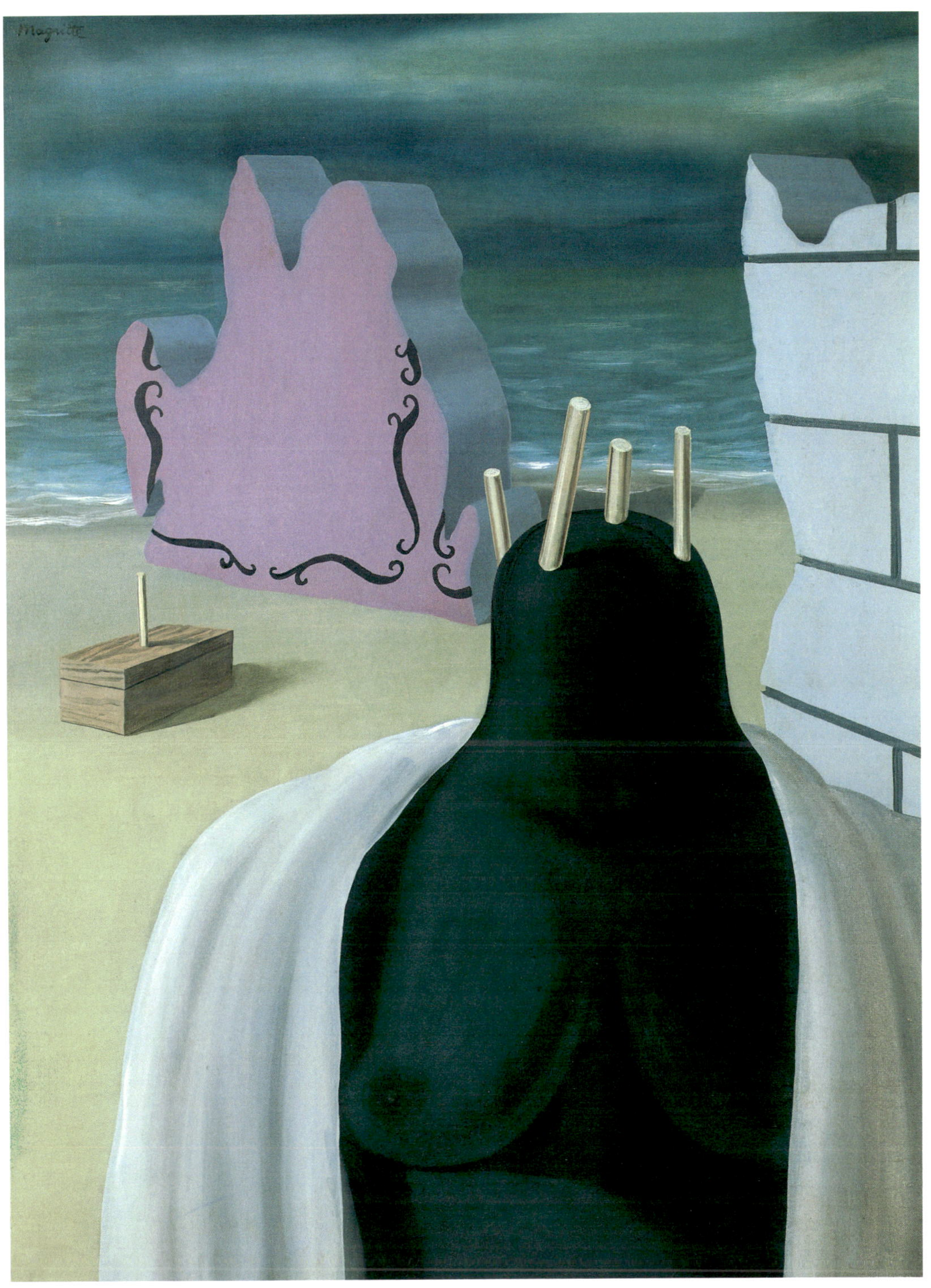

The Torturing of the Vestal Virgin
Le Supplice de la vestale 1927, oil on canvas, 97.5 × 74.5 cm.
Collection Isy Brachot and Christine Duchiron-Brachot, CR 134

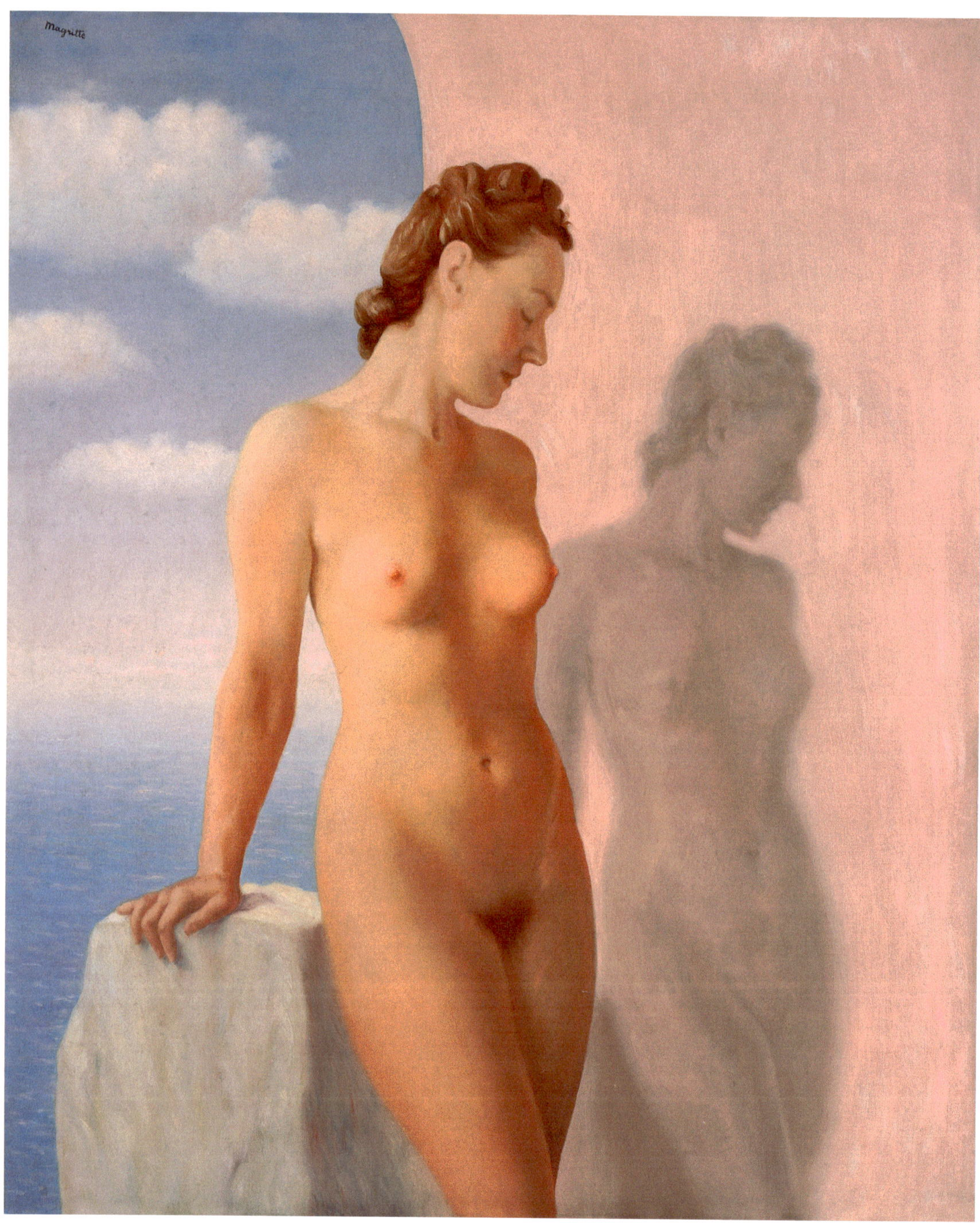

The Dream
Le Rêve 1945, oil on canvas, 83 × 69 cm.
Utsunomiya Museum of Art, Japan, CR589

Female Form: Magritte's fascination with the female body manifests itself in his paintings in a whole variety of ways. In contrast to his male figures, which are always clothed and clearly situated, his female figures are generally depicted as nudes: lifeless, doll-like creatures, sometimes fragmented and reduced to no more than body parts, such as in *Representation* 1937 and *The Rape* 1934; with no physical form as such, but in the guise of a **fetish**, for example *Philosophy in the Boudoir* 1947; or in the idealised sensual form of *Black Magic* 1934 (and its variants). Whatever the case, these compositions are always concerned with **metamorphosis** and Magritte's striving to grasp the female figure in its entirety and in its very being. He reduces his figures to standardised abstract pictorial signs, as he stated: 'A human being is a visible phenomenon like a **cloud**, like a tree, like a house, like all the things we see. I do not deny its importance, but even so I do not give it pride of place in the hierarchy of things that the world visibly offers us. In fact, if I portray a person, it is his existence which is in play and not any activity of his.'[69] Accordingly, the female figure is presented in Magritte's paintings as though carved from marble, reified and immobile, a cool beauty, far removed from the pleasures of the senses. Magritte's approach to the female form is ambiguous – an approach that never goes beyond an endeavour to imbue the human form with real life, for instance in *Attempting the Impossible* 1928. (**GF**)

See also: ***Bilboquet*; Double; Eroticism; Mannequin; Object; Visual Fracture**

Fetish: The concept of fetishism combines two distinct ideas: that of overvaluation, per Marx's 'commodity fetishism', and that of one thing standing in place of another. **Sigmund Freud's** influential text *Fetishism* 1927 proposed that 'the fetish is a substitute for the woman's (the mother's) penis that the little boy once believed in,' with the fetish being a defence against castration anxiety.[70] With Magritte it is the mother herself who suddenly disappeared, her suicide by drowning in 1912 being an enigma explored in his work of 1926–27. Magritte's supposed witnessing of the recovered corpse, with the head swathed in the nightdress, implies a sighting of his mother's lower body, suggesting the impact of fetishism on the work. Freud claimed that 'the last impression before the uncanny and traumatic one is retained as a fetish', as though freezing time at that point. With

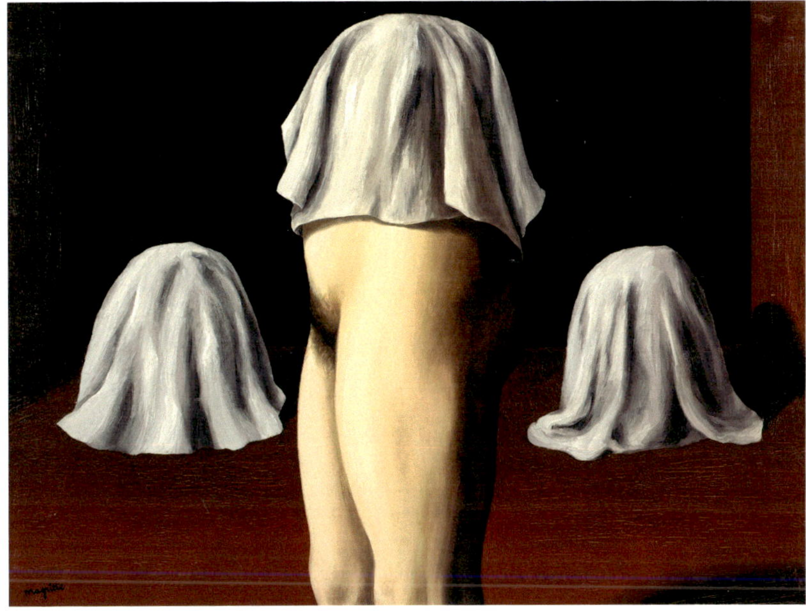

The Symmetrical Trick
La Ruse symétrique
1928, oil on canvas,
54 × 73 cm.
Private Collection,
Switzerland, CR 227

Magritte we might suggest that the veil plays such a role, halting time at the moment before the fatal sighting of the corpse itself.[71] The numerous veiled figures, as in *The Lovers* 1928 and *The Symmetrical Trick* 1928, with its truncated lower female torso topped with a veil, all suggest anxieties relating to both castration and the lost mother. (**NM**)

👁 **See also: Léopold and Régina Magritte; Mask and Masquerade**

The Fidelity of Images: It was under this title, invented by **Louis Scutenaire** in reference to Magritte's *The Treachery of Images* 1929 and *The Subversion of Images* 1929, a photographic series by **Paul Nougé**, that in 1976 the photographs and short films made by Magritte were exhibited together for the first time. With the sole aim of rediscovering a familiar Magritte, Scutenaire titled every photograph, whose imagery sometimes corresponds to and sheds light on the world of his pictures. For example, *Love* 1928 is the direct source of *Attempting the Impossible* 1928; *The Destroyer* 1943 relates to *Universal Gravitation* 1943; *God, the Eighth Day* 1937 being the basis for *The Healer* 1938. Other negatives showing **Georgette Magritte** were used as the basis for advertising projects for Studio Dongo, Magritte preferring this method to the constrained poses and expense of professional models. Other more singular photographs revealed a taste for the facetious and for improvisation, with Magritte and his friends seen eating paving stones in *The Feast of Stones* 1942, sleeping on a railway line in *The Good Trip* 1933, or contemplating a glove in *The Enigma* 1950. Numerous negatives invert the very function of photography by refusing the notion of the portrait, showing sidekicks masked, from behind, or hiding their faces, for example in *The Giant* 1937. The status of these photographs is ambiguous. Magritte never saw these amateur photographs as a valuable mode of expression and he hardly ever showed them.

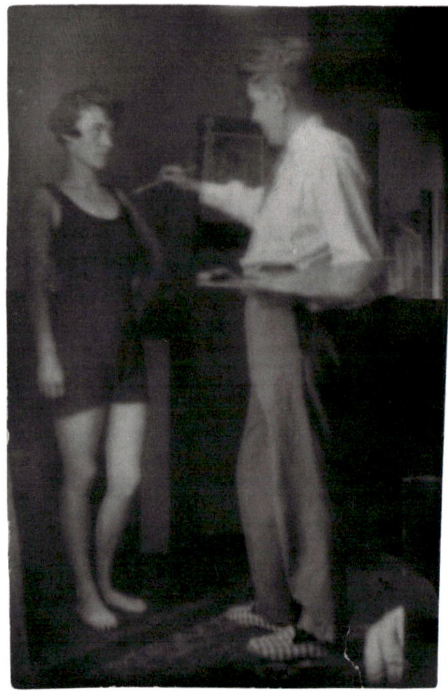

Love
L'Amour, Georgette and René Magritte, Le Perreux-sur-Marne, Paris, 1928, photograph, gelatin silver print, 10.5 × 7 cm. Private Collection

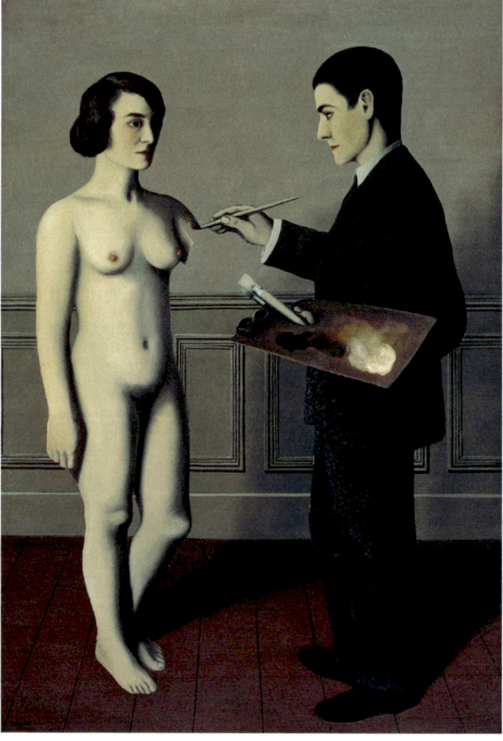

Attempting the Impossible
Tentative de l'impossible 1928, oil on canvas, 116 × 81 cm. Toyota Municipal Museum of Art, Toyota Aichi, CR 284

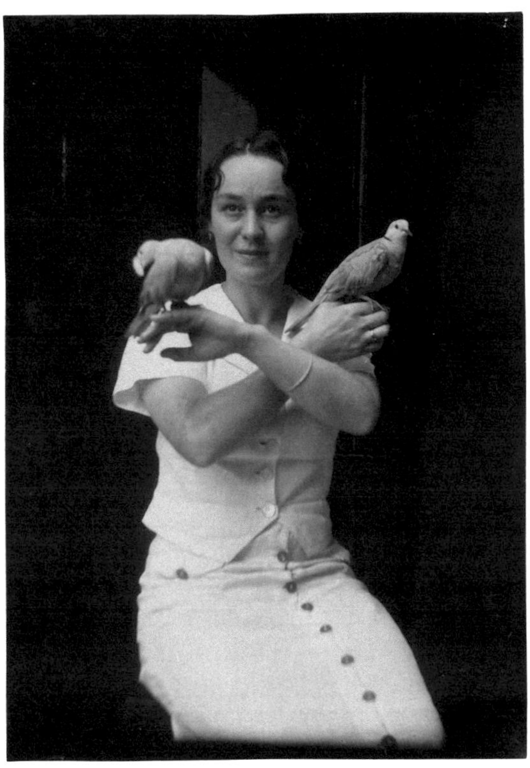

The Meeting
Le Rendez-Vous, Georgette Magritte, Brussels, Rue Esseghem, 1938, photograph, gelatin silver print, 11.5 × 8.2 cm. Private Collection

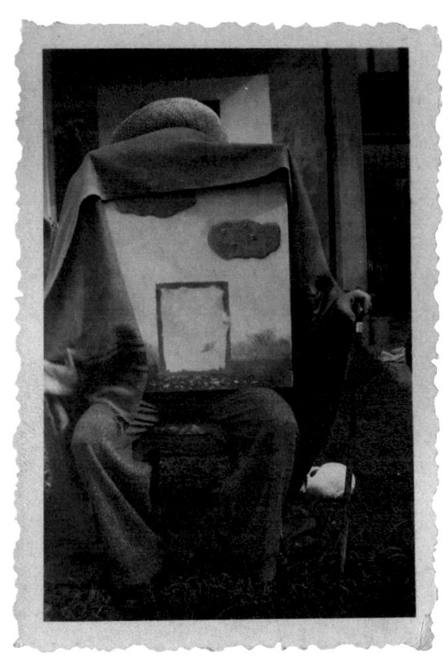

God, the Eighth Day
Dieu, le huitième jour, René Magritte, Rue Esseghem, Brussels, 1937, photograph, gelatin silver print, 8.5 × 5.7 cm. Private Collection

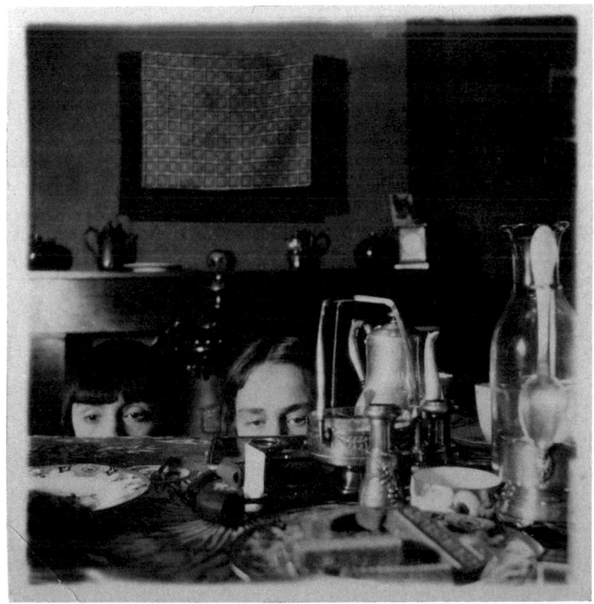

The Seers
Les Voyants, Marthe Nougé and Georgette Magritte, Brussels, 1930, photograph, gelatin silver print, 9 × 9 cm. Private Collection

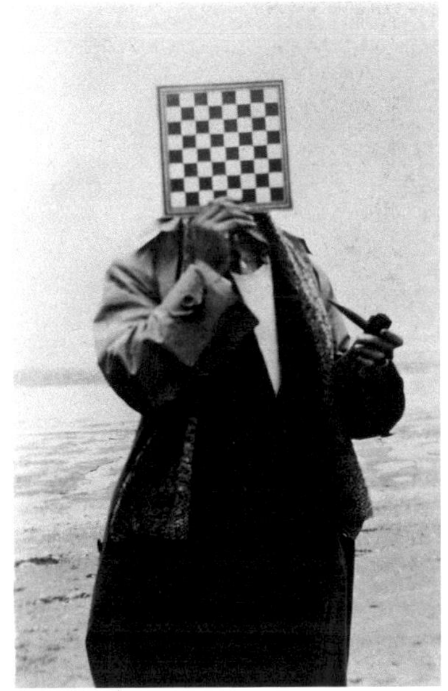

The Giant
Le Géant 1937, photograph, gelatin silver print, 8.8 × 6 cm. Collection Isy Brachot

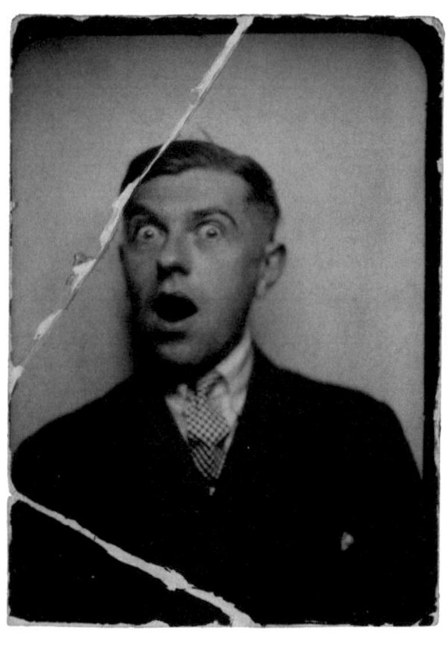

Flirtaciousness

La Coquetterie, self-portrait of René Magritte, Paris botanical gardens, 1928, photograph, gelatin silver print, 5 × 3.7 cm. Private Collection

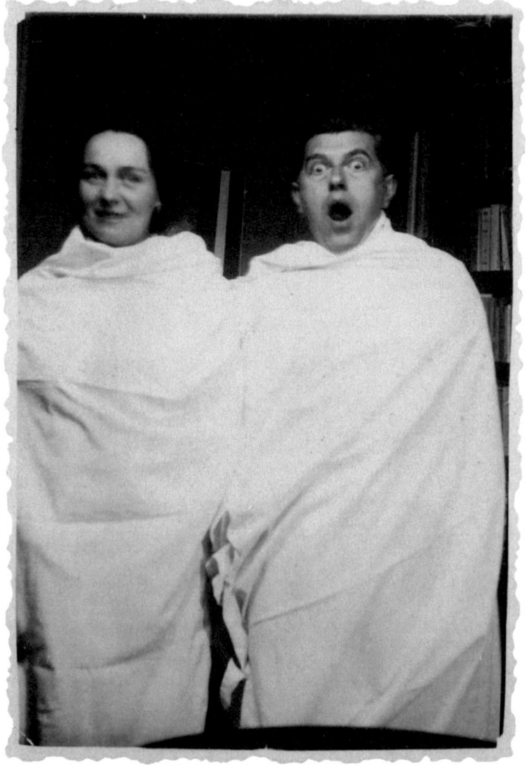

The Bouquet

Le Bouquet, Georgette and René Magritte, Rue Esseghem, Brussels, 1937, photograph, gelatin silver print, 8.5 × 5.8 cm. Private Collection

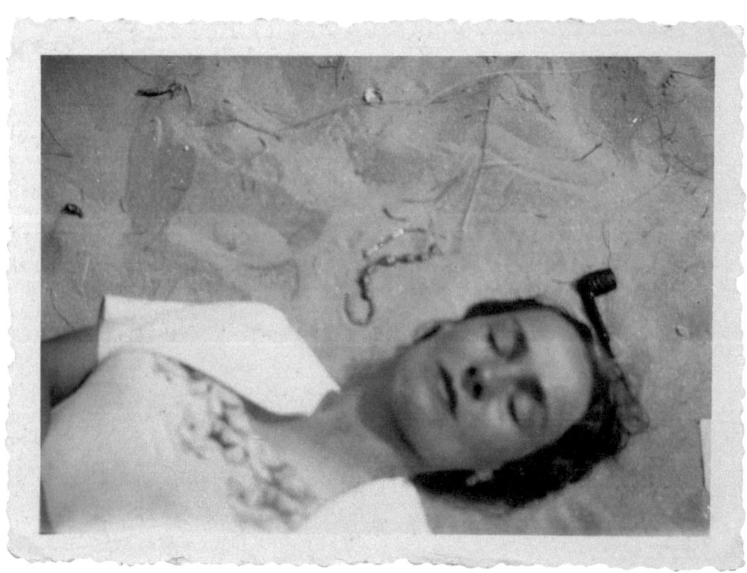

The Oblivion Seller

La Marchande d'oubli, Georgette Magritte, Belgian coast, 1936, photograph, gelatin silver print, 8.5 × 6.2 cm. Private Collection

They should be seen as works influenced by the burlesque and by comedy, the equivalent of those short super-8 films made in an afternoon, a distant reminiscence of Magritte's cinematographic memories from a time when the cinema was silent and when it aspired to be no more than popular entertainment. (XC)

See also: **Film; Photography;** *The Treachery of Images*

Film: Invented only a few years before his own birth in 1898, Magritte grew up with cinema, closely following the adventures of **Fantômas**, Laurel and Hardy, and particularly the work of the director Georges Méliès.[72] The significance of cinema for Magritte is signalled in an early canvas, *Cinéma bleu* 1925, in which a fashionably dressed woman stands before a classical façade, flanked by deep red curtains, a sign in the foreground directing the reader towards the cinema. In the background of this typically theatrical image floats an air balloon. This recalls the dramatic incident from Magritte's childhood when a balloon landed on the roof of the family home – the sudden eruption of the 'marvellous' within the everyday, which the artist associated with the magic of cinema.

Besides drawing on early serial films such as Louis Feuillade's *Les Vampires* 1915 and *Judex* 1916 for the themes and characters in his works, Magritte also borrowed their theatrical melodrama and vivid pictorialism to organise his compositions. Magritte also wrote a number of short film scripts, as in this first scene from *The Obsession*, c.1936:

The countryside towards evening –
Threatening sky – Empty landscape.
1. A young man on a horse seems to be wandering.
2. He can see in the distance, by a road, a burning object.
Close-up: a tuba on fire, the countryside in the background.[73]

This scenario refers to both *The Lost Jockey* image and *The Discovery of Fire* 1934–5. Whereas Magritte wrote of basing his works on striking still images, the film scenarios also suggest a *time* element to his works, as with short fantasy scenarios that unfold

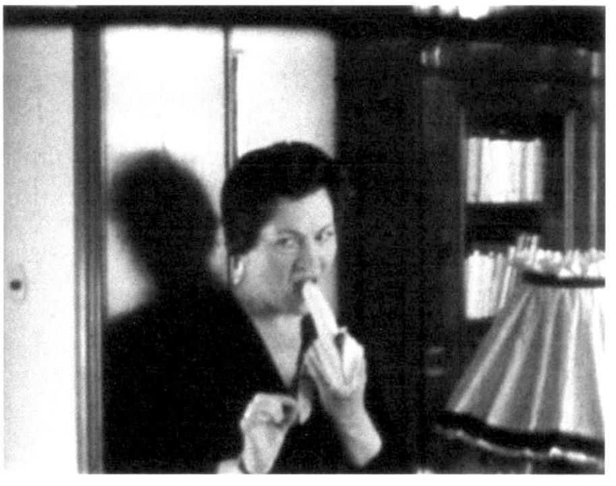

The Antillean Dessert
Le Dessert des Antilles 1957, 8mm film, black and white, duration: 2 minutes 29 seconds (with Irène Hamoir and Louis Scutenaire). Archives of Belgian Arts Letters and Documents, Belgium

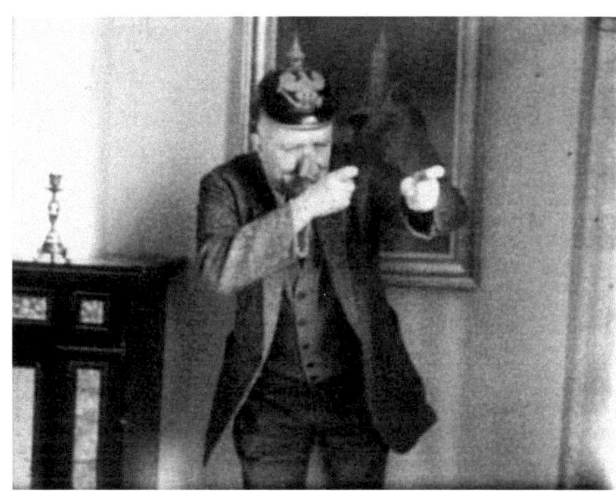

The Total Scenario
Le Scénario total 1956–7, 8mm film, black and white, duration: 2 minutes 39 seconds (with Georgette Magritte, Irène Hamoir and Louis Scutenaire). Archives of Belgian Arts Letters and Documents, Belgium

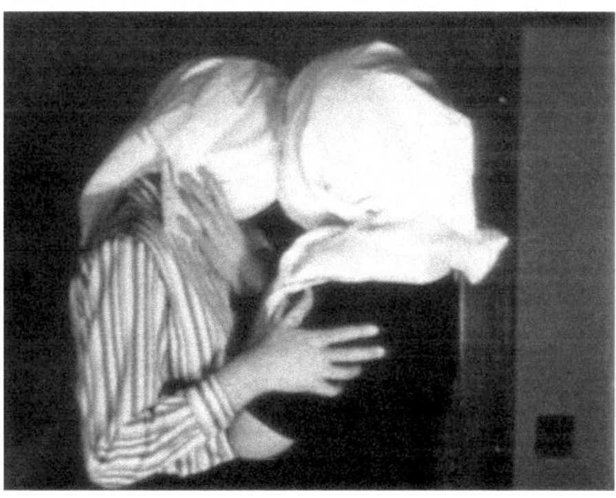

Tuba (Interior)
Tuba (intérieur) 1960, 8mm film, colour, duration: 5 minutes 40 seconds (with Irène Hamoir, Louis Scutenaire, Georgette and René Magritte, Nicole Desclin, Suzi Gablik, and Alan Schmeer). Archives of Belgian Arts Letters and Documents, Belgium

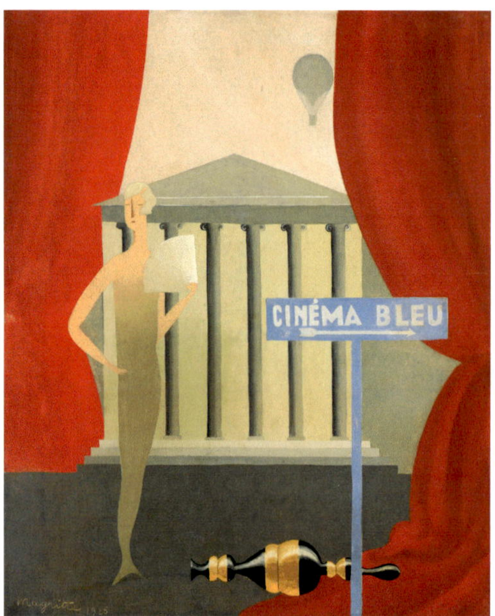

Cinéma bleu
1925, oil on canvas, 65 × 54 cm. Private Collection, CR 68

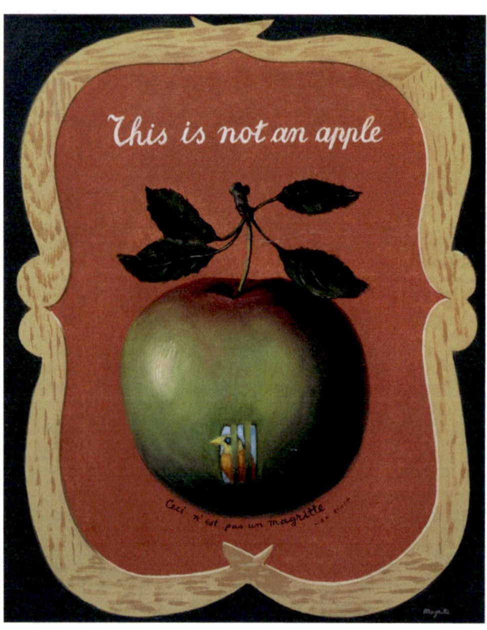

Force of Habit
La Force de l'habitude 1960, oil on canvas, 61 × 50 cm.
Private Collection, CR 914

like films over time. This time dimension was ultimately realised in Magritte's super-8 films produced between 1956 and 1960. *Tuba (Interior)* 1960, for example, re-stages the veiled kissing figures of *The Lovers* 1928. (**NM**)

See also: **Detective Stories**

Fire: In his 1938 lecture 'La Ligne de vie', Magritte expounded his ideas on what he described as **Elective Affinities**, in particular how he struggled in his paintings with the 'problem of fire'. He stated: '*The Discovery of Fire* afforded me the privilege of feeling the same as the first people to create fire by hitting two pieces of stone together.'[74] In order to heighten the effect and impact of this feeling, Magritte reduced the various objects – paper, chair and tuba in *The Ladder of Fire* 1934 and *The Discovery of Fire* 1936 – to just one object, namely the tuba, made from the material least capable of catching fire. Suzi Gablik also connects fire – 'one of the principles of universal explanation' – with sexual associations.[75] For, when Magritte painted *The Invention of Fire* in 1946, he stated: 'The astonishing discovery of fire. Because of the rubbing of two bodies, suggests the physical mechanism of sexual pleasure.'[76] (**GF**)

See also: **Eroticism; Metamorphosis**

Forgery: Plagiarism and forgery are integral to **Surrealism**, evidenced by the Surrealists' admiration for Comte de Lautréamont, himself a fervent plagiarist who asserted 'Plagiarism is necessary, progress implies it.'[77] **Marcel Mariën's** autobiography *Le Radeau de la Mémoire*, published in 1983, claimed that Magritte funded his first monograph by producing and selling, between 1942 and 1946, forgeries of Titian, Meindert Hobbema, Pablo Picasso, Georges Braque, **Giorgio de Chirico** and **Max Ernst**. David Sylvester and Sarah Whitfield later linked Ernst's infamous inscription on Magritte's *Force of Habit* 1960 to Magritte's supposed forgery, in 1943, of Ernst's *The Forest*:

In Max Ernst's dining room in Paris there was a painting by Magritte, entitled *Force of Habit*, in which a heraldic image of a large green apple is inscribed, in English, 'This is not an apple.' Max and Magritte had exchanged pictures, as artists often do. And Max, in the middle of the apple,

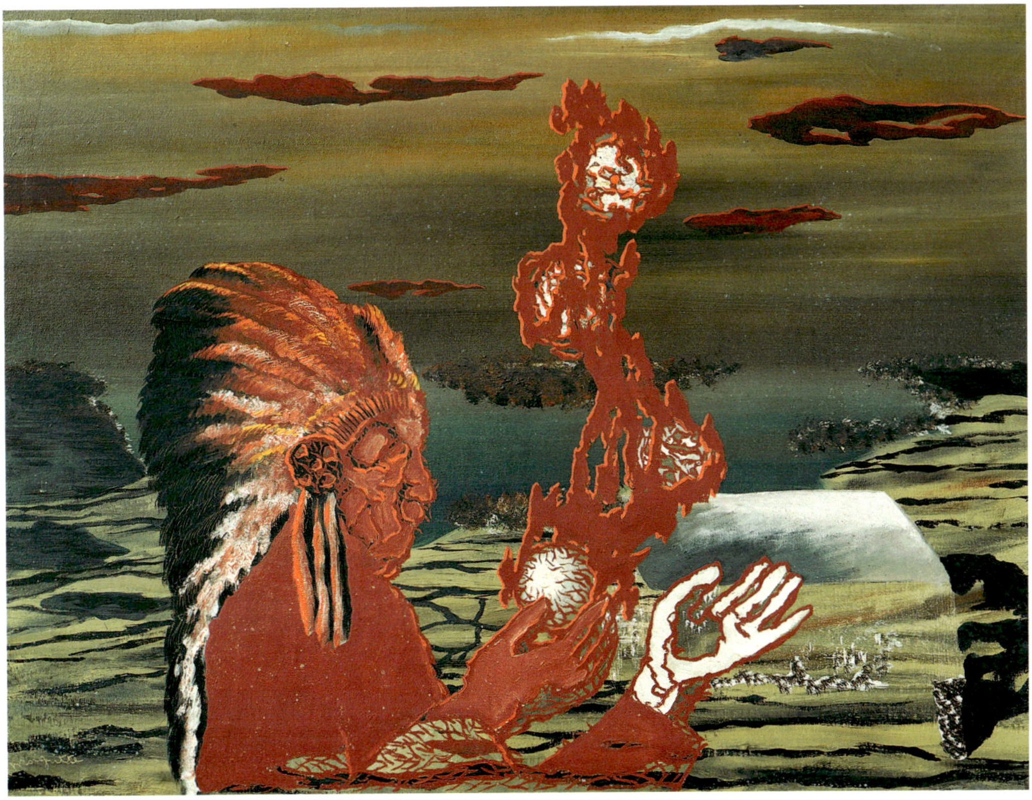

The Age of Fire
L'Âge du feu 1927, oil on canvas, 73 × 100 cm.
Private Collection, CR 150

had painted a cage with a bird inside. Below this cage, Max had written, '*Ceci n'est pas un Magritte – signé Max Ernst*.'[78]

As Mariën explained, three months before Magritte's death in 1967, the forged version of *The Forest* reappeared in Brussels at an exhibition. Magritte, passing by the painting, exclaimed 'This is a famous Max Ernst!'[79] Ernst's inscription unearths the subversive character of Magritte beneath his appearance as a commercial artist, revealing him as being 'like a worm in the apple … changing what is within, without touching the surface'.[80] Plagiarism and forgery are intriguing dimensions of Magritte's art, subverting conventional notions of originality, authenticity and value. **(PA)**

👁 See also: **Artifice; Ersatz; Parody and Pastiche**

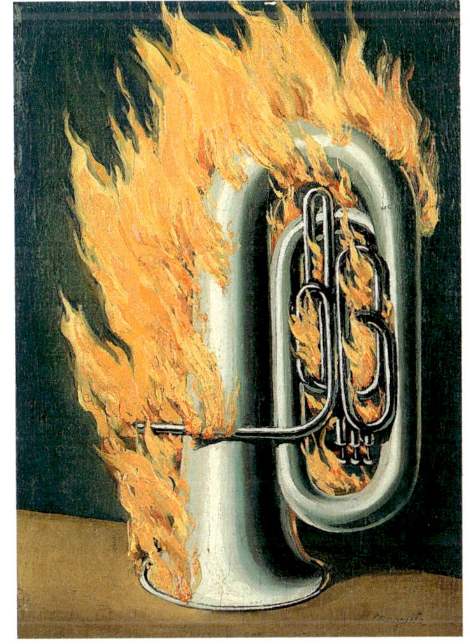

The Discovery of Fire
La Découverte du feu 1936, oil on board, 22 × 16 cm.
Mr and Mrs Gilbert Kaplan, New York, CR 393

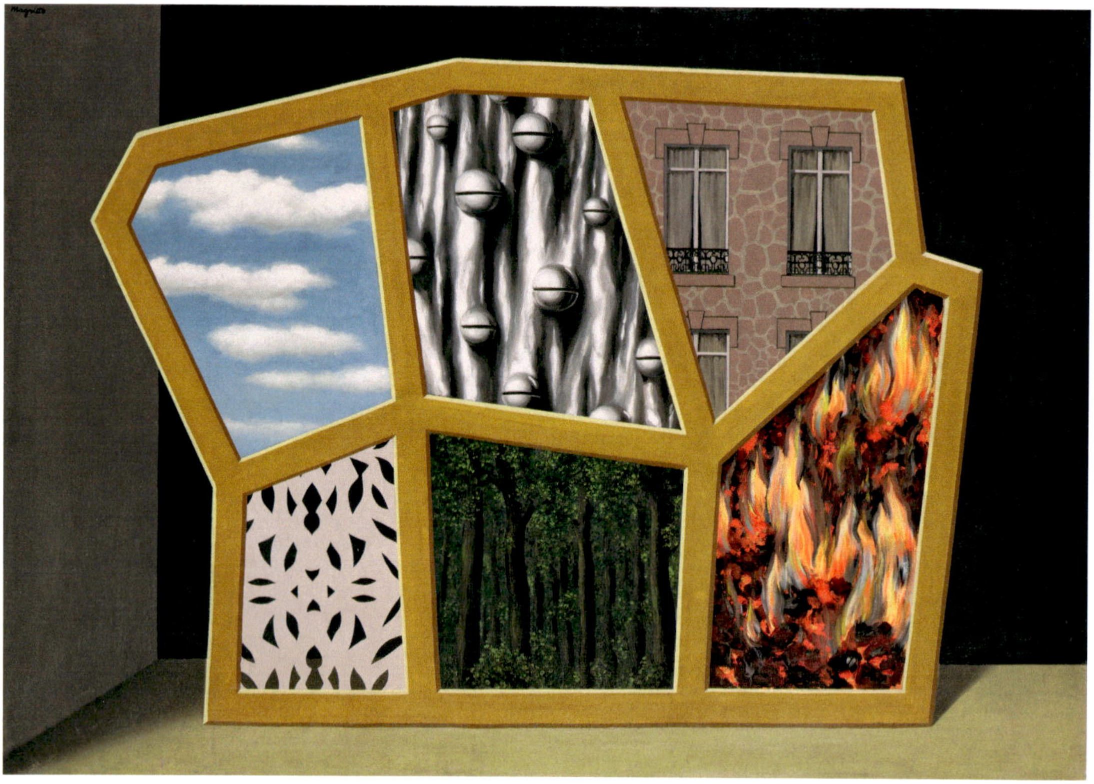

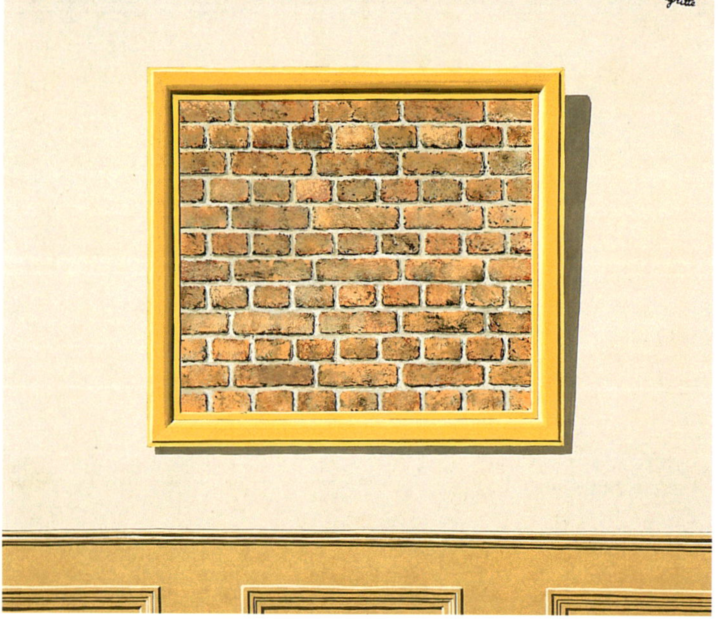

The Empty Mask
Le Masque vide 1928, oil on canvas,
81 × 116 cm. National Museum of
Wales, Cardiff, CR 285

Blood-Letting
La Saignée 1938 or 1939,
gouache on paper, 35.5 × 41.6 cm.
Museum Boijmans Van
Beuningen, Rotterdam, CR 1149

Michel Foucault (1926–1984) French philosopher
and critic. Foucault was one of a number of French
philosophers grouped under the Structuralist
mantel known for their critical perspectives on the
human sciences who came to prominence in the
mid-1960s. Foucault's 1966 essay *The Order of Things
(Les Mots et les choses)* constitutes his most important contribution to the history and theory of art.
The text offered a powerful analytical interpretation
of Diego Velázquez's *Las Meninas* 1656, Foucault
interpreting the painting as allegorising the very
processes of **representation**. Having read the book,
Magritte engaged in an exchange with Foucault,
his letter of 23 May 1966 expressing his belief that
Foucault had inadequately differentiated between
resemblance and similarity. 'Peas share a relationship of similarity … only thought has resemblance,'
he opined.[81] This contact led to Foucault's 1973 essay
This is not a Pipe, which questioned received notions
of representation by engaging specifically with
Magritte's painting. The essay played an important
role in the critical re-evaluation of Magritte's work,
emphasising the profoundly philosophical enquiry
that underpinned the artist's practice. (**DP**)

See also: **Language; Meaning; Philosophy;** *The
Treachery of Images*

Frame, draws a border around one sort of reality
– a painting, for example – and sets it apart from
the larger and perhaps very different reality that
surrounds it. Magritte uses frames in a number of
different ways in his work. In *The Empty Mask* 1928,
a grid of irregularly shaped frames holds various
fragments – forestation, a house façade, a fire – as
if to create a sense of order that is nevertheless quite
arbitrary. Sometimes, the frame seems to refer to
and undercut its traditional role in separating the
work of art from the outside world. In *Blood-Letting*
1938–9, a frame surrounds the section of brick
wall that lies – normally unseen – behind the wall
of the gallery. Yet, at the same time, we well know
that this separation is an illusion, that what is in
the frame and outside it are both made of the same
substance – paint.

   In a number of works Magritte moved out from
the internal illusion of his painting to work with its
actual framing. *The Eternally Obvious* (1930 and 1948)
consists of five small framed paintings stacked

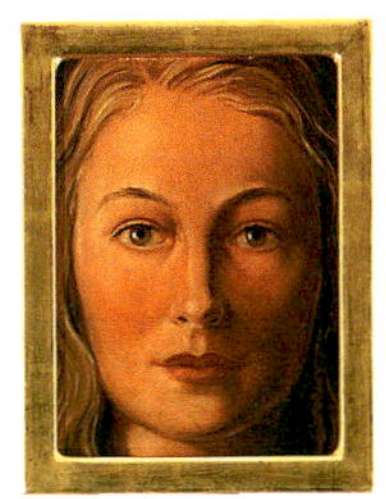

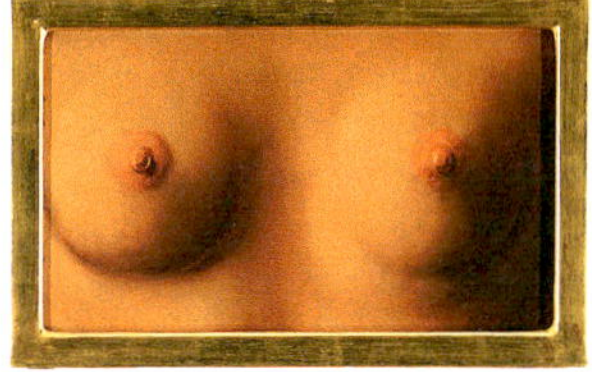

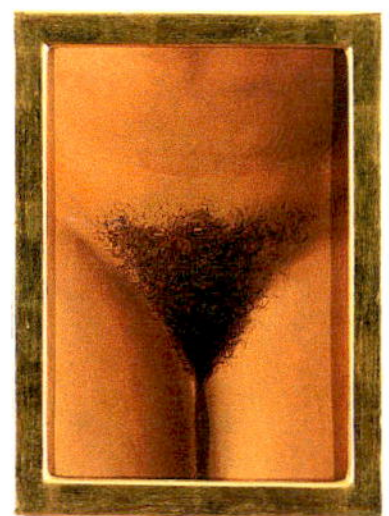

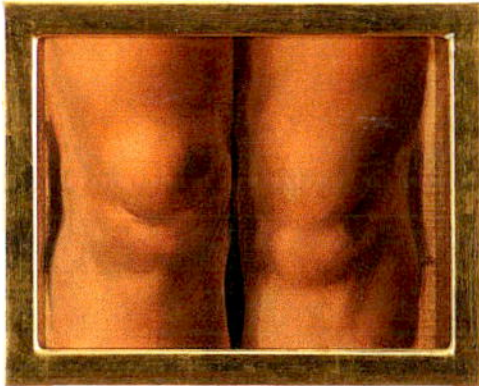

***The Eternally
Obvious***
L'Évidence éternelle
1948, oil on canvas laid
on board. Five panels,
framed and mounted
on glass: 25.5 × 19.5;
19.3 × 32; 27 × 20.2;
20.5 × 26.6; 26 × 18 cm.
The Metropolitan
Museum of Art, New
York. The Pierre and
Maria-Gaetana Matisse
Collection, 2002, CR 640

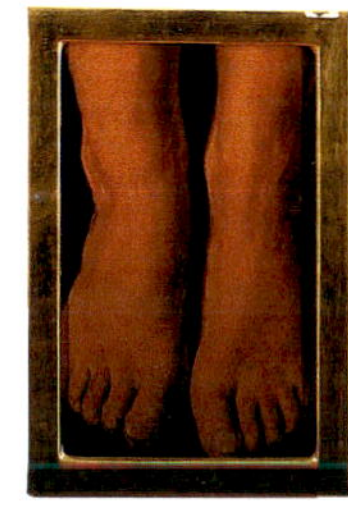

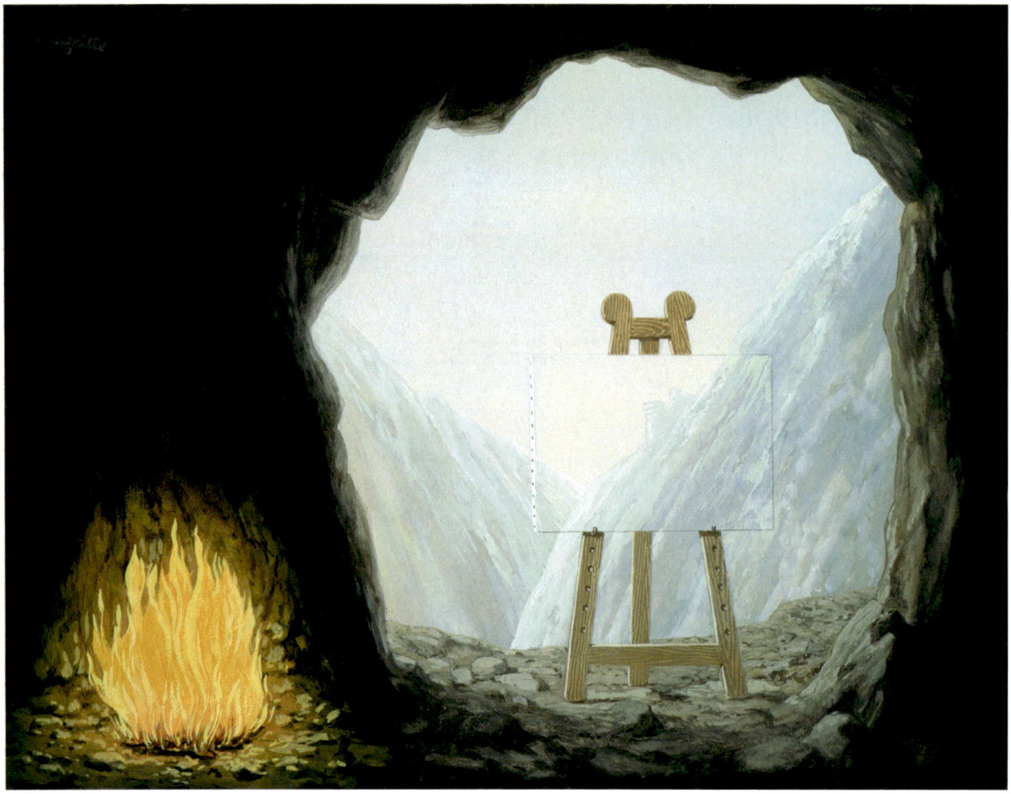

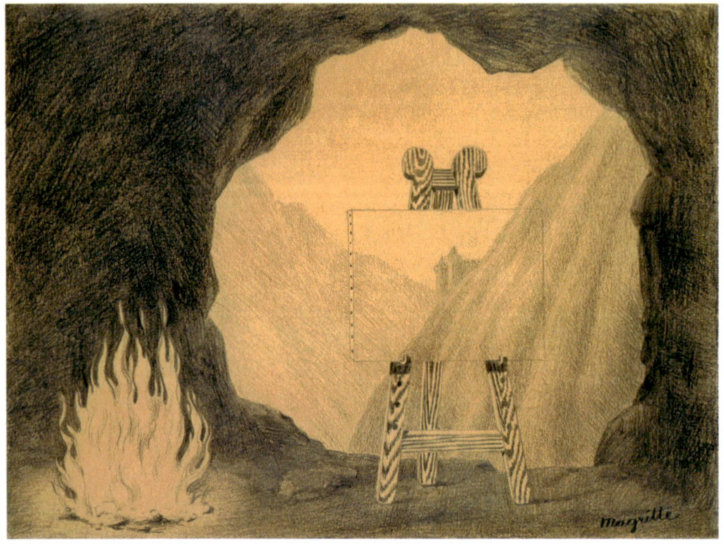

The Human Condition
La Condition humaine 1948,
gouache and pencil on paper, 36 × 46.5 cm.
Collection Jasper Johns, CR 1301a (1316)

The Human Condition
La Condition humaine 1948,
pencil on paper, 23.8 × 32.7 cm.
Collection Jasper Johns

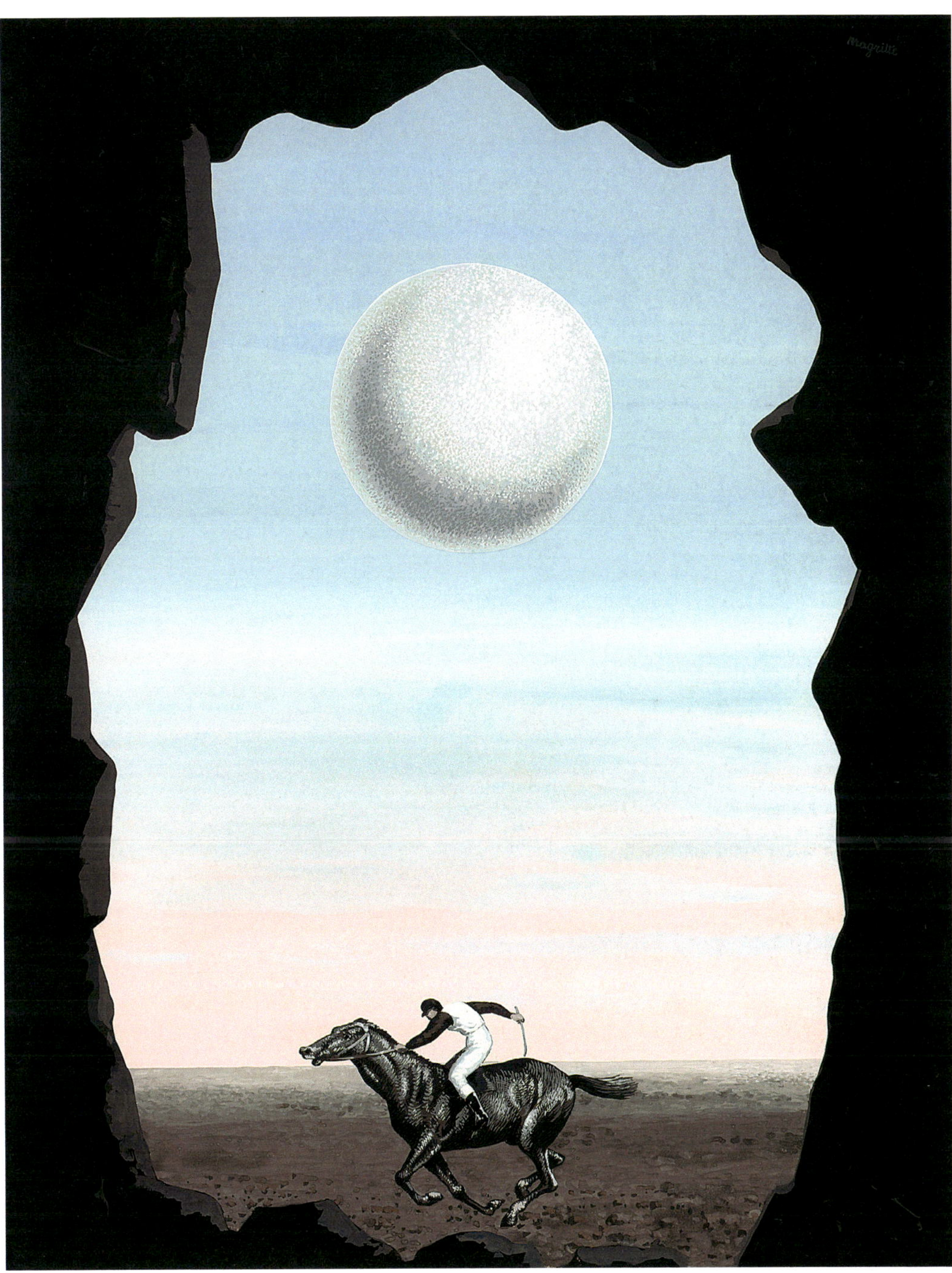

The Lost Jockey
Le Jockey perdu n.d., gouache on paper,
64.8 × 50.5 cm. Private Collection

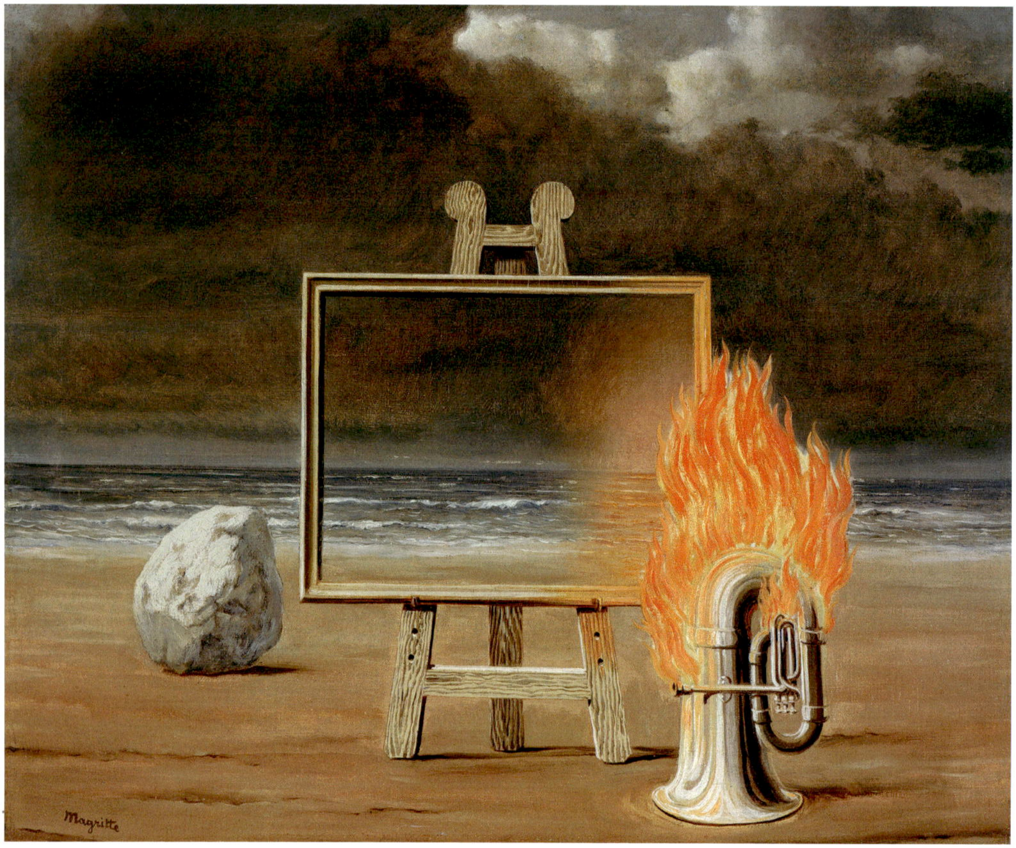

The Fair Captive
La Belle Captive 1948, oil on canvas, 54 × 65 cm.
Private Collection, CR 641

vertically and depicting from top to bottom the face of a woman, her breasts, her pubic area, her knees and her feet. The five frames are placed so as to depict the actual relationships of these parts and to give the illusion that the rest of the body might continue outside the frame and connect into a whole. This three-dimensional physicality was always important (there is a photograph where René holds the object as he might hold his wife **Georgette**, whose image formed the basis of the work), adding an additionally unnerving element to the work. (**IW**)

👁 See also: **Absence; Object; Visual Fracture; Window**

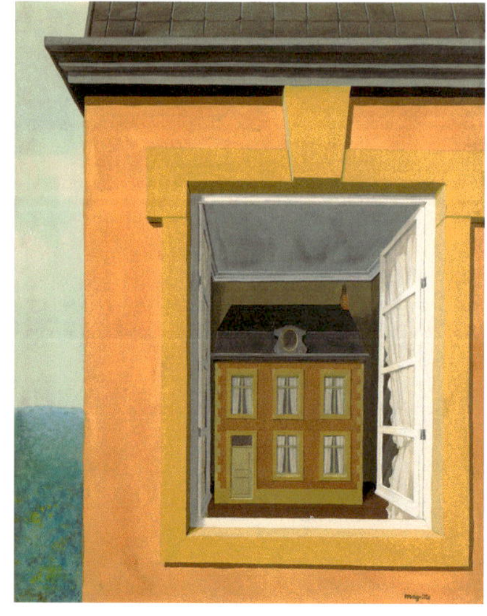

In Praise of the Dialectic
Éloge de la dialectique 1937, gouache on paper, 38 × 32 cm. Musée d'Ixelles, Brussels, CR 1120

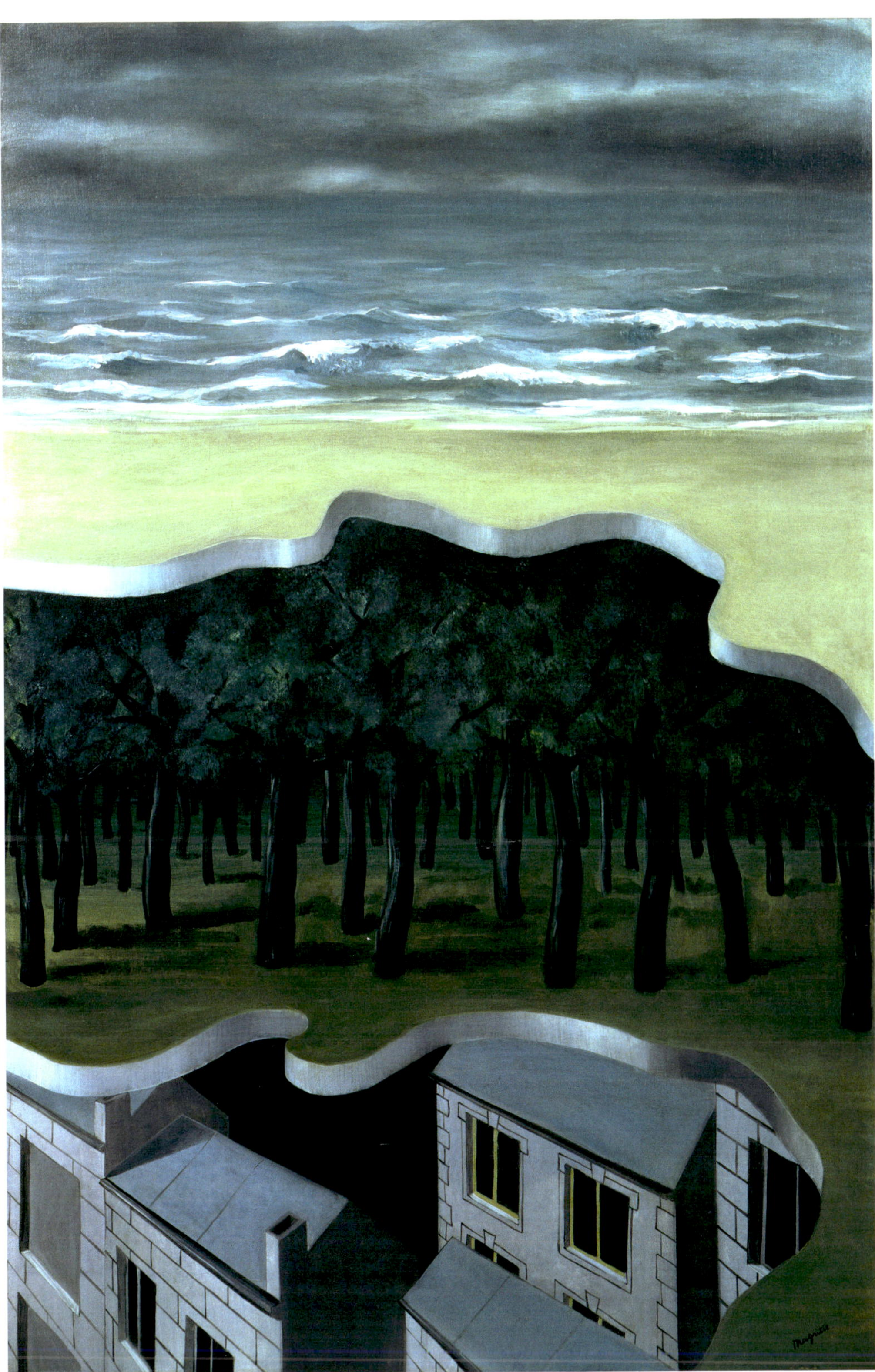

Panorama for the Populace
Panorama populaire 1926, oil on canvas, 120 × 80 cm.
Kunstsammlung Nordrhein-Westfalen, Düsseldorf, CR 122

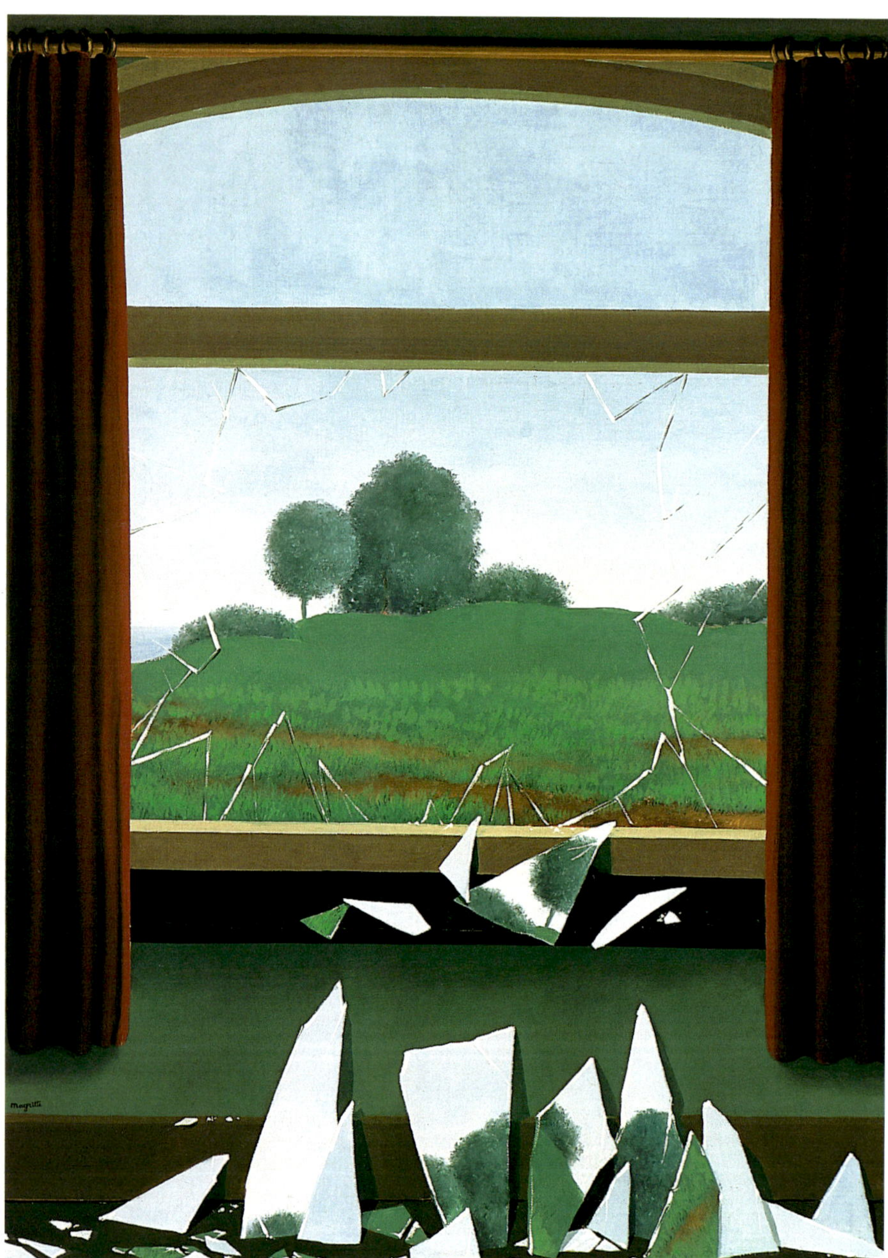

The Key to the Fields
La Clef des champs 1936, oil on canvas, 80 × 60 cm.
Museo Thyssen-Bornemisza, Madrid, CR 411

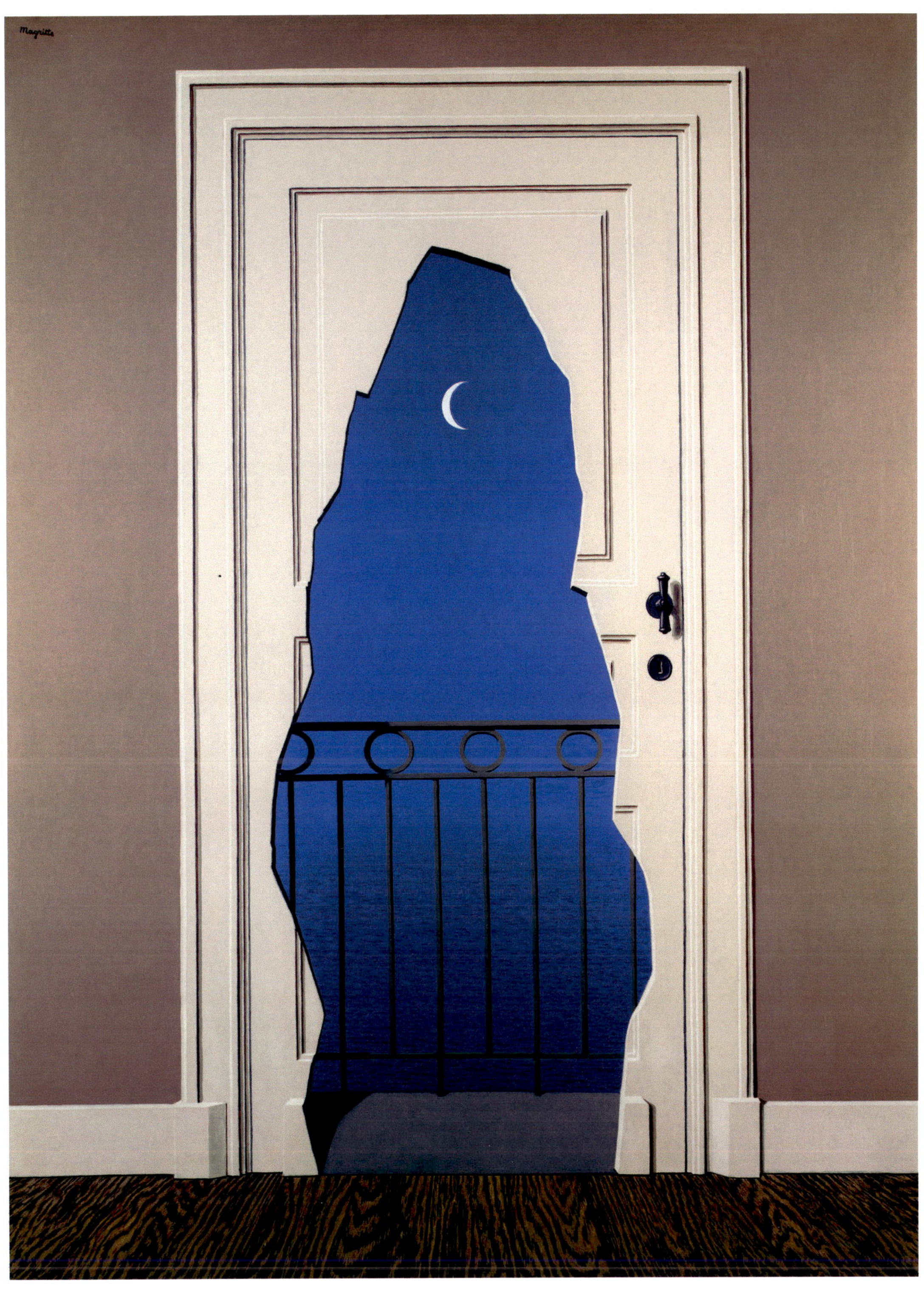

The Act of Faith
L'Acte de foi 1960, oil on canvas, 130 × 97 cm.
Private Collection, CR 925

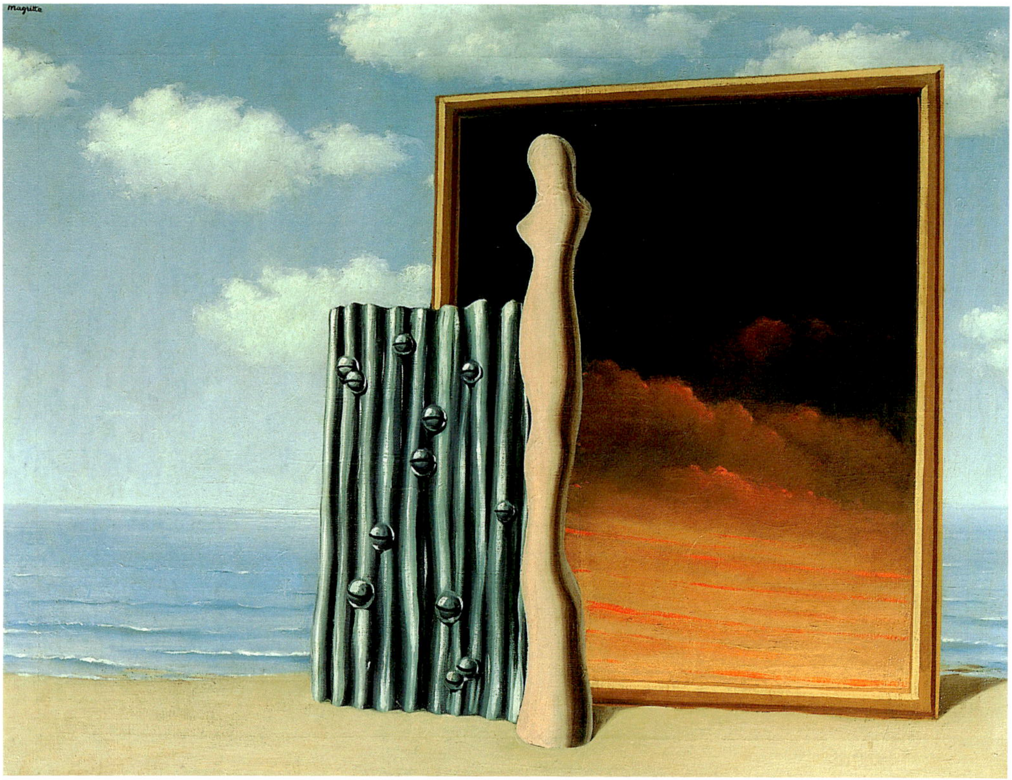

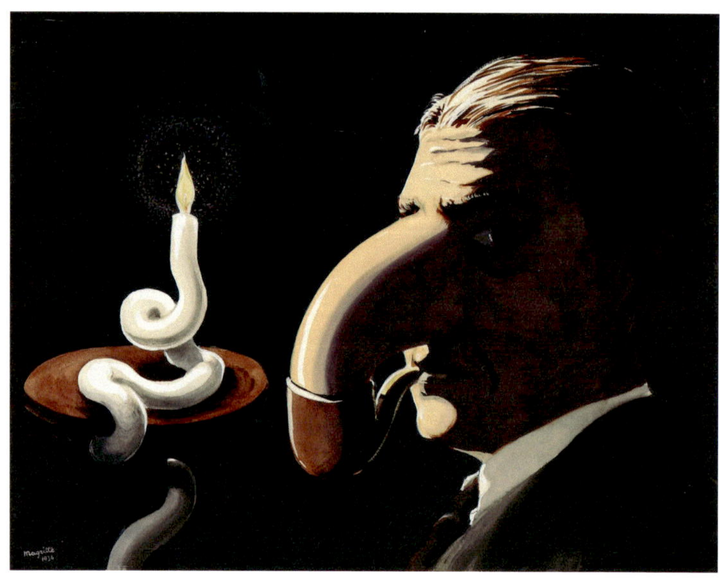

Composition on a Sea Shore
Composition sur la plage 1935–6,
oil on canvas, 54.5 × 73.5 cm.
Collection Mr and Mrs Wilbur
Ross, CR 391

The Philosopher's Lamp
La Lampe philosophique 1936,
gouache on paper, 23.5 × 30.6 cm.
Collection Mr and Mrs Wilbur
Ross, CR 1114

Sigmund Freud (1856–1939) Austrian neurologist, the father of **psychoanalysis**, and one of the most influential thinkers of the twentieth century. His ideas were critical to the development of **Surrealism**. In his psychoanalytical studies Freud developed a theory of art posited on **dreams** and the imagination and a concept of art as a substitute world to compensate for unsatisfactory reality. This was wholly at odds with Magritte's thinking, the artist setting great store by being totally alert when he was involved in the creative process, concentrating on representing visible reality rather than hoping to draw inspiration from subconscious dream images.[82] 'I don't believe in the unconscious,' he stated, 'nor do I believe that the world presents itself to us as a dream, except for when we are asleep. I don't believe in waking dreams. Nor do I believe in the imagination. It is arbitrary, and I am searching for the truth, and the truth is the mystery.'[83] Magritte thus distinguished between dreams as a 'sub-reality' and his paintings, which pass by virtue of their **poetry** into 'sur-reality' – a reality that 'we perceive at certain privileged moments when we have presence of mind'.[84] Magritte resisted any form of psychoanalytical interpretation of his works. In his view, this mode of interpretation attributed symbolic meaning to pictorial motifs, whereas, for him, 'a cloud in a picture is no more than a cloud'.[85] His paintings engage directly with the visible to achieve precision in his description of a thought. One thing Magritte did, however, recognise early on in Freud's theories, was the relationship between sexuality and artistic activity.[86] Freud's concept of 'sublimation' as the transformation of instinctive drives into intellectual achievement was in keeping with his own artistic motivations. This was also a tenet of the Surrealists, who drew on Freud's theories in their championing of the liberation of sexual desires. **(GF)**

See also: **Automatism and Automatic Writing; Double; Fetish**

Futurism: Movement founded in 1909 by the Italian poet Filippo Tommaso Marinetti (1876–1944), which denounced the art and culture of the past, celebrating instead the modern world of industry and technology. Magritte's interest in Futurism came before his engagement with Surrealism and was catalysed by **E.L.T. Mesens**, who tended to take the

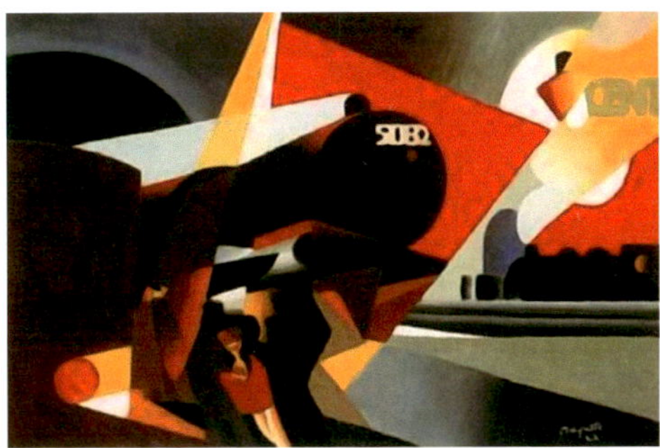

The Station
La Gare 1922, oil on canvas, 40 × 60 cm.
Whereabouts unknown, CR 35

lead in their shared intellectual and artistic pursuits. In 1920, shortly after they first met, the two wrote to the Futurist headquarters in Milan. In response, they received a letter from Marinetti, and parcels of manifestos whose 'fiery proclamations' excited them greatly. The correspondence inspired Magritte to create a series of Futurist-influenced paintings and gouaches, of which only a handful survive, for example *The Station* 1922. Their interest was extinguished shortly after, both rejecting the inhumane and violent imperialistic spirit of the Futurist movement. **(DP)**

G

Camille Goemans (1900–1960) Along with **Paul Nougé** and **Marcel Lecomte**, Goemans established ***Correspondance***, a series of tracts which constitute the first manifestation of the future Brussels Surrealist group. A medical student and fellow student of poet Henri Michaux (1899–1984) at Saint-Michel College in Brussels, in 1924 he published a collection of poems entitled *Périples* before collaborating with Nougé and Lecomte for the review ***Marie: Journal bimensuel pour la belle jeunesse***. In 1927 he established Galerie Goemans in Paris where he presented **Max Ernst's** earliest collages and the first joint exhibition of René Magritte and **Salvador Dalí**. Goemans also originated with Magritte the five tracts entitled *Le sens propre*, each illustrated with one of the artist's works, produced under contract in 1929. Close to the Parisian group, Goemans was photographed, eyes closed, with Magritte, Nougé and the Parisian **Surrealists** in the twelfth issue of ***La Révolution surréaliste*** (December 1929) around Magritte's picture *The Hidden Woman* 1929. His gallery closed in 1930 for financial reasons. Maintaining his close relations with the members of the group, little by little Goemans distanced himself from

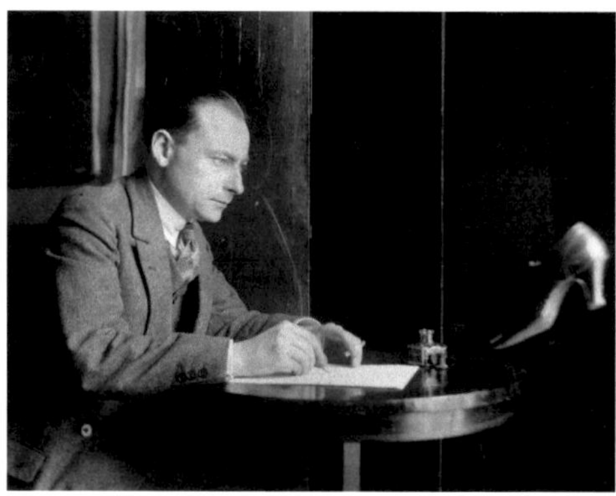

Camille Goemans, Paris, 1928

collective activity, while participating in monthly meetings aimed at giving **titles** to Magritte's paintings, of which he owned several significant examples. His entire poetic output, of great quality, was published by **Marcel Mariën** in 1970. (**XC**)

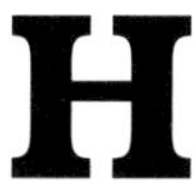 See also: ***Distances***; **Paris**

H

Martin Heidegger (1889–1976) German philosopher and theologian. With his distinction between being and beingness (*Being and Time* 1927) and his exploration of likenesses and reality, in other words, the relationship between truth and art (*The Origin of the Work of Art* 1935, published 1950) Heidegger addressed two issues that are central to the work of Magritte, who became interested in the philosopher's ideas in 1953.[87] Heidegger's example of a pair of peasant's shoes painted by Vincent van Gogh (and subsequently paraphrased in Magritte's series of *The Red Model*, first created in 1935) can be seen to affirm Magritte's epistemological 'principle of resemblance' as opposed to mere (imitative) sameness.[88] He observed a difference between the painted depiction of the shoes, which epitomise the particularity of the peasant world, and the real **objects**. For him, their function as something that is used, designed for a purpose and subordinated to an individual's personal interest, means that they cannot conjure up the real world. Heidegger concludes that everyday objects have to be transposed into the context of art in order for their true being to emerge. Heidegger's 'setting-into-work of truth', equivalent to his 'setting up a world', corresponds to Magritte's – inspired – 'unaccustomed order of things', which in turn evokes the **mystery**. (**GF**)

See also: **Meaning**; **Philosophy**; **Representation and Resemblance**

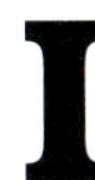

Alexandre Iolas (1908–1987) Of Greek origin, Iolas was a dancer before becoming an art dealer in New York, receiving the support of Elizabeth Arden and the **de Menil** family. Aware of the interest in Surrealist art in the United States, he contacted Magritte in February 1946. In 1947 Magritte staged his first exhibition in the United States, at Iolas's Hugo Gallery in New York. Over the next twenty years, they collaborated, Iolas in particular encouraging the artist to produce variations and copies of previous works for the American market. Iolas also suggested that Magritte transform some of his paintings into three-dimensional objects, which were cast in bronze after the artist's death.[89] (GF)

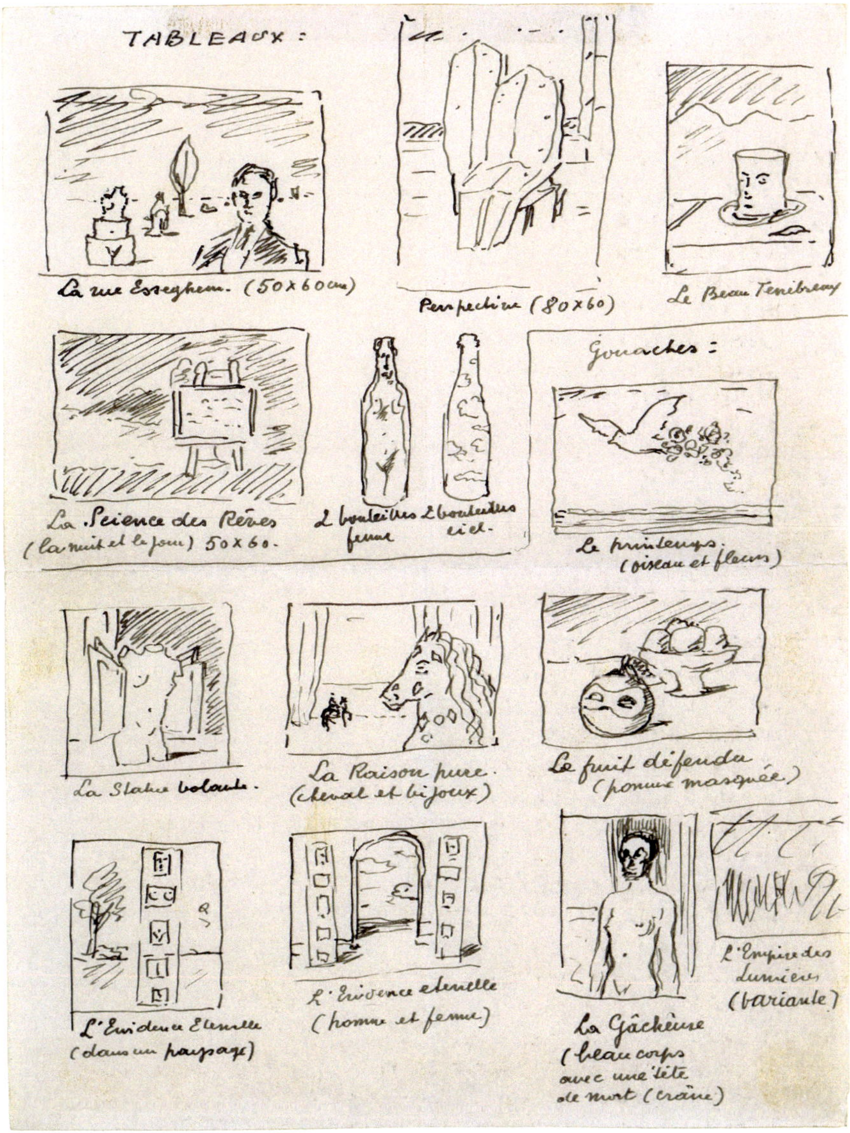

Tableaux: Sheet of 18 ink sketches
c.1950, ink on paper, 27.7 × 21 cm. Collection Leslee and David Rogath

J

Edward James (1907–1984) English aristocrat renowned for his patronage of Surrealist artists. Counting **Marcel Duchamp** and Pablo Picasso amongst his friends, he was an important patron of **Salvador Dalí** and his collection was exemplary, notably rich in works by women artists including Leonora Carrington. James also financially supported *Minotaure*, the Surrealist journal published between 1933 and 1939. An aspiring poet, his wealth enabled him to pursue aesthetic interests. He regarded his relationship with artists as one of collaboration rather than patronage. It was this that led him to invite Magritte to stay at his London home at 35 Wimpole Street in early 1937 to undertake a commission for three large paintings: *The Red Model*, *Youth Illustrated* and *On the Threshold of Freedom*. London evidently made a great impression on Magritte. 'London is a Revelation,' he wrote. 'True, I am only beginning to discover it. But so far everything is perfect … there is <u>something</u>.'[90] Later that year James purchased additional works including *The Pleasure Principle*, based on Man Ray's portrait of James, and *Not to be Reproduced*, both 1937, whose composition was based on a photograph of James standing in front of *On the Threshold of Freedom*. James stopped collecting Magritte's work in mid-1938. (**DP**)

See also: **England; Poetry; Portraiture**

Juxtaposition: In order to induce the **shock** to the system which allows us to perceive what he regarded as a hidden reality, Magritte's images juxtapose incompatible events or **objects**. In 1959 Magritte defined his 'principle of resemblance' in connection with the thoughts that emerge as we move towards the perception of poetic mystery, the basis for this being the juxtaposition of apparent opposites and the ensuing convergence or growing resemblance. For Magritte 'a thought resembles by becoming what the world offers it and by reinstating what it is offered into the mystery'.[91] Whereas his earliest Surrealist paintings juxtaposed wilfully contradictory items, in 1936 he began seeking out **Elective Affinities** such as the connection between feet and shoes in *The Red Model* (1935, and its variants). Rather than being juxtaposed with each other, things now encounter each other and coexist in a new order arising from the artist's inspiration. (**GF**)

See also: **Chance; Poetry; Representation and Resemblance**

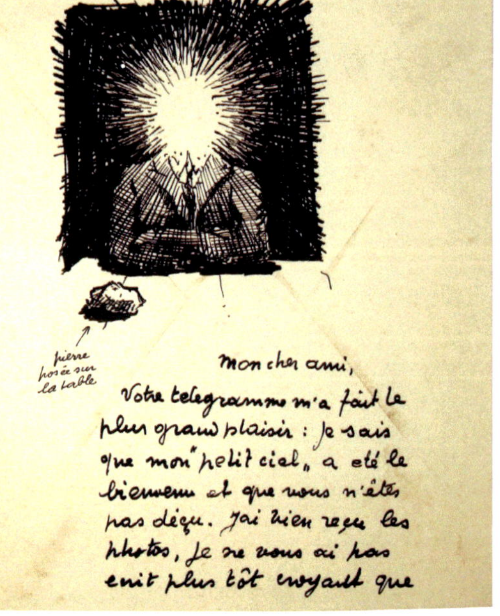

Letter from René Magritte to Edward James with sketch for *The Pleasure Principle*, 18 May 1937, ink on paper, 14 × 24 cm. The Edward James Trust, West Dean

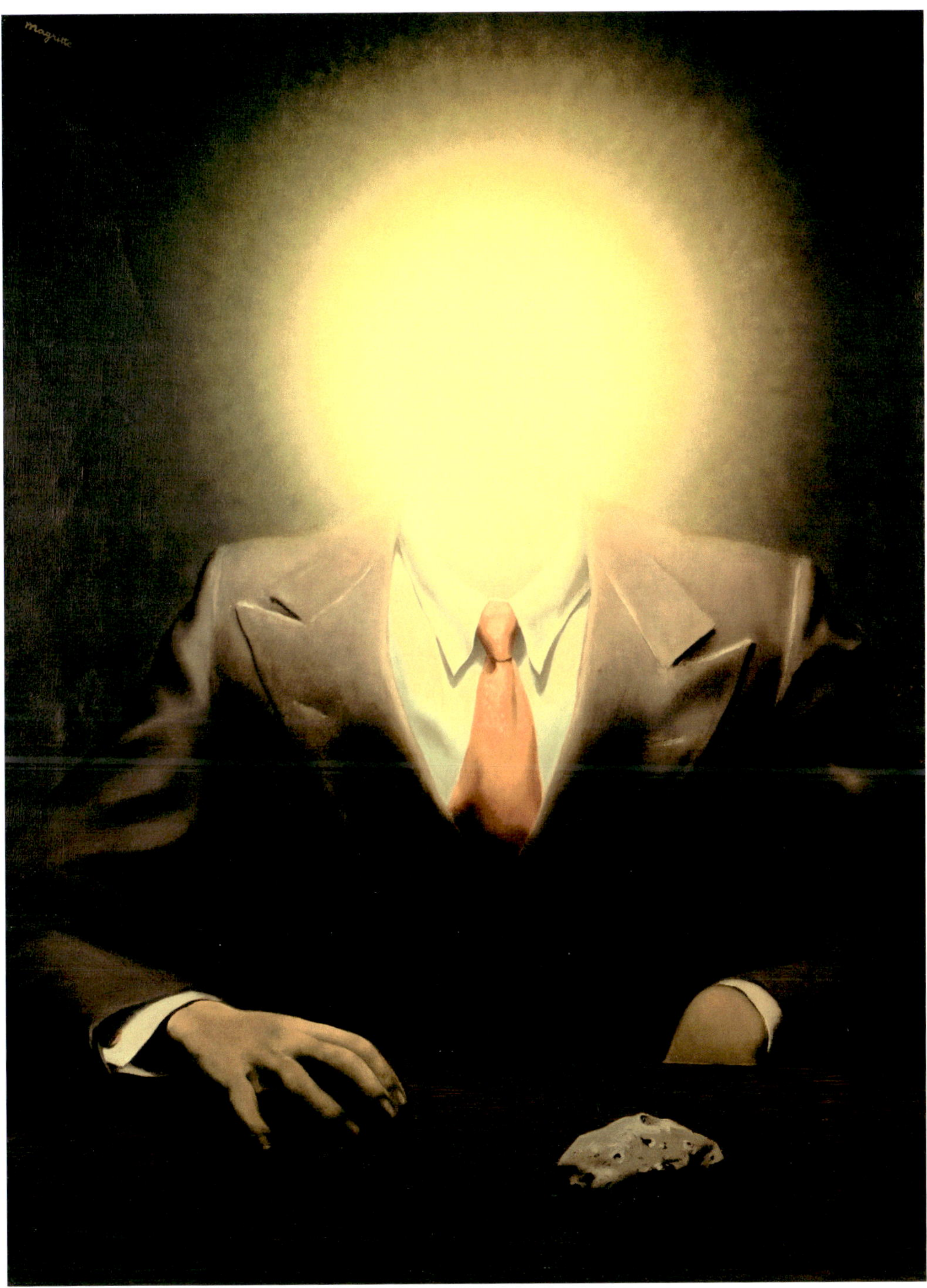

The Pleasure Principle
Le Principe du plaisir 1937, oil on canvas,
73 × 54 cm. Private Collection, CR 443

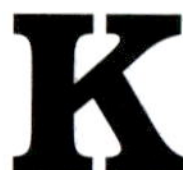

K

Kitsch denotes an unselfconscious aberration of taste, characterised by exaggerated sentimentality, theatricality, vulgarity and pretentiousness. Magritte consciously made use of elements of Kitsch in his art: in the adherence to the conventions of heightened realistic representation and a smooth academic style of painting, evoking bourgeois realism of the nineteenth-century Salon; through the modification of stock subjects of assumed good taste and high art such as classical nudes, idyllic landscapes, blue skies and sunsets; and, at times, through apparently cheap visual puns and effects such as the **metamorphosis** of a nose into a penis or doves silhouetted against the sky. One of the key features of Kitsch is its lack of authenticity as materials, objects, taste and feelings are simulated or cheaply reproduced. Magritte's paintings display a deliberated proximity to reproductions, the artist proudly proclaiming: 'I don't create paintings, I create reproductions in oil.'[92] In the 1940s he painted a number of excessively colourful and painterly flower still lifes which, significantly, were used for advertising and violated the sacred barrier between fine and popular art (*Forethought* 1943).

In particular his late work, with its occasionally pronounced use of pastel colours (intense pink sunsets) and overtly sentimental motifs (horses with flowing blond manes, *Pure Reason* 1948; Pre-Raphaelite beauties, *The Novelette* 1944), deliberately flirts with Kitsch subject matter and form. As other Surrealists, he further played with what Walter Benjamin described as 'the revolutionary energies that appear in the "outmoded"', the appropriation of out-of-fashion models and styles of

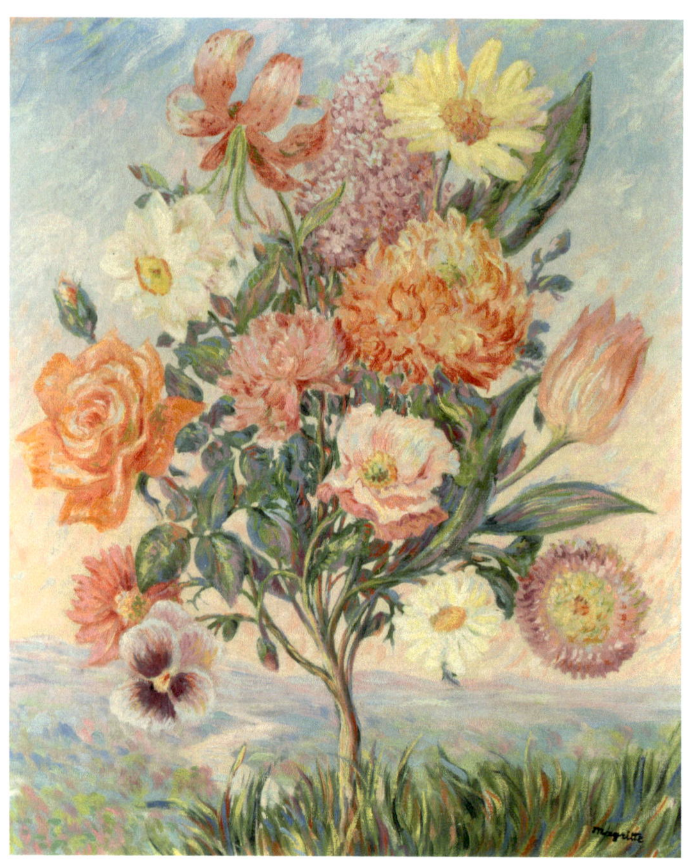

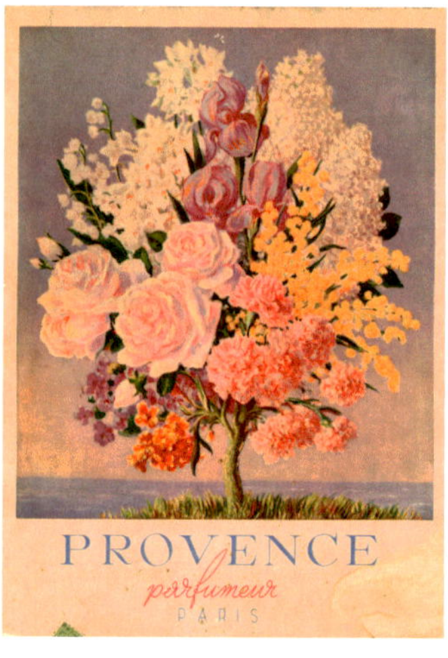

Provence perfumier Paris advertisement mid-1940s, photogravure on paper, 41.2 × 30.7 cm, Royal Museums of Fine Arts of Belgium, Brussels

Forethought
La Préméditation 1943, oil on canvas, 55 × 46 cm. Private Collection, USA, CR544

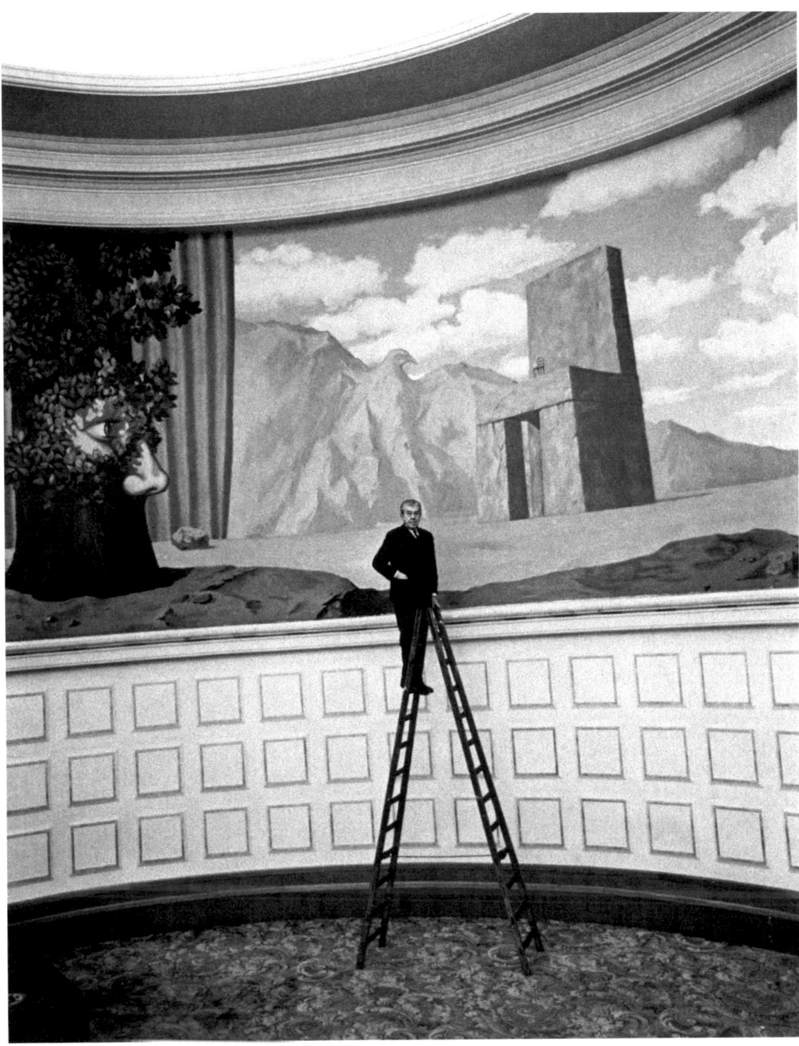

René Magritte standing in front of his mural *The Enchanted Spot*, in the Casino at Knokke, 1953

the previous generation as in his so-called **Renoir Period**.[93] Magritte's critical reputation has been affected by his association with Kitsch and his perceived lack of conceptual acumen, his widespread popularity and the pervasive appropriation of his imagery and visual techniques in art, advertising, illustration and popular culture. However, Magritte's employment of and play with Kitsch was one of his most successful devices as it created an ambiguity which unsettles and challenges received assumptions of taste, style and subject matter. **(CG)**

See also: **Appropriation; Artifice; Commercial Art; Ersatz; Legacy**

Knokke Casino Mural: In 1953 Gustave Nellens, owner of the Casino Communal at Knokke, commissioned Magritte to decorate its chandelier room. He created a vast panoramic mural entitled *The Enchanted Spot*, based on a number of his previous works. The location of the Casino would have appealed to Magritte, not least for its links with the serialised **Fantômas** novels by Marcel Allain and Pierre Souvestre, in particular *La main coupée* (November 1911) whose cover illustration portrays a severed hand grasping at a roulette wheel. **(NM)**

L

Language: Magritte's views about language are twofold and steer an intermittently calculated course between its conditions as a complex structural system, on the one hand, and its capacities to crystallise or denote meaning, on the other. The first of these possibilities, which he considered too abstract, prompted, we could reasonably infer, some of the suspicions about the anti-poetic, 'age-old stupidity' of abstract art to which Magritte gave vent several times in his career.[94] The symbolic insistence often brokered by the second operational arena of language, especially when couched in the false 'precision' of the 'language of symbols', was, conversely, usually too specific or reductive for the semantic taste of the artist. 'To the extent that my pictures have any value,' he wrote in 1957, 'they do not lend themselves to analysis.'[95] The same letter also underlines the artist's equivocation with the whole linguistic enterprise of criticism and history (with its potential for 'facile labelling') as well as his own reluctance 'to give a name to the images I paint'. At the same time he guardedly expressed the hope that 'language and writing can bring out the unpredictable possibilities suggested by a picture'.[96]

In the **titles** of his works Magritte often invoked different forms, genres, materialities – even grammars – of language as they might be deployed in everyday exchange. While there are important indications of the artist's attitude towards language in his earlier work – notably his striking use of text within the image in a series of paintings made during the late 1920s, beginning with *The Use of Speech* 1928, it was in the 1950s that his interest in language took a signal turn. Magritte painted works named after conversations, promises or pledges, poetry and poets, politeness, explanations, parts of speech and writing types, as well as the very notion of an 'active' voice itself: *The Art of Conversation* 1950 (several versions); *The Pledge* 1950; *The Explanation* 1952 (and its variants); and *The Active Voice* 1951. In the same years he alludes to different qualities of speech or language, as in *Fine Language* 1952, or locations where speech can be heard and experienced, as in *The Listening Room* 1952, with versions from 1953 and 1958.

These commitments to various kinds of language in action, and to the texture and effects of particular speech acts themselves, furnish an important context for Magritte's provision of larger and more speculative questions about the nature of language or speech, clearly – if allusively – evidenced in *The Literal Meaning* 1929, and its variations, *The Origins of Language* 1955, *The Voice of Air* 1935 and *The Voice of the Absolute* 1955. But Magritte's concern with particular, declarative, uses of language, on the one hand, and its more abstruse appearances on the other, must be understood in relation to his equal commitment to various forms of restraint, silence, secrecy and, of course, **mystery**. Images investigating the linguistically non-declarative aspects of an exchange system are sometimes addressed to the incommunicado of individual figures, as in the **Giorgio de Chirico**-inspired floating heads, probably male (with eyes closed) and female (with eyes open) of *He is Not Speaking* 1926; sometimes proffered under cover of the artist's ubiquitous commitment to secrecy in people-less, almost empty landscapes or interiors, as in *The Secret Life* 1928 and its variants; and sometimes governed by states of distraction as in *Faraway Looks* 1929, or passivity, for instance in *The Impassive Bust* 1926. The Magrittean *silentium* is, however, more often referred to in the

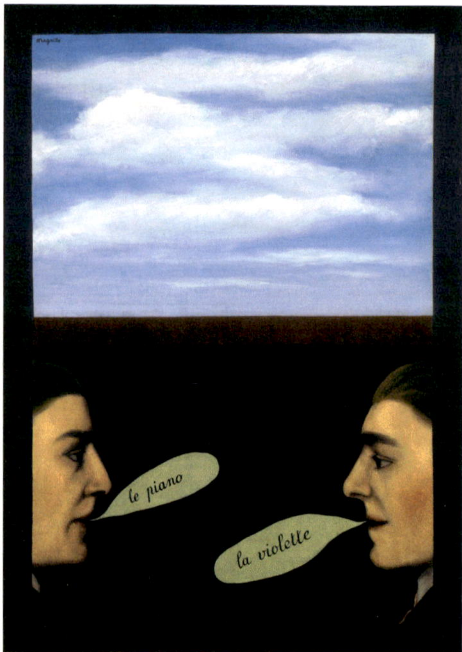

The Use of Speech
L'Usage de la parole 1928, oil on canvas, 73 × 54 cm.
Private Collection, CR 275

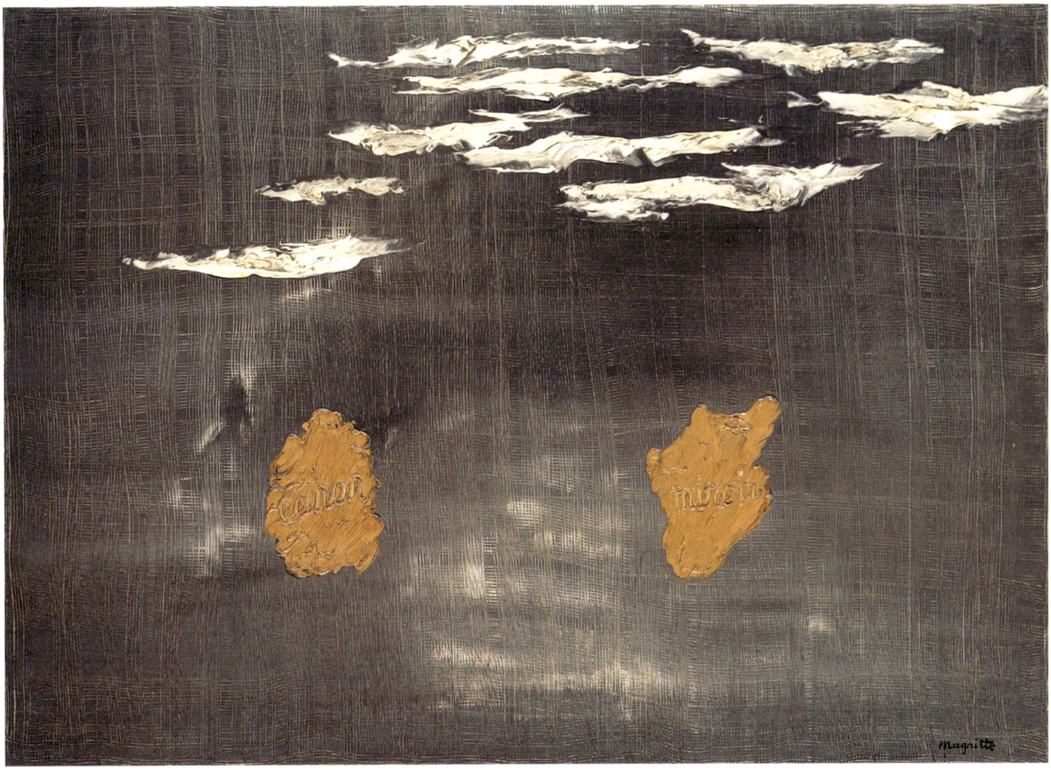

**Untitled (Sky with
Biomorphs and Words)**
1928, oil on canvas, 81 × 116 cm.
Private Collection, London,
CR 278

The Literal Meaning
Le Sens propre 1929, oil on canvas,
54 × 73 cm. Private Collection,
courtesy Keitelman Gallery, CR 311

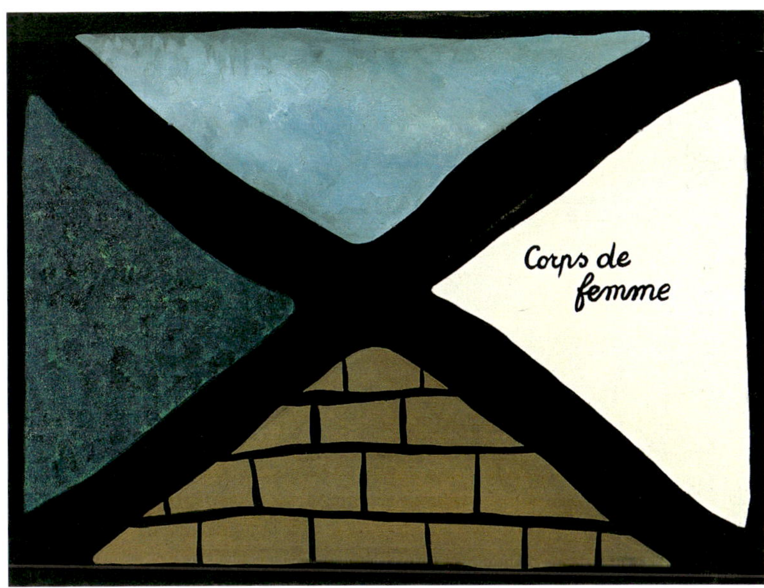

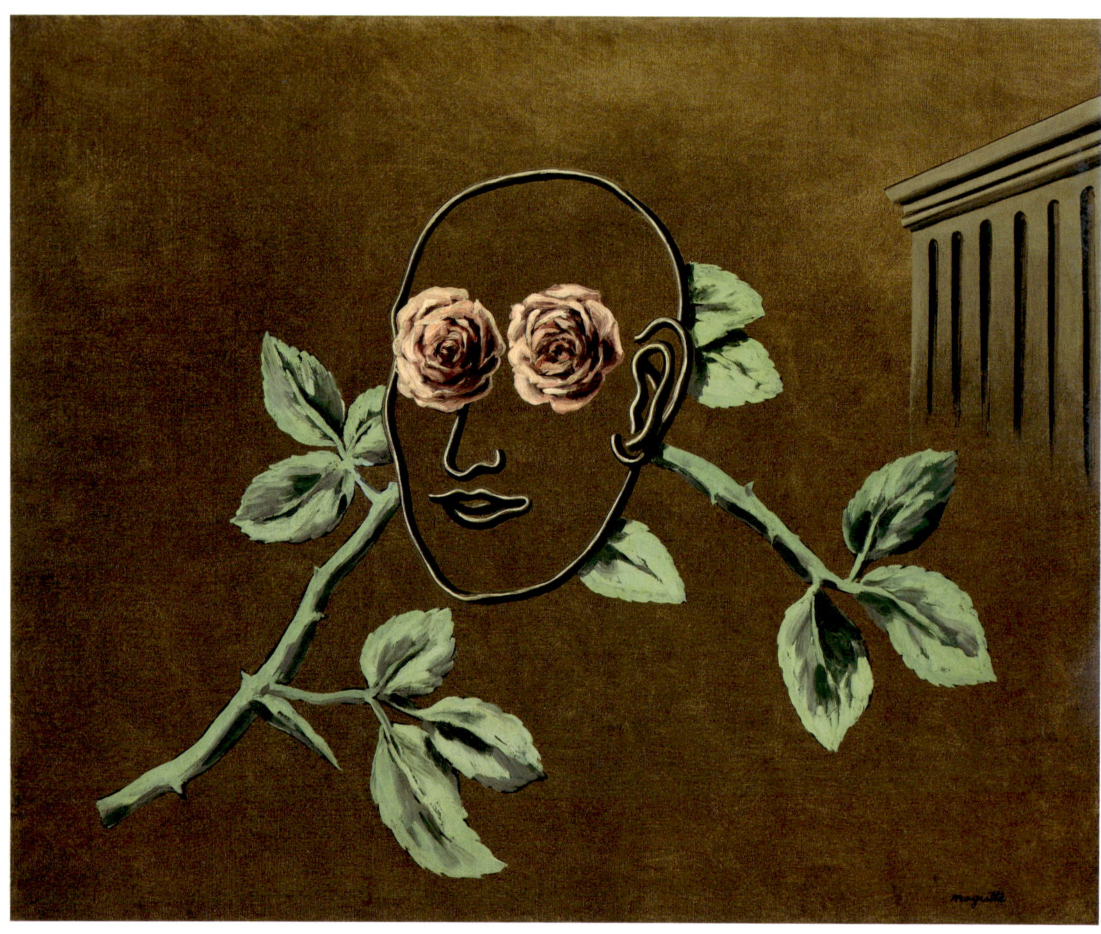

The Journey of the Flowers
Le Voyage des fleurs 1928, oil on canvas, 73 × 92 cm.
Isidore Ducasse Fine Arts, CR 211

echoing, interiorised and atmospheric conditions in which even the widest spectra of enunciation are rendered ineffable, as in *The Uncertainty Principle* 1944; *The Echo* 1944; *The Mind's Gaze* 1946; and *The Mental Universe* 1947. (**JW**)

See also: **Absence; Juxtaposition; Meaning; Poetry; Representation and Resemblance**

Marcel Lecomte (1900–1966) Belgian poet. Having associated with Clément Pansaers, one of the rare representatives of **Dada** in Belgium, Lecomte joined with **Paul Nougé** and **Camille Goemans** for the edition of ***Correspondance*** tracts published during 1924 and 1925, the first manifestation of the Brussels Surrealist group, later contributing to the journals ***Marie*** 1926 and ***Distances*** 1928. Magritte illustrated his Surrealist **poetry** collection *Applications* 1925, the two remaining lifelong friends. Lecomte dedicated several texts to the painter, who depicted some of them in his pictures. Whilst not definitively breaking with the Brussels Surrealists, Lecomte had a certain independence from the 1930s onward, turning towards Oriental art and philosophy or art criticism, continuing the publication of his texts and poems in a precise and measured style with a restrained lyricism. (**XC**)

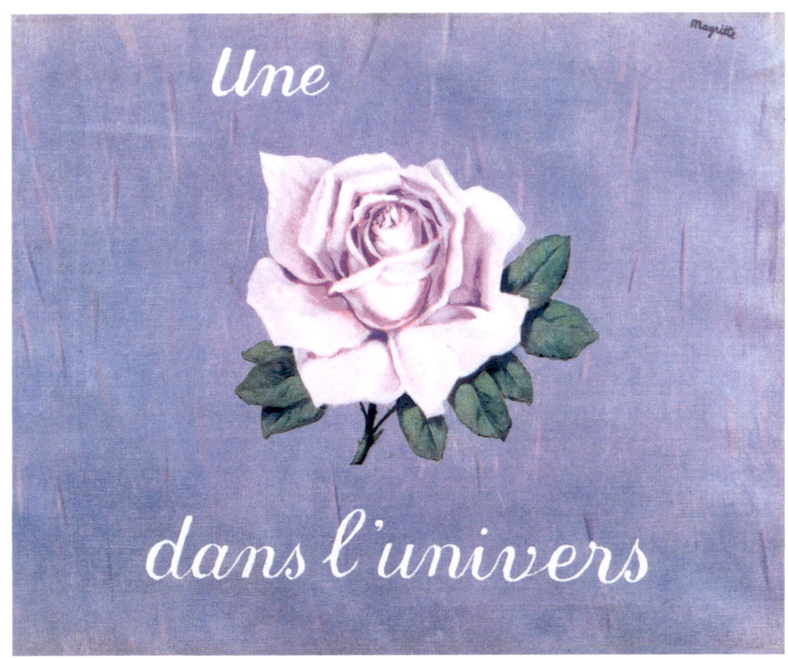

The Voice of the Absolute
La Voix de l'absolu 1955,
oil on canvas, 40 × 50 cm.
Private Collection, Brussels,
CR 829

Legacy: One of the most popular and imitated, socially influential and culturally lionised of Modern artists, Magritte's legacy has several dimensions. One arises from his extraordinary and sustained impact on the areas of advertising and design in which he worked himself at the beginning of his career, again in the early 1930s, and intermittently throughout it. While many of the posters and **music score** and magazine covers he made from the late 1910s to the mid-1930s had little impact beyond their relatively limited circulation, in December 1965 Sabena Airlines commissioned an emblem from Magritte which resulted in the painting *Sky Bird* 1966 – the image of which was incorporated in a 'prestige advertising' campaign, 'a series of notices, posters, leaflets, placards, labels' designed to 'introduce *Sky Bird* to the public', which would be followed up by 'sales advertising (brochures, window displays, etc.)'.[97] At the time of its sale for £2.3 million in 2003, following the Belgian airline's bankruptcy two years earlier, the value of what Magritte referred to as 'butter' for his 'spinach' had risen so precipitously that the image was seen not just as a highly visible airline logo but as a kind of national icon.

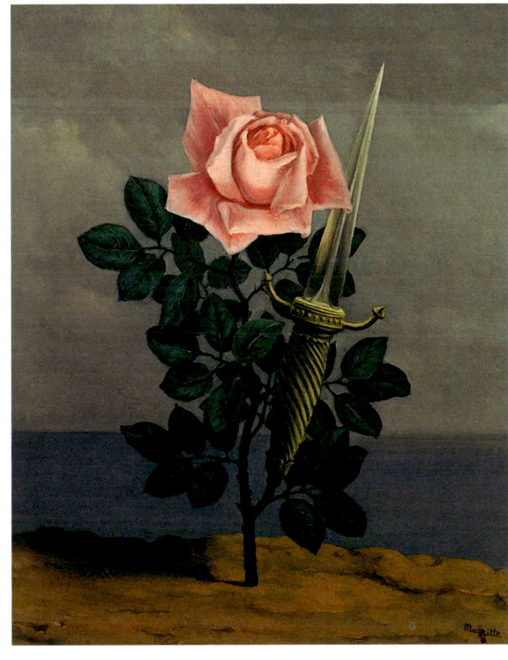

The Blow to the Heart
Le Coup au cœur 1952, oil on canvas, 46 × 38 cm.
Private Collection, Brussels, CR 777

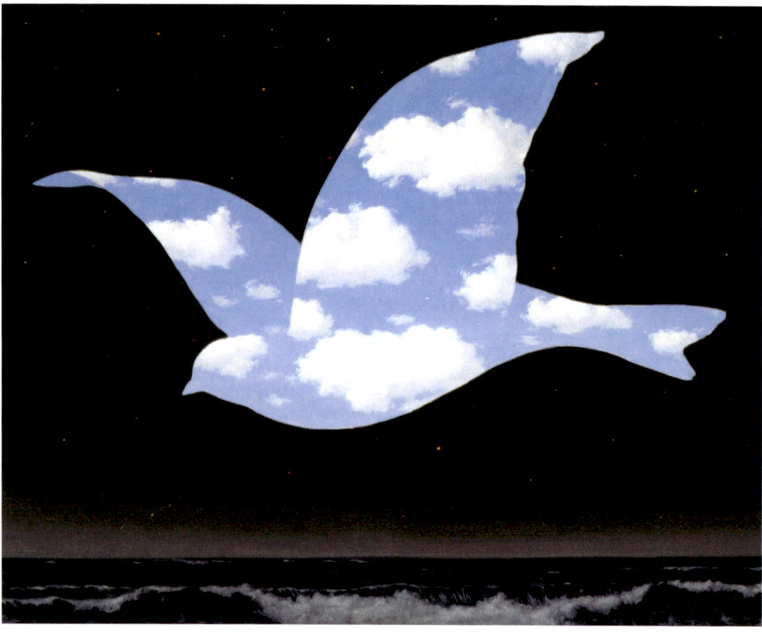

The Kiss
Le Baiser 1951, oil on canvas,
65 × 80 cm. The Museum
of Fine Arts, Houston.
Gift of an anonymous
donor, CR 769

On numerous occasions Magritte's images have been taken and adapted without permission, as with *The Healer* 1937.[98] These borrowings are legion and range from William Golden's eye-and-cloud logo for CBS Television in 1952, to covers for albums by The Jeff Beck Group (*Beck-Ola* 1969), Jackson Browne (*Late for the Sky* 1975), Styx (*The Grand Illusion* 1977) and many others. On celluloid, directors such as Jean-Luc Godard, **Alain Robbe-Grillet**, Bernardo Bertolucci and Nicolas Roeg all glanced across to Magritte's work; while playwright Tom Stoppard wrote *After Magritte* in 1970.

A second dimension of Magritte's cultural impact must be measured, of course, by his influence on a wide range of other visual artists and movements during the last half-century, from later incarnations of Surrealism itself, to Pop Art in the 1960s (which he disparaged), Conceptualism in the late 1960s and 1970s, a variety of practices based on appropriation in the 1980s to 1990s, as well as more contemporary in installation, video and new media. This legacy was assessed most recently in the 2006 exhibition *Magritte and Contemporary Art: The Treachery of Images* at the Los Angeles County Museum of Art, designed by the Los Angeles Conceptual artist John Baldessari who rolled out cloud-patterned carpeting, painted freeways on the ceilings, and sent bowler-hatted invigilators into the galleries. The relation between Magritte and the thirty or so artists represented in the show took very different forms, ranging from a few individuals – notably his compatriot, **Marcel Broodthaers**, for whom Magritte was 'a father who ate his children',[99] and Duane Michaels who took photographs of him every day for a week in August 1965 – whose careers were marked by extensive or intensive dialogue with Magritte, to others who made occasional works directly citing him, as with Vija Celmins' *Untitled (Comb)* 1970, a giant facsimile from Magritte's *Personal Values* 1952, or Sherrie Levine's *A Pipe* 2001, a cast copper simulacrum of the pipe from *The Treachery of Images*. The case is made for the impact of Magritte's images on the scalar modulations of Claes Oldenburg and Celmins; on **trompe l'oeil** and fake surface in the work of Richard Artschwager and Roy Lichtenstein; on Jasper Johns' investigation of the relations between seeing and thinking, and **language** and perception; on Robert Gober's sculptural physicalisation of Magrittean motifs; and even on Ed Ruscha's cultivation of what he termed the 'huh?' quality in art.[100] (**jw**)

See also: **Appropriation; Commercial Art; Kitsch; Scale**

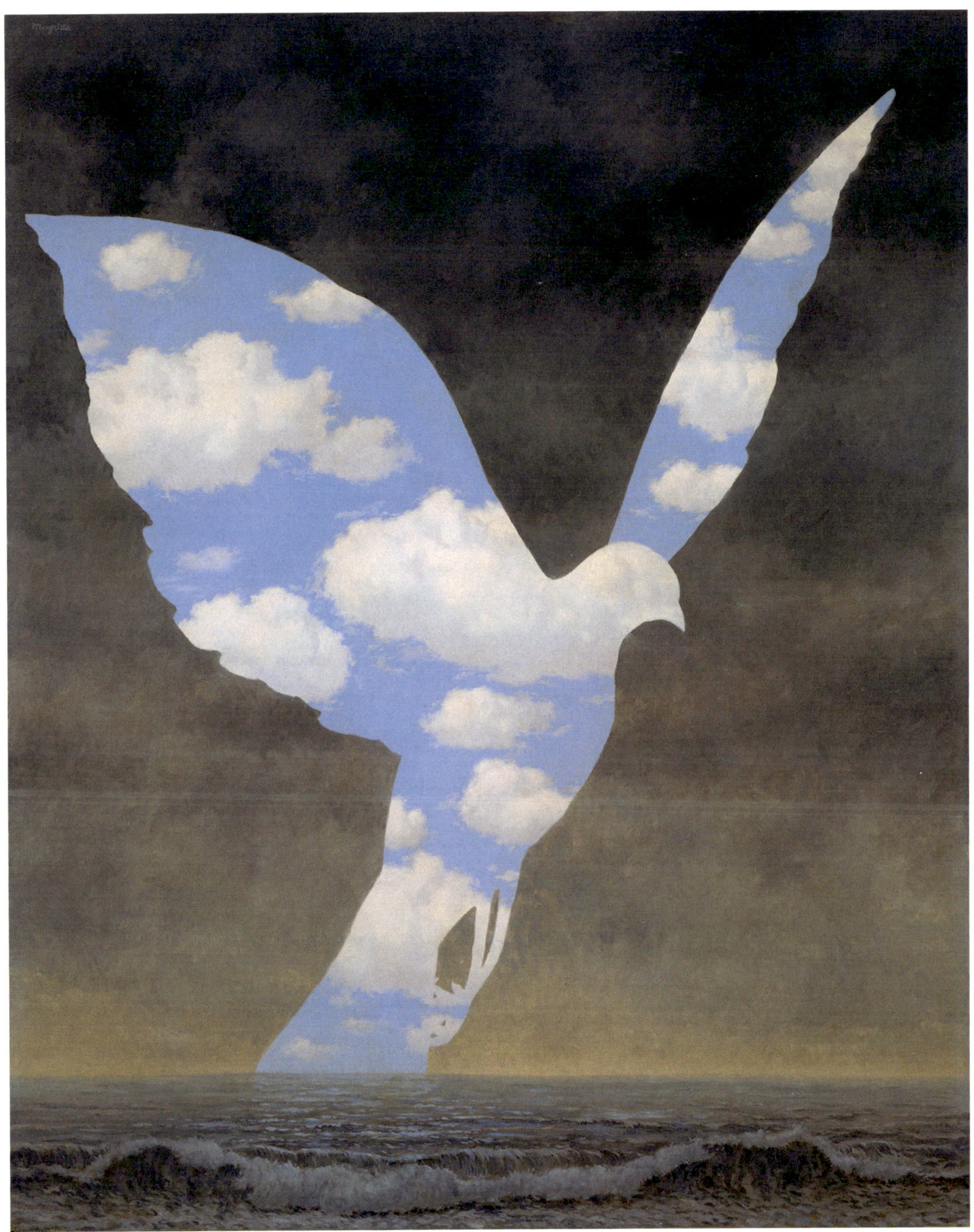

The Great Family
La Grande Famille 1963, oil on canvas, 100 × 81 cm.
Utsunomiya Museum of Art, Japan, CR 972

Letters: For Magritte, written correspondences with friends, collaborators, philosophers and collectors, often accompanied by drawings and sketches, were a major means to explore philosophical questions, to elaborate on his artistic intentions and creative processes, and to find **titles** for his artworks. He wrote in total a couple of thousand letters, often writing a number of letters a day. Collections of Magritte's letters include **Marcel Mariën's** exchanges with Magritte, all published by Les Lèvres Nues, Brussels: *Le Fait accompli* 1973; *Lettres Surréalistes (1924–1940)* 1973; and *La Destination – Lettres à Marcel Mariën (1937–1962)* 1977. Magritte's written correspondences also constitute a major part of André Blavier's *Écrits complets*, and **Harry Torczyner** collected his writerly exchanges with Magritte in *Magritte/Torczyner – Letters Between Friends* (H.N. Abrams, 1994; originally published as *L'Ami Magritte: Correspondance et Souvenirs* 1992). The significance of written correspondences for Magritte closely relates to his artistic oeuvre, which also comprises correspondences in its dialogic relations with other texts and images. Notably, Magritte's letters tie in with and are part of a wider concern of the Brussels Surrealists with written correspondence, evident in **Paul Nougé**, **Camille Goemans** and **Marcel Lecomte's** publication in 1924–25, *Correspondance*. (PA)

See also: **Language; Postcards**

London Gallery: In early 1938 **E.L.T. Mesens** left Brussels and the Palais des Beaux-Arts, where he had been a salesman for the Société Auxiliare, and relocated to London. In partnership with **Roland Penrose**, he became director of the London Gallery, 28 Cork Street. Its inaugural exhibition was devoted to Magritte, with the accompanying issue of the *London Gallery Bulletin* carrying texts by Herbert Read, Humphrey Jennings and **Paul Nougé**. Under Mesens' directorship the London Gallery became the headquarters of Surrealism in England. (DP)

See also: **England; George Melly**

The Lost Jockey: Magritte regarded *The Lost Jockey* 1926, as being his first successful Surrealist painting. Depicting a jockey within a mysterious forest of **bilboquet** trees, the image became a kind of archetypal Magritte composition. As Suzi Gablik points out, its creation marked the moment where Magritte was liberated from his formal investigations and concerns with mere 'aesthetic specialities', turning instead to the mode of poetic research which sustained his practice for the rest of his career. Magritte also created **collage** versions of *The Lost Jockey*, with two further paintings created in 1942 and 1948. (DP)

See also: **Giorgio de Chirico; Mystery; Theatrical Display**

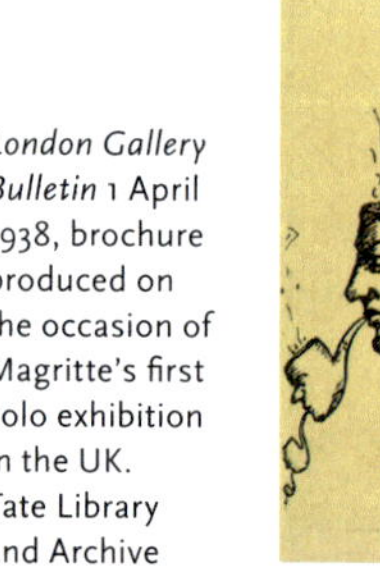

Good News
La Bonne Nouvelle 1928, oil on canvas, 80 × 61 cm.
The Menil Collection, Houston, CR 210

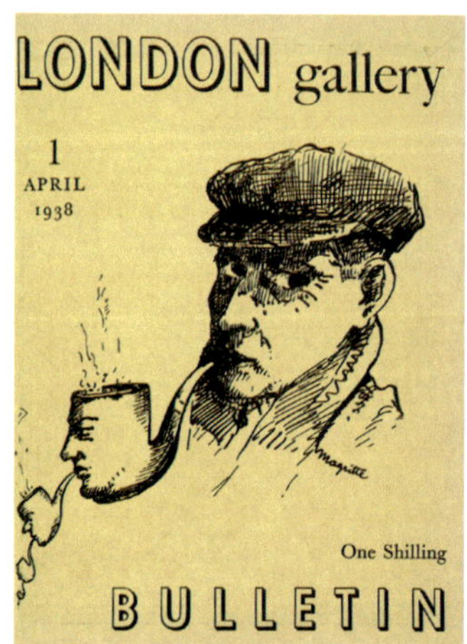

London Gallery Bulletin 1 April 1938, brochure produced on the occasion of Magritte's first solo exhibition in the UK. Tate Library and Archive

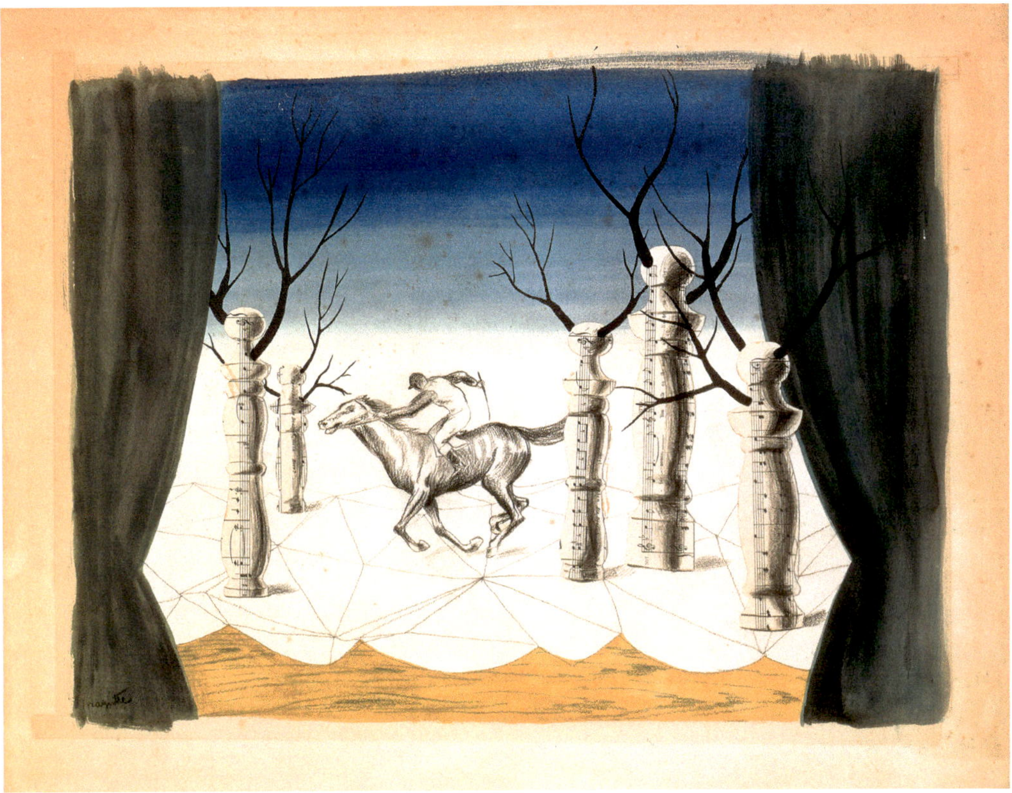

The Lost Jockey
Le Jockey perdu 1926,
printed paper, watercolour,
ink and pencil on paper,
39.3 × 54.2 cm.
Collection Gale and
Ira Drukier, CR 1605

The Lost Jockey
Le Jockey perdu 1926,
printed paper, gouache,
watercolour and pencil
on paper, 41.2 × 57.7 cm.
Private Collection,
courtesy Hauser & Wirth,
CR 1606

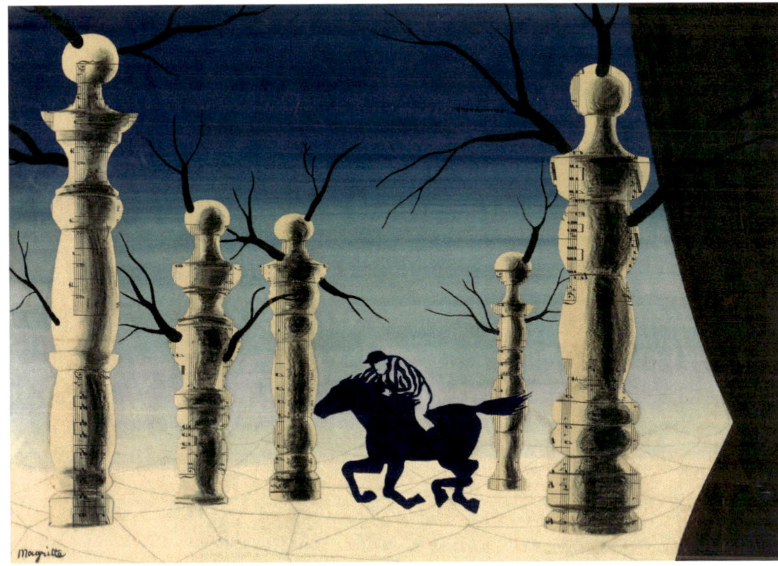

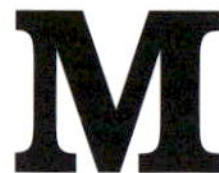

M

Georgette Magritte (1901–1986) A native of Marcinelle, Georgette Marie Florence Berger, a butcher's daughter, met the man who would become her husband at a fair in Charleroi in 1913. World War I and the Magritte family's relocation to Brussels meant that the two did not meet again until January 1920, Georgette having moved in with her sister in Brussels following the death of their mother. They married on 28 June 1922 and moved to Rue Ledeganck in Laeken, with Magritte designing and making the furnishings. As Magritte's only wife, having no children, Georgette played her part in her husband's career as model, serving as inspiration for numerous paintings including *Attempting the Impossible* 1928, *Girl Eating a Bird (Pleasure)* 1927 and *Black Magic* 1945. She also appeared in **Paul Nougé's** photographic series *The Subversion of Images* 1929 as well as being an improvising and amusing actress in her husband's photographs and short films. Magritte would use the name of her father, Florent Berger, as a signature for several articles in the left-wing press. In September 1927, she accompanied her husband to Le Perreux-sur-Marne in the Parisian suburbs at the invitation of **Camille Goemans** who had opened a gallery in Paris. It was in the company of Goemans that the couple visited **Salvador Dalí** in 1929 at Cadaqués, met there by Gala and **Paul Éluard**. In 1929 Georgette became the centre of a quarrel between Magritte and **André Breton**, the latter objecting to her wearing a cross around her neck. Returning to Brussels in 1930, the couple lived in Rue Esseghem in Jette until 1954, then Boulevard Lambermont and finally Rue des Mimosas in 1957, the couple's final residence. Georgette worked at the Maison Berger, her employment lasting until the late 1950s, at which time the recognition of Magritte's oeuvre rendered work unnecessary. In 1965 she would accompany her husband around the exhibitions he had in the United States and in 1966 on a trip to Israel. (**XC**)

See also: Banality; Belgium; Paris

Léopold and Régina Magritte (1870–1928; 1871–1912) Magritte's parents, the artist being their eldest of three sons. Léopold Magritte is recorded as holding a number of occupations, including being a tailor and a commercial traveller. He established a stock cube factory around 1917–18, this most likely connected to Magritte being commissioned in 1918 to design a poster advertising 'Pot au Feu Derbaix' stock cubes, his earliest known piece of commercial design. He married Régina Bertinchamps on 2 March 1898. Magritte's mother was a depressive and on 24 February 1912, after several unsuccessful

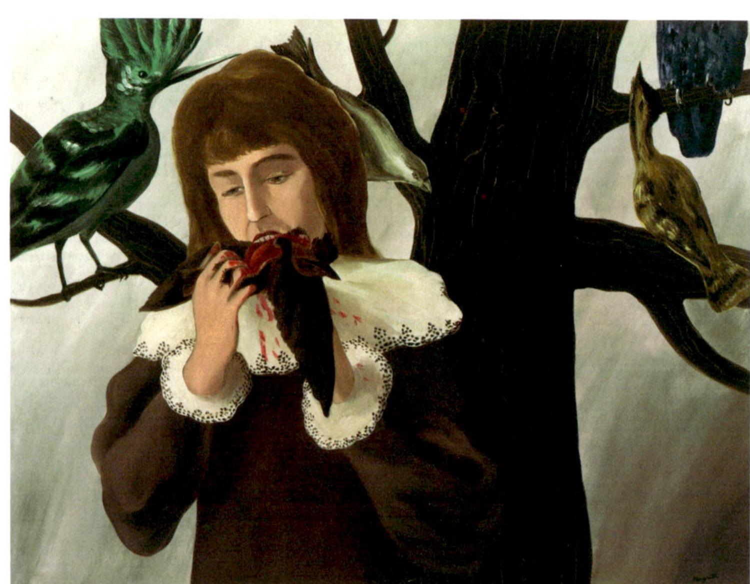

Girl Eating A Bird (Pleasure)
Jeune Fille mangeant un oiseau (Le Plaisir) 1927, oil on canvas, 74 × 97 cm. Kunstsammlung Nordrhein-Westfalen, Düsseldorf, CR 145

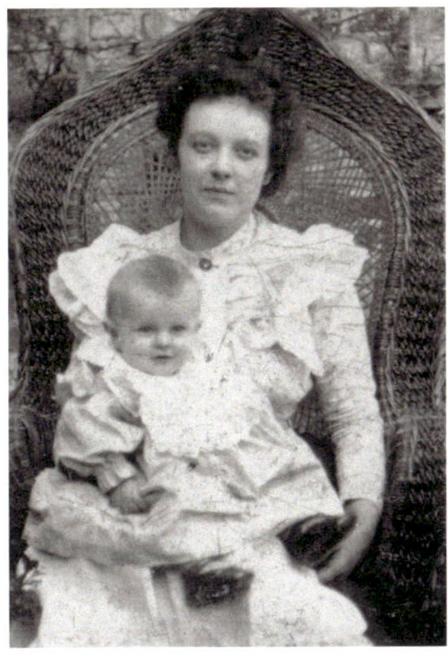

René Magritte on his mother's lap, 1899

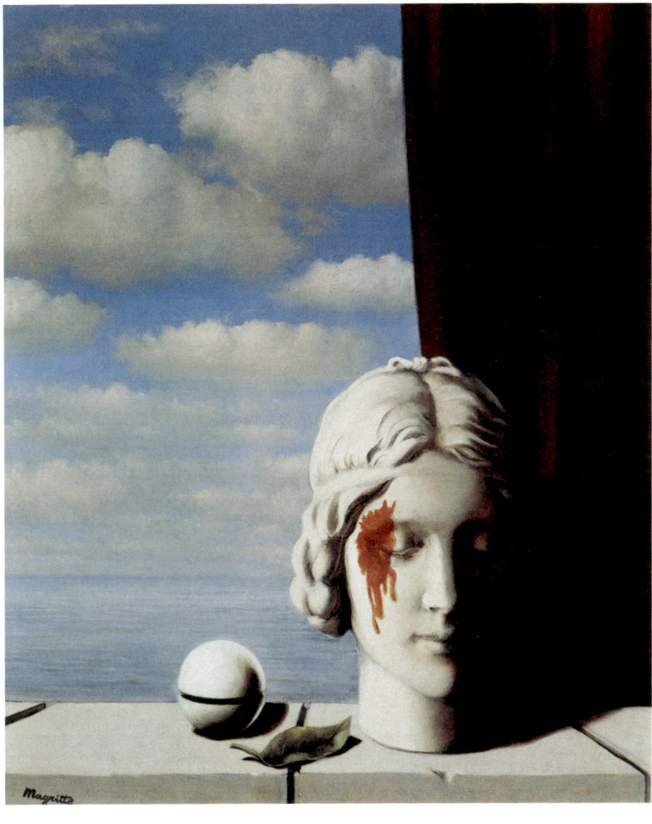

Memory
La Mémoire 1948, oil on canvas, 60 × 50 cm.
Collection de la Communauté française
de Belgique, CR 666

suicide attempts, she drowned herself in the River Sambre near to the family home in Châtelet. According to **Louis Scutenaire**, Magritte – then aged thirteen – witnessed his mother's body being recovered, her face apparently hidden by her nightdress. He wrote: 'It was never known whether she had hidden her eyes with it in order not to see death which she had chosen, or whether the swirling currents had thus veiled her.'[101] Magritte himself never concealed the manner of his mother's death, yet chose not to talk about it. Léopold Magritte, who took another partner after his wife's death, died in Brussels on 24 August 1928. (**DP**)

👁 See also: **Commercial Art; Fetish**

Paul Magritte (1902–1975) Nicknamed 'The Marquis' by his friends, the youngest of the three Magritte brothers was a dandy and witness of the whole **Surrealist** adventure, though loath to give his official

signature to the movement. He joined his brother in **Paris** between 1927 and 1930 and after returning to Brussels the two founded Studio Dongo, a studio of advertising projects. In 1936 he also composed musical pieces such as *Marie Trombone Chapeau Buse*, based on a poem by **Paul Colinet**, as well as various more commercial compositions in the 'Jazzy' style of the era. Collagist and author of darkly humorous poems, he was an accomplice of René Magritte and **Marcel Mariën** in 1953 in making false banknotes. Described by Rachel Baes as 'a formidable sloth', Paul Magritte was held in high esteem by Colinet and **Louis Scutenaire**. (**XC**)

👁 See also: **Commercial Art; Music scores**

Mannequin: A sense of cool indifference emanates from the mannequin-like human figures depicted in Magritte's Surrealist paintings of 1926–27. Generally naked figures bereft of individuality and

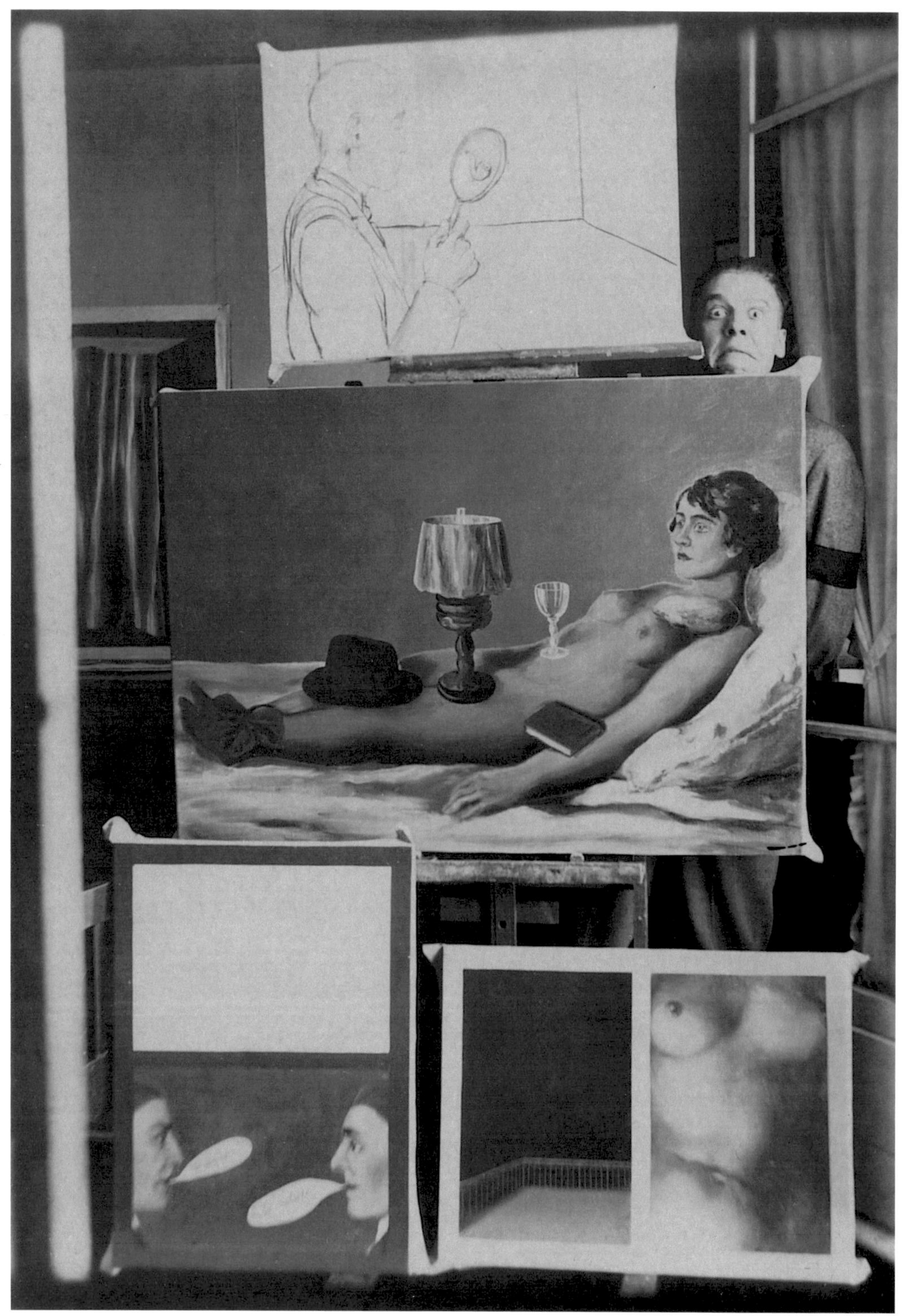

Paul Magritte in Black Armband
Le-Perreux-sur-Marne, Paris, 1928, photograph,
gelatin silver print, 12.7 × 8.8 cm. Private Collection

unapproachably distant, they appear as lifeless detached protagonists in mysterious pictorial worlds. Like display-window mannequins in rigidified poses, they seem incapable of action or movement – many are encased in netting, for example in *The Magician's Accomplices* 1926 – and trapped in absurd scenarios. Like ghosts, yet with a disturbing element of familiarity about them, they occupy the 'real space' of the painting even as they elude reality. Their eyes closed, or with a fixed blank gaze, they appear to be blind. Magritte presents the world to us as a stage or substitute world – like a theatre – and peoples it with actors and marionettes. This approach is very evident in his early narrative paintings, such as *The Menaced Assassin* 1927. Like cut-outs, symbolically deposited within a scenario, these figures' movements seem to have no real connection to their surroundings. Despite being in motion, they appear frozen, momentarily arrested.

Magritte plays on the notion of the mannequin as being a *doppelgänger* of a human being. In the same sense that an **apple** in a Magritte painting is only ever a model of an apple, his visual representation of the human form lays bare various aspects of his intellectual approach. On one hand, there is the sense of abandonment that ensues from our being 'thrown into the world', as the Existentialists would have it, trapped in existence. On the other hand, Magritte's universalised figures appear to be interchangeable props in a constantly changing world. As such they might be seen to represent the liberation necessary for recognising the true nature of the world. In this isolation the figure appears as an exemplar of a possible existence, which, in its function as a model, reveals a norm, something universal. (**GF**)

See also: **Commercial Art; Double; Eroticism; Female Form; Shop Window Display**

Marcel Mariën (1920–1993) It was in 1937 that Mariën first met Magritte, who introduced him to the principal members of the Brussels group. The youngest member of the Surrealists, he was constantly engaged in multiple activities: his earliest collages and objects included the celebrated *The Thin Man*, a pair of glasses with a single lens, created in 1937. Also in that year he participated in the exhibition *Surrealist Objects and Poems* at the **London Gallery**, contributing to **E.L.T. Mesens**' *London Bulletin*.

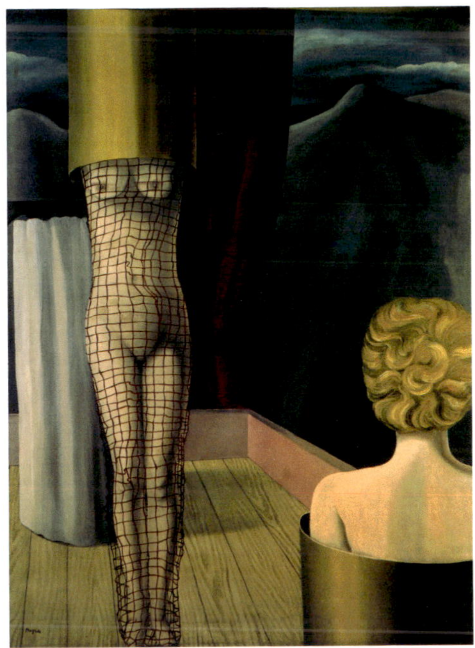

The Magician's Accomplices
Les Complices du magicien 1926, oil on canvas, 139 × 105 cm. Collection Ulla & Heiner Pietzsch, Berlin, CR 92

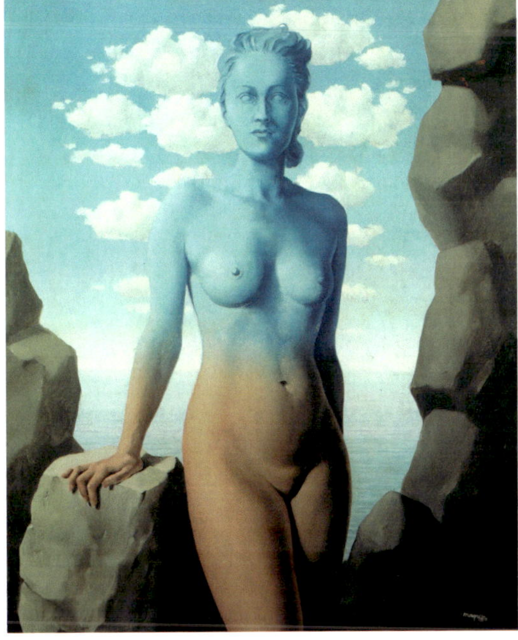

Black Magic
La Magie noire 1942, oil on canvas, 65 × 54 cm. Private Collection, CR 507

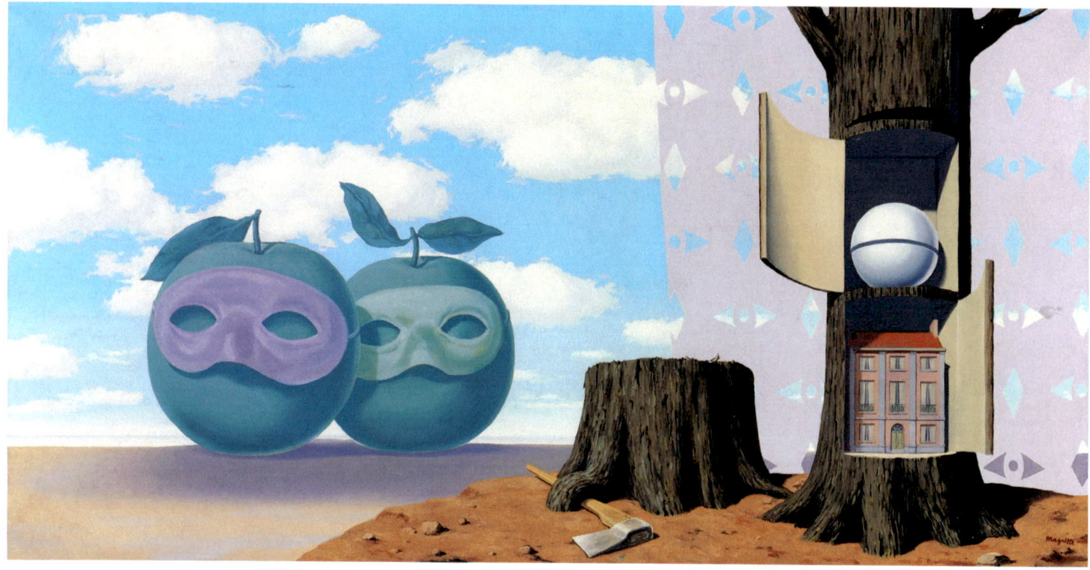

The Enchanted Spot
Le Domaine enchanté 1953, oil on canvas, 68 × 134.8 cm.
Albertina, Vienna / Batliner Collection, CR 791(7)

An unconditional admirer of Magritte – penning the painter's first biography in 1943 – and of **Paul Nougé** whose then unknown literary oeuvre he revealed, Mariën would extend his editorial activities, mainly with the journal *Les Lèvres nues* 1954–58, which he created with Jane Graverol and Nougé. In 1959, with meagre resources, he made the film *L'imitation du cinéma* (which would be censored in Belgium and banned in France). In 1962, he created the tract *Grande Baisse* with his associate Leo Dohmen, allegedly signed by Magritte, in which the painter apparently announced the slashing of the prices of his paintings: the quarrel between the two men would be definitive. An uncompromising character, afraid of letting go of the spirit of **Surrealism**, he became an historian, publishing *L'activité surréaliste en Belgique 1924–1950* in 1979, maintaining an extensive output as author and editor. (**XC**)
See also: **Belgium; Jacqueline Nonkels**

Marie: *Journal bimensuel pour la belle jeunesse*: Bimonthly Surrealist arts review launched by **E.L.T. Mesens** and first published in June 1926. Magritte contributed texts and illustrations. The issue dated 8 July 1926 features the earliest example of Magritte's black-swathed **Fantômas** figure. The final **Paul Nougé**-edited issue *Adieu à Marie* appeared in February 1927. (**DP**)

Mask and Masquerade: Taking advantage of its capacity to both reveal and conceal, Magritte used the mask – a black band with openings for the eyes – to mask men or **apples**, for example in *The Enchanted Spot* 1953. Magritte, his wife and some friends also posed in masks in *The Extra Terrestrials*, a series of photographs of 1935. Magritte's inspiration for this kind of masking was perhaps taken from the fictional villain **Fantômas**, who was pictured in evening dress, with a top hat and black eye-mask. Notably, Fantômas – who appears in Magritte's painting *The Flame Rekindled* 1943 – had the ability to transform himself into almost any other character. The ephemeral appearance of the phantom also corresponds to Magritte's image of the figure as a possible existence, in flux and endlessly elusive.

Masks can also be about disappearance, the evanescence of a persona or their transition to a different level of reality. Traditionally the mask elevates the subjective world into a state of objectivity. It allows the wearer to assimilate with the outside world, at the same time as protecting him or her by concealing their real self. People also hide their weakness behind the mask, in the hope that it may also help them to grow beyond themselves.[102] As such, Magritte might be seen to use the mask as a kind of mirror-image of our perceptions, which are torn between semblance and reality. As in his 'failed portraits', the mask allows him to avoid falsification: the individuality of a particular figure recedes behind its objectified appearance, with the result that the image is spared accusations of imitation. **(GF)**

See also: **Absence; Curtain; Detective Stories; Portraiture; Self-Reference and Self-Portraiture**

Meaning: Magritte wrestled throughout his life with the problem of meaning, whether literal or symbolic (which he generally disavowed) or secret or circumvented (which he usually cultivated), reaching the conclusion in 1953 that 'my pictures are not reducible to a meaning, they are a meaning'.[103] The route to this declaration was not an easy one, however, for at different stages in his career his semantic philosophy is sometimes definite, even doctrinaire, sometimes maddeningly equivocal – and not occasionally both at once. But Magritte did reach consensus with himself on at least one signal proposition, the contention that 'images, ideas and words are *different* determinations of a *single* thing: thought ['la pensée']'.[104] Magritte regarded thought as a productive organising process, the raw material of all expression and activity, conditioning language and image alike. Encouraging a continuous interchange between the materials and devices of his paintings, thought becomes something akin to a ringmaster in the circus of exchange to which they give rise. Magritte's prioritisation of thought and the corollary notion that images and words should be referred back to thought as well as apprehended through its operating system (of which they were only a part) relates to the reflections on this subject by contemporary philosophers including **Martin Heidegger** and **Michel Foucault** – with both of whom Magritte engaged in the later part of his career.[105] Magritte would probably have concurred with the suggestion that 'it is the very function of thought [for Heidegger] to bring inner-worldly phenomena back into their truth'.[106]

At the same time, Magritte's understanding of the relationship between thought and **language**

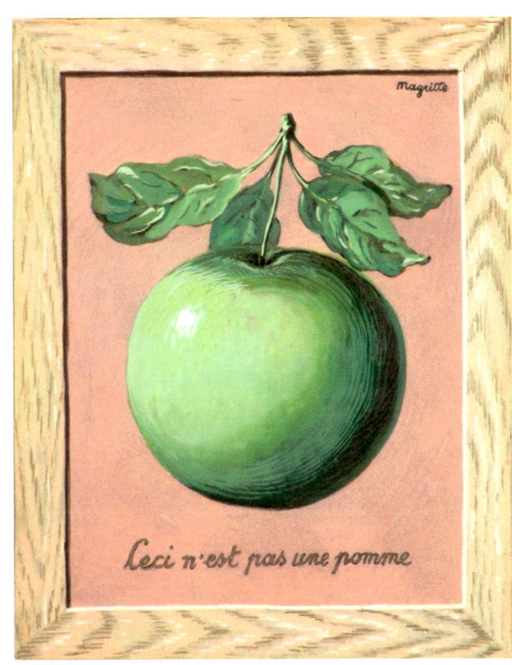

This is not an Apple
Ceci n'est pas une pomme c.1959, gouache on paper, 19.7 × 15.9 cm. Collection Triton Foundation, The Netherlands, CR1468

offers to invert the more imperious claims made by structuralist theorists and related ideas of the pre-eminence of language in the development of what the anthropologist and linguist Edward Sapir termed 'all the cultural asset[s] of man'. In his only general book on language, however, Sapir reflected on the nature of thought and its relation to the linguistic order, positing the existence of a domain of thought relatively independent of the rule of language. 'One may go so far,' he wrote, 'as to suspect that the symbolic expression of thought may in some cases run along outside the fringe of the conscious mind, so that the feeling of a free, nonlinguistic stream of thought is, for minds of a certain type, a relatively, but only a relatively, justified one.'[107] Magritte makes the same concessions for language that Edward Sapir makes for thought. But while both artist and linguist use different predicates and terms, and work out their ideas with differing degrees of sophistication, there still remains a modelled similarity between their theories of governance linking thought and language.

LES MOTS ET LES IMAGES

9/96

— Un objet ne tient pas tellement à son nom qu'on ne puisse lui en trouver un autre qui lui convienne mieux :

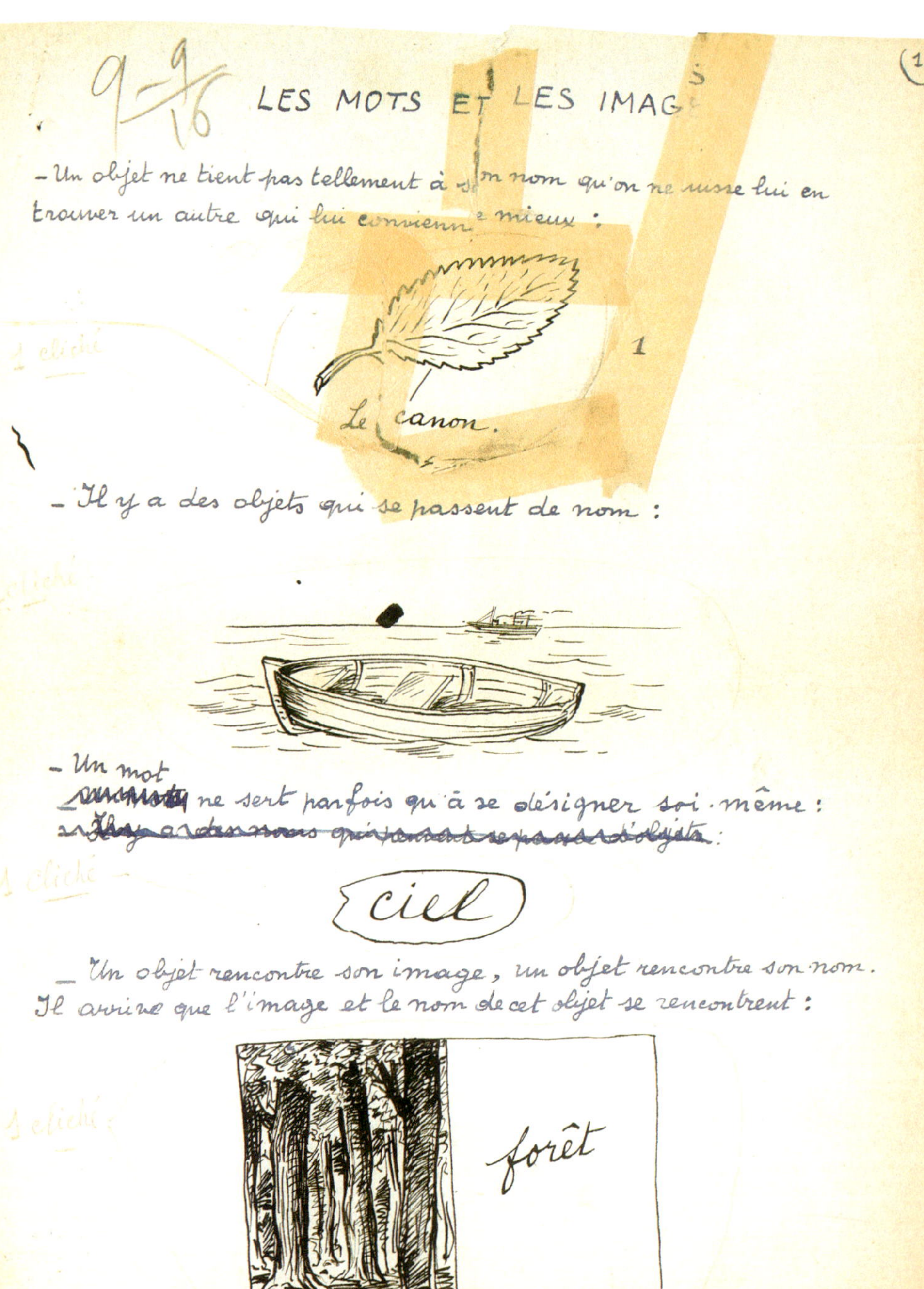

Le canon.

1

— Il y a des objets qui se passent de nom :

— Un mot ne sert parfois qu'à se désigner soi-même :

ciel

— Un objet rencontre son image, un objet rencontre son nom. Il arrive que l'image et le nom de cet objet se rencontrent :

forêt

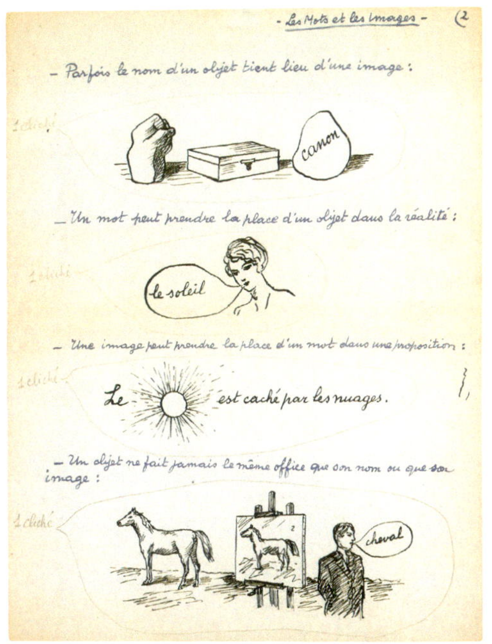

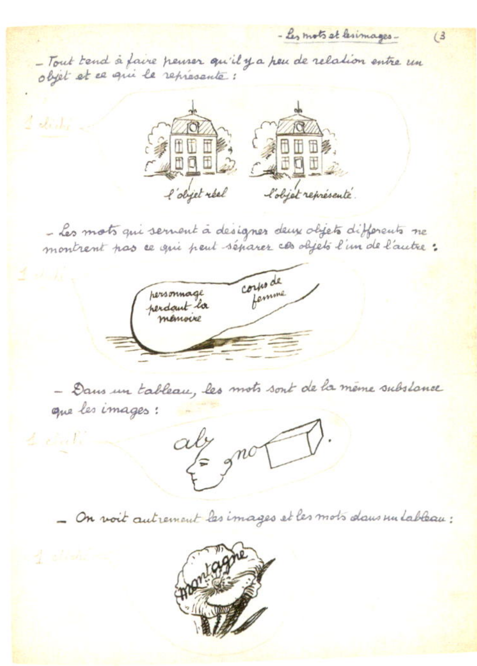

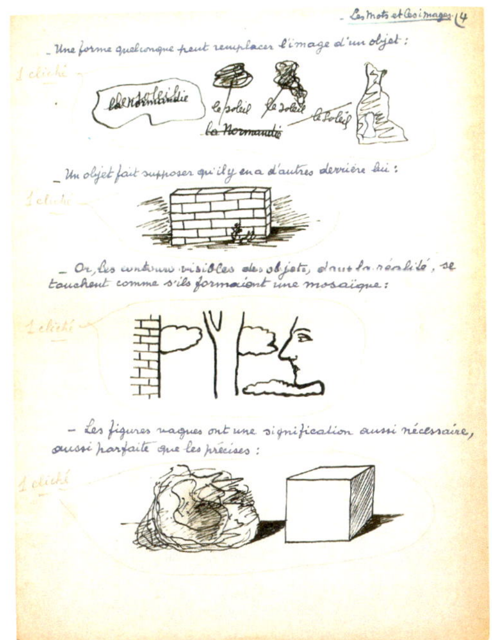

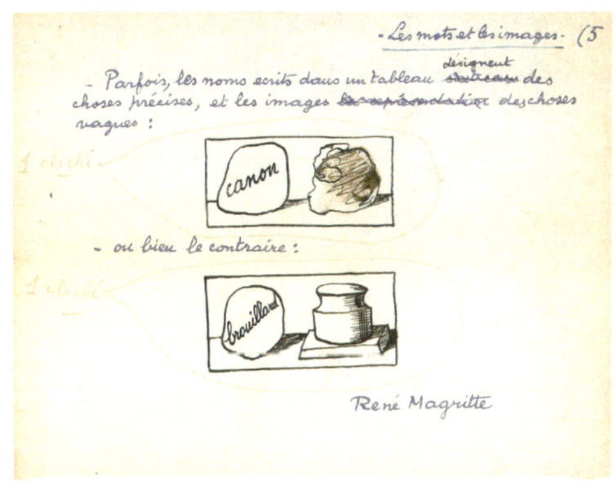

Words and Images
Les Mots et les images 1929,
ink and pencil on paper.
Five sheets, each 27.2 × 28 cm.
Private Collection

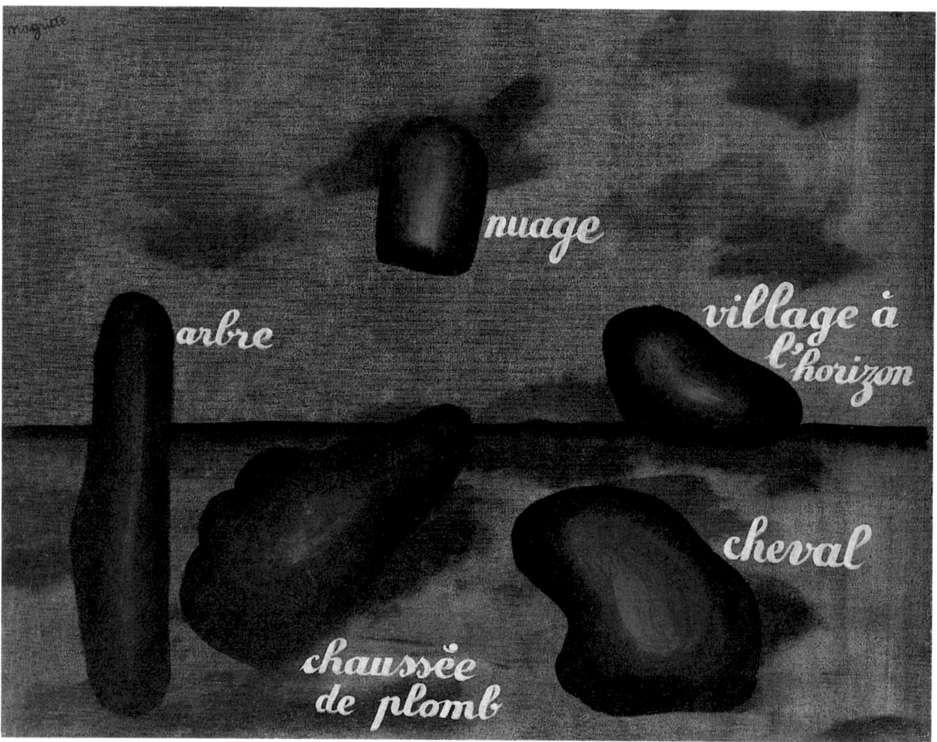

Swift Hope
L'Espoir rapide 1927, oil on canvas, 49.5 × 64 cm.
Hamburger Kunsthalle. On extended loan from the Stiftung
zur Förderung der Hamburgischen Kunstsammlungen, CR 191

Magritte and Sapir are not alone in making this connection. In her discussion of Surrealist photography, Rosalind Krauss begins by locating the origin of the Surrealist valorisation of thought processes and '*purely* internal models' in **André Breton's** declarations of the mid-1920s in which he disparages both literary realism and the deceptions of modernist notions of autonomy.[108] The tendency to see the photographic activity of Surrealism as a kind of writing fills in the picture of visual Surrealism considered as text, which Krauss develops here and in her other writings, exemplifying the structuralist desire to make broad comparisons governed by language. Elsewhere Krauss uses metaphors from writing to characterise the frenzied calligraphy of André Masson. She describes it as 'cursive' and 'scriptorial' and defends its literal similarity to **automatic writing**. Likewise, the veristic style of Magritte and **Salvador Dalí** is regarded as being textually based in so far as

it is narrative and literary. It is the presupposition of this criticism that language becomes the ghost that animates the thought machine of Surrealist generality. Magritte resisted the logic of linguistic overdetermination with a kind of knight's move in which he affirmed the 'validity' of 'the linguistic attempt to say that my pictures were conceived as material signs of freedom of thought'.[109] (**JW**)

See also: **Philosophy; Titles**

George Melly (1926–2007) Liverpool-born jazz musician, writer, critic and bon vivant. A lifelong interest in **Surrealism** began during his National Service. After demobilisation in 1947, he worked at the **London Gallery** under **E.L.T. Mesens**, who persuaded Melly's father to invest in gallery stock on behalf of his son. This formed the basis of Melly's renowned Surrealist art collection. Works held by Melly included *The Black Flag* 1938 and

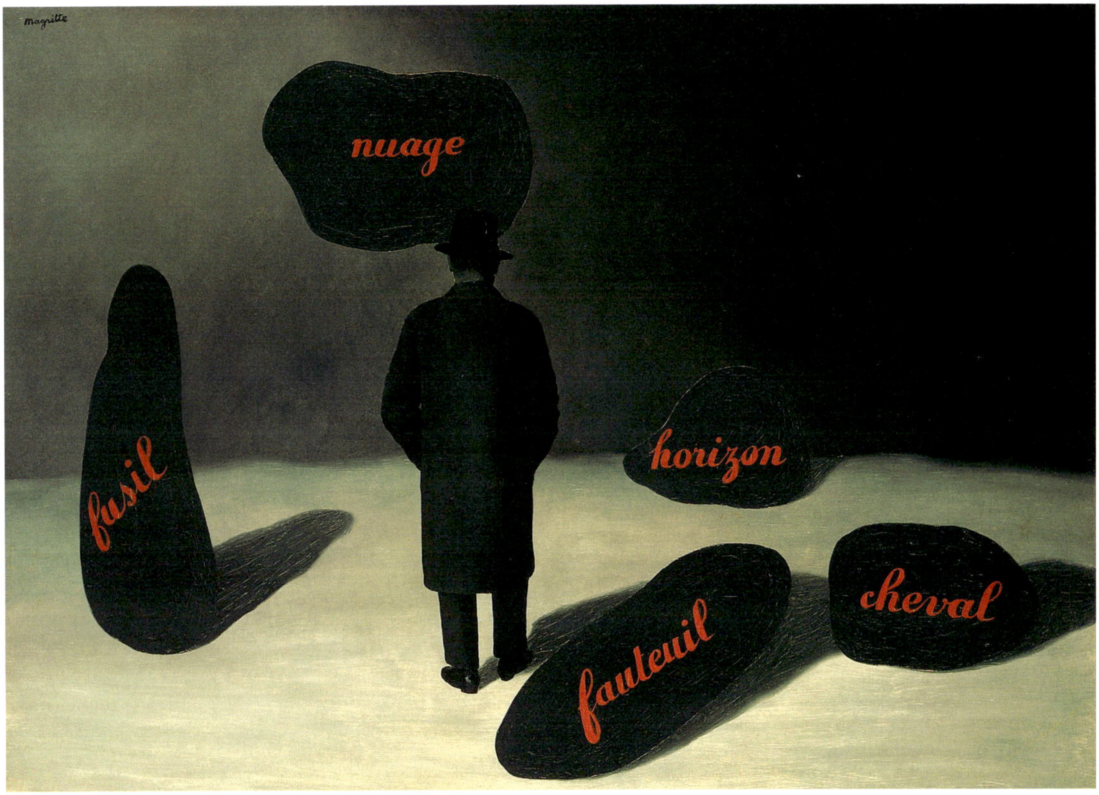

The Apparition
L'Apparition 1928,
oil on canvas, 81 × 116 cm.
Staatsgalerie, Stuttgart,
CR 220

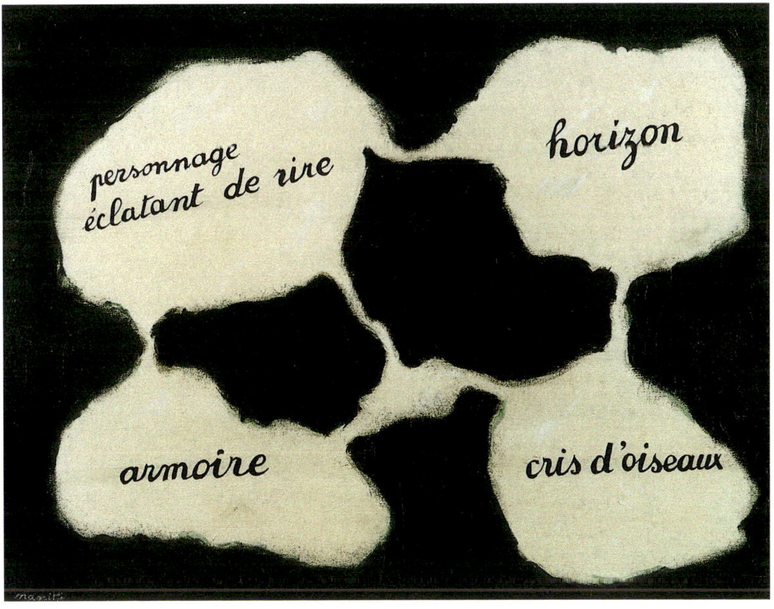

The Living Mirror
Le Miroir vivant 1928,
oil on canvas, 54 × 73 cm.
Private Collection, CR 295

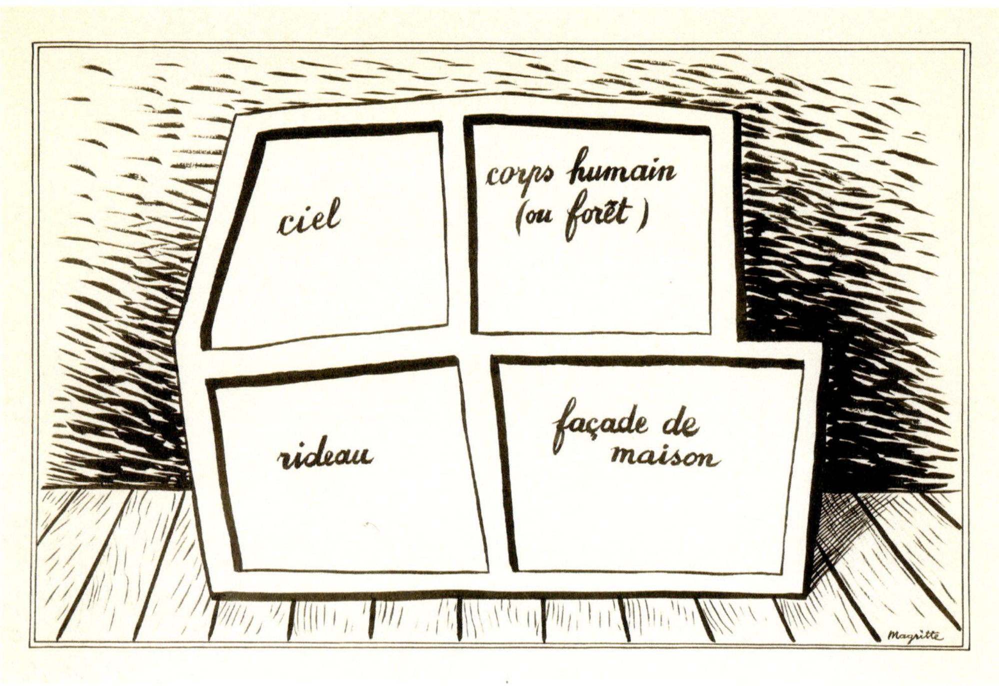

The Empty Mask
Le Masque vide 1928, ink on paper, 32 × 46 cm.
Collection Sylvio Perlstein, Antwerp

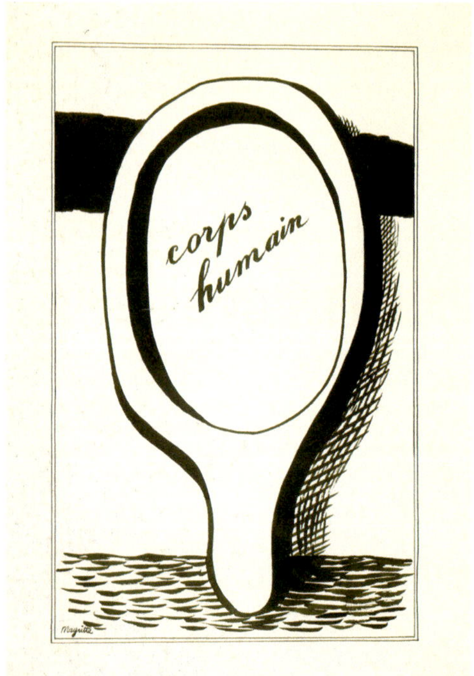

The Magic Mirror
Le Miroir magique 1928, ink on paper, 46.7 × 32.7 cm.
Collection Sylvio Perlstein, Antwerp

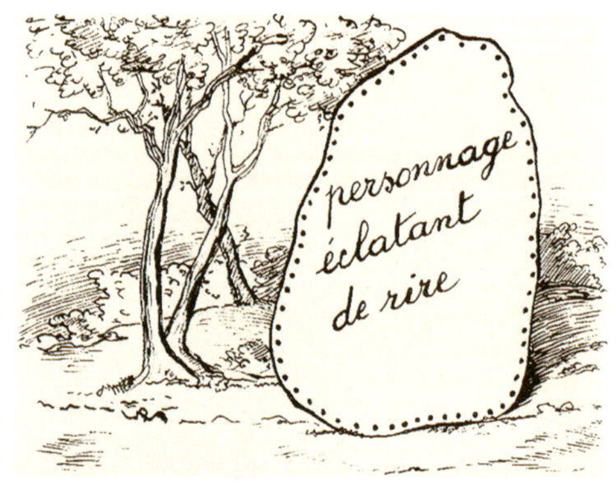

Person Bursting out Laughing
Personnage éclatant de rire c.1929, ink on paper, 11 × 14.4 cm.
Galerie Ronny Van de Velde, Antwerp

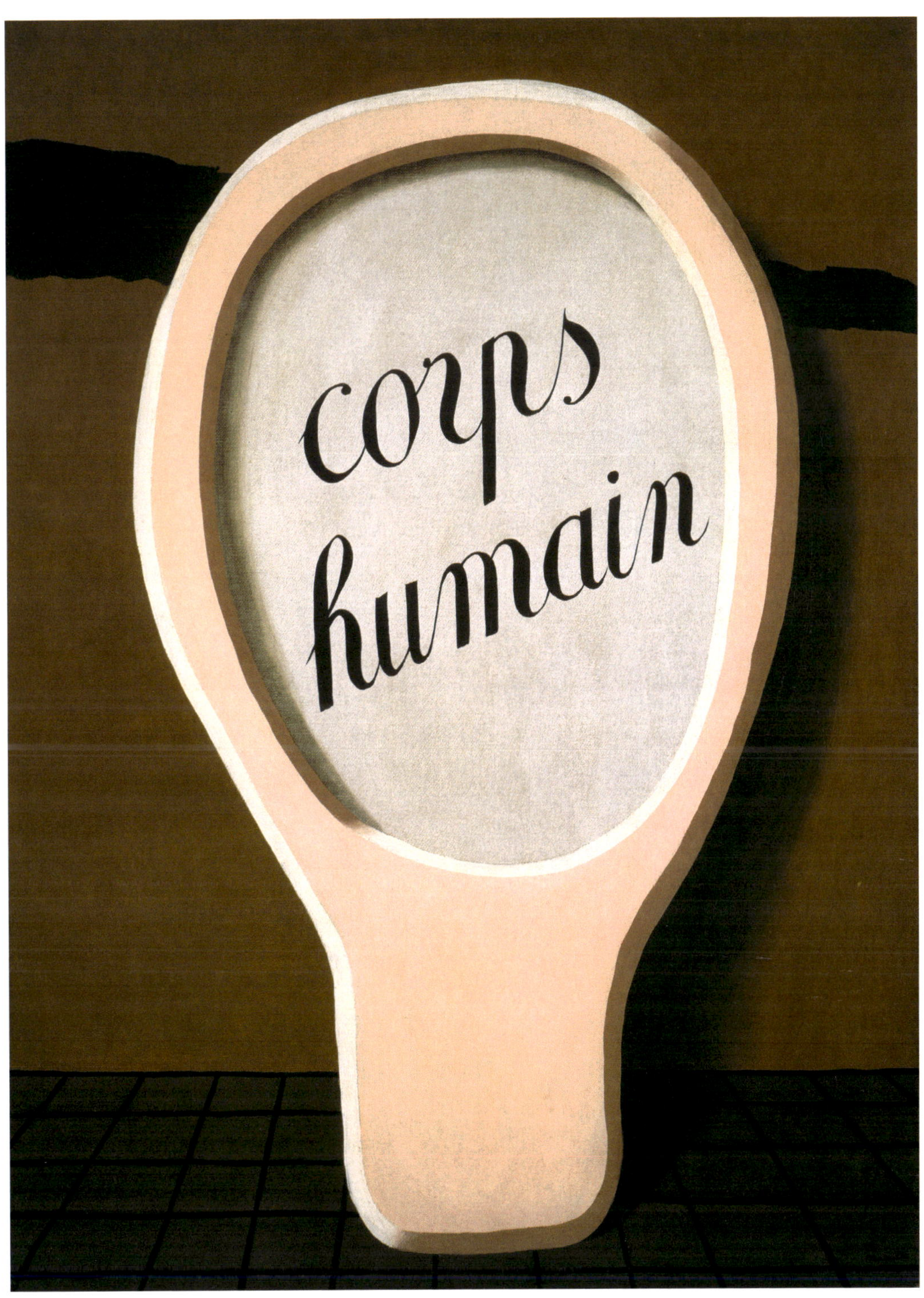

The Magic Mirror
Le Miroir magique 1929, oil on canvas, 73 × 54 cm.
Scottish National Gallery of Modern Art, Edinburgh.
Bequeathed by Gabrielle Keiller 1995, CR 308

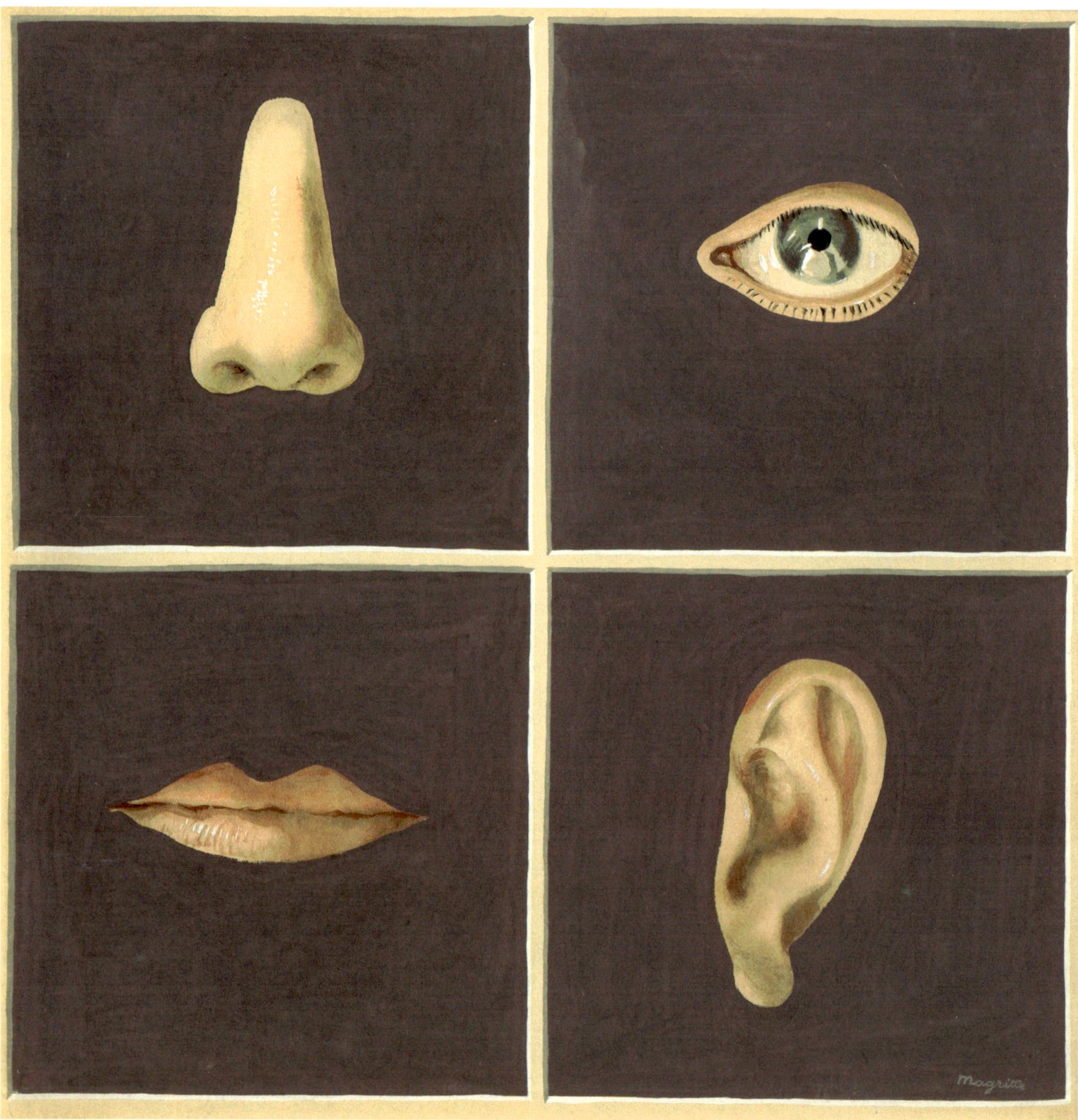

The White Race
La Race blanche 1937, gouache on paper, 26 × 26 cm.
Private Collection, CR 1130

The Rape 1934. Melly sold part of his collection in 2000 to fund the purchase of a section of the River Usk in mid-Wales, enabling him to indulge his passion for fly-fishing. (**DP**)

See also: **England**

John and Dominique de Menil (1904–1973; 1908–1997)

American art collectors and philanthropists of French birth. The de Menils fled Nazi Europe in 1941 and settled in Houston, Texas, where they relocated Schlumberger Ltd, Dominique de Menil's family business. They began collecting art shortly after. In a general sense, their extensive collection is bound by religious, political and social concerns and includes art from the Palaeolithic period to the twentieth century. The dealer **Alexandre Iolas** introduced them to **Surrealist** art and artists, and today the collection holds fifty-four Magritte works. In June 1987 the Renzo Piano-designed Menil Collection was opened to house and present their collection. (**DP**)

See also: **Harry Torczyner**

E.L.T. Mesens (1903–1971)

In 1919, Édouard-Léon-Théodore Mesens enrolled in the Brussels Conservatory, being drawn to music and having already written a range of works for piano. Early in his career he sought contact with avant-garde writers, artists and musicians in Paris such as Tristan Tzara, Erik Satie and **Marcel Duchamp**. In 1920 Mesens met Magritte at an exhibition of poster designs, which Magritte held together with Pierre Flouquet. Mesens subsequently became the piano teacher of Magritte's brother **Paul**, a close associate of the Brussels Surrealist group. In 1925, Mesens and Magritte created a number of reviews including *Œsophage* and *Marie*. In 1927 they joined **Paul Nougé's** group, including André Souris and **Camille Goemans**, around the publication *Correspondance*, marking the formation of the Brussels Surrealist group. In Brussels, Mesens directed the Galerie L'Époque in 1927, was editor of the 1929 special issue *Variétés*, one of the most important collaborations between Belgian and French **Surrealists**, and the review *Violette Nozières*, and in 1931 became Magritte's dealer. He was also a key mediatory figure between Surrealist groups, establishing links between French and Belgian Surrealists, as well as later between

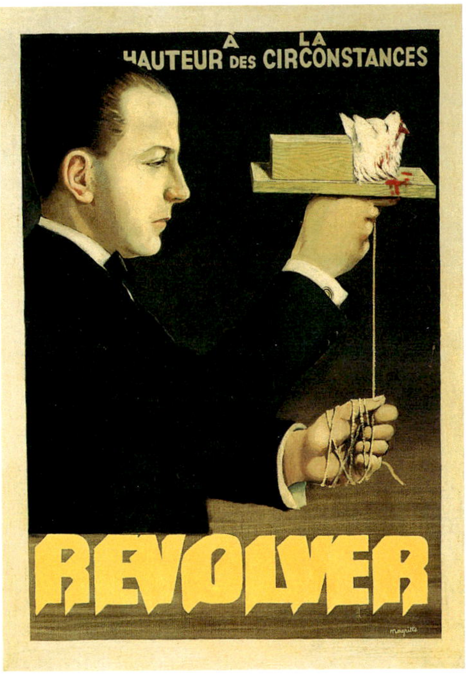

Portrait of E.L.T. Mesens
Portrait de E.L.T. Mesens 1930, oil on canvas, 73 × 54 cm. Private Collection, CR 333

Surrealists in Britain, France and Belgium. In 1938 Mesens moved to London, becoming a leading figure in British Surrealism. His artistic contribution to the avant-garde is diverse, ranging from **poetry** and writing to music and **collage**. (**PA**)

See also: **England; London Gallery**

Metamorphosis:

'I have found a new potential inherent in things,' wrote Magritte in 1927, 'their ability to become *gradually* something else, an object *merging into* an object other than itself ... This seems to me to be something quite different from a composite object, since there is no break between the two substances, and no limit.'[110] Magritte cites the example of 'a naked woman' with parts that 'change into a different substance'. This technique of metamorphosis is enacted in *Discovery* 1927, where the body of the woman is partly transformed into wood – but a highly ambiguous form of *faux bois* suggestive of tiger fur. This recalls Gilles Deleuze's concept of 'becoming-animal', a term used in his books on Francis Bacon and on Franz Kafka's

Metamorphosis to suggest a *'zone of indiscernibility … between man and animal'*,where, as with Magritte, there is 'never a combination of forms, but rather … the common fact of man and animal'.[111] Magritte's image also combines a picture postcard of a naked woman with the symbolism of Fernand Khnopff's *Art*, or *The Sphinx*, or *The Caresses* 1896, where Oedipus is caressed by a lascivious Sphinx with the head of a woman and the body of a leopard. What is radical in Kafka is his new use of language, just as with Magritte we see a new visual language emerge as part of his sustained critique of the nature of **representation**. (NM)

See also: **The Petrified Image**

Joan Miró (1893–1983) Spanish painter, sculptor and printmaker. A defining figure of mid-1920s French **Surrealism's** emphasis on spontaneous and automatic creative production, the vivid carnivalesque imagery of Joan Miró appears at first sight to embody completely different preoccupations from those of Magritte. Beneath the playful invention of Miró's technique, however, lies a poetic re-imagination of the everyday, of unexpected but definitive

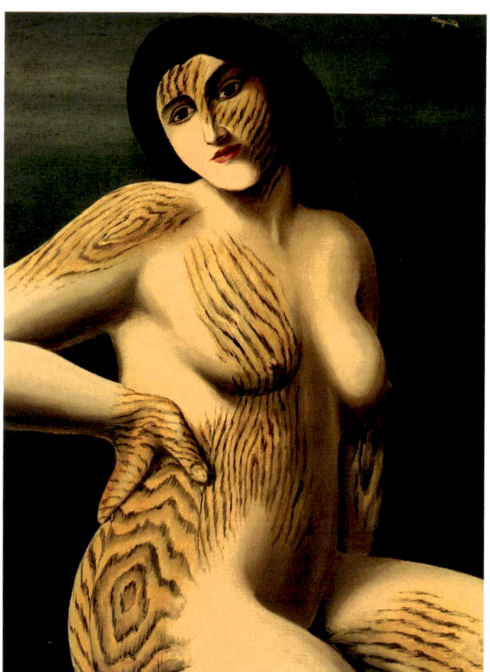

Discovery
Découverte 1927, oil on canvas, 65 × 50 cm.
Royal Museums of Fine Arts of Belgium, Brussels, CR 187

encounters, making his artworks the exuberant kin of the apparently more sober intellectual reflections of Magritte's paintings. Miró's 'painting-poems', which combine biomorphic painted elements with text, influenced Magritte's text-image paintings of the late 1920s. (KF)

See also: **Abstraction; Automatism and Automatic Writing; Dreams; Metamorphosis; Poetry**

Mirror, a fragile reflection of reality which turns it round rendering it intangible, was of great interest to Magritte. There are many moments when, viewing one of his images, there is a sense that one might be looking into a mirror. A fragment of the world placed within a **frame** or apparently seen through a window might, by a twist of perception, be seen as a reflection in a mirror, a perception that suddenly turns the space of the picture inside-out.

In *Not to be Reproduced* 1937, Magritte directly addresses what he might have called 'the problem of the mirror'. The painting was commissioned from Magritte by **Edward James** in 1937 and is usually taken to be a portrait of James. He stands with his back to us facing into a mirror but instead of seeing his face in the mirror, we see once more the back of his head. Perhaps, then, this is not truly a mirror but a cunningly painted **trompe l'oeil**. As he does with his window paintings, Magritte includes one small element which blocks our attempt to explain this image within the image as anything other than what it seems to be: a mirror. At bottom right on the ledge in front of the mirror rests a book, which is reflected correctly – that is, reversed. It is a French edition of **Edgar Allan Poe's** *The Narrative of Arthur Gordon Pym of Nantucket* (1838), a fact which may or may not be useful in explicating the painting but cannot deflect the proposition of the image: this is indeed a mirror that, when you look into it, shows you a view of yourself that you yourself can never actually have. (IW)

See also: **Absence; Double; Elective Affinities; Portraiture; Repetition and the Encounter; Window**

Moon: The image of the moon was the conceptual hinge for works such as *The Sixteenth of September* 1956. Here the crescent moon in front of a tree constitutes one of the artist's most succinct statements

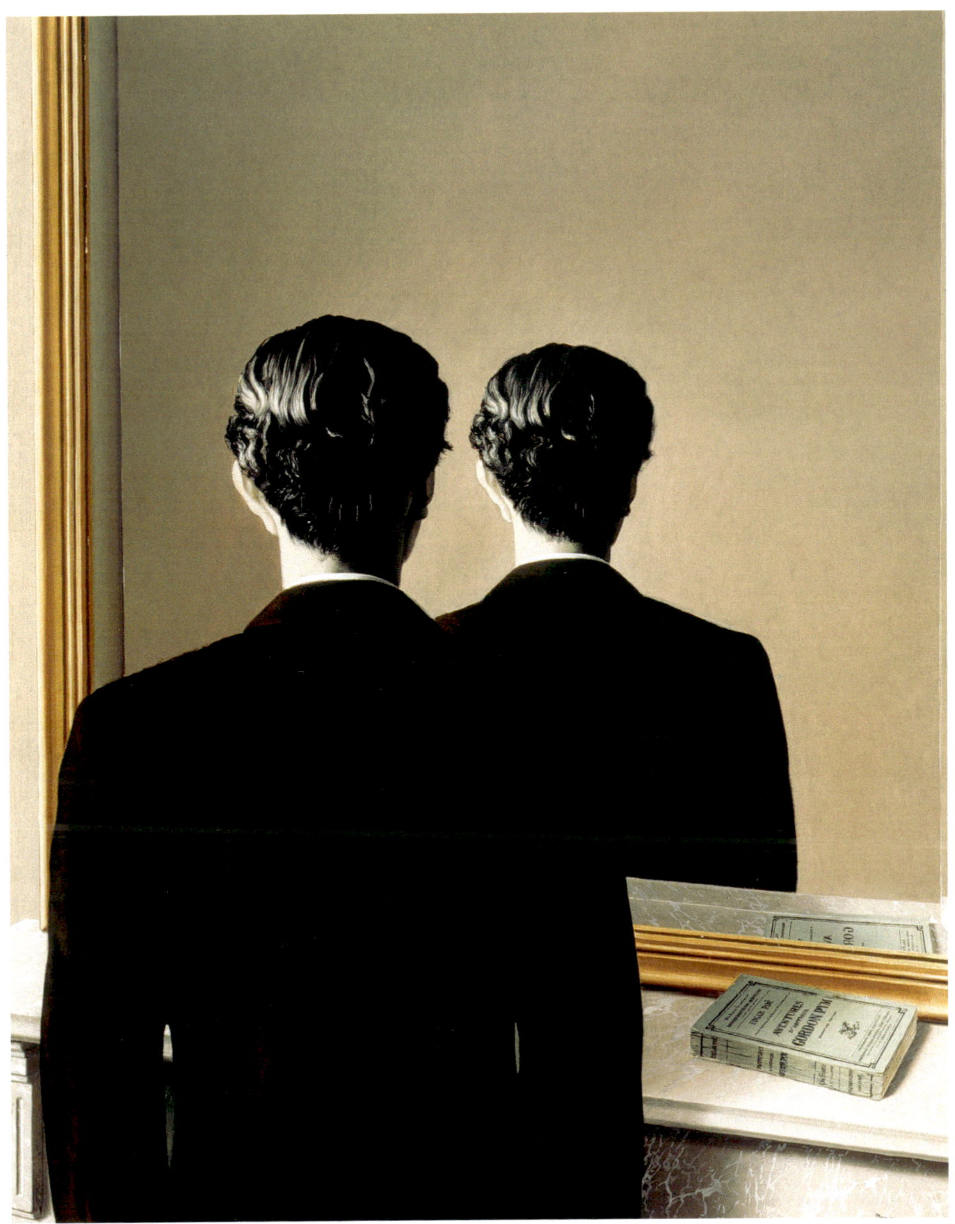

Not to be Reproduced
La Reproduction interdite 1937, oil on canvas, 81 × 65 cm.
Museum Boijmans Van Beuningen, Rotterdam, CR 436

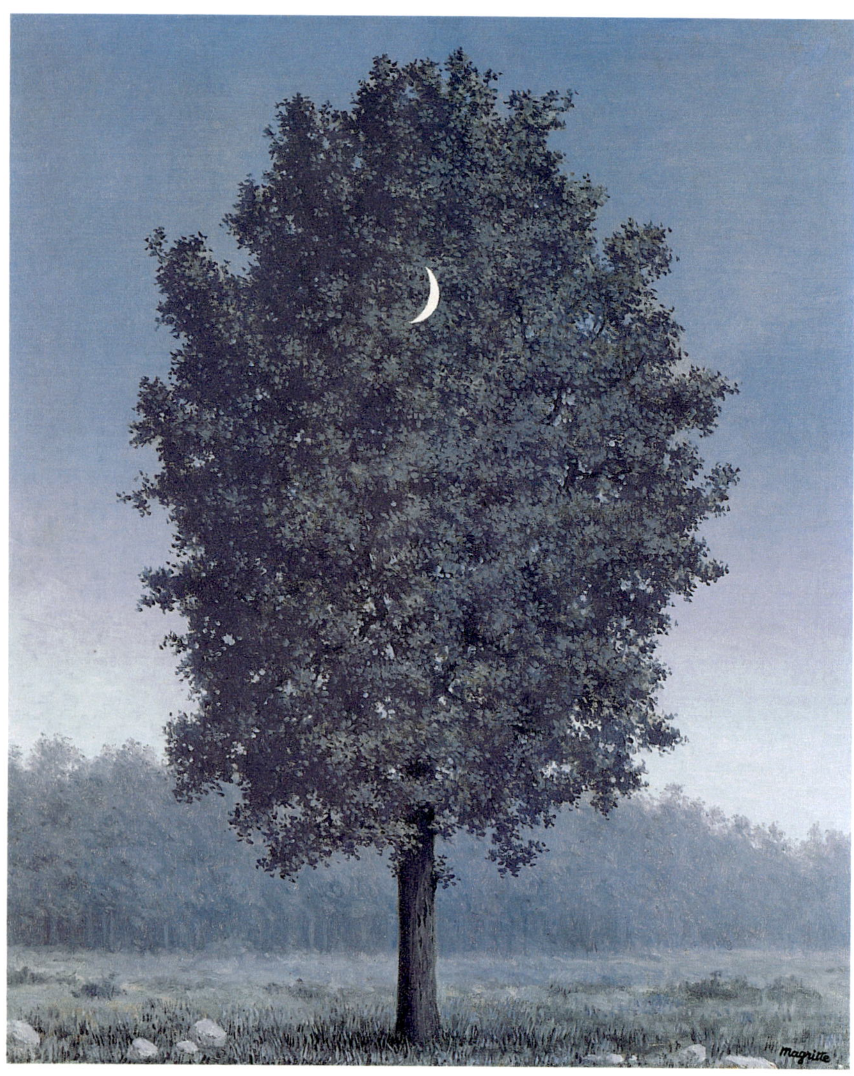

**The Sixteenth
of September**
Le Seize Septembre
1956, oil on canvas,
60 × 50 cm.
Kunsthaus Zurich,
Walter Haefner
Donation, CR 834

on the idea of the 'hidden visible'. A philosophical concern is also evident in *The Masterpiece or the Mysteries of the Horizon* 1955, of which he stated 'when a man thinks about the moon, he has an idea of it … it becomes his moon. So I did a painting showing three men, each with his own moon over his head … This is a philosophical problem – how to divide the unity.'[112] (**DP**)

See also: ***The Dominion of Light***; **Meaning**; **Mystery**

Music scores: Between 1924 and 1938 Magritte designed cover illustrations for around sixty-three sheet music scores. The designs of some music scores show the influence of the art nouveau poster designs produced by Gisbert Combaz (1869–1941), who taught Magritte when he was a student at the Académie royale des Beaux-Arts. In July 1925 *Norine Blues*, a song composed by Magritte's brother Paul with lyrics by René and **Georgette Magritte** (using the pseudonym René Georges), was performed by

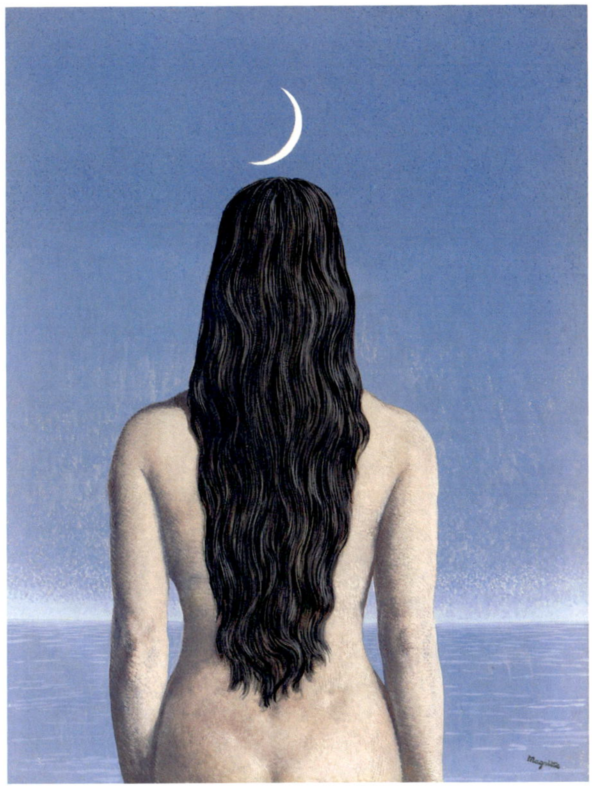

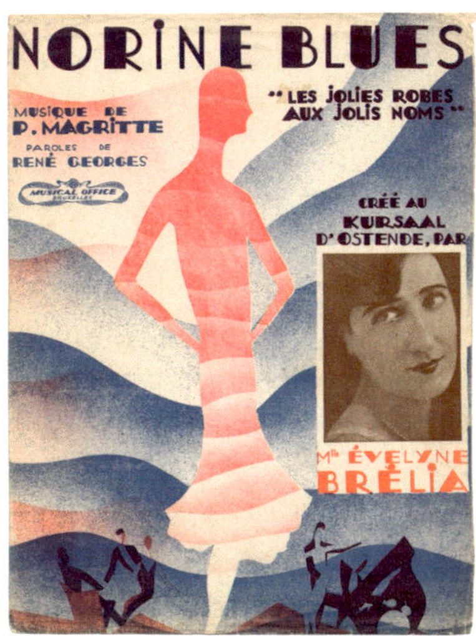

Norine Blues
René Magritte designed music score cover, n.d.
(copyright dated 1925), zincograph on paper,
34.8 × 26.9 cm. Archives of Contemporary Art
in Belgium / Royal Museums of Fine Arts of
Belgium, Brussels

The Evening Gown
La Robe du soir 1955, gouache on paper,
44 × 33.5 cm. Collection Mr and Mrs Wilbur
Ross, CR vol.IV, app.no.168

Évelyne Brélia at the Norine fashion show at the
Casino in Ostend. The cover of the score was also
designed by Magritte. **(DP)**

👁 See also: **Commercial Art**; **Paul Magritte**

Mystery is at the core of Magritte's art, the focus of
all his pictorial inventions. Unlike the **Surrealists**,
he did not equate mystery with a subconscious,
transcendental world. On the contrary, Magritte
regarded it as life itself. He stated: 'The mystery is
not one of the possibilities of the real. The mystery
is that which is absolutely necessary for there to be a
real.'[113] In Magritte's terms, mystery coincides with
the concept of existence and being, as defined by
twentieth-century Existentialists, who specifically
distinguished it from beingness (the nature or essence of things) – a distinction that excludes any
hint of determinism from 'being' Magritte took
the same view as Wittgenstein, who declared 'Not

how the world is, is the mystical, but *that* it is.'[114]
Magritte used his paintings to search for other ways
of portraying the world, in order to come closer to
its very existence. Concepts such as inspiration,
poetry and resemblance were central to this search.
He championed freedom of thought as opposed to
regulated possibilities and strove to portray immediate, spontaneous thinking unconstrained by feelings,
emotions, habits, memories or experiences. His
intent was to portray the moment when thinking
comes to a halt, a moment of accord and harmony
that neither words nor pictures can explain.[115] 'One
cannot speak about mystery,' he declared, 'one must
be seized by it.'[116] **(GF)**

👁 See also: **Dreams**; **Sigmund Freud**; **Representation and Resemblance**

N

Jacqueline Nonkels (1916–2007) In early 1926 the Magrittes moved to an apartment at 113 Rue Steyls, Laeken, living above a shop run by the Nonkels family. Their then young daughter Jacqueline was to become a lifelong friend. Whilst not a member of the Surrealist group, she can be seen in some of *The Fidelity of Images* photographs and in Magritte's portrait of 1944. It was at Magritte's house that Nonkels met **Marcel Mariën**. Captivated by her beauty, between December 1937 and August 1938 he wrote her passionate surrealist letters. Although his love was unrequited, the letters were anthologised in *Magritte, Mariën: My Accomplices*, and published by the King Baudouin Foundation in 2008. **(DP)**

See also: **Letters**

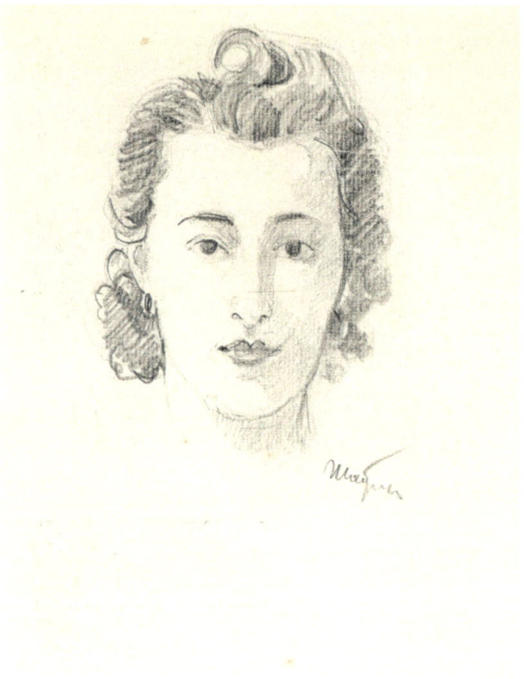

Portrait of Jacqueline Nonkels
Portrait de Jacqueline Nonkels n.d., pencil on paper, 21 × 17.5 cm. Collection King Baudouin Foundation, gift of Jacqueline Nonkels

Paul Nougé (1895–1967) A key figure in Belgian Surrealism. Leader of the Brussels group, whether or not he always cared to be thought of as such, Nougé was the figurehead, along with Magritte, of **Surrealism** in **Belgium**. A trained biochemist, interested in many art forms, Nougé was not, however, an aesthete. Interrogating the conditions of creation and the role of the artist within society with an unwavering scepticism and an extreme lucidity, his interest in the encounter between words and images was coupled with a great mistrust of them. For Nougé, artists or writers were always liable to be acting as undercover revolutionaries – Nougé became one of the co-founders of the Communist Party in Belgium in 1919 – not to say terrorists. It was with this logic that Nougé rejected the capacity of **automatic writing** to privilege an 'effective poetry' against the 'skinny exercises or little hacks who believe themselves to be causing a rupture of literature and who believe they can really change the world with this innocent play of mute syllables'.[117] Nougé was instead concerned with the realm of the real, far from the comforts of the imagination. It is in this sense that we must understand his interest in the oeuvre of Magritte, on which Nougé would have a considerable influence, being responsible for the creation of numerous **titles** for paintings, and dedicating his first biography to the painter. The series of nineteen photographs *The Subversion of Images* 1929 came close to Magrittean research in the roles given to everyday objects, by which they revealed their independence and peculiar existence. Though he was an enlightening defender of Magritte's oeuvre, including his most startling formulations such as the concept of 'Sunlit Surrealism', devised in 1946 during the artist's **Renoir Period**, Nougé and Magritte experienced a definitive quarrel in 1952. **(XC)**

See also: **Communism**; *The Fidelity of Images*; **Language**; **Object**; **Photography**; **Poetry**

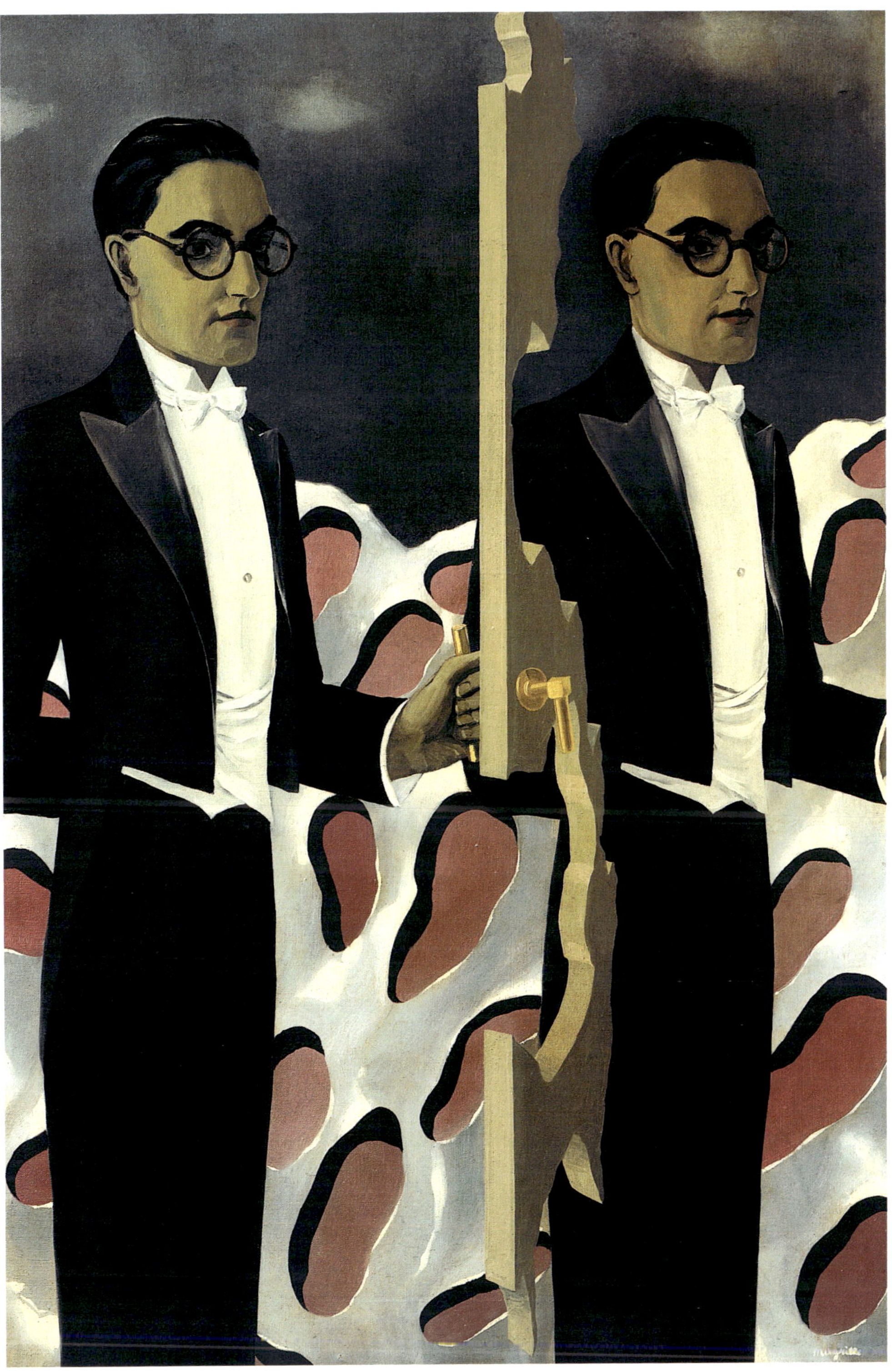

Portrait of Paul Nougé
Portrait de Paul Nougé 1927, oil on canvas, 94.3 × 64.5 cm.
Royal Museums of Fine Arts of Belgium, Brussels, CR 151

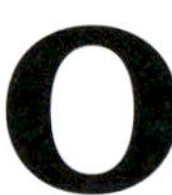

O

Object: According to **Paul Nougé**, the power of Magritte's work stems above all from the operation it performs upon the object.[118] His creation of 'objets bouleversants' – staggering, overwhelming objects – allows a reorientation of thought and experience, through the processes of **juxtaposition**, abrupt changes in **scale** or context, or of an object's structure and materials, and by challenging its names. First of all, however, comes the object's isolation from the hurly-burly of the everyday. For Nougé, 'the charm of an object lies in direct relation to its **banality**', an ordinary item being imbued with the most power to upset our understanding of the world.[119] The result is a disruption of our perception of the object at its deepest, philosophical level, as an emissary of that reality whose apparent stability Magritte seeks fundamentally to question and realign.

Magritte's insights take place alongside **Surrealism's** wider enquiry into the world of the object, above all in its propositions for 'Surrealist objects', assemblages of found or made items whose interruption of sense and utility fed the movement's assault on the values of logic, rational order and the tyranny of the commodity. Though Magritte rarely ventured into this domain directly – his best-known object consists precisely of a miniature painting of a piece of Camembert stood in a glass cheese dish, entitled *This is a Piece of Cheese* 1963 or 1964 (first created in 1936) – the profound re-examination of the object in his art has helped to construct our contemporary understanding of the obscure realm of things. (**KF**)

See also: Marcel Duchamp; *Objet trouvé*; The Petrified Image; Poetry

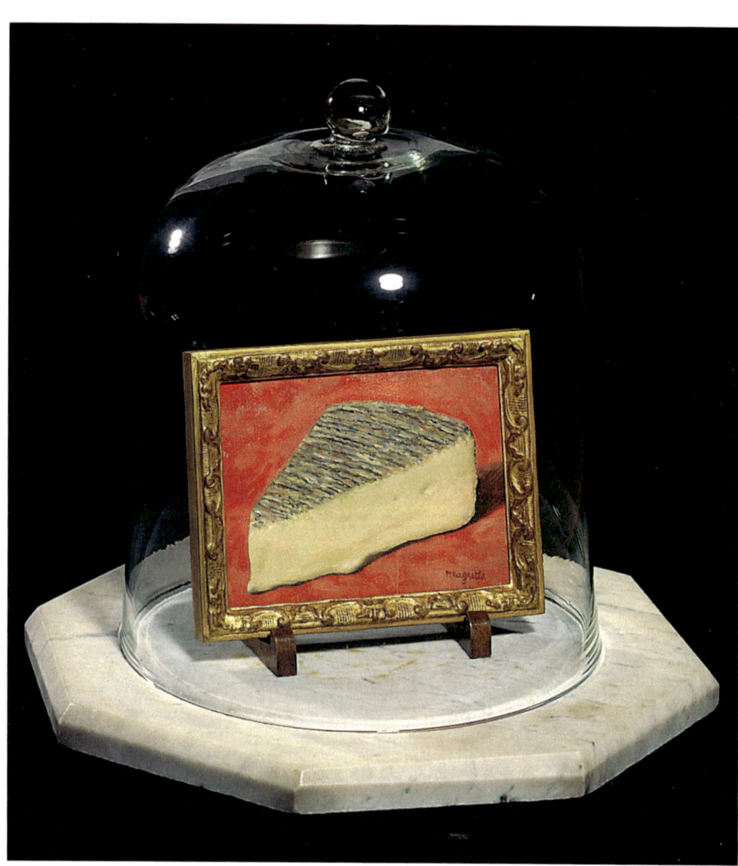

This is a Piece of Cheese
Ceci est un morceau de fromage
1963 or 1964, oil on masonite,
with glass dome, painting
dimensions 11.1 × 15.1 cm.
Collection Mr and Mrs Wilbur
Ross, CR 1083

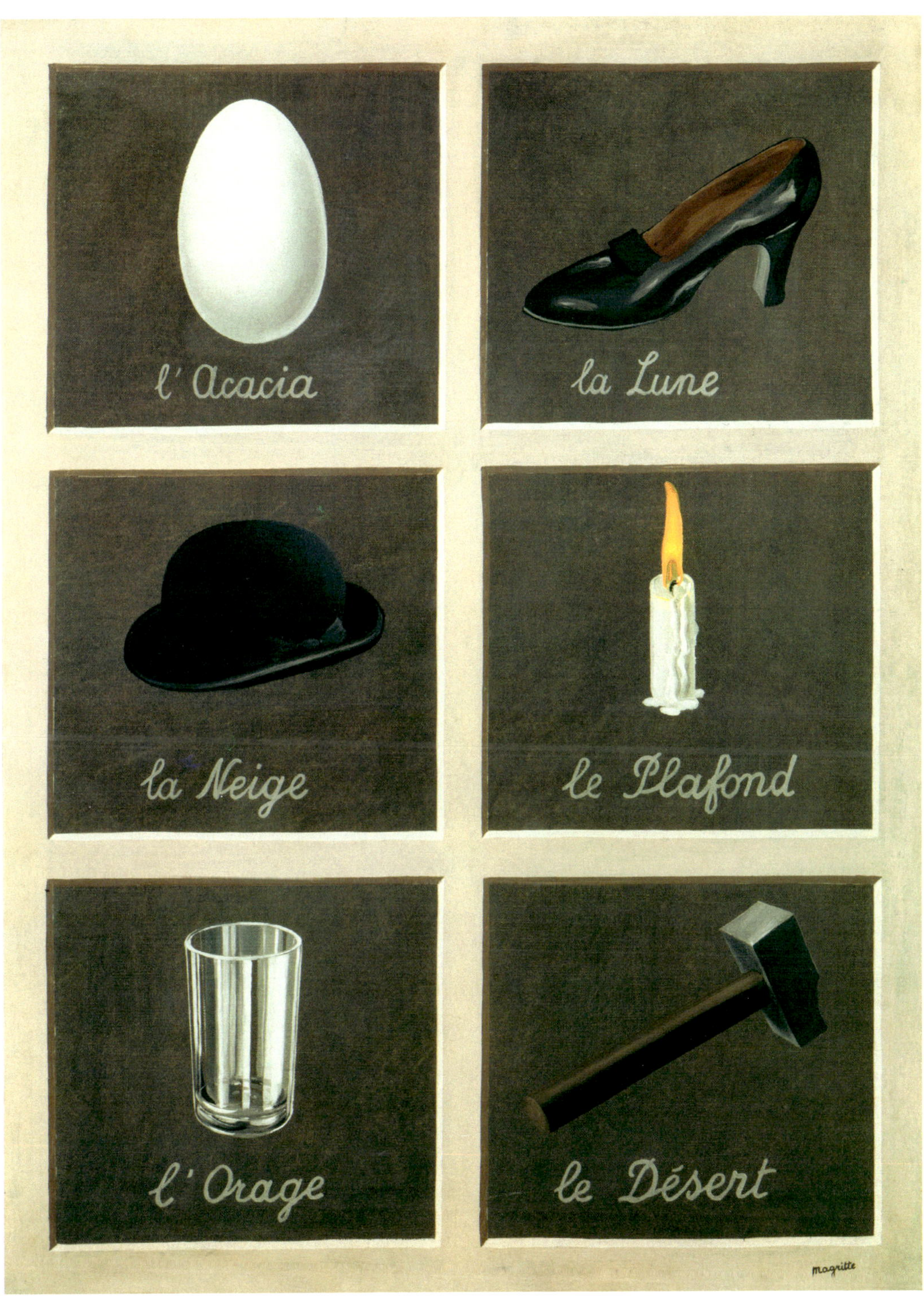

The Interpretation of Dreams
La Clef des songes 1930, oil on canvas,
81 × 60 cm. Private Collection, CR 332

Objet trouvé: One of **André Breton** and the French **Surrealists**' favourite activities was drifting through the Parisian flea markets in search of the *objet trouvé*, the found **object**. As Breton remarks in his 1928 novel *Nadja*: 'I often go there, in search of those objects that one can find nowhere else: outmoded, broken, useless, nearly incomprehensible – in short perverse, in the way that I understand and love this word.'[120] The found object possesses an inexplicable, unconscious draw, making it distinct from all other objects.

Unlike Breton, Magritte was not interested in the perception of the object as a manifestation of unconscious drives and desires. He instead focused on mundane, even banal, everyday objects. In Magritte's art, these everyday objects exemplify his theories of word, image and **representation**. This is evident in Magritte's word-and-image paintings such as *The Interpretation of Dreams* 1927, where words designate images (and vice versa) in four compartments – while in three word-and-image do not match, the fourth compartment's word designates the image. The painting seems to be an exercise in grammar to illustrate Magritte's theory. In contrast to the uniqueness of Breton's *objet trouvé*, the objects here are demonstration tools. They are examples, replaceable and exchangeable. (PA)

👁 See also: **Automatism and Automatic Writing; Cabinet of Curiosities; Chance; Dreams**

Œsophage: Dadaist review edited by Magritte and **E.L.T. Mesens**. *Œsophage* was a unique edition published in Brussels in March 1925. Bringing together various collaborations such as those of **Max Ernst**, **Francis Picabia**, Kurt Schwitters and Tristan Tzara, it was a slightly chaotic attempt by Magritte and Mesens to work independently before they joined the trio behind ***Correspondance***, their collective action leading to the journal ***Marie***. (XC)

👁 See also: **Dada**

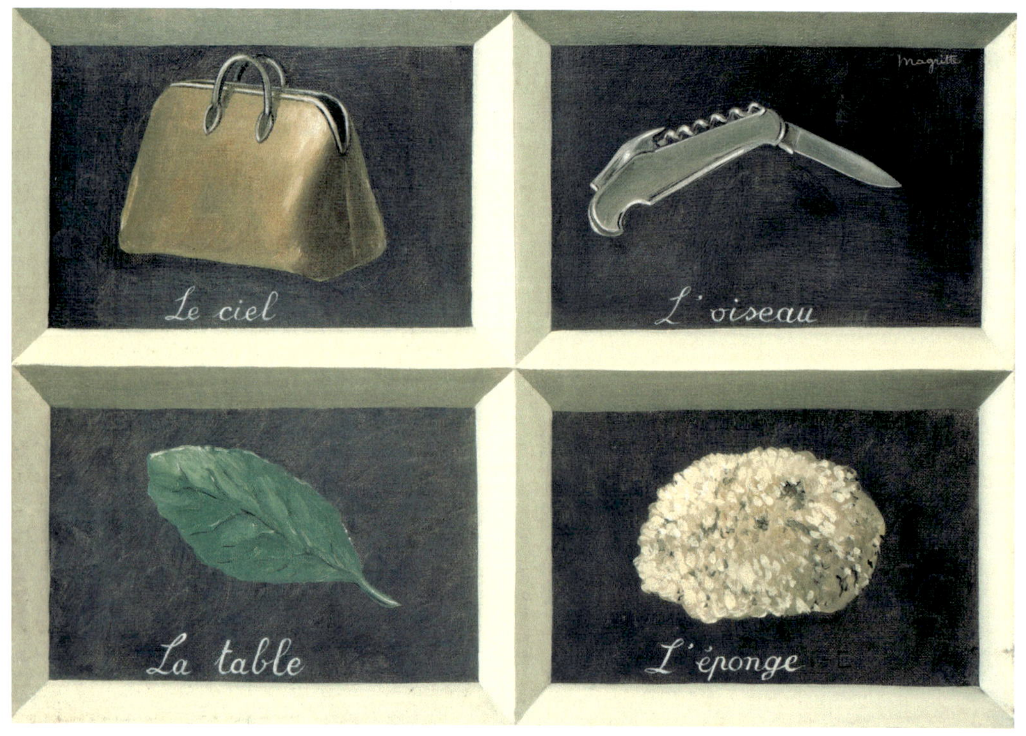

The Interpretation of Dreams
La Clef des songes 1927, oil on canvas, 38 × 55 cm.
Bayerische Staatsgemäldesammlungen München – Pinakothek der Moderne (Sammlung Theo Wormland), CR 172

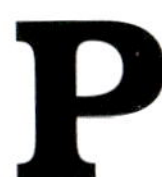

P

Paris: The period that Magritte and his wife Georgette spent between 1927 and 1930 in Paris, close to the Surrealist headquarters, was one of mixed fortunes. The couple moved to Paris in September 1927, after Magritte's dealer, the writer **Camille Goemans**, had settled there, eventually establishing his own gallery. The Magrittes lived modestly in the suburb of Le Perreux-sur-Marne, some 12 km from central Paris, in many ways continuing **Belgium's** marginal relationship with metropolitan **Surrealism**. Although a highly productive period for Magritte – it was there, for example, that he produced his first text-image paintings – he maintained only sporadic contact with **André Breton's** group.

A combination of the economic depression and personal problems led to the collapse of Goemans' gallery just before a major Magritte exhibition scheduled for early 1930. The final straw for Magritte had come when, at a meeting of Surrealists held at André Breton's apartment shortly before Christmas, Breton suddenly objected to Georgette wearing a crucifix, prompting the couple to walk out and leading to their departure from Paris in July 1930. The incident initiated a breach with Surrealism that endured until May 1933, when Magritte eventually contributed to *Surrealism in the Service of the Revolution*. It was not until 1948, however, with the **Vache** exhibition that Magritte would present a solo exhibition in the city. (**NM**)

Parody and Pastiche: To parody is to imitate the style of a particular work or genre by means of exaggeration, or satiric imitation. Perhaps it is inevitable that an artist concerned with the resemblance of things should adopt a philosophy of mimicry that appears simultaneously sincere yet satirical. Magritte's trademark style, in which questions of genre and technique are either absent or, more rarely, foregrounded as a matter of ironic choice, oversees a body of work in which the very act of painting becomes one of parody. The apparent invisibility of style – sometimes mistaken for a lack of ability – both privileges parody and pastiche as the means to challenge convention, and mimics their effects so as to make it impossible to separate the imitation from the thing being imitated. In the end, these exist in the mental rather than visual domain. 'To resemble is an act,' he would write, 'that belongs only to thought.'[121]

Magritte's tendency to return to earlier themes, or to repeat images with minor variations, points to a willingness to treat his own work as material to be manipulated and endlessly re-staged.

It is the codes of representation themselves that are Magritte's target, highlighted in his overt borrowings from other artists, or his adoption of outmoded styles. The startling **Renoir** (1943–47) and **Vache** (1948) periods, drawing on Impressionist

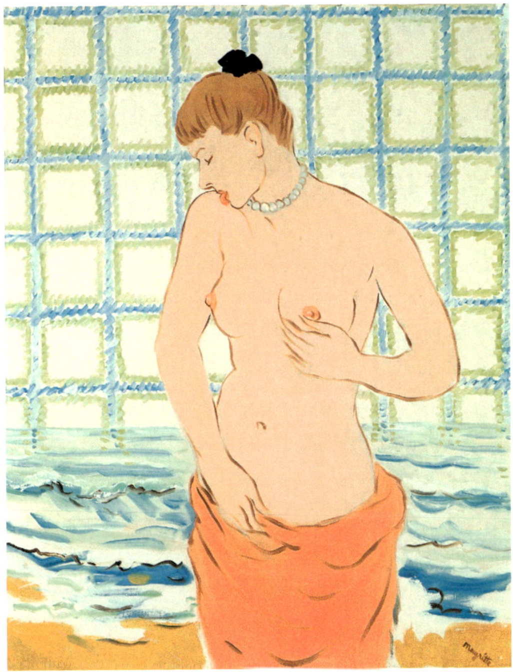

The Pebble
Le Galet 1948, oil on canvas, 100 × 81 cm.
Royal Museums of Fine Arts of Belgium, Brussels.
Gift of Georgette Magritte, CR 656

and popular culture sources, stand in marked contrast to the rest of his mature work; they attracted a hostile reception, and coincided with a period when the paths of Belgian and French **Surrealism** were at their most divergent. Theorised as part of a newly 'optimistic' Surrealism during and after **World War II**, Magritte's apparent desire was to scandalise the public and his supporters alike, and to produce work whose power as pastiche derives in part from a refusal to admit its comic status.

This sense in which the artist's oeuvre may be read, in Georges Roque's words, as a 'representation of representation'[122] hints at how doublings, **repetitions**, intertextuality and a labyrinthine play of **meaning** are all implicated in a complex, ambiguous gamble with the very comprehension of life itself. To the outside world, even Magritte's scrupulously 'normal' suburban lifestyle may be viewed as a kind of pastiche of daily existence, one so seamlessly bonded to its double that the two cannot be separated or distinguished. (**KF**)

See also: **Banality; Double; Ersatz; Forgery; Kitsch**

Pattern: Given Magritte's stated disdain for the applied arts, expressed in his declaration that 'applied art kills art', it is perhaps perverse to discuss the theme of decorative patterning in relation to his oeuvre.[123] A correspondence between Magritte's artistic concerns and his commercial designs has been suggested by a number of critics. Richard Calvocoressi, for example, relates the split-screen composition of *Man with a Newspaper* 1928 to **wallpaper** and fabric pattern repeats, both of which Magritte designed.[124] Magritte's use of simulated 'paper cut' patterning, deployed in *The End of Time* 1927 and *The Annunciation* 1930, reads as hand-painted collage, suggesting that the

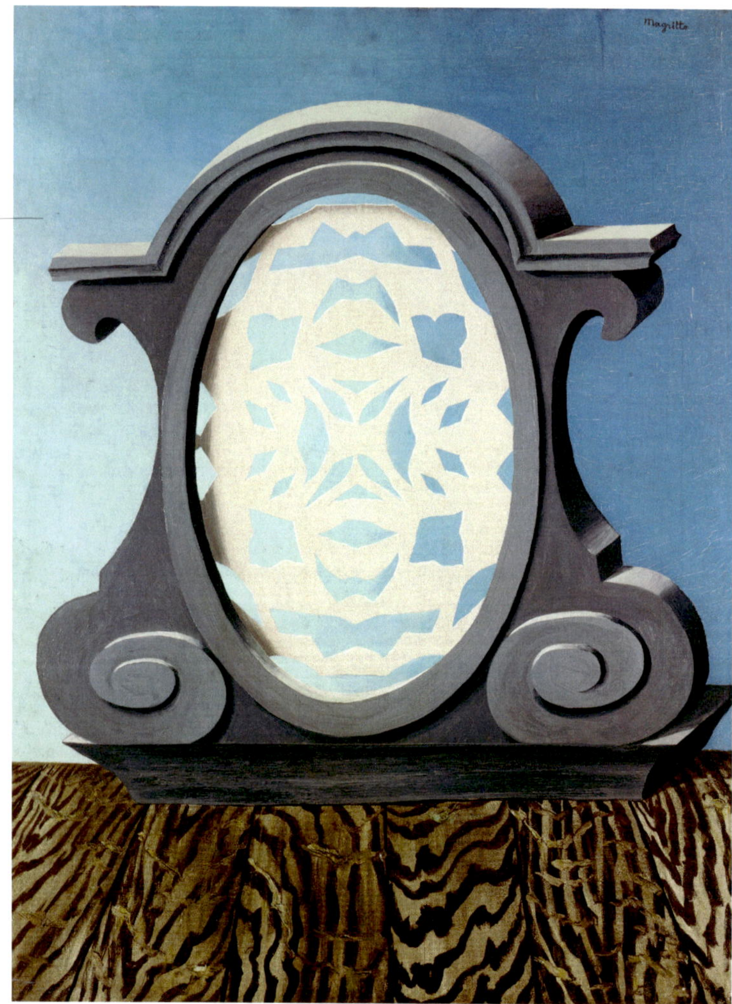

The End of Time
La Fin du temps 1927,
oil on canvas, 73 × 54 cm.
Private Collection, USA, CR 179

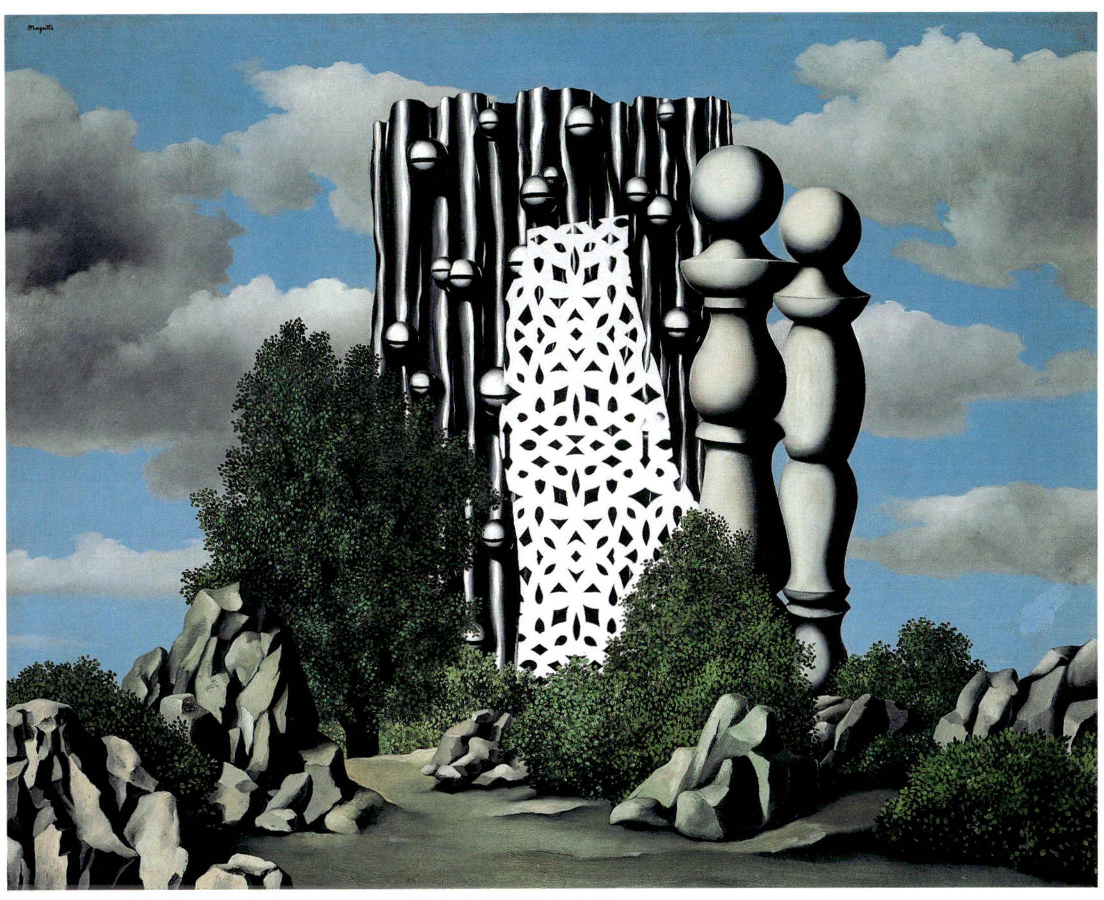

The Annunciation
L'Annonciation 1930, oil on canvas, 113.7 × 145.9 cm.
Tate. Purchased with assistance from the Friends of
the Tate Gallery 1986, CR 330

artist created actual cut outs from paper to use as
a stencil. Magritte's exposition of resemblance, and
concern with testing the world of appearances, led
to a preoccupation with surface pattern and artifice,
explored extensively through the illusionist device
of **trompe l'oeil**. *Pink Bells, Tattered Skies* 1930, for
example, constitutes a kind of decorative trompe
l'oeil diptych, a pictorial statement which displays
the dual elements of supposed reality and artificiality side by side, with neither demonstrating verac-
ity over the other. Other works play with similar
notions of illusionism, revelling in the depiction
of false materials such as wood-grain, marble and
wallpaper. As Calvocoressi points out, 'there are
plenty of occasions when Magritte reminds us of his
taste for trompe l'oeil decoration ... prompting him

to ask "Is it real or fake?" – a question which has little
meaning within the context of painting'.[125] **(DP)**

👁 See also: **Abstraction; Artifice; Collage; Commercial Art**

Roland Penrose (1900–1984) English artist and
collector. Penrose, together with Herbert Read and
David Gascoyne, was instrumental in introducing
Surrealism to Britain with the 1936 International
Surrealist Exhibition. As a collector, Penrose established an important collection of modern art and
with **E.L.T. Mesens** took over the **London Gallery**
in 1938, making it a showcase for Surrealism and
dedicating their inaugural show to Magritte. During
the late 1930s Penrose developed a new collage
technique, using picture **postcards** to create bands

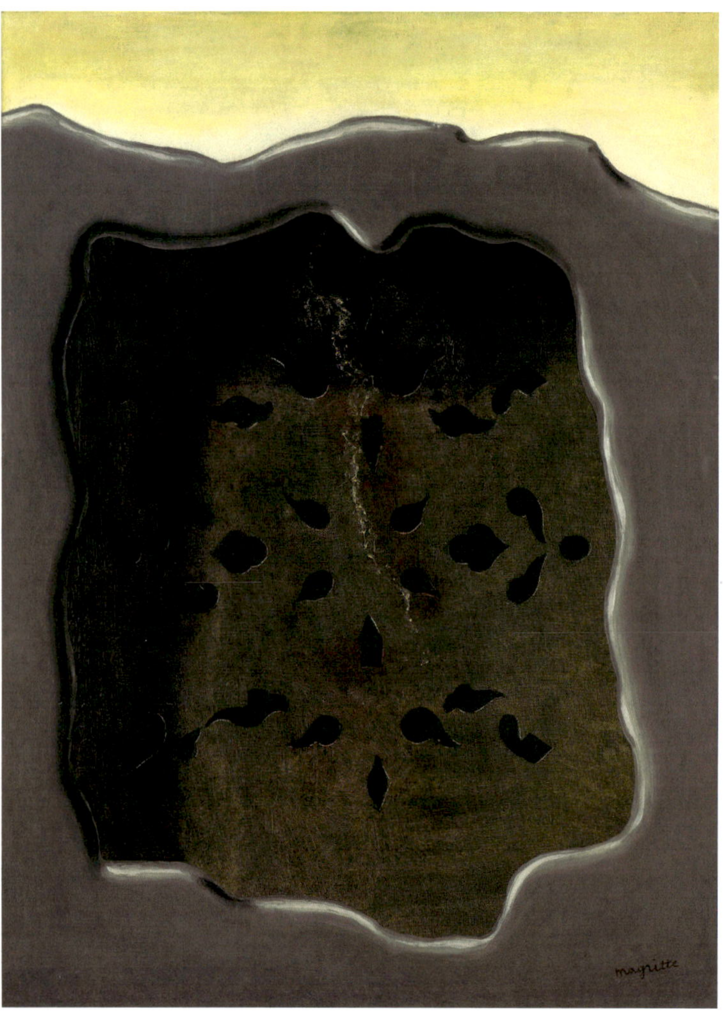

The Literal Meaning
Le Sens propre 1927, oil on canvas, 73 × 54 cm.
Private Collection, CR 194

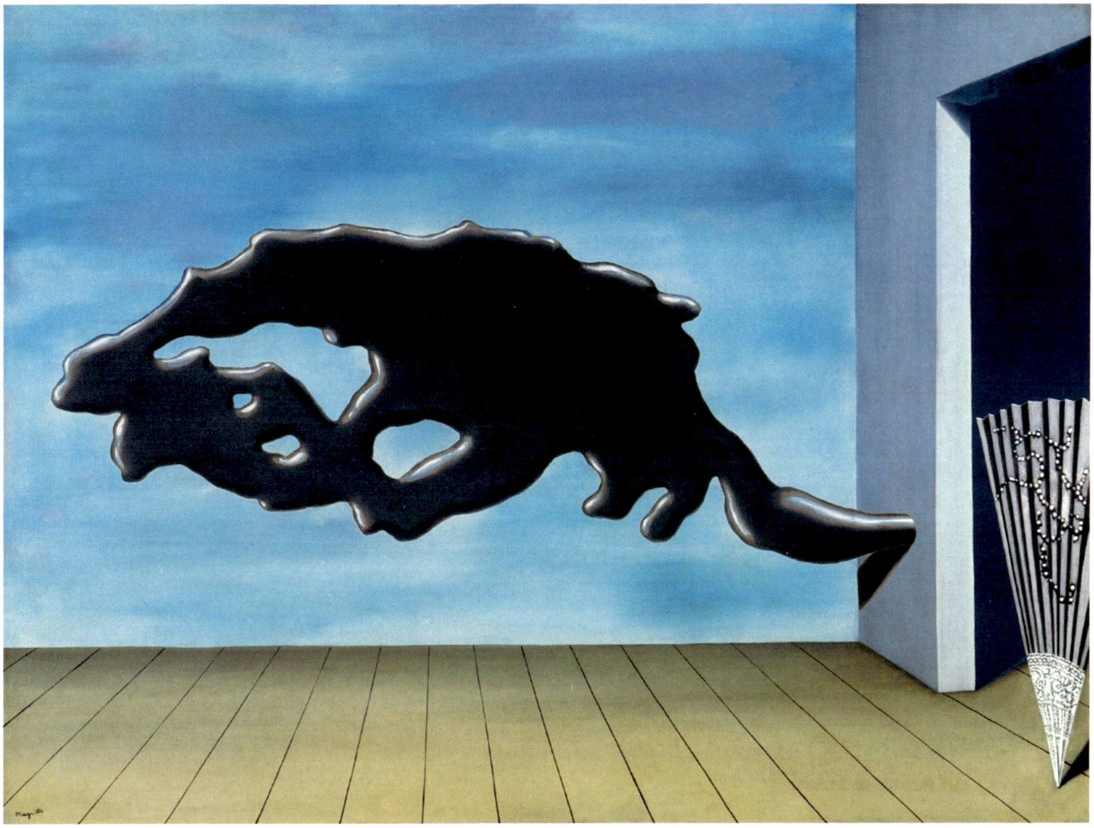

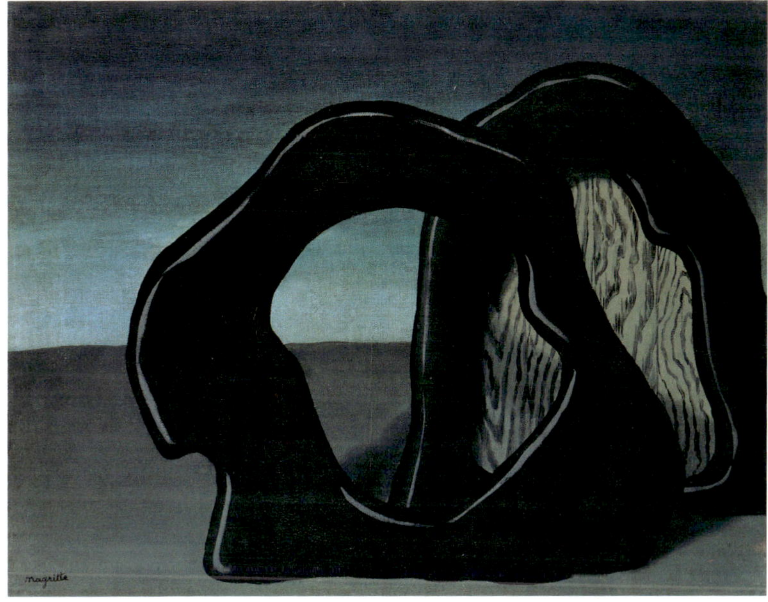

Let out of School
La Sortie de l'école 1927,
oil on canvas,
73 × 100 cm.
Private Collection,
Switzerland, CR 158

In the Face of Murmurs
En face des murmures 1927,
oil on canvas, 50 × 65 cm.
Private Collection, London,
CR 181

of **colour** in his artworks. Magritte collaborated with **Paul Nougé** on the essay *Colour–Colours, or an Experiment by Roland Penrose*, published in the *London Bulletin* in June 1939. The article roots the technique of collage in André Derain's *Le Chevalier X* 1914, a key image for Magritte that originally incorporated a real newspaper, thus effecting 'the union between two realities'.[126] What fascinates the writers in Penrose's technique is his focus on 'the *problem of colour*' and his use of '*the image of the objects to create colour*'. Their claim is that, in cutting up postcards and imposing some new 'structure' on the pieces, the image is transformed in its 'very nature'. Their conclusion is the interdependence of colour and structure, suggesting vast new possibilities for the medium. (**NM**)

See also: **Collage; England; Edward James**

Période: The journal *Période* was never published. Only the prospectus announcing its planned publication bears witness to its misfortune. In October 1924 **E.L.T. Mesens** set about establishing a journal in collaboration with Magritte, **Camille Goemans** and **Marcel Lecomte**. In response, **Paul Nougé** created a parody prospectus, which disconcerted Mesens and his collaborators to the extent that they put the publication of their planned journal on hold. Nougé took advantage of the situation, attracting Lecomte and Goemans to the task of the **Correspondance** tracts which appeared from November 1924. It was not until six months later that Mesens and Magritte published **Œsophage** before joining the *Correspondance* trio on *Adieu à Marie*, thereby forming the nucleus of Surrealism in Belgium. (**XC**)

The Petrified Image: In 1950 Magritte began creating works on the theme of petrification. Exploring a range of subject matter, including living and mythical creatures, as well as still life and landscape compositions, they depict a world and individual elements within a world transformed into stone. Inherent in these images is the idea of transformation, relating them to earlier works concerned with processes of **metamorphosis**. In the petrified works, however, the process of transformation has been completed, creating a scenario fixed in stone. *The Haunted Castle* 1950, for example, depicts a lightning

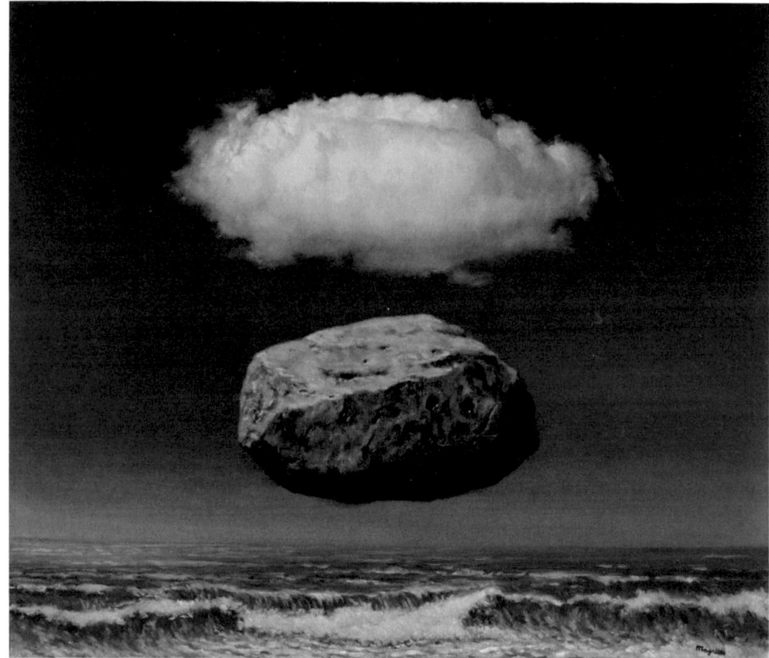

Clear Ideas
Les Idées claires 1955,
oil on canvas, 50 × 60 cm.
Private Collection, USA,
CR 885

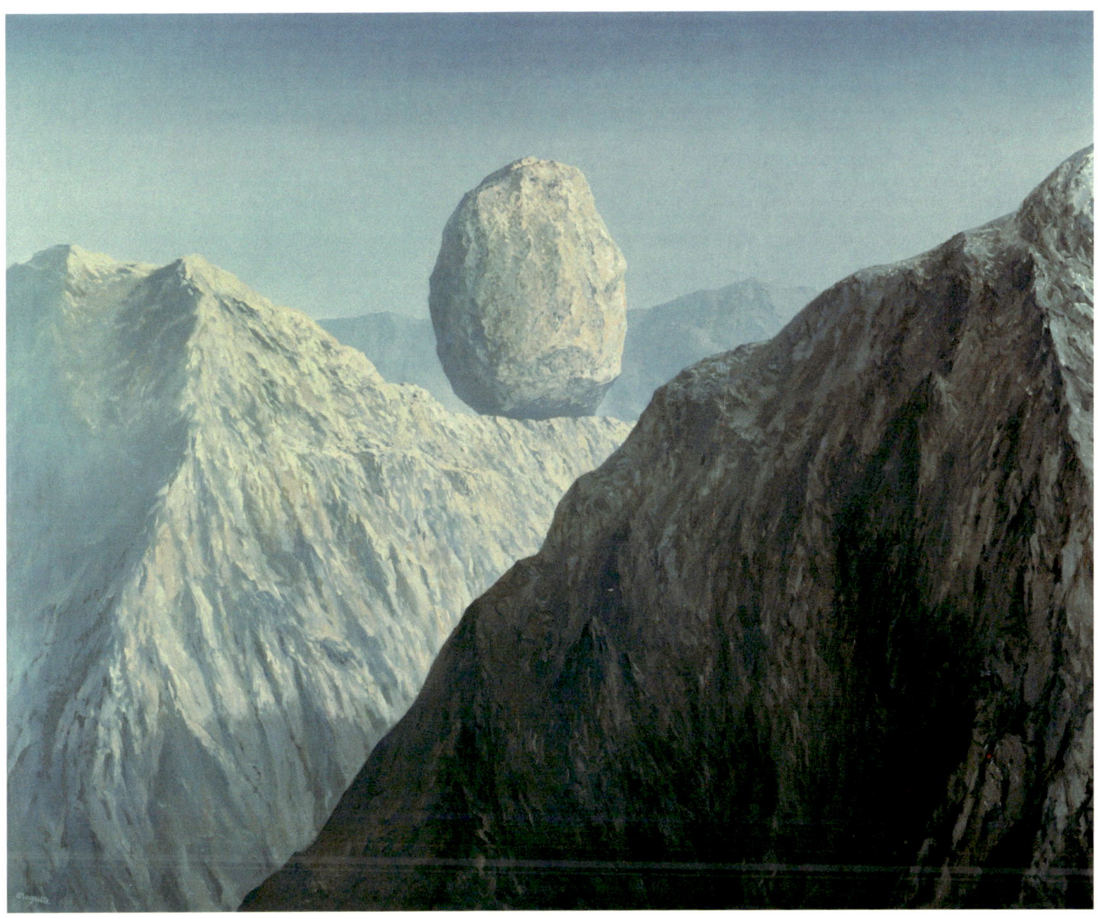

The Glass Key
La Clef de verre 1959, oil on canvas, 130 × 162 cm.
The Menil Collection, Houston, CR899

flash created from rock, the entire composition belonging to a material oneness. When describing this image Magritte alluded to cinematic imagery, stating 'on the screen, thanks to a simple trick effect, the spectator could see a really motionless flash of lightning in a tempestuous sky'.[127] In a similar vein *The Art of Conversation* 1950 belongs to a small series of works sharing the same title, each redolent of imagery from popular culture. The depiction of a pile of rocks arranged to form the word 'RÊVE' (dream) was likened by **David Sylvester** to the gigantic lettering of Hollywood film iconography, suggesting a further relationship to the series of commercial advertisements for Odol mouthwash, which were widespread across Europe in the early 1900s.

Many of the petrified paintings depict a solitary boulder, an object chosen by the artist because of its lack of allegorical or symbolic significance. Such neutrality – meaninglessness, even – is presented in *The Glass Key* 1959, an image of a boulder of seemingly monumental proportions balanced atop a mountain within a rocky wilderness. As with so many of his compositions, Magritte seems to have based the image on a real location, yet has selected an entirely nondescript locale in which to set his philosophical proposition. For Magritte, the boulder suspended in the air (*Clear Ideas* 1955) or balanced and dislocated from the effects of gravity enables us to have an 'active' and heightened conceptualisation of such phenomena. 'What is evoked is weight, not its laws …

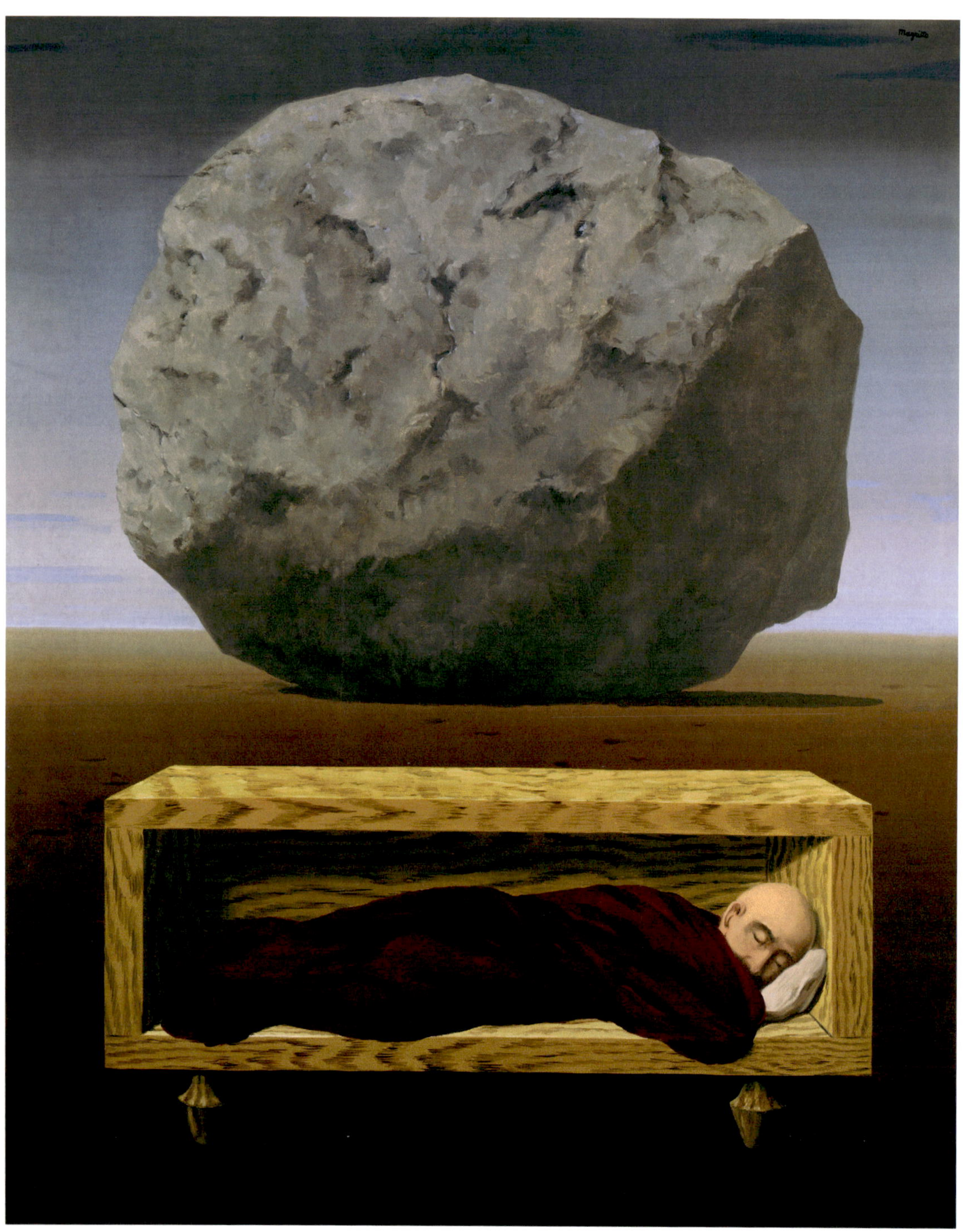

The Cape of Storms
Le Cap des tempêtes 1964, oil on canvas, 100 × 81 cm.
Koninklijk Museum voor Schone Kunsten, Antwerp, CR 992

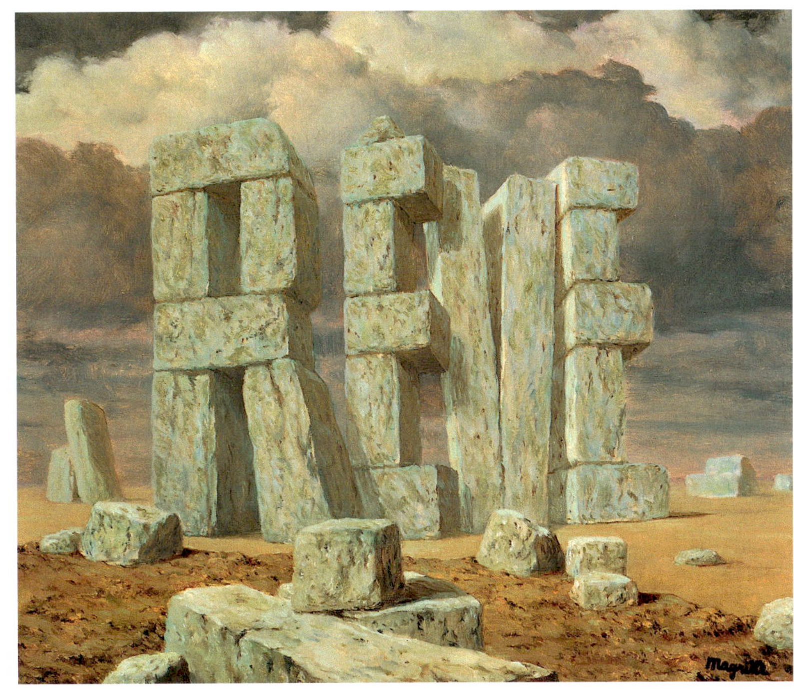

The Art of Conversation
L'Art de la conversation 1950,
oil on canvas, 50 × 60 cm.
New Orleans Museum of Art.
Gift of William H. Alexander,
CR 743

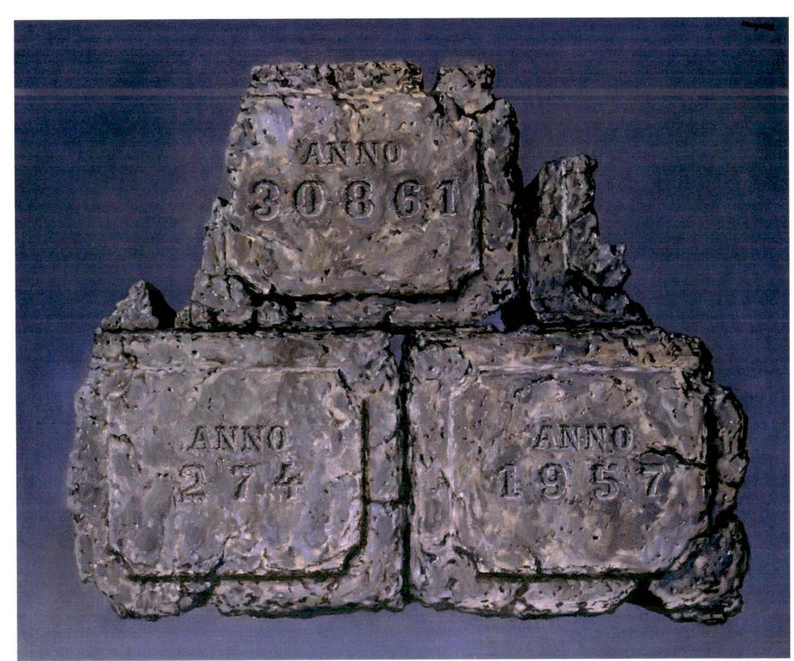

The Smile
Le Sourire 1951,
oil on canvas, 65 × 80 cm.
Private Collection, CR 762

the sensation, feeling, or idea of weight is enough for poetry.'[128] By creating such images – or 'material signs of freedom of thought' as he put it – Magritte was intent on making man responsible for the conceptualisation of the world in which he lives.[129] (DP)

See also: **Commercial Art; Object; Postcards**

Philosophy: Magritte regarded himself as neither an artist nor a philosopher, just as a 'man who thinks and who communicates his thoughts by means of painting'.[130] For him painting was an 'instrument to deepen our knowledge of the world'.[131] Magritte's

thinking touches on the expanses of Existential philosophy and his own theoretical interests were eclectic. In later life he read the work of René Descartes, Immanuel Kant, Georg Wilhelm Friedrich Hegel and **Martin Heidegger**, and he sought advice from philosophers such as Alphonse de Waelhens. However, his own engagement with philosophical problems was only ever poetic.

The question as to the relationship of the reality of concepts and names to the real **object**, posed by Magritte in 'La Ligne de vie' (1938), was discussed in Magritte's own time in the context of structural

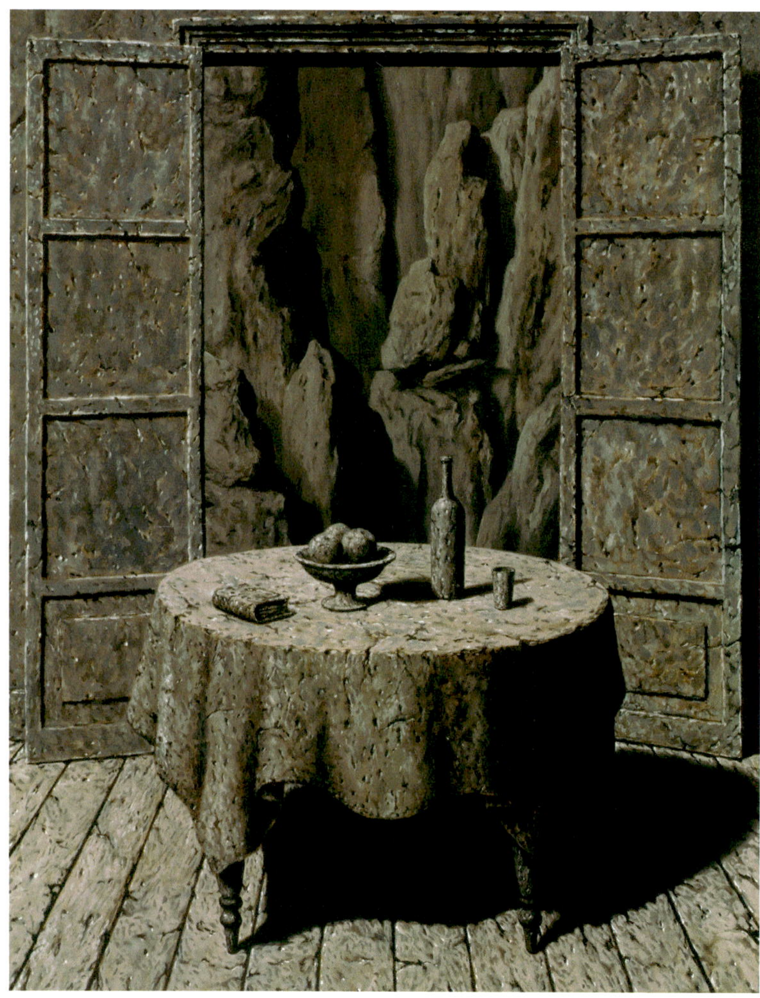

Memory of a Journey
Souvenir de voyage 1951,
oil on canvas, 80 × 65 cm.
Private Collection, New York,
CR 760

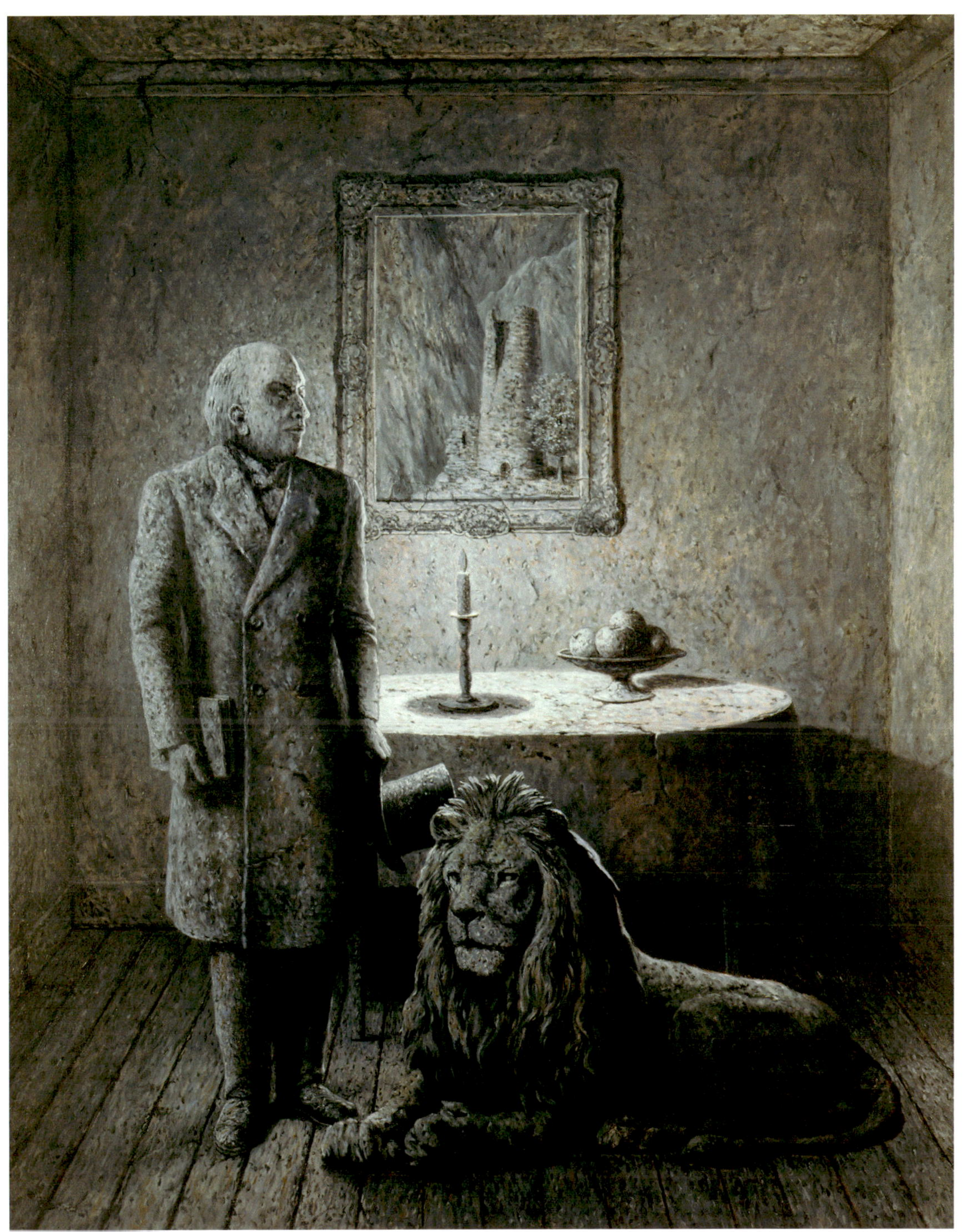

Memory of a Journey
Souvenir de voyage 1955, oil on canvas,
162 × 130 cm. The Museum of Modern Art,
New York. Gift of D. and J. de Menil, CR 827

linguistics by philosophers such as Charles Sanders Peirce, Ferdinand de Saussure and Ludwig Wittgenstein. Magritte drew on these debates in his own search for '**mystery**' – a concept of his own devising that in a sense approximated to the concept of 'existence' in the work of Heidegger. His endeavour to challenge our view of the world by unsettling our understanding of it echoes Descartes' methodological doubt. Hegel's dialectics provided him with another, equally creative tool.[132] The latter's concept of eternal 'becoming' corresponded with Magritte's own aim to change the world by means of 'dialectical movement'. Consequently his paintings find no solution to the mystery. 'We know nothing,' he stated, 'and that's heartening. Mystery allows hope and despair. Since it is question [sic] of the absolute, one may have hope.'[133] (**GF**)

Photography: Magritte's photographs were unseen in his lifetime. It was only in 1978 that a small volume containing 62 photos was published with the title ***The Fidelity of Images***; each photo was titled by Magritte's old companion **Louis Scutenaire** in the same way that he had previously assigned **titles** to many of his paintings.[134] From the start the status of the photographs was ambiguous. As Scutenaire noted with a gentle irony, the publication of these modest and private images was entirely due to Magritte's fame, but in fact many of the photos were not 'by' Magritte, but rather made collectively by the Belgian Surrealist group, with scenarios suggested and the camera operated by whoever happened to be present.[135] In fact, there seems to be a wide range of reasons why these photographs were made. Many seem to be snapshots recording a group of friends out for a walk or playing around at the beach, where they enact some perverse Surrealist rituals – eating bricks or posing on an empty plinth. At the other end of the spectrum are the photos that lie closest to Magritte's paintings. Sometimes, he was using the photograph as a visual aid for the painting, but more interesting are those images where he makes a photographic variation of a painting. *Attempting the Impossible* 1928 shows a painter in suit and tie standing before a nude woman whom he is bringing to life through his paint brush. In a photograph of the same year, which Scutenaire titled *Love*, René stands before **Georgette** making the same gesture. She is

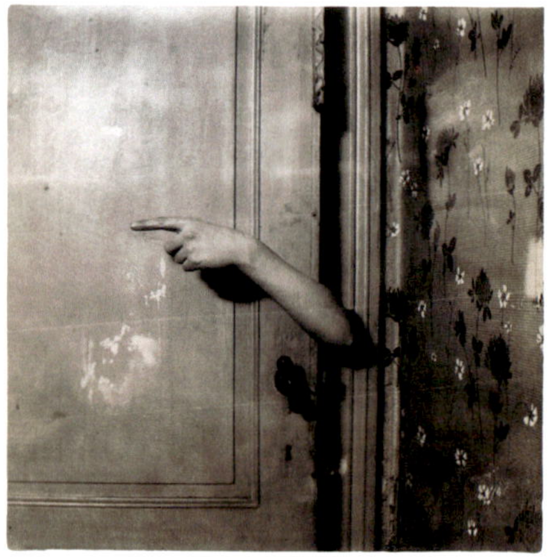

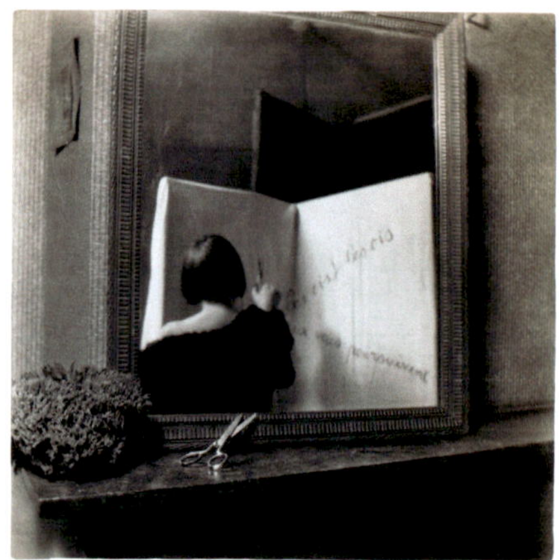

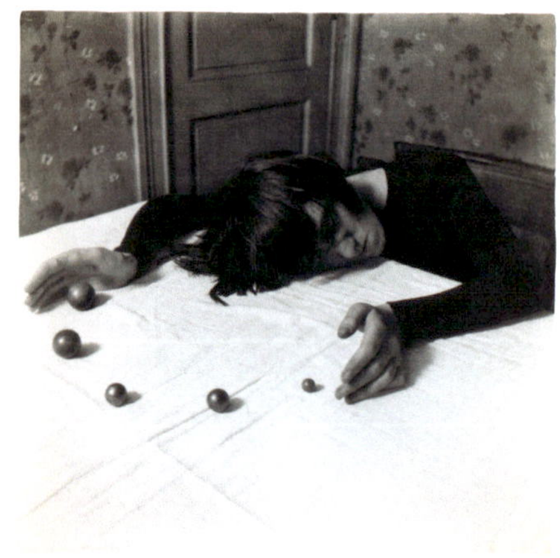

Paul Nougé (1895–1967): (top–bottom) *Le bras révélateur*, *...les oiseaux vous poursuivent* and *La jongleuse* from the series *Subversion des images* 1929–30, photographs, gelatin silver print from original negative, each 30 × 30 cm. Archives et Musée de la Littérature, Brussels

wearing a bathing costume; he is in shirt-sleeves and wearing his slippers.

These referential images in turn shade over into another sort of photograph, where Magritte seems to be investigating the properties of photography as much as he investigated the properties of painting. The most extraordinary of these images is *The Shadow and its Shadow* 1932. René and Georgette both stare into the camera, but he is behind her so that only one of his eyes is visible next to her ear.

It is an image that says much about the intimacy of their relationship. If this were real life, one could step sideways to see the other eye; if it were a painting, one would know that there was no other eye. But a photograph is both a slice of reality and a fixed, two-dimensional image and we are caught between what we see and what we know. This is also an ambiguous image in terms of authorship. Christine de Naeyer, in her study of **Paul Nougé** and photography, suggests that *The Shadow and its Shadow* was

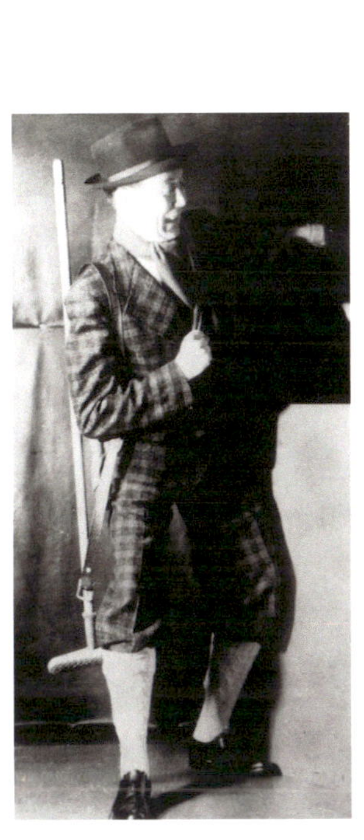

The Destroyer
Le Destructeur 1943, photograph, gelatin silver print, 40 × 19 cm. Private Collection

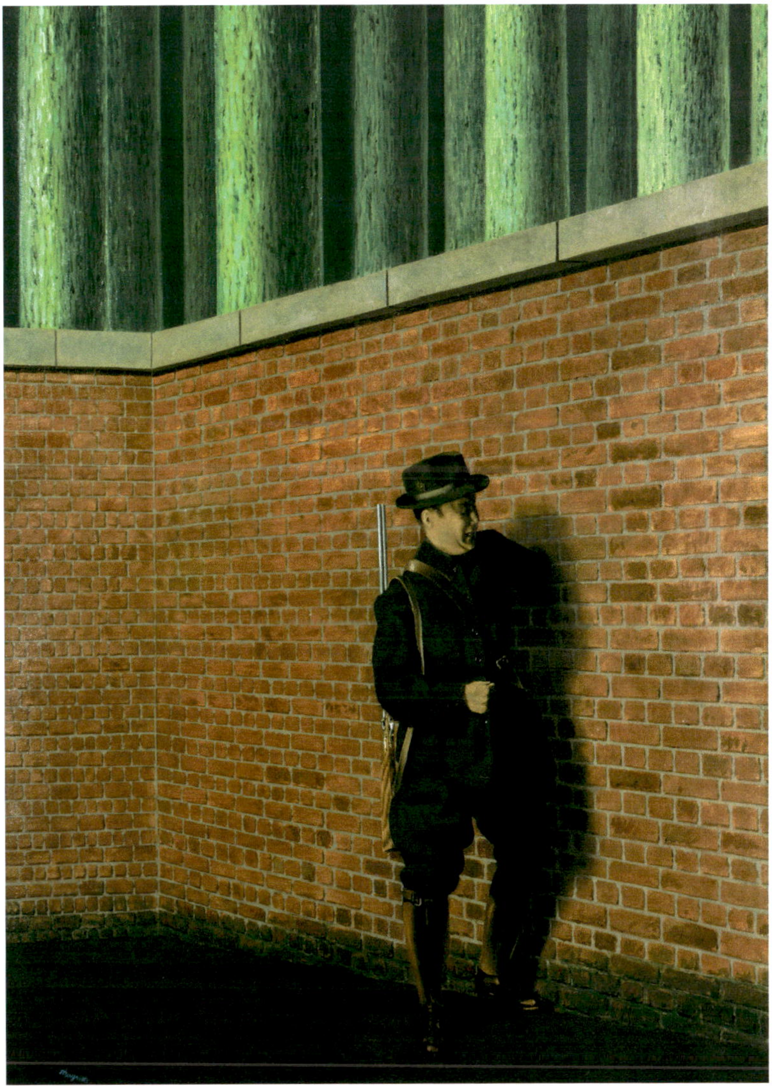

Universal Gravitation
La Gravitation universelle 1943, oil on canvas, 100 × 73 cm. Private Collection, CR 518

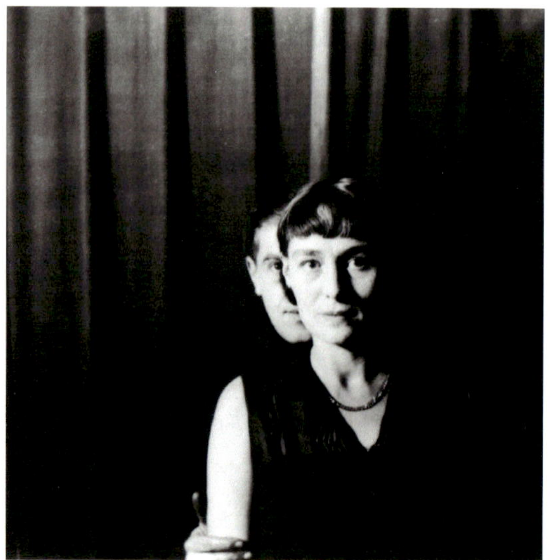

The Shadow and its Shadow
L'Ombre et son ombre 1932, photograph, gelatin silver print,
9 × 6.3 cm. Private Collection

made jointly by Magritte and Nougé.[136] Indeed, the rigorousness of the image is closer to the sequence of photographs that Nougé made in 1929 with the title *The Subversion of Images*.[137]

Finally, this play with photography is also a major feature of the later situations where Magritte worked in collaboration, actively or passively, with other photographers. In a book like Duane Michals' *A Visit with Magritte*, published in 1981, an elegant series of variations is played on Magrittean themes, Magritte lending himself to the project with (one suspects) an amused and appreciative forbearance.[138]

Magritte's photographs remain enigmatic, sometimes nudging at profundity but often rather charmingly banal. If we are overly familiar with the main body of Magritte's work, perhaps it is when we turn to some of his more peripheral productions – his scratchy **drawings**, his deadpan texts, the slapstick of the home movies and, not least, the photographs – that we get a fresher sense of Magritte's true subversiveness. (**IW**)

See also: **Film**

Francis Picabia (1879–1953) French Dadaist painter and writer. **E.L.T. Mesens** was introduced by Erik Satie into Dadaist circles in Paris and he and Magritte subsequently contributed to the October

1924 issue of Picabia's journal *391*. Under Picabia's influence they published **Œsophage** in 1925, followed by **Marie**, which on 8 July 1926 featured an image of Picabia's *Optophone*. Magritte would again contact Picabia in 1946. **David Sylvester** suggests he may have seen Picabia's **Kitsch** nudes based on magazines like *Paris Sex Appeal* – work that may well have influenced Magritte's **Vache Period** works and works such as *The Invention of Fire* 1946, in which a naked woman squats while a phallic **bilboquet** lurks behind.[139] (**NM**)

See also: **Dada**

Pipe: Perhaps Magritte's most emblematic 'banal object'. It made its first appearance in *The Treachery of Images* 1929, and was deployed extensively in his work throughout his career. *The Philosopher's Lamp* 1935, for example, depicts a man in profile, possibly Magritte himself, his nose morphing with the pipe. The pipe also appears as a visual element in his 'failed portraits', for example in *Good Faith* 1964–5, in which it partially obstructs the face of a bowler-hatted man. (**DP**)

See also: **Banality**; **Object**; *The Treachery of Images*

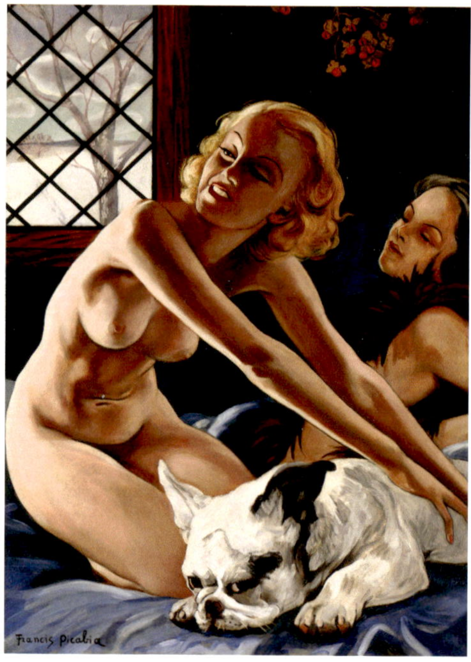

Francis Picabia (1879–1953): *Women with Bulldog*
(*Femmes au bull-dog*) 1941–2, oil on canvas, 106 × 76 cm.
Centre Georges Pompidou / Musée national d'Art moderne /
Centre de Création industrielle, Paris

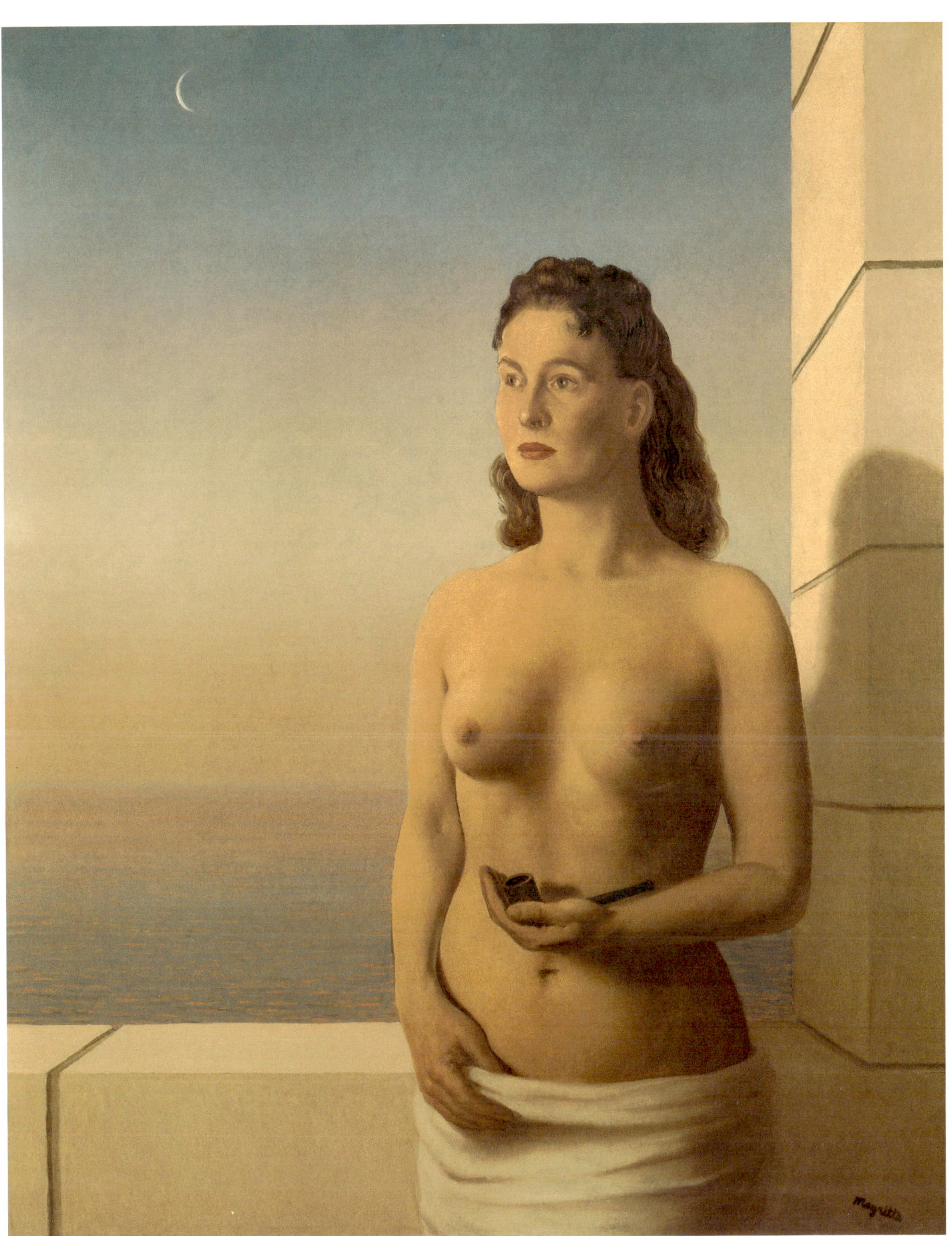

Freedom of Mind
La Liberté de l'esprit 1948, oil on canvas, 100 × 80 cm.
Collection Musée des Beaux-Arts de Charleroi, CR 667

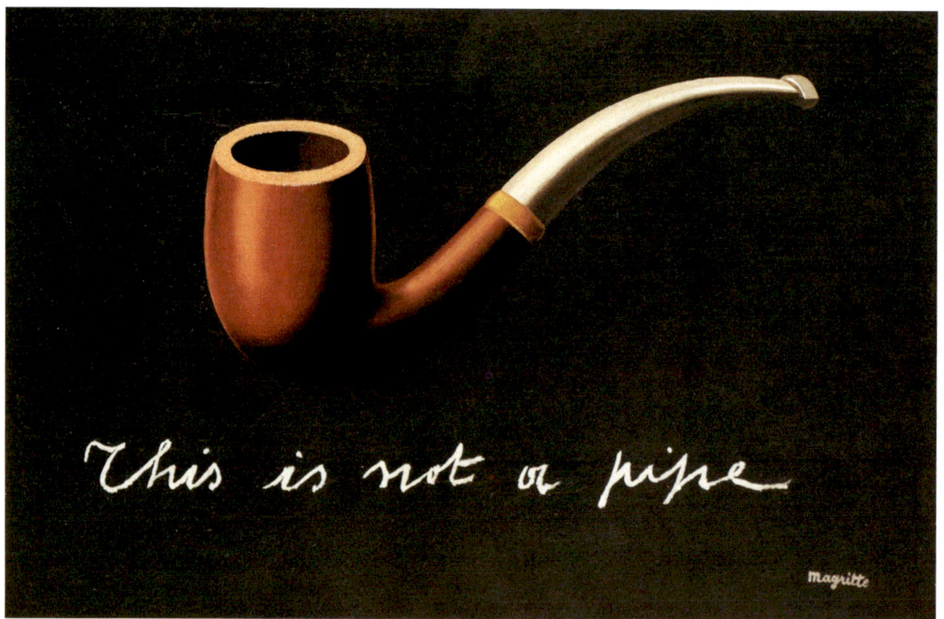

The Treachery of Images
La Trahison des images 1935, oil on canvas, 27 × 41 cm.
Private Collection, CR 369

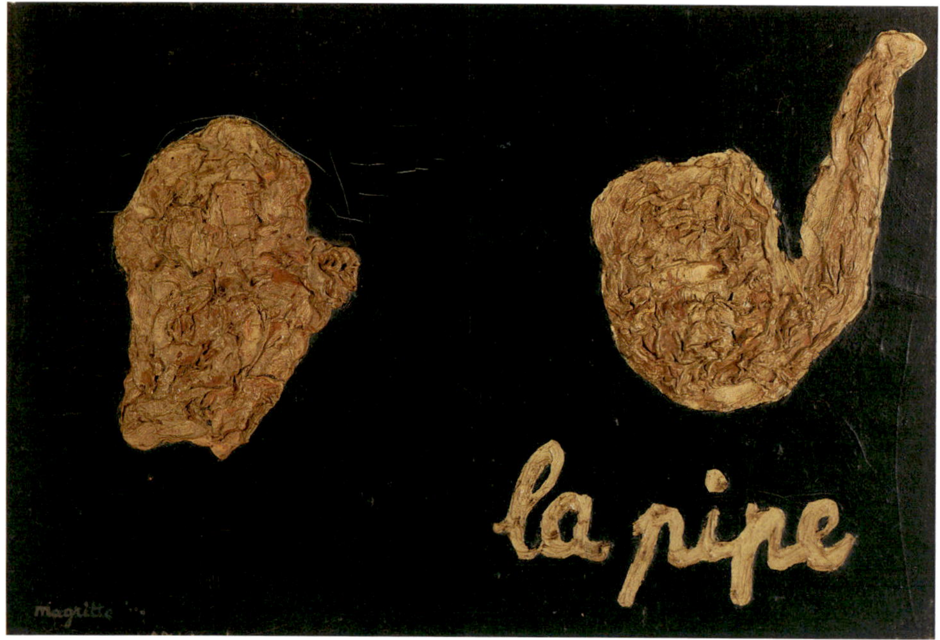

Biomorphs with Words (The Pipe)
Sans titre (La Pipe) 1928, oil on canvas, 27 × 41 cm.
Collection Sylvio Perlstein, Antwerp, CR 279

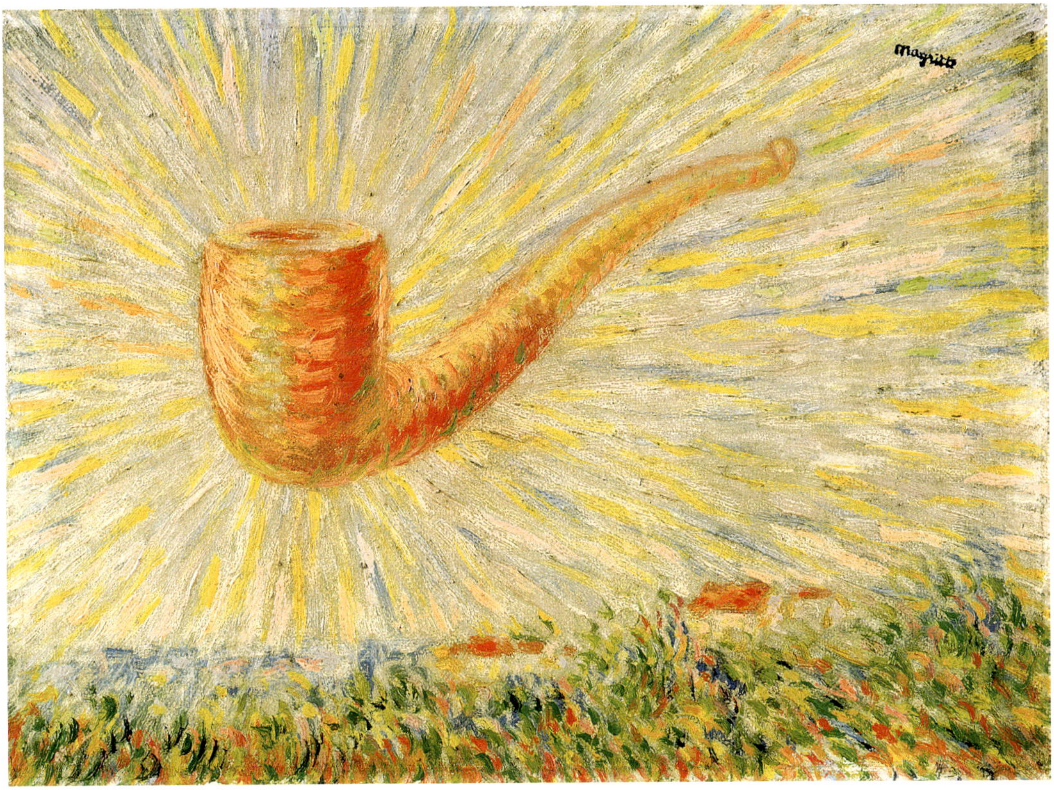

The Freedom of Worship
La Liberté des cultes 1946, oil on board, 24 × 33 cm.
Private Collection, courtesy Galerie 1900–2000, Paris, CR 605

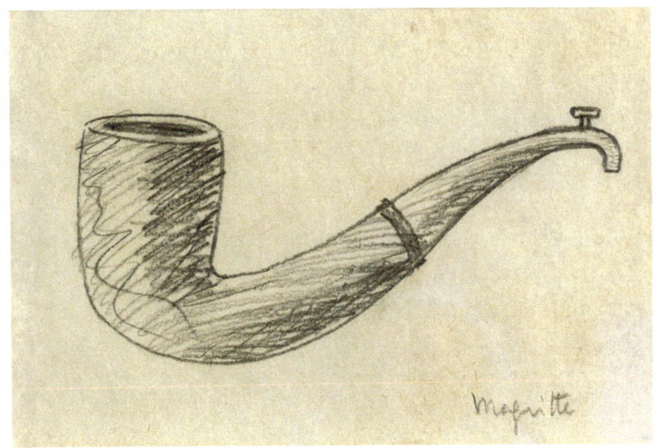

Untitled (Pipe)
1944, pencil on paper, 8 × 11 cm. Private Collection, USA

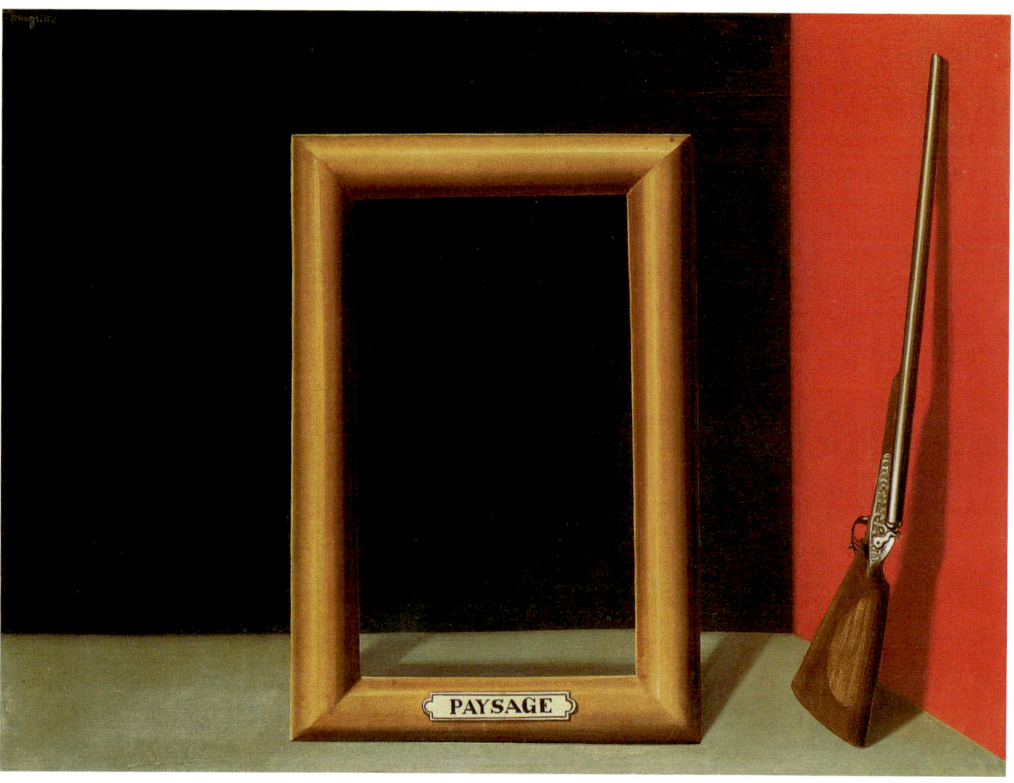

The Delights of Landscape
Les Charmes du paysage 1928, oil on canvas, 54 × 73 cm.
Private Collection, London, CR 273

Pleasure: In Magritte's early work, pleasure – which he in part derived from his interest in the unknown and the unfathomable – was often conflated with a sense of **shock**, for example in the macabre-eroticism of *The Menaced Assassin* 1927, or the voracity of the young girl devouring a bird in *Pleasure* 1927. A more explicit engagement with pleasure underpinned Magritte's **Renoir Period** which began in 1943 and lasted until 1947. At this time, as a reaction to the pessimism that prevailed immediately following **World War II**, Magritte devised his concept of 'Sunlit Surrealism' in which he declared that pleasure should be the guiding principle for life and art, and a reason to face the world with open minds and heightened perceptions. He declared that 'pleasure and charm must be our aims, because our desire for the extraordinary cannot be satisfied by our present world, which has nothing more to offer than the sad spectacle of ruins and foolish anxieties'.[140] Magritte's passionate plea for a 'more intense life of pleasure' by avoiding unpleasure echoes **Freud's** 'pleasure principle' (*Beyond the Pleasure Principle* 1921). Freud's theory of sublimation can similarly find correspondence with Magritte's interest in transformation and **metamorphosis**. (GF)

See also: **Eroticism; Fetish**

Edgar Allan Poe (1809–1849) American writer, poet and literary critic. Edgar Allan Poe was a favourite figure of the **Surrealists**, and particularly of Magritte. Magritte borrowed Poe's titles for his paintings, for example *The Fall of the House of Usher* 1949, *The Imp of the Perverse* 1927, *Bérénice* 1948, and *The Domain of Arnheim* 1938 and its variations. A copy of Poe's *The Narrative of Arthur Gordon Pym of Nantucket* 1838 appears on the mantelpiece in *Not to be Reproduced* 1937. Magritte's theoretical and painterly engagements with **absence** and nothingness drew on Poe's texts. *The Perfect Image* 1928 and *The Delights of Landscape* 1928, showing **frames** 'framing' void and absence, evoke Poe's line in *The Pit and the Pendulum*: 'It was not that I feared to look upon things horrible, but that I grew aghast lest there should be *nothing* to see.' (PA)

Poetry: There is a sense in which Magritte could have expressed his ideas just as well through poetry as through painting. His collaborations and close friendship with poets such as **Louis Scutenaire**, **Paul Éluard** and **Jacques Wergifosse**, and admiration for the work of **Charles Baudelaire** and Stephane Mallarmé and others testify to his belief in the potency of written **language**.[141] Effective poetry, he felt, was derived from reality, 'absolutely *that which is thought*', rather than from anything imaginary.[142] He regarded poetry as something that intervened in the flux and negotiation of everyday life. 'When I gaze at a starry night,' he wrote in 1963, 'I find among the other aspects of this spectacle a "poetry" of the stars.'[143] Summoned forth at certain moments through cognition, it constituted a '*description* of absolute thought'. As such, it corresponded and coincided with his belief about the poetic truth expressed in his own painting. Magritte also was commissioned to produce illustrations for books of poetry, and his 1932 painting *The Giantess* incorporates a poetic text by **Paul Nougé**, which is rendered 'anonymous' by being signed 'Charles Baudelaire'. The artist also titled works after poems, including *Sentimental Conversation* 1945, which derives from a poem by Paul Verlaine. (DP/GF)

See also: **Book Illustration; Titles**

Portraiture: While Magritte disavowed traditional modes of portrait representation – which he once referred to as 'total portraits' – he engaged with two sometimes overlapping modes of figurative imaging which relate in different ways to the genre of portraiture. The first and most conventional is a series of largely commissioned paintings of family members, friends, patrons or collectors. These, though purged of the welter of particularising detail and 'meaningless information' associated with a 'total' image, are clearly recognisable as portraits of individuals or family groups.[144] Magritte occasionally painted portraits between the early 1920s and the end of the decade, including of his wife **Georgette** (1923 and 1926) and in 1928 his then patron **Paul-Gustave Van Hecke**, but produced very few between the late 1920s and 1935. His commissioned portraits commenced in earnest in the mid-1930s and developed roughly in proportion to the artist's increasing reputation – and fame – in the last two decades of his career. That the artist was not uniformly sympathetic to the necessity of accepting commissions nor to some of the wealthy patrons who handed them out is clear from a letter he wrote in 1956 in which he admits that he 'obeys' with some reluctance 'their idiotic caprice that I paint their portraits'.[145]

Almost all the commissioned portraits share a number of traits, tending to reduce background detail to a minimum, for instance a wall or abstracted landscape, whilst in the portraits of Georgette, **Jacqueline Nonkels** and Lou Cosyn from 1944 the background is reduced to the facture of circumambient paint marks themselves. Another trait is to position the head or figure in apposition to a range of specific or familiar **objects**, whilst some works offer one or more forms of discrepancy in the formal adjudication of the head or body – such as doubling or inversion – or in the provision of a normative context. In general, however, the portraits affirm the social legibility of their subject(s).

The Pleasure Principle 1937, 'a picture representing a man whose head is a light', as Magritte wrote to **Edward James** in June 1937, is of special importance in the genealogy of Magritte's so-called failed portraits. Magritte notes that a preliminary version of the work was 'done very quickly' for an exhibition in the Netherlands, but that 'the real picture as I envisage it is still to be painted'. What Magritte notes next – in the future conditional – is of crucial importance for the concept of the *portrait manqué* (**Paul Colinet**), as the artist attempts to convert an image that was not in fact conceived as a specific portrait into a kind of commission in advance, a painting that actively sought an identity for its defacialised 'sitter' *post factum* by reattaching itself to a commissioning subject (James himself) who had not yet offered any commission. 'Since it would be intended for you,' Magritte wrote, 'do you not think your person could be recognisable in it as well?'[146]

The second aspect of Magritte's address to the body and the face can be seen, then, in works that

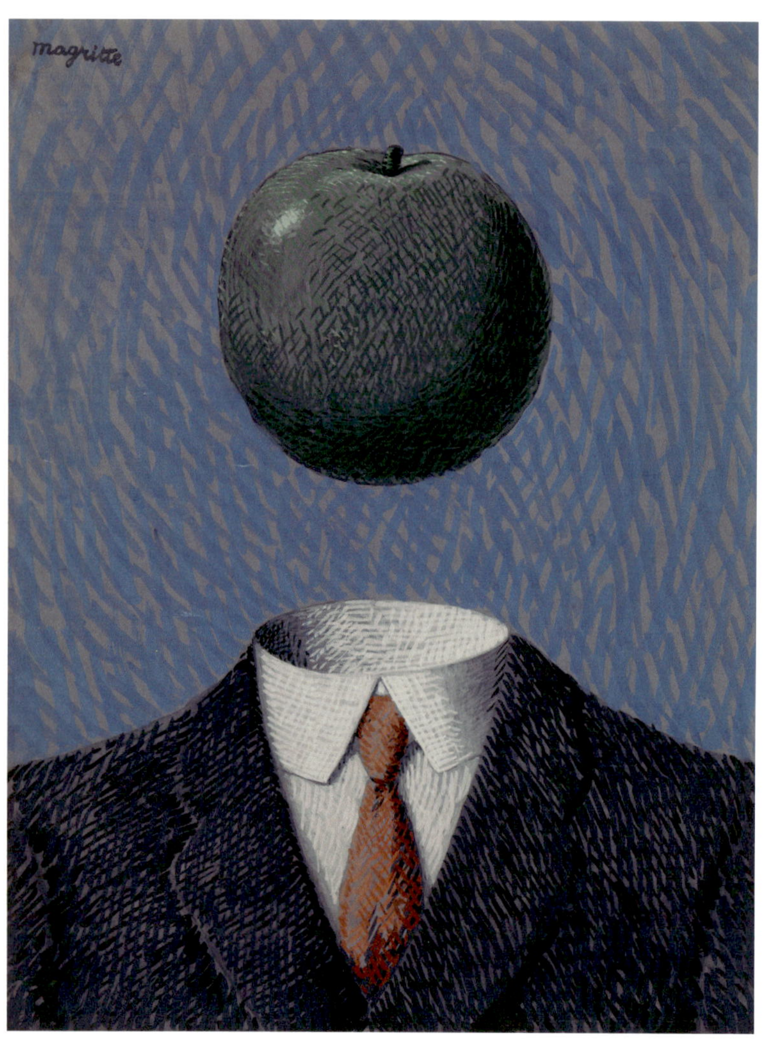

The Idea
L'Idée 1967, gouache on paper, 38.5 × 29.5 cm.
Private Collection, CR 1593

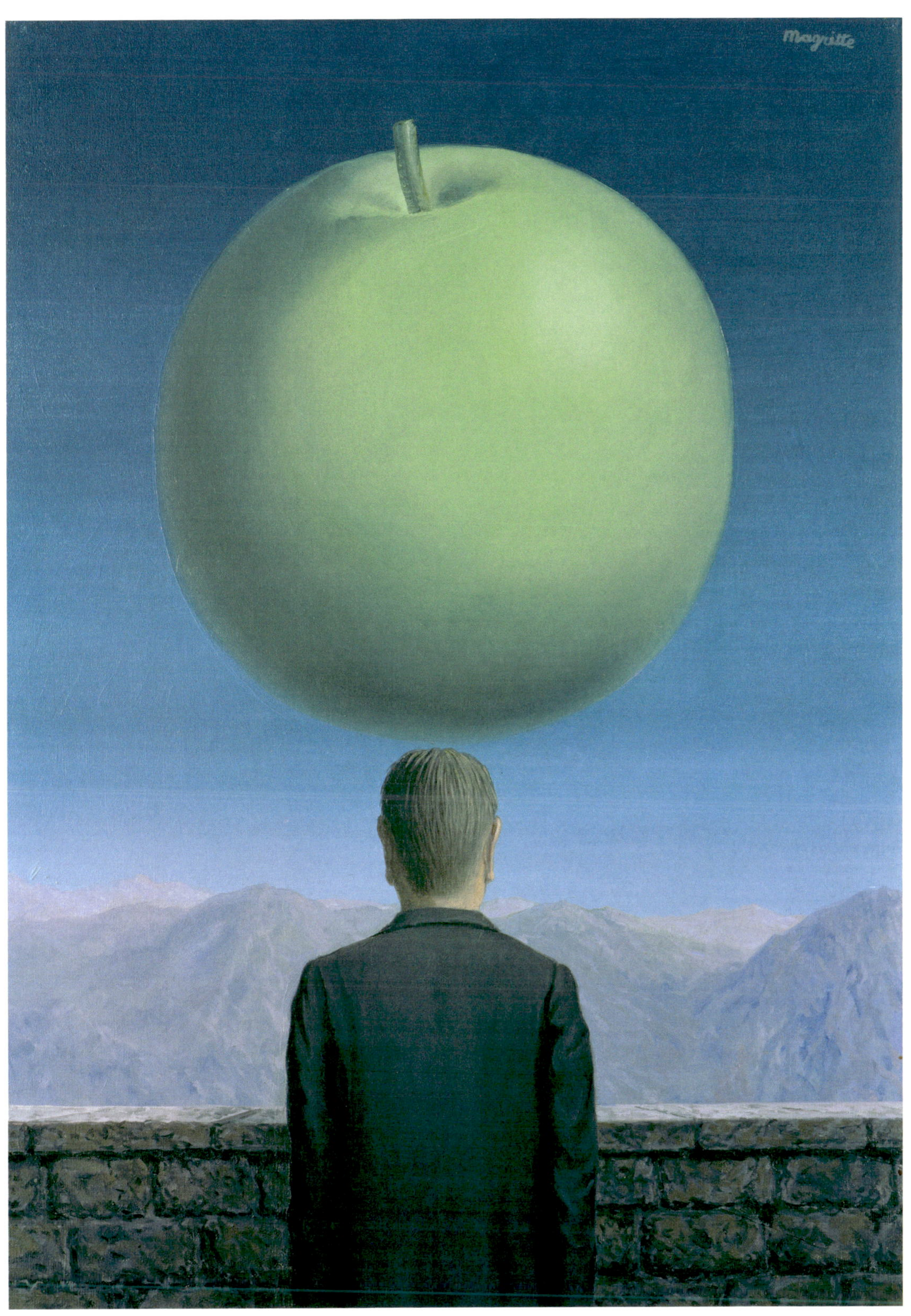

The Picture Postcard
La Carte postale 1960, oil on canvas,
70 × 50 cm. Private Collection, CR 921

are not specified as portraits, but in which the figure is considered as one object or pictorial zone within a wider field of other objects and locations. With these images the artist participates in the multiple trajectories of a general logic of effacement that underwrites much avant-garde art in the late nineteenth and early twentieth centuries, ranging from **Francis Picabia's** dissident portraiture of machine-diagrams to the counter-human abstractions of the *pittura metafisica* of **Giorgio de Chirico** and his followers which were so important to Magritte in the mid-1920s. In contrast to most of the commissioned portraits, one of the governing modes of facial representation in this group of works is offered in a negative economy, so that faces are covered over by cloths, for instance in *The Central Story* 1928, or masked or blurred into other forms or patterns. In some portraits the face is blocked out by various objects, for instance an apple in *The Son of Man* 1964, a painting in *The Liberator* 1947, while in others it is eradicated altogether – a process that appears to commence in *Moderne* 1923.[147]

These obfuscations of the face were applied by Magritte to many different forms of investigation, including the question of visibility and invisibility and what the artist termed 'the eternal struggle between the gaze and objects'. In an interview with Otto Hahn in November 1964, in which he discussed *The Great War* 1964, for example, Magritte asserted that he painted 'only the visible' and that 'it would be wrong therefore to look for the invisible'. In *The Great War*, he continued, 'you can see a man with a face, which is something visible. You can also see an apple which is itself visible. However, there comes a time when one visible prevents you seeing another visible.'[148] But gestures of erasure and the eclipse of visibility were met in Magritte's figure-based work by an equally powerful current of dissident facial reconstitution, including a sequence of works that re-conjugate one or more of the facial elements, the most disturbing example being the jolting reconfiguration of a face as a naked female torso in *The Rape* 1934 and its variants. (**JW**)

See also: **Absence; Double; Representation and Resemblance**

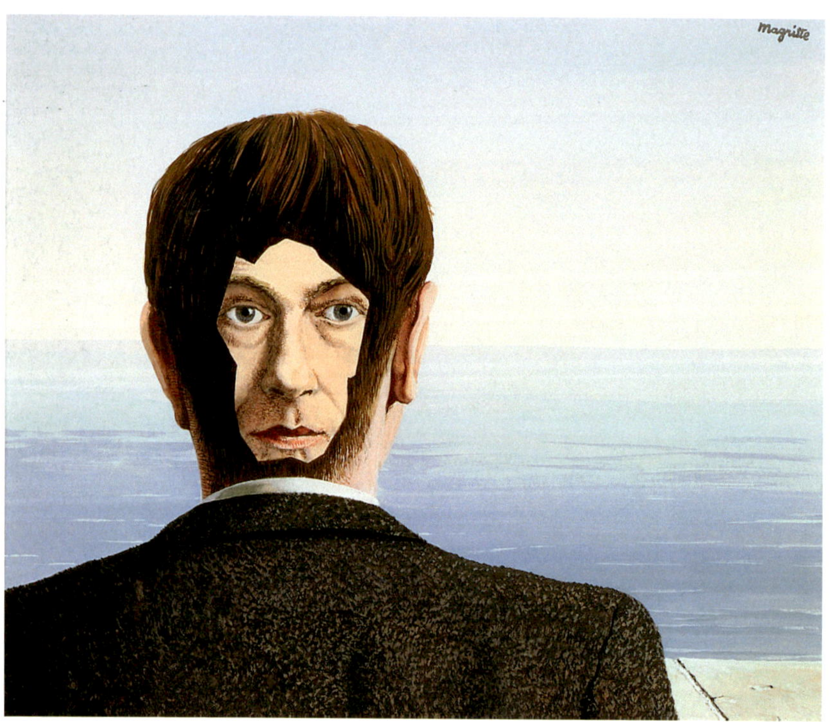

The Glass House
La Maison de verre 1939, gouache on paper, 32.3 × 38.6 cm.
Museum Boijmans Van Beuningen, Rotterdam, CR 1158

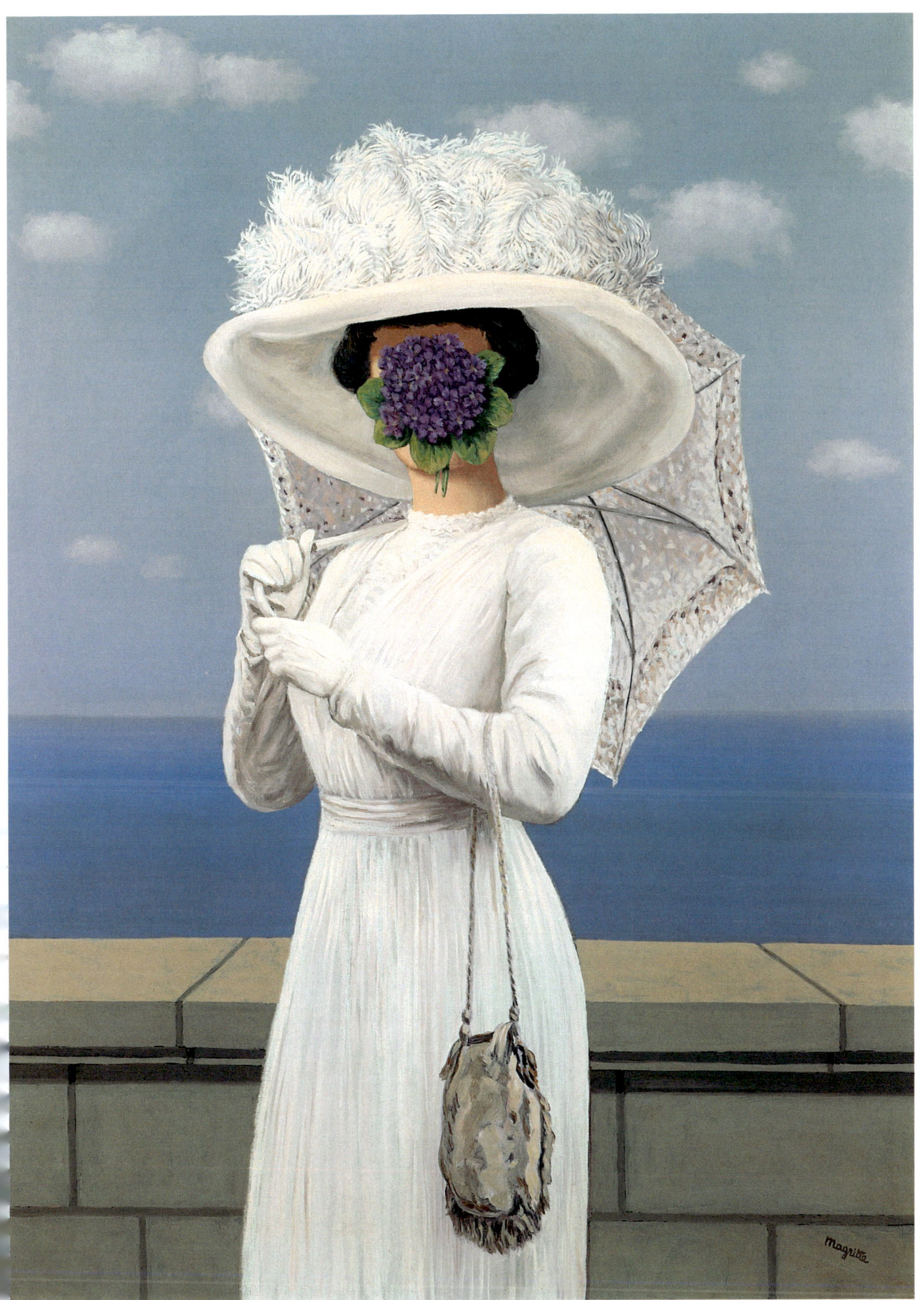

The Great War
La Grande Guerre 1964, oil on canvas,
81 × 60 cm. Private Collection, CR 1001

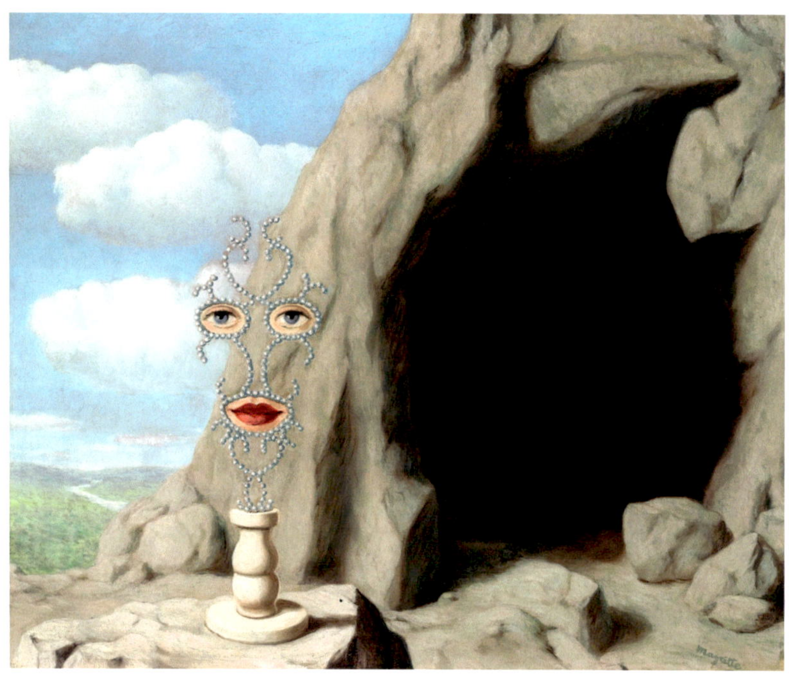

High-level Meetings
Les Grands Rendez-Vous
1947, oil on canvas,
54 × 65 cm.
Collection Leslee and
David Rogath, CR 631

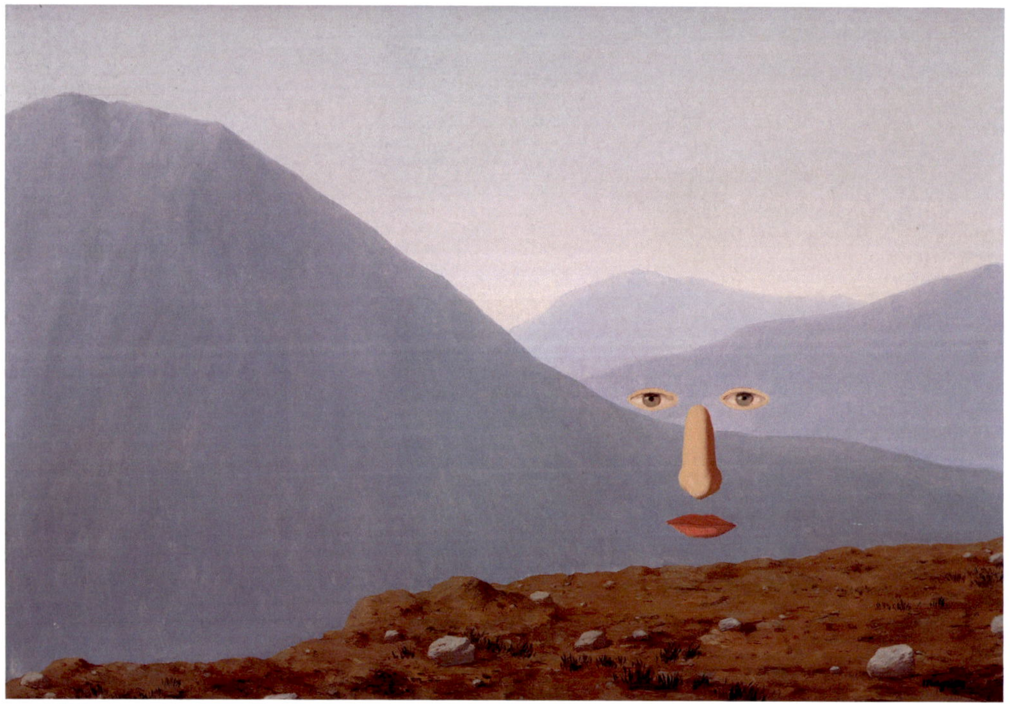

Every Day
Tous les jours 1966, oil on canvas, 50 × 73 cm.
Isidore Ducasse Fine Arts, CR 1052

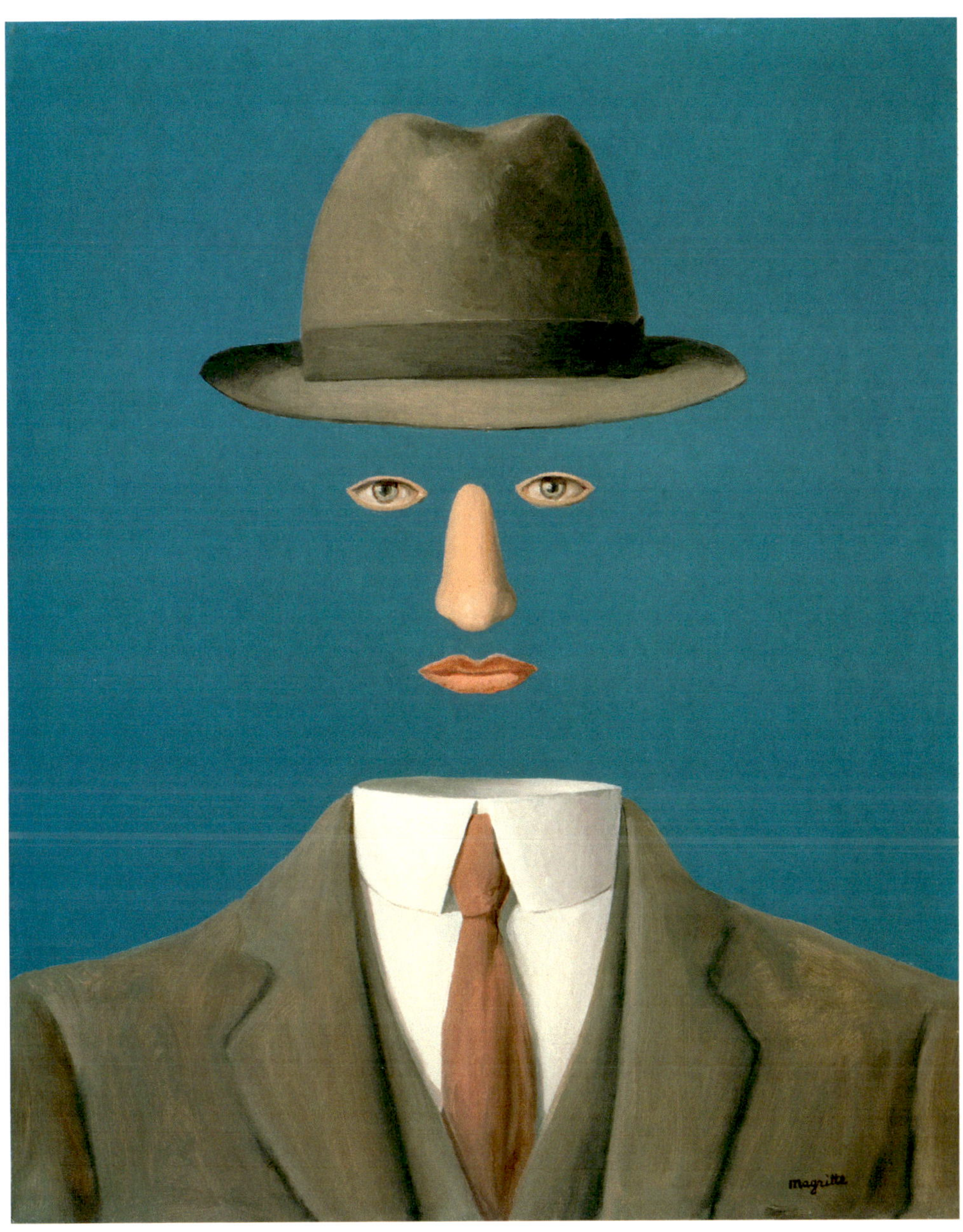

Baucis's Landscape
Le Paysage de Baucis 1966, oil on canvas, 55 × 45 cm.
The Menil Collection, Houston, CR 1032

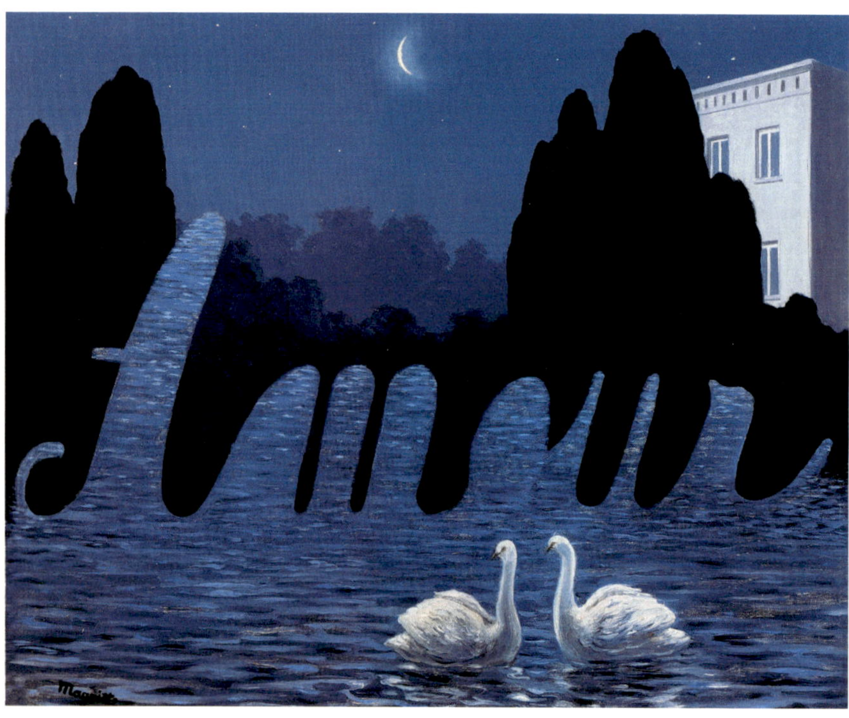

The Art of Conversation
L'Art de la conversation 1950, oil on canvas, 50 × 60 cm. Private Collection, CR 744

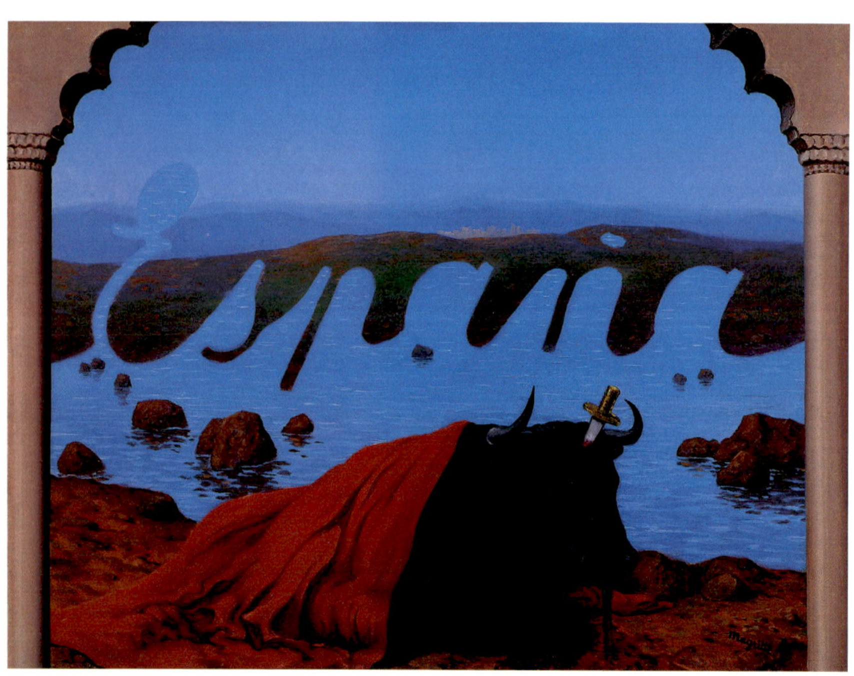

The Art of Conversation
L'Art de la conversation 1950, oil on canvas, 50 × 65 cm. Collection de la Communauté française de Belgique, CR 745

Postcards: The postcard crops up in Magritte's oeuvre in many guises. It occurs as the title of a painting from 1960 and a range of Magritte's paintings created in 1928 that reproduce scenes or elements of scenes from picture postcards, such as *The Subjugated Reader*, *The Lovers* and *The Spy*. Other works draw on the aesthetics of postcards, in particular *The Art of Conversation* 1950, which evokes a scene from a holiday postcard. Magritte's interest in postcards ties in with his painterly exploration and use of reproductions such as photographs, images from encyclopaedias, film scenes, posters and book covers. As Magritte states: 'I have seen the Uffizi in Florence, not bad, but it looks better on postcards.'[149] He was attracted to the postcard's ability, as a form of mass-reproduced image, to subvert and challenge conventional, bourgeois notions of the uniqueness of the artwork and the originality of the artist. It is a symbol of endlessly reproducible ephemerality, and of modern technologies of communication that imply a publicly readable discourse rather than the private communication implicit in the sealed letter.

Magritte's interest in postcards connects with a wider Surrealist concern with the medium. The Brussels Surrealists published *La Carte d'après nature*, a review founded in 1952 and edited by Magritte, which was mostly produced in the format of postcards; Georges Hugnet's series *La carte surréaliste* 1937, to which Magritte contributed, consists of twenty-one postcards featuring artworks by the Surrealists, and **Roland Penrose** made collages with holiday postcards. These works are discussed in an article by Magritte and **Paul Nougé** entitled *Colour–Colours*.[150] (**PA**)

👁 See also: **Appropriation**; **Commercial Art**; **Letters**

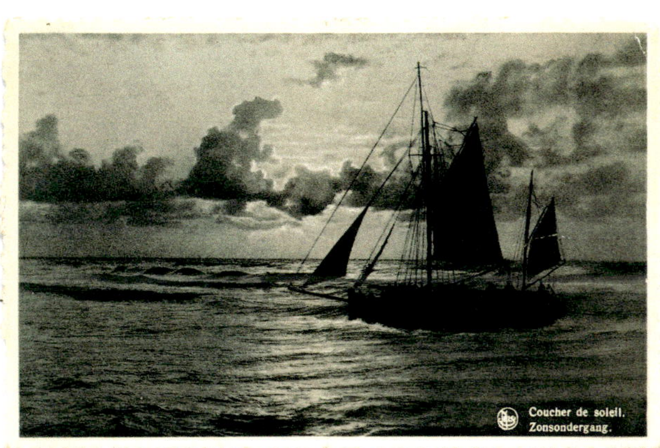

Postcard from René Magritte to Marcel Mariën 20 June 1953, Private Collection, courtesy Keitelman Gallery

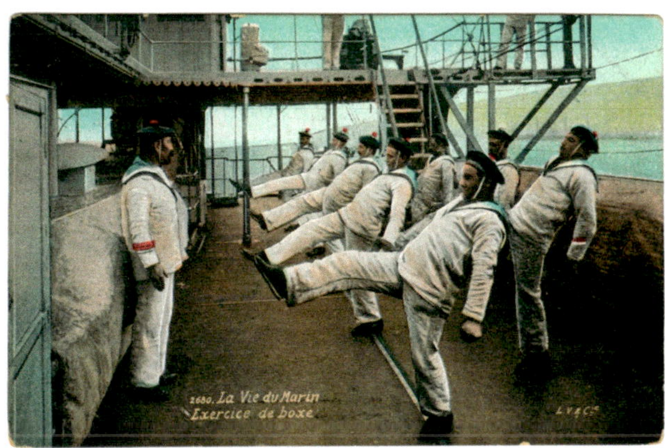

Postcard from René and Georgette Magritte to Marcel Mariën 27 April 1949, Private Collection, courtesy Keitelman Gallery

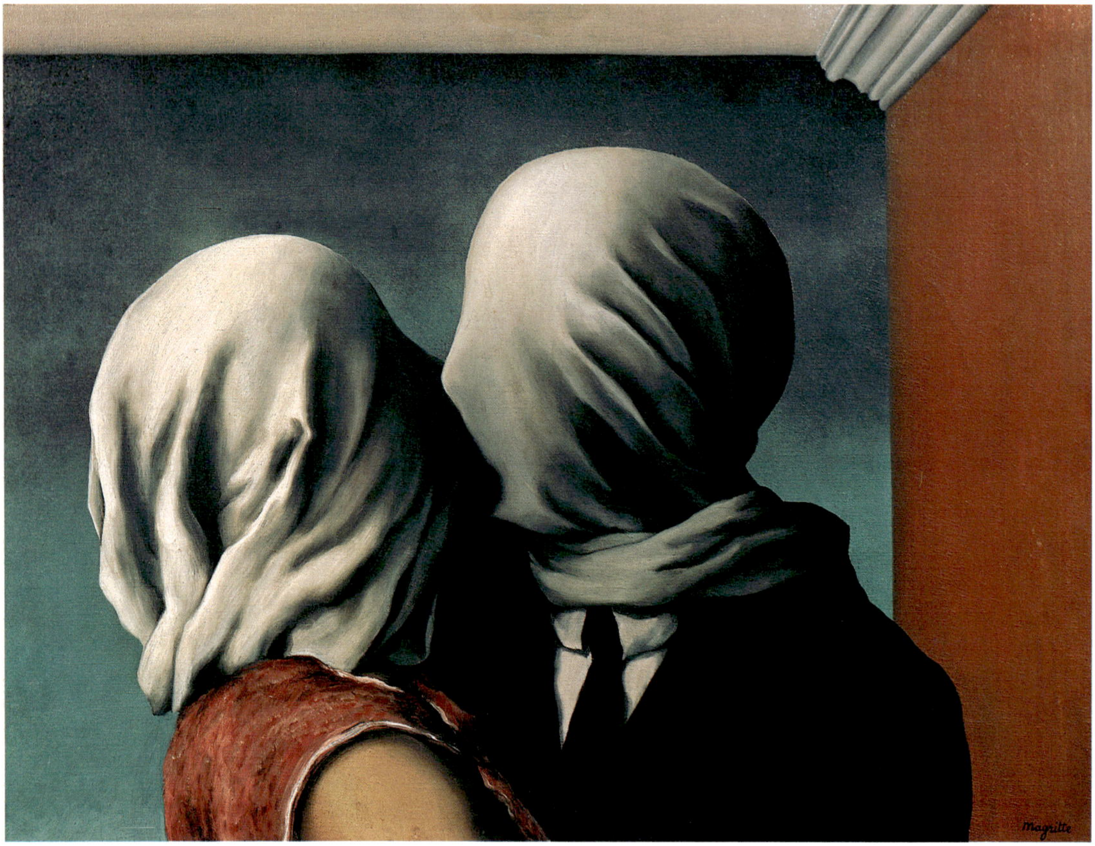

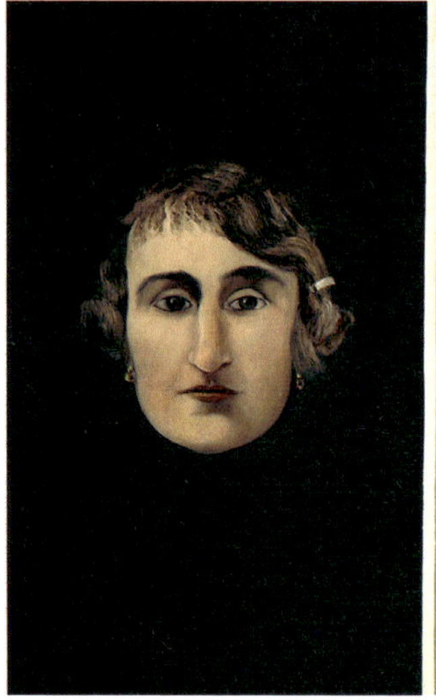

The Lovers
Les Amants 1928, oil on canvas,
54 × 73 cm. The Museum of
Modern Art, New York. Gift of
Richard S. Zeisler, CR 250

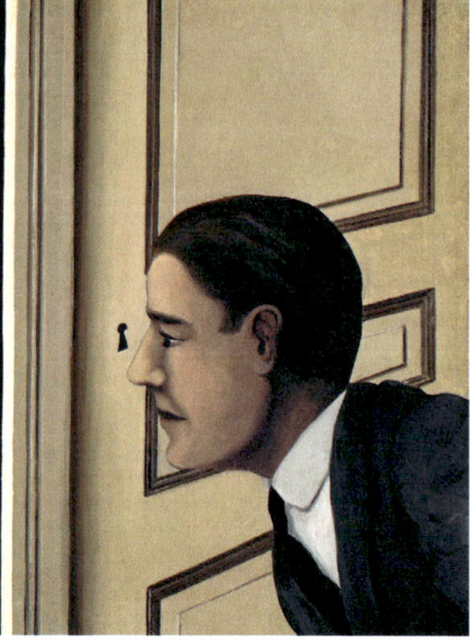

The Spy
L'Espion 1928, oil on canvas,
54 × 73 cm. Private Collection,
CR 215

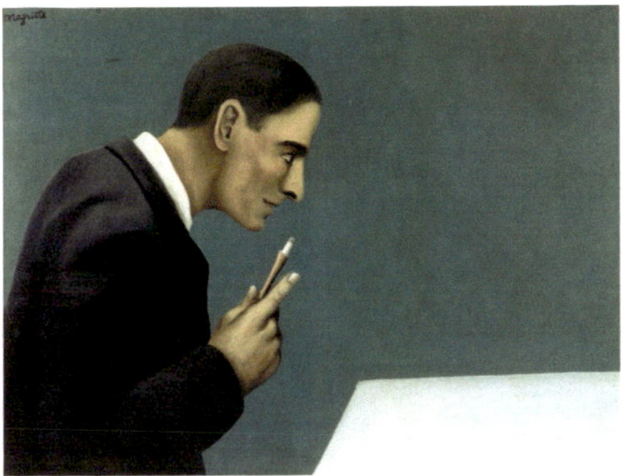

Figure Brooding on Madness
Personnage méditant sur la folie 1928, oil on canvas, 54 × 73 cm.
Royal Museums of Fine Arts of Belgium, Brussels, CR 283

Psychoanalysis: Founded by **Sigmund Freud**, psychoanalysis describes the analysis of the unconscious through the interpretation of **dreams** and verbal slips and through the use of free association. Whereas **André Breton** had been introduced early on to the work of Freud, through his wartime medical training, Magritte always showed antipathy towards psychoanalysis, arguing that 'no sensible person believes that psychoanalysis could shed light upon the mystery of the world'.[151] In 1928, though, whilst in Paris, Magritte produced a series of images that seem to evoke psychopathological states. In *The Dark Suspicion* 1928, a man stares obsessively at his open palm, anticipating a similar scene in Luis Buñuel and **Salvador Dalí's** *Un Chien andalou* of the following year. **Shock** verging on hysteria is suggested by the open-mouthed reader in *The Subjugated Reader* 1928, while hallucination is suggested by Magritte's *Figure Brooding on Madness* 1928, as a man intently examines some invisible object. It was also in 1928 that Dalí, with whom the Magrittes stayed at Cadaqués in the summer of 1929, began to develop his own theory of 'Paranoid-Critical Activity' on the model of paranoia. Magritte's images also anticipate the celebrated simulations of more extreme mental states of 'The Possessions' contained in Breton and **Paul Éluard's** *The Immaculate Conception* 1930. (**NM**)

See also: **Automatism and Automatic Writing**

R

Renoir Period: In 1943, during the occupation of Belgium, Magritte felt the desire to produce artworks which would evoke pleasure and charm. 'Since the beginning of this war,' he wrote, 'I have had a strong desire to achieve a new poetic effectiveness … I leave to others the business of causing anxiety and terror and mixing everything up as before.'[152] Magritte was referring to a new style in his paintings of the time, which drew on the Impressionists, and specifically on the style and imagery of Pierre-Auguste Renoir. The Renoir period emerged from Magritte seeing a reproduction of Renoir's *The Bathers* c.1918–9 which inspired the artist to paint *Treatise on Light* 1943. Magritte's Renoir works can be interpreted as a covert expression of loyalty to French cultural traditions during the Nazi occupation of France and Belgium. The Impressionists were deemed 'degenerate artists' alongside the Surrealists and other Modernist avant-gardes, by the Nazis.

Magritte's art dealer **Alexandre Iolas** was dismayed by this new style, asking Magritte 'not to break with the mysterious, poetic quality of your former pictures, which by their compact technique were much more Magritte than those in which the Renoiresque technique and colouring strike everyone as outmoded. Outmoded is really not the word I should use … I should say rather "less Magritte-like".'[153] Magritte's Renoir period finished in 1947. (PA)

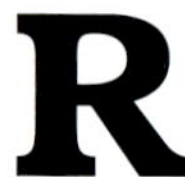 **See also: Colour; Kitsch; Pleasure; World War II**

Repetition and the Encounter: Throughout Magritte's oeuvre can be found sustained engagement with ideas of repetition in visual and conceptual terms. Repetition can be seen in Magritte's creation of multiple painted variations based on a single image or theme, for example the 27 versions of **The Dominion of Light** created between the late 1940s and the early 1960s, and in his use of multiplied and standardised imagery, such as the **bilboquet** motif. Repetition of a single visual element features

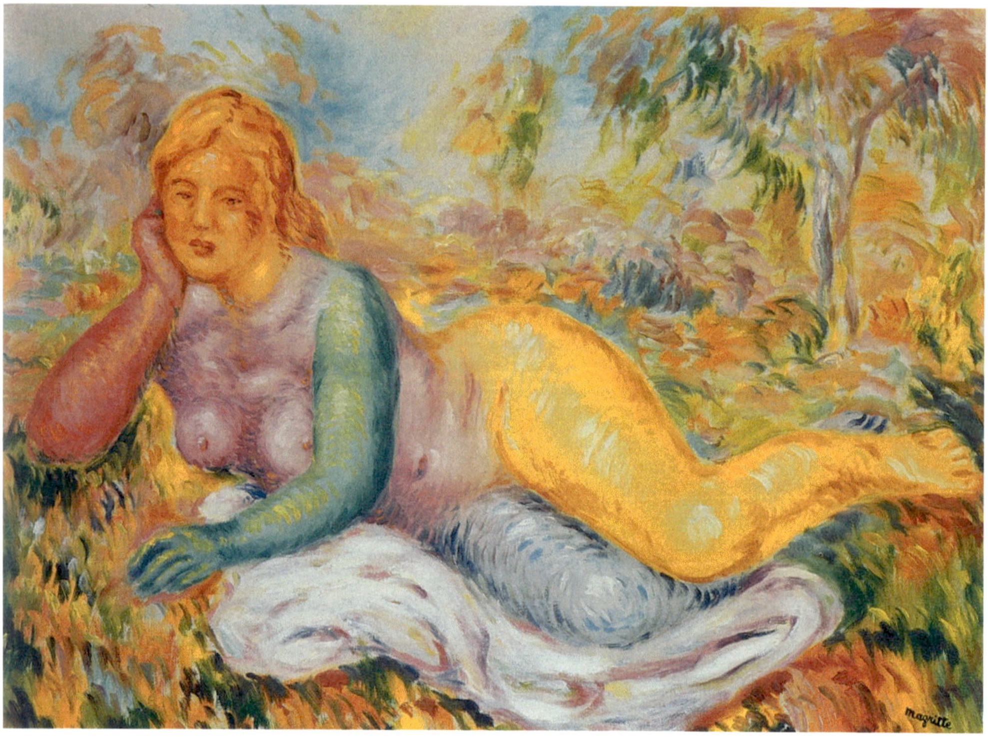

Treatise on Light
Le Traité de la lumière 1943, oil on canvas, 55 × 75.5 cm.
Whereabouts unknown, CR 521

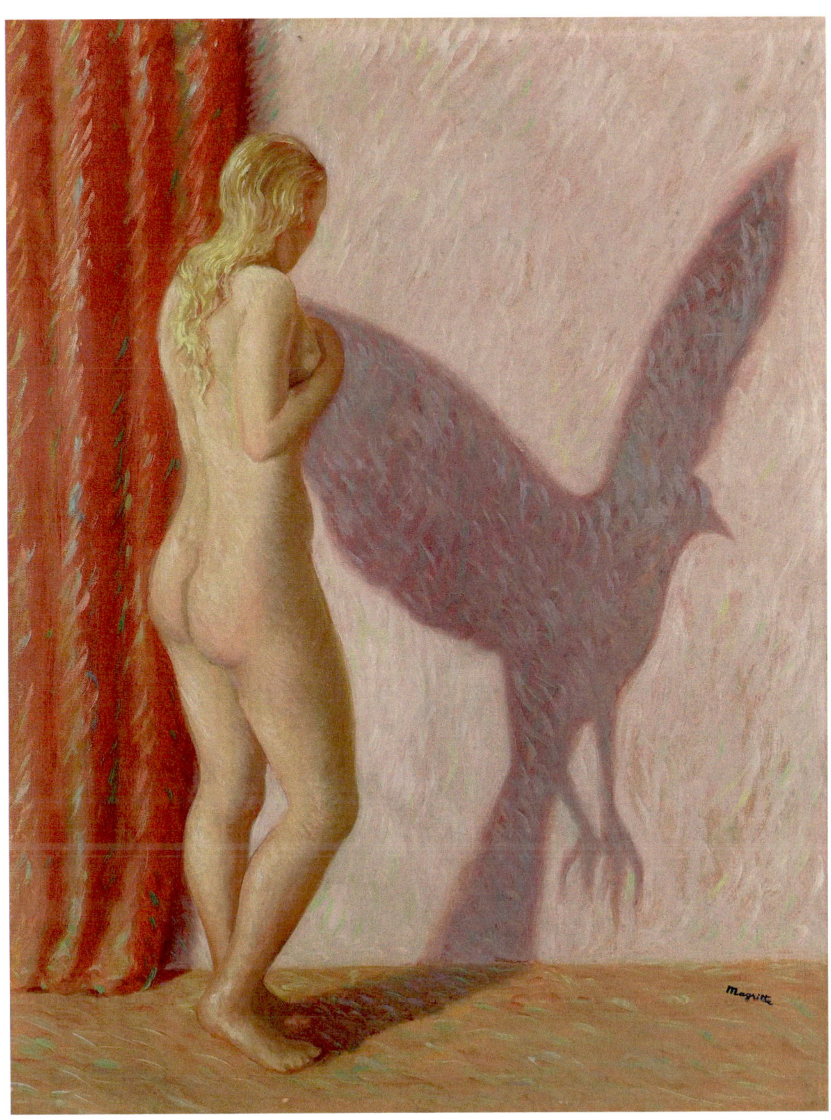

The Uncertainty Principle
Le Principe d'incertitude 1944, oil on canvas, 65 × 50 cm.
Collection Mr and Mrs Wilbur Ross, CR 557

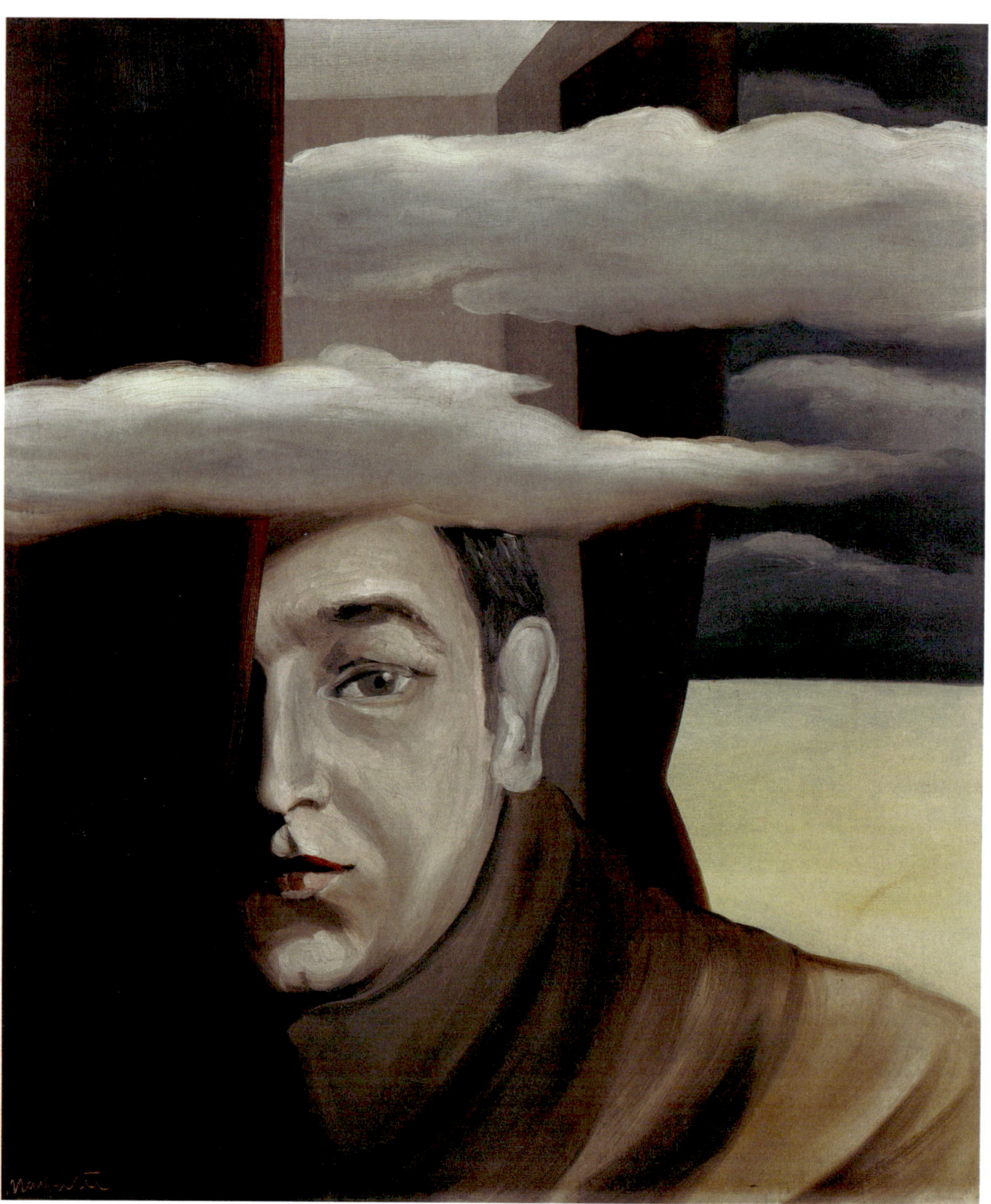

Portrait of Paul Max
Portrait de Paul Max 1926, oil on canvas, 75 × 65 cm.
Private Collection, courtesy Keitelman Gallery, CR 109

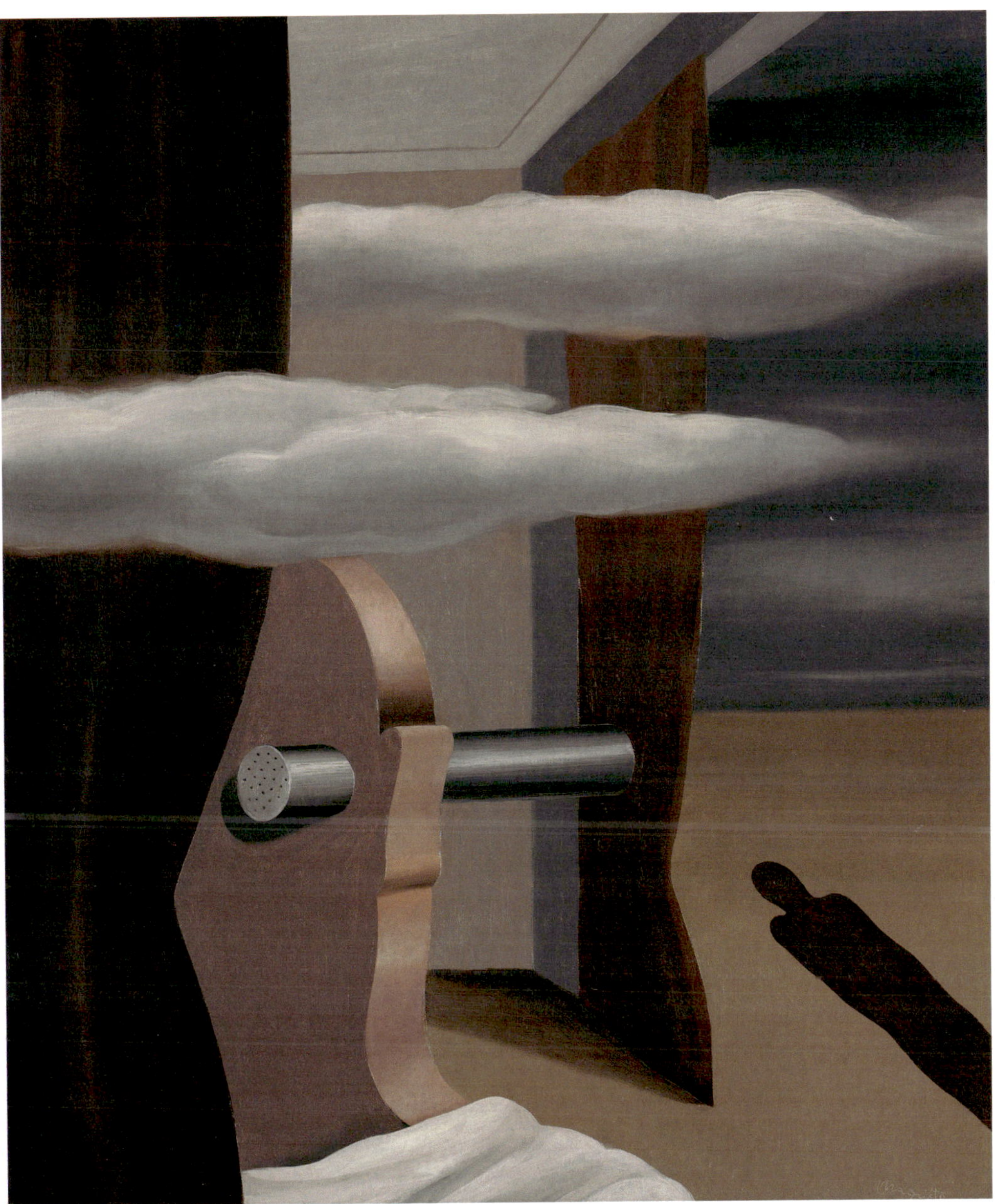

The Desert Catapult
La Catapulte du désert 1926, oil on canvas, 75 × 65 cm.
Private Collection, courtesy Hauser & Wirth, CR 108

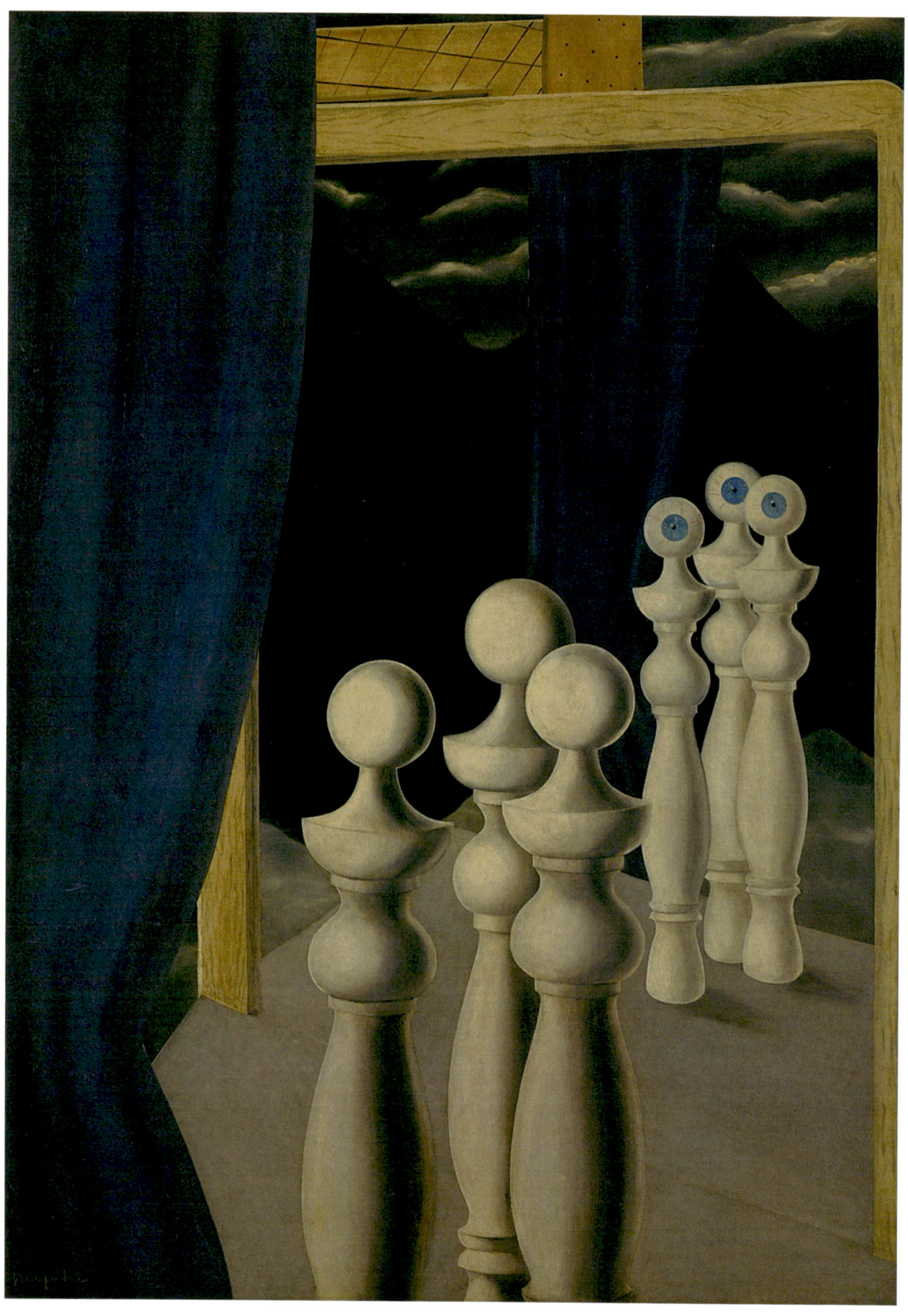

The Encounter
La Rencontre 1926, oil on canvas, 139.5 × 99 cm.
Kunstsammlung Nordrhein-Westfalen, Düsseldorf, CR 99

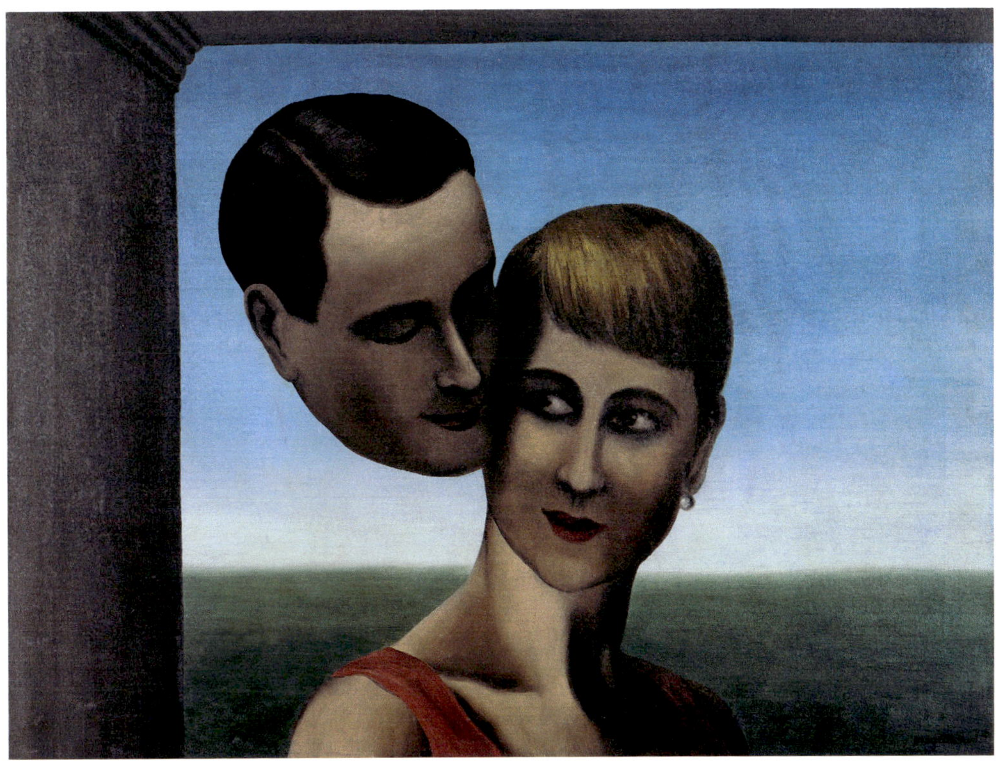

The Lovers
Les Amants 1928, oil on canvas, 54 × 73 cm.
Galerie Haas, Zurich, CR 252

in Magritte's panelled 'comic strip' composition *Man with a Newspaper* 1928, an image derived from an illustration in a German health manual of 1895.[154] The artist also created a series of double portraits, for example *Portrait of Paul Nougé* 1927 and *The Double Reality* 1936. As Silvano Levy describes, the double portrait draws on a resemblance derived from a model, yet simultaneously asserts a 'more compulsive affinity with a second image … the portrait's duplicate' which effectively severs its referential relationship with the original model.[155] Magritte himself described the double portraits as images which present a resemblance of a person alongside their reflection. 'If it were *alone*,' he stated, 'it would not evoke what it has in common with every other person, that is to say their mystery.'[156] Similarly explored in his 'pictured picture' works, the concern with the self-referencing image which simultaneously asserts its own legitimacy whilst disclaiming

the authenticity of its corresponding model in the real world, was one of Magritte's primary artistic preoccupations, engaging with ageless debates about illusion and reality, whilst also commenting on the nature and status of painting itself.

Magritte often repeated a visual motif within a single work, for example the *bilboquet* forms depicted in *The Encounter* 1926. The *bilboquets* are here arranged like skittles, transformed into figurative motifs with a single unblinking eye, shocked by an unexpected encounter with its own reflected image. Magritte's concern with the Surreal encounter dovetailed with his interest in the detective and murder mystery genre, in particular Marcel Allain and Pierre Souvestre's **Fantômas**. This inspired a series of quasi-filmic 'murder mystery' paintings including *The Menaced Assassin* 1927 and *The Night Owl* 1928, the latter based on a photograph of Magritte himself in which the artist, perhaps, effectively casts

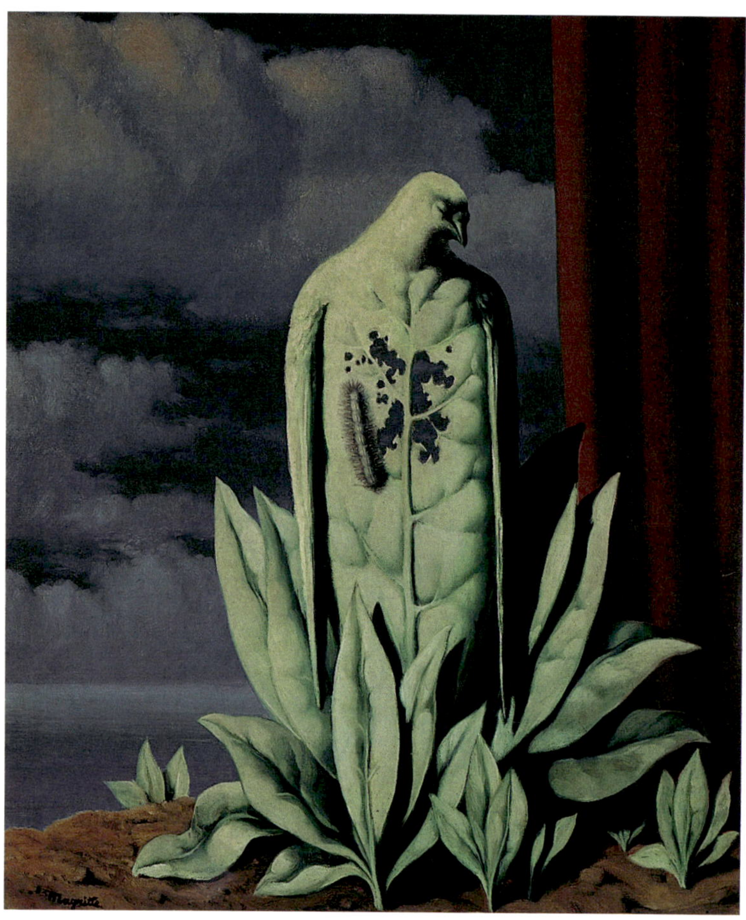

The Flavour of Tears
La Saveur des larmes 1948,
oil on canvas, 60 × 50 cm.
Royal Museums of Fine Arts
of Belgium, Brussels, CR 664

himself as a hard-boiled cop at the scene of the crime. Magritte's **appropriation** of pop cultural imagery is also evident in *The Lovers* 1928 and its variations. In this work a sense of dislocation between the two kissing figures is evoked due to their heads being covered with fabric. As David Sylvester pointed out, the painting derives from an image found by Magritte in a 'Nick Carter' detective dime novel, a particular favourite of the artist's.[157] In one such story a body is discovered in mysterious circumstances, its head wrapped with fabric. (**DP**)

See also: **Commercial Art; Detective Stories; Double; Portraiture; Representation and Resemblance; Theatrical Display**

Representation and Resemblance: For Magritte the kind of resemblance 'which can be made visible through painting' was a self-evident form of reference underwritten by identification and common knowledge. Pictorial resemblance, he noted, 'only deals with figures as they appear in the world: people, curtains, weapons, stars, solids, inscriptions, etc.' – all of which, and hundreds of other everyday objects besides, are clearly legible in his paintings. Magritte used associative clusters of singular words in the language of ready identification to outflank the hold of resemblance on representation. By creating discrepant syntactical relations among specific objects he attempted to defeat the simple, itemised

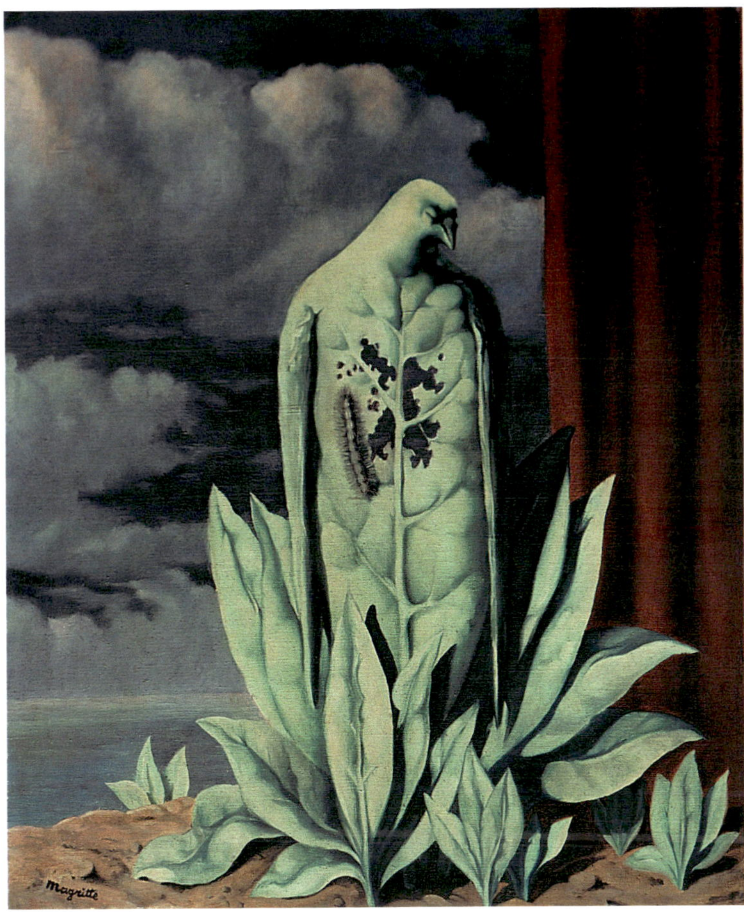

The Flavour of Tears
La Saveur des larmes
1948, oil on canvas,
60 × 50 cm. The Trustees
of the Barber Institute of
Fine Arts, The University
of Birmingham, CR 665

legibility that informed them. Often similar and recurring, objects were 'spontaneously united in the order wherein the familiar and the strange are restored to mystery'.[158] Perhaps as a result of the famous exchange with **Michel Foucault** towards the end of his life, Magritte seemed to modify his understanding of resemblance, referring its more literal aspects to the notion of 'similarity'. The discussion with Foucault offers a partial demonstration that visual and textual discourse can neither be fully separated (as in 'Western painting from the fifteenth to the twentieth century')[159] nor mutually superimposed. When text and image come together, neither material nor its mode of signification will ever be separable from a supplementary trace of the other. The word-image underlines the difference between a plastic and a visual sign by never fully fusing them or eclipsing one behind the other. As Foucault put it, 'designation and design do not overlap'.[160]

Foucault used the model of the calligram as a focus for his discussion of Magritte. While **The Treachery of Images** is not actually described as a calligram, some of its properties were regarded as being structurally similar to the doubling of text and image written in this mode of text-image conjunction. In a step-by-step itemisation and re-diagramming of the plural and conflicting messages of Magritte's painting, Foucault argues that

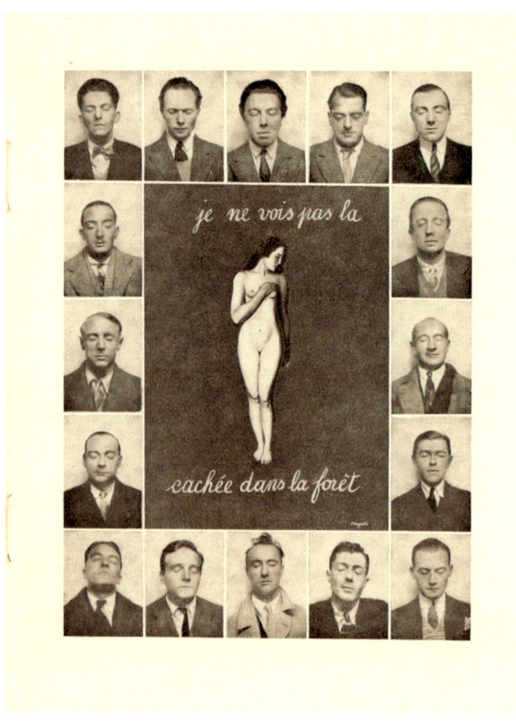

Photomontage with image of *The Hidden Woman* 1929 (CR 302), published in *La Révolution surréaliste*, no.12, 15 December 1929

the break marked by Magritte's ambiguous images and word-images is founded on a 'disassociation' of 'resemblance' (epitomized by **trompe l'oeil**) from 'similitude'. The order of resemblance is one in which a form of 'rigid designation' takes place such that an object and image, on the model of persons and their proper names, are related by identity. The precise differences between resemblance and similitude are sufficiently nuanced that Foucault details their disassociation in seven types of gesture and device in the fifth section of his essay – which concludes with a rather opaque and self-referential formula. For Magritte similitude, according to Foucault, is 'restored to itself and unfolding from itself and folding back upon itself … [in] infinite games of purified similitude'.[161] On its own, this new formalism is insufficient, and Magritte expressed his awareness of the problem by objecting to the artificial separation of 'resemblance' and 'similitude' in his first letter to Foucault, written in May 1966. 'Green peas have between them relations of similitude, at once

visible … and invisible,' he wrote. 'Things do not have resemblances, they do or do not have similitudes. Only thought resembles … by being what it sees, hears or knows; it becomes what the world offers it.'[162]

Magritte made several works that seem to refer to the questions before us, including two paintings entitled *Resemblance* 1954 and 1964–5. He used the title *Representation* for paintings made in 1937 and 1962, both of which are unusual. The earlier painting, referred to by the artist as 'a rather surprising object', is Magritte's only shaped canvas, its contours following the curves of a female body cut off above the navel and in the middle of the thighs. It is surely no coincidence that while 'resemblance' would later be associated with a rather neutral and nondescript female face, 'representation' comes down on the side of the body parts associated with sex and reproduction. On the other hand, Magritte somewhat confounds this association in an earlier letter which likely refers to a preliminary stage in the conception of this piece when he writes of using 'the maximum trompe l'oeil effect I could muster' – thus posing representation in an uneasy alliance with similitude.[163] The 1962 piece is notable for several reasons. First it seems to have been the object of intense nominal competition among some seven titles outlined and discussed in a letter from Magritte to **André Bosmans** in July 1961. Secondly, during the long gestation period for the painting which began almost a year earlier, Magritte expressed his excitement at having discovered the subject matter suitable for 'a picture containing "impossible" images: those of *Football-players!*'[164] 'Representation' is here associated with semantic equivocation and complexity and then crossed with partly wilful, partly absurd, iconographic impossibility. (**JW**)

See also: **Language; Meaning**

La Révolution surréaliste: Parisian Surrealist journal first published December 1924. Magritte's marginal relationship to Parisian **Surrealism** meant that he did not contribute to *La Révolution surréaliste* until its final issue of 15 December 1929. Using the Photomaton machines newly installed in Paris, he created a photomontage of 'dreaming' male Surrealists surrounding his painting *The Hidden Woman* 1929. In this work the image of a naked woman irrupts mid-sentence: 'I do not see the …

hidden in the forest.' Key to the montage is **André Breton**, located directly above the woman, who had written the previous year in *Nadja* that: 'I have always, beyond belief, hoped to meet, at night and in a woods, a beautiful naked woman.'[165] Breton's fantasy is thus realised in Magritte's painting, a work that Breton long owned. (**NM**)

See also: **Paris**

Rhétorique: Edited in Tilleur-lez-Liège by **André Bosmans**, *Rhétorique* comprised thirteen issues between 1961 and 1966. It was realised as a collaboration with Magritte, who organised and financed it and formed its contents by soliciting collaborations. Alternating between a collective and a monographic approach, *Rhétorique* was dedicated to the oeuvre of Magritte who found there, after *La Carte d'après nature* (his review which appeared at irregular intervals between 1952 and 1954) a final journal wherein to express his ideas. (**XC**)

Alain Robbe-Grillet (1922–2008) French writer and film-maker best known for his contribution to the *Nouveau Roman* of the 1950s in France. In 1975, he published the novel *La Belle Captive* (*The Beautiful Captive*), illustrated with 77 works by Magritte. The title of the novel is inspired by a series of six paintings, an investigation into the nature of reality, perspective and **representation** by layering pictures on easels in front of what appears like matching landscapes. The images do not function as illustrations but 'are used instead as pulsative forces, as generative themes for an imaginary discourse that parallels the paintings, glosses over them, and contradicts them'.[166] Magritte's work thus reflects and enhances the open, playful and discontinuous nature of Robbe-Grillet's self-reflective fiction. In 1983, Robbe-Grillet also wrote and directed a film of the same title, again using Magritte's paintings to evoke fantastic visions. (**CG**)

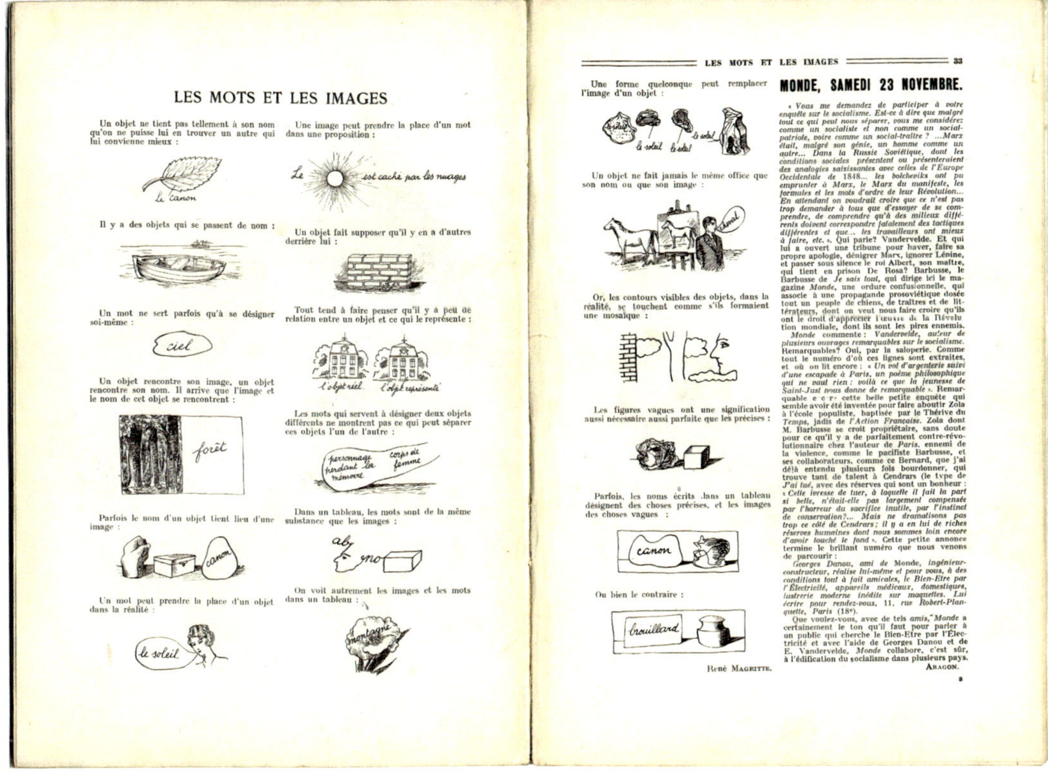

Words and Images
Les Mots et les images in *La Révolution surréaliste*, no.12, 15 December 1929

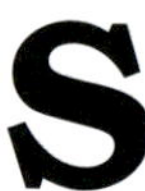

S

Scale: Magritte's images deploying distortions of scale aimed to destabilise the viewer's habitual perception of the world, whilst heightening the dramatic power of the picture. Exaggerated shifts in scale, evoking dream states, can be seen for instance in the erotically charged *The Giantess* 1931. Later works such as *The Tomb of Wrestlers* 1960, an image of a flower whose scale is spectacularised to room-filling proportions, contributed to Magritte being regarded as a precursor and inspiration to the Pop artists in the 1960s. This was an association he was keen to refute, stating: 'They [Pop artists] say they like me … But they are of their own time – neon, posters, technology … Me, I feel I am into truth.'[167] Magritte's images of isolated oversized everyday objects express a concern with utility and use value. He described the staged ensemble of personal effects depicted in *Personal Values* 1952 as being imbued with 'social character'. For Magritte, the focusing on 'superfluous luxury objects' represented an assault on the processes of social exchange and behaviours within a rational society. He stated: 'The social individual needs a repertory of ideas [that] permit him … to act in accordance with movements intelligible to society.' His imagining of an oversized and entirely useless comb reveals the hidden true reality rather than the mere symbolic reality represented by the object.[168] The undermining of rational logic through shifts in scale was consistent with the primary aim of Surrealism, namely to disrupt and derange accepted modes of communication and conduct. (**DP**)

See also: **Apple; Object**

Sculpture: Magritte's first large-scale retrospective at the Palais des Beaux-Arts, Brussels, in 1933 included the cloudscape-painted plaster death-mask of Napoleon entitled *The Future of Statues* c.1932. Also presented was a painted plaster miniature of the Venus de Milo, whose title was provided by **André Breton**, and which is now destroyed. A fragile medium, Magritte is known to have created many more works in plaster than have survived. In 1940 a shortage of canvas during **World War II** led Magritte to begin creating his painted **bottles** – a readymade 'banal' **object** – adorned with wittily Surrealist imagery. An element of Duchampian subversiveness is discernible in *This is a Piece of Cheese*, the first version of which was created in 1936. Its programmatic title refers to a framed painting of a piece of Camembert which simultaneously declares its own falsehood and seeks to affirm legitimacy by being positioned under a glass cheese dome. In 1967, a few months before his death in August that year, a discussion with his dealer **Alexandre Iolas** spurred Magritte to begin making sculptures based on existing paintings. Magritte selected a number of images which could be adapted to three-dimensional form. The casting of the works in bronze was not completed until after his death. (**DP**)

Louis Scutenaire and Irène Hamoir (1905–1987; 1906–1994) The writings and **poetry** of Louis Scutenaire and Irène Hamoir are significant contributions to **Surrealism** in **Belgium**. They married in 1930 and were close friends and accomplices of Magritte. Scutenaire's relationship with the Brussels Surrealists began in 1926 and he contributed texts to a range of journals and publications such as **Distances** and *Documents 34, Invention Surréaliste*. His collage novel *Les Jours dangereux: Les Nuits noires,*

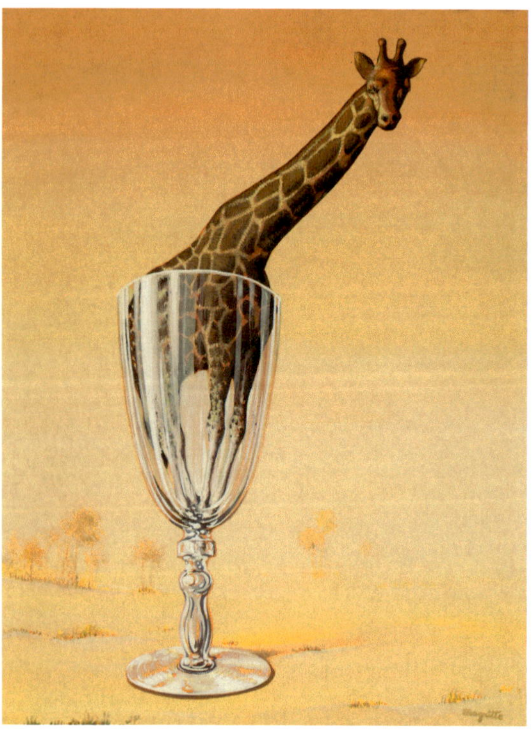

The Cut-glass Bath
Le Bain de cristal 1949, gouache on paper, 46 × 36 cm.
Private Collection, CR 1312a

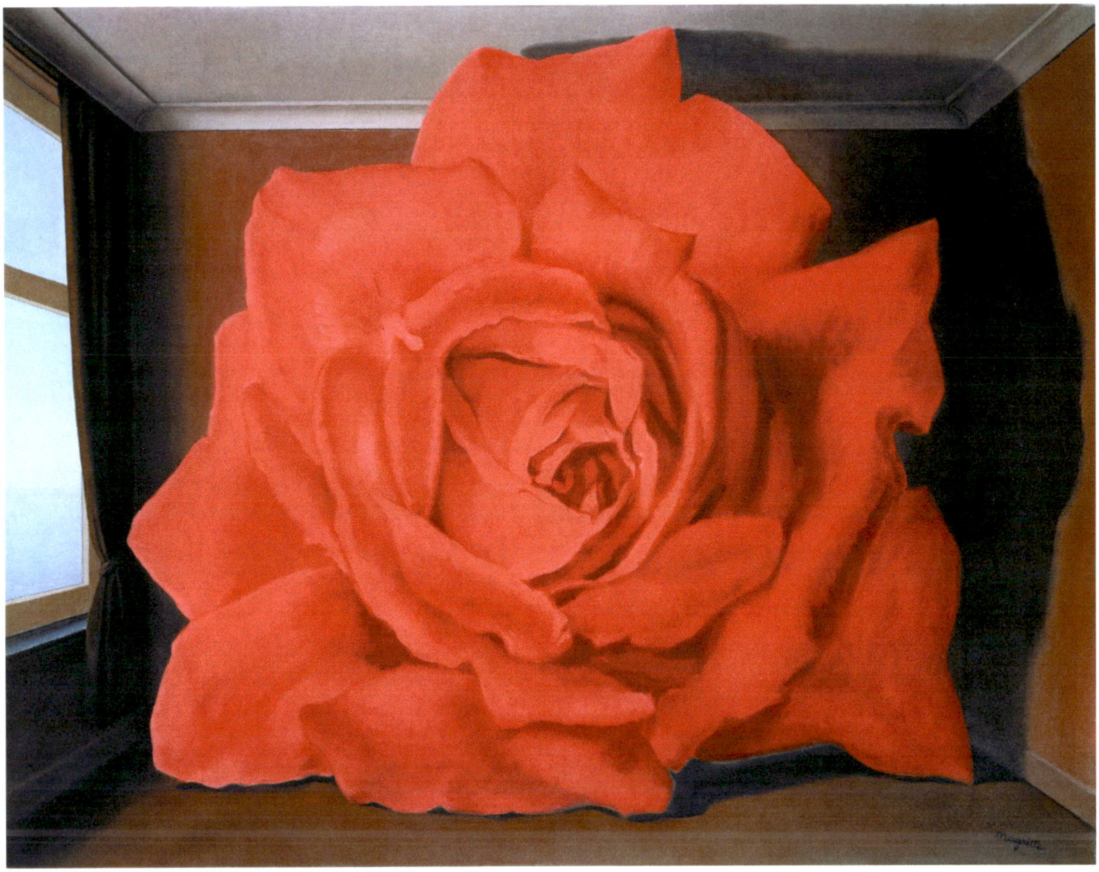

The Tomb of the Wrestlers
Le Tombeau des lutteurs 1960, oil on canvas,
89 × 116 cm. Private Collection, CR 912

based on quotations, borrowings and plagiarisms, was published in 1934. His writings closely tie in with Magritte's paintings and he provided **titles** for over 170 works, with Magritte illustrating several of Scutenaire's poetry collections including *Les Haches de la vie* 1937 and *Frappez au miroir* 1939. Scutenaire's book *René Magritte* was published in 1947.

Irène Hamoir, the only female writer in the Brussels Surrealist group, was a militant member of the Young Socialist Guards from 1924. She contributed to a range of Brussels Surrealist publications including *Documents 34* and *Le Ciel bleu*. In 1937 she received the Prix de l'Image for her screenplay for the film *Le Fort d'Orio*. Many of her poetry

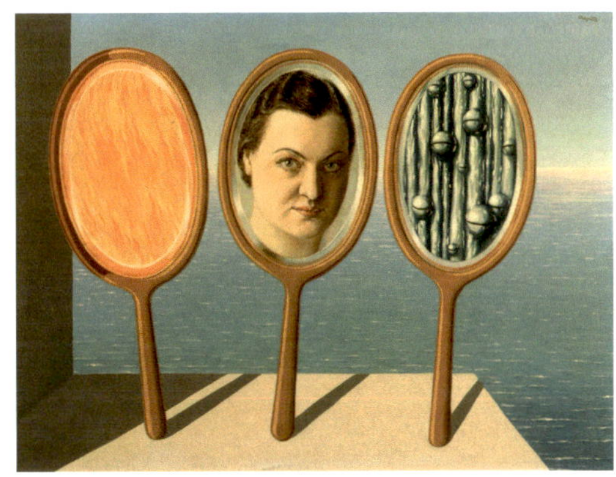

Portrait of Irène Hamoir
Portrait d'Irène Hamoir 1936, oil on canvas, 54 × 73 cm.
Royal Museums of Fine Arts of Belgium, Brussels, CR 397

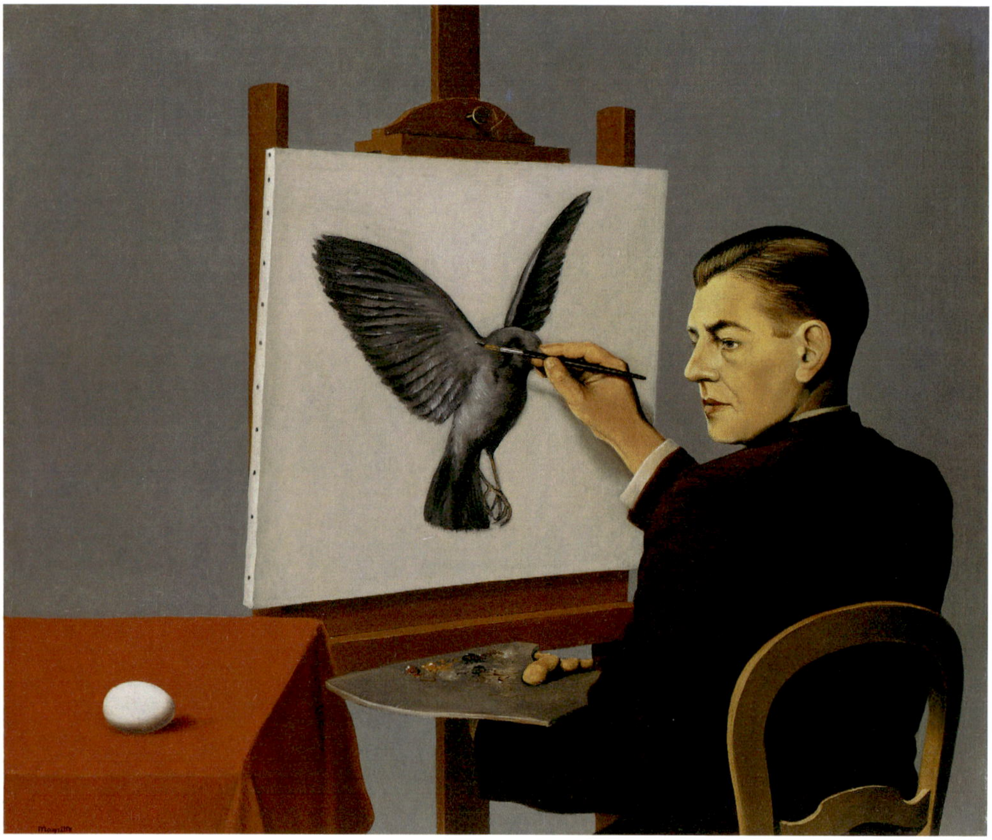

Clairvoyance
La Clairvoyance 1936, oil on canvas, 54 × 65 cm.
Private Collection, CR419

pamphlets were published under the pseudonym 'Irene'. In 1949, these were collected in *Œuvre poétique 1930–1945*, and later in 1976 in *Corne de brune*. Her novel *Boulevard Jacqmain*, published in 1953, is set in a circus and includes the appearance of the Brussels Surrealists as hooligans. Scutenaire and Hamoir repeatedly appear in Magritte's paintings and photographs, and were also actors in his short films. (**PA**)

Self-Reference and Self-Portraiture: Magritte

made very few paintings in which he was clearly the subject of the image, noting in 1946 that he had depicted himself in a picture only 'three times' and that even on these occasions there was, at the 'outset … an idea for a picture, not for a portrait'.[169] **David**

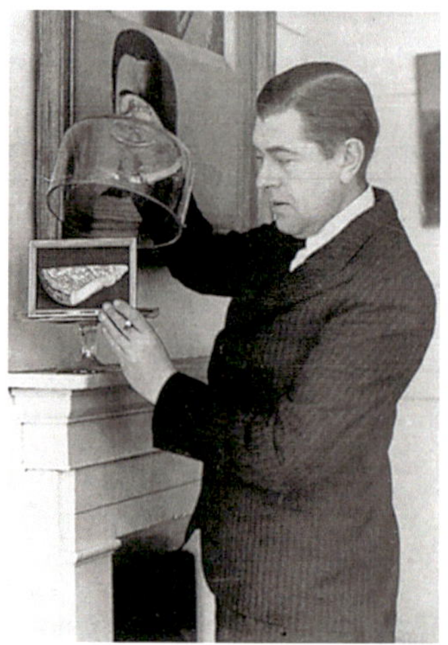

Publicity photograph showing René Magritte with with *This is a Piece of Cheese* 1936 or 1937, London Gallery, 1938

Sylvester and Sarah Whitfield add one more painting to this inventory, identifying four self-portraits in oil. The first is *Attempting the Impossible* 1928, an updated version of the Pygmalion and Galatea myth in which the artist, standing with his palette in the dining room of the Magrittes' house in Le Perreux-sur-Marne, paints a naked woman (his wife, **Georgette**). Jack J. Spector and others have argued that a second work, probably the painting omitted from Magritte's own list of three, *The Philosopher's Lamp* 1936, should also be considered as a self-portrait. It represents an 'absent-minded, obsessive philosopher' whose elongated nose droops into the bowl of his pipe, together with a lit candle on a simple stand, the lower registers

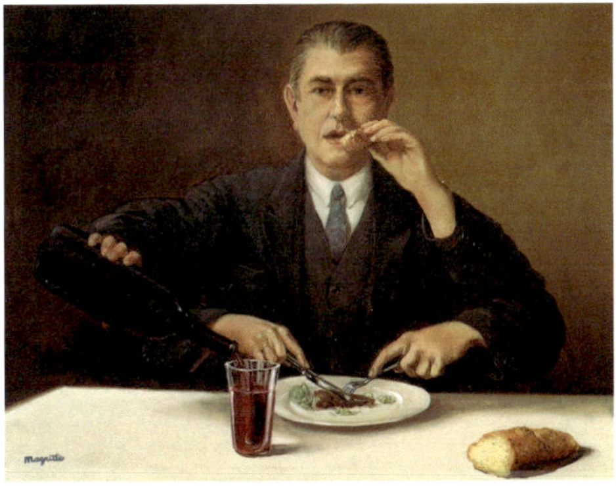

The Magician
Le Sorcier 1951, oil on canvas, 35 × 46 cm.
Private Collection, CR 766

of which also morph into a snake-like tube.[170] Thirdly, as is made clear from a photograph of the artist taken by **Jacqueline Nonkels**, *Clairvoyance* 1936 shows Magritte looking at his 'model', an egg set on a table to his left, while putting the finishing touches with the brush in his right hand to a spread-winged bird on the easel-supported canvas in front of which he sits. Finally, *The Magician* 1951, as Magritte put it, 'is simultaneously the *auto (mobile) portrait* (self-portrait) of its author' and conventionally bears the subtitle 'Self-portrait with four arms'.

The most cited investments in self-referentiality by Magritte, however, have long been associated with – or imposed on – the figure of a man wearing a **bowler hat** who appears in many works, especially in the last two decades of the artist's career.[171] By the 1960s the bowler-hatted figure had become so ubiquitous that it appears as a silhouette standing for everyman and infilled with various grounds: **clouds** in *The Granite Quarry* 1964, a house within a landscape in *The Happy Donor* 1966, and a pattern of foliage in *Man and the Forest* c.1965.

The situation is somewhat different in several photographs of the artist in which he is shown in proximity to a particular work, often looking back at the camera. Such is the case with a photograph of Magritte at his one-person exhibition at the **London Gallery** in 1938 in front of a lost work, *The Vicious Circle* 1937.[172] The artist holds the bottom of the frame with his left arm, and probably the side of the frame with his unseen right hand, as if in the process of hanging or adjusting the piece, or even gesturing to climb into it and become a participant. As the painting represents the profile of a woman embracing a body imaged as a flat, anatomical cross-section of the head and shoulders, Magritte's posture could be interpreted as a second embrace – offering another mode of his entry into the composition. That these suggestions are not purely speculative is attested by the silhouette of the artist's intrusion into the right side of the painting, which clearly makes a pair with the shape of the single curtain painted on the left. In like manner, Magritte has ensured that the light source for the photograph casts his shadow onto the painting in continuity with the pronounced shadows behind the two figures, which are also lit by raking light from the right. Finally, another photograph of this exhibition, captioned as a 'publicity photograph', shows Magritte lifting a glass dome from its pedestal to reveal the small oil on canvas board that, together with the cheese keep, make up his '**object**' *This is a Piece of Cheese* 1963 or 1964 (first created in 1936) – attesting once again to his willingness, at this point in his career at least, to insinuate himself into his own works.[173] As he noted a few years later, Magritte always hoped that rather than a portrait trying to resemble its model, 'this model' (himself) 'will try to resemble its portrait'.[174] (JW)

See also: **Anonymity; Photography; Portraiture**

Victor Servranckx (1897–1965) Painter, sculptor and furniture maker. In 1922, after his studies at the Académie royale des Beaux-Arts, Servranckx, then artistic director in a paint factory, co-authored with

René Magritte an unpublished manifesto entitled *L'Art pur. Défense de l'esthétique*. A contributor to **7 Arts**, his paintings were influenced by Purism. After 1927, he rejected geometric rigour, his painting becoming increasingly abstract with Surrealist influences. (**XC**)

See also: **Wallpaper**

7 Arts: Avant-garde journal published in Brussels between 1922 and 1929. *7 Arts* sought to be a meeting point between architecture, painting and **poetry**, music and cinema. Led principally by **Victor and Pierre Bourgeois**, both friends of Magritte, the journal was informed by the ideas of Purism, an important artistic influence for the artist at this time. It sought the collaboration of numerous painters and artists including **E.L.T. Mesens** and Magritte before they began to distance themselves from it. Relations between *7 Arts* and **Correspondance** deteriorated in the mid-1920s, with **Paul Nougé** regularly attacking the journal and its collaborators. (**XC**)

Shock: The concept of 'shock' was a highly topical one within **Surrealist** circles during 1928. At the conclusion of *Nadja* 1928, the tale of his relationship with an increasingly deranged woman, **André Breton** likens 'beauty' to 'a train that ceaselessly roars out of the Gare de Lyon' – a series of 'jolts and shocks … destined to produce one *Shock*'.[175] Magritte's *The Subjugated Reader* 1928, produced that same year during his period in Paris, depicts a female reader, face aghast, as she stares wide-eyed at the book she holds closely in front of her. Magritte isolates the figure against a plain, deep blue background, on which a shadow falls, suggesting the reader is pinned against a wall. This effect is further heightened by the powerful lighting and deep shadows, suggesting – somewhat sadistically – that the absorbed woman is literally 'under the spotlight'. We cannot know what text has produced such a reaction in the reader – perhaps Comte de Lautréamont or Marquis de Sade, Surrealist beacons of the period. That this work was the companion image of *The Dark Suspicion* 1928, in which a man stares obsessively at his hand, suggests this image too represents some mental disturbance, particularly given Surrealism's celebration in March 1928, in *La Révolution surréaliste*, of the '50th Anniversary of Hysteria'. (**NM**)

See also: **Violence**

Shop Window Display: Aspects of the shop window display or department store vitrine find their way into Magritte's work in three overlapping dimensions. First, the frontality and symmetrical framing of the display is evident in the composi-

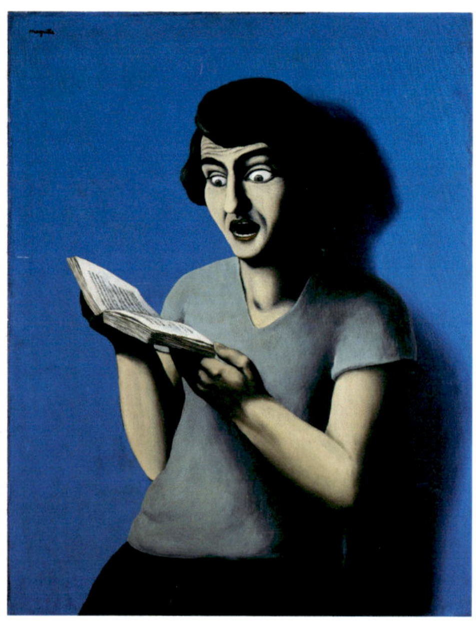

The Subjugated Reader
La Lectrice soumise 1928, oil on canvas, 92 × 73 cm. Ivok Braka Ltd, London, CR 230

tional formats of the artist's paintings in which an ordered object, or series of objects – such as the brick wall in *Blood-letting* 1939, or an interior, or vista – are presented square-on from the point of view of a spectator looking at the work immediately in front of its own centre. Sometimes less apparent in a singular painting, this effect is magnified when studiously frontal images are shown adjacent to another compositional type featuring similarly simplified perspective, such as *The Fair Captive* 1931. Certain paintings, such as *The Human Condition* 1935, produce their discrepant points of view precisely by modulating between frontality and perspective. The fact that this group of works is almost uniformly interested in the manipulative effects of the technique of perspectival rendering with which it engages – interrogating the very constructs of its

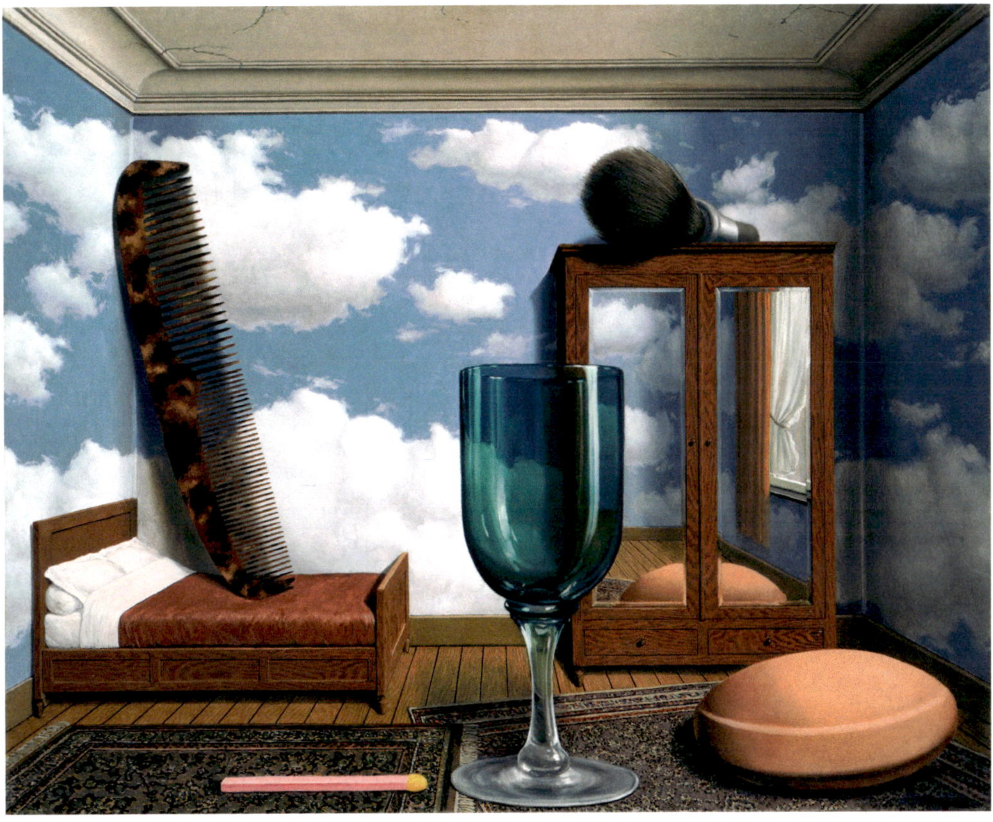

Personal Values
Les Valeurs personnelles 1952, oil on canvas, 80 × 100 cm.
San Francisco Museum of Modern Art, CR 773

artifice – produces, by inference and association, a renewed sense of oddness and counter-seduction as we are somehow surreptitiously solicited to view frontality itself as a device.

Secondly, the vitrine model, as several commentators have observed, corresponds with the historical **cabinet of curiosities** (or *Wunderkammer*)[176] through a mode of compartmentalised organisation. This is readily apparent in works such as *The Six Elements* 1928 and *The Empty Mask* 1928, though most obvious, perhaps, in the six compartments of the 1946 advertising image for men's toiletries which brings the artist's aesthetic innovation, already predicated in this instance on window display, back into the commercial domain.[177] The sectioned appearance has several consequences: it helps to confer, on object sets in particular, a kind of equivalency in the sense that scalar differences are eradicated, as well as a sense of availability as objects offer their seemingly unadulterated 'thingness'.

Perhaps the widest relational horizon is constituted by Magritte's negotiation with the practice, everyday appearance and even the theory of commercial culture itself, for which the shop window offers a point of entry and enticement as well as being a paradigm spectacle. At the beginning of his career, Magritte worked as a commercial artist, producing book covers, **music score** covers and other designs. He took up again with such practices for financial reasons on his return from **Paris** to Brussels in 1930, establishing a business called Studio Dongo with his brother, **Paul**. Magritte was, therefore, one of several twentieth-century artists who made work specifically for display vitrines, including **Salvador Dalí**

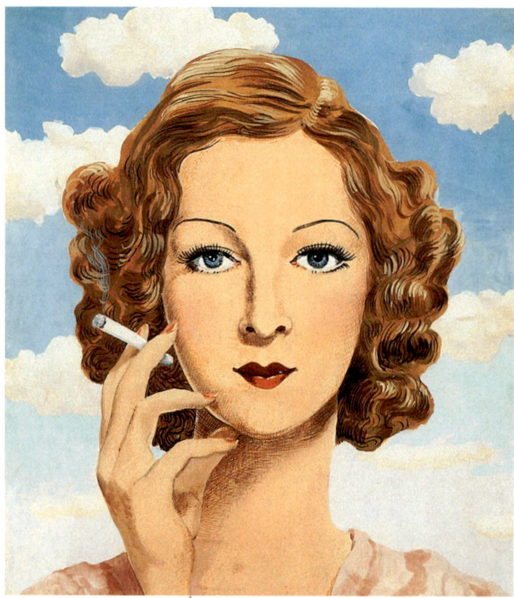

Woman with Cigarette
Femme à la cigarette 1935, design for a cigarette advertisement,
gouache on paper, 32 × 29 cm. Collection Province de
Hainaut, Belgium, CR X26

(who produced 'screwy' windows for Bonwit Teller
in New York in March 1939) and Andy Warhol (who
worked for the same store in the early 1960s).[178]
He was responsible, for example, for the window
decorations of the Graineterie de Boendael, a shop
opened in Brussels in 1946 by **Jacqueline Nonkels**
– known to the artist since 1926 – and her husband
Maurice Delcourt.[179]

That the artist was aware of the reach of his work
between commercial and artistic realms is attested
in several ways. In 1934, when **André Breton's** book
What is Surrealism? was published featuring a tinted-
paper cover image by Magritte based on *The Rape*,
painted in the same year, the artist wrote: 'I hope
you will be pleased by this cover-project, I also think
it is excellent from the publicity point of view. An
image of this kind is not likely to pass unnoticed in
a bookstore window.'[180] **David Sylvester** underlines
the nexus of relations present here between advertising and avant-gardism by pointing to the similarity between Magritte's cover and a 'Belga' cigarette
poster designed by the artist, noting that 'it seems
to share the self-assured, even audacious, air of the

commercial image'.[181] A second moment in which
the commercial and the aesthetic were convened
took place nearly two decades later, when a version
of Magritte's most famous image, captioned *This
is not a Pipe* 1952, was produced as a hand-painted
poster for a window display at La Fleur en Papier
Doré, a bar owned by **Geert Van Bruaene** in Brussels.
A fragmentary inscription on a label attached to the
verso suggests that the artist intended the image
to 'teach people' about the 'display of […] poetic
thought'.[182] (**JW**)

👁 See also: **Commercial Art; Mannequin**

Surrealism and Surrealists: André Breton
defined Surrealism as:

> SURREALISM, *n.* Psychic automatism in its
> pure state, by which one proposes to express
> – verbally, by means of the written word, or in
> any other manner – the actual functioning of
> thought. Dictated by thought, in the absence of
> any control exercised by reason, exempt from
> any aesthetic or moral concern.

> ENCYCLOPEDIA. *Philosophy.* Surrealism
> is based on the belief in the superior reality
> of certain forms of previously neglected asso-
> ciations, in the omnipotence of dream, in the
> disinterested play of thought. It tends to ruin
> once and for all other psychic mechanisms and
> to substitute itself for them in solving all the
> principal problems of life.[183]

Magritte and the Brussels Surrealists' theories dif-
fer in a number of ways from Breton's definition.
They were little interested in **Freud**, the unconscious
or **automatism**, as Magritte notes: 'contrary to the
fondness of the Surrealists for dream-accounts,
they leave me indifferent'.[184] Instead, Magritte
and the Brussels Surrealist group aimed to 'cast
doubt on reality through the use of reality itself',
investigating the very texts and textures of reality as
unreliable, illogical and ideological, often employing
methods such as **pastiche**, borrowing, referencing
and plagiarism.[185]

Another major difference between the Brussels
and the Parisian Surrealists, and specifically Breton,
is the former's passion for music. As Magritte notes

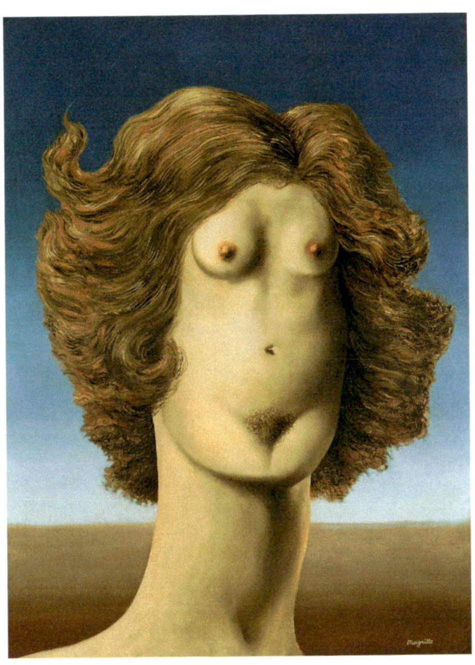

The Rape
Le Viol 1934, oil on canvas, 73 × 54 cm.
The Menil Collection, Houston, CR356

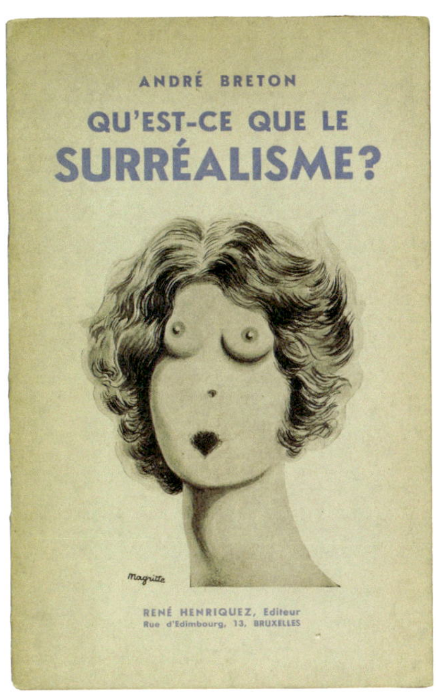

André Breton, *What is Surrealism?* 1934.
Tate Library and Archive

on Breton, in a conversation with **Harry Torczyner**: 'I had difficulty in getting on with a man who didn't like music.'[186] Breton had a life-long distaste for music, while the Brussels group promoted music in publications such as ***Correspondance***, adored Erik Satie and other avant-garde composers, and included in its membership composers such as **E.L.T. Mesens**, André Souris and **Paul Magritte**.

Perhaps Breton eventually did find the best definition of Surrealism:

What is Surrealism?
It is the Cuckoo's egg laid in the nest
(whose brood is lost) with the
complicity of René Magritte.[187]
(PA)

David Sylvester (1924–2001) British art critic, writer and curator. Sylvester was influential in promoting modern British art, in particular Francis Bacon and Lucien Freud. The catalogue raisonné of Magritte (5 vols. published 1992–97) which he edited and co-wrote with Sarah Whitfield, and which was commissioned by the Menil Foundation in Houston, remains the essential resource and foundation-stone for all Magritte scholarship. Sylvester curated important Magritte exhibitions at the Tate Gallery, London, 1969, and co-curated with Whitfield the retrospective at the Hayward Gallery, London, in 1992. (DP)

👁 See also: **John and Dominique de Menil**

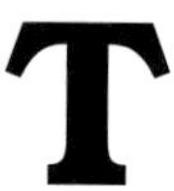

Yves Tanguy (1900–1955) French painter. Perhaps the purest, most visionary of the first generation of Surrealist painters, Tanguy discovered his vocation after a chance encounter in 1923 with the work of **Giorgio de Chirico**, finding the same door to **Surrealism** Magritte would open soon afterwards. The early work of the two artists perhaps has the most in common, staging disorienting encounters between half-recognised objects in stage-set landscapes, painted in a deliberately unsophisticated style. A shared sense of enigma lies at the heart of both sets of work, Magritte's oriented towards the waking realm of knowledge, Tanguy's towards imaginary worlds and the classic Surrealist topos of the dream landscape. (**KF**)

See also: **Chance; Pattern; Theatrical Display**

Theatrical Display: An enigmatic stage-set quality is evident in certain Magritte compositions of 1926 and 1927. Demonstrating the influence of **Giorgio de Chirico** in its atmosphere and compositional logic, in *The Difficult Crossing* 1926 theatricality is coded through the depiction of the **bilboquet** which reads like a figure centre-stage, and evoked further through the depiction of **curtains** drawn back as a framing device, wooden floorboards, **mirrors**, exaggerated perspective, and painted flimsy stage panels and backdrops. The space and place of the image is presented within a claustrophobic boxed interior. Every individual element presented is familiar, yet their combined **juxtaposition** creates a scene that is instantly unreal and artificial.[188] As with **trompe l'oeil** painting, which Jean Baudrillard describes as oscillating between the realms of artificiality and the 'realist' hallucination in its depiction of typically banal **objects**, the scene seems illuminated by what is described as a 'mysterious light which has no source and whose oblique incidence no longer has anything in common with reality'.[189] *The Birth of the Idol* 1926 similarly displays a distinct sense of *mise-en-scène*, whilst *The Silvered Chasm* 1926 presents an entirely theatrical and unrealistic scene. In this work we see the first appearance of the *grelot*, or bell, a standardised mass-produced object which was to be an important motif in Magritte's oeuvre until the end of his career.

The idea of isolating and presenting an individual mass-produced object – such as the *grelot* – or group of objects in special arrangements was reflected in the work of a number of artists including Fernand Léger as well as Magritte. The focusing on a mass-produced object in isolation – perhaps tracing back to his early interest in Purism – was evident in his commercial design work, in particular the fashion plates of 1927 captioned by **Paul Nougé** for the furrier Maison Samuel which depict free-floating furs and coats with **collage** elements and objects whose **scale** is inverted. The compositional strategies in these images bear a close relationship to his 'stage-set' paintings created around the same time. In *Let out of School* 1927, we see a decorative fan on a wooden stage with a mysterious molten lead-like substance pouring into view, seemingly solidified into a fixed and mysterious presence. Magritte's concern with theatrical display extends to the vitrine-like composition of *Personal Values* 1952. (**DP**)

See also: **Artifice; Cabinet of Curiosities; Frame; Shop Window Display**

Titles play a key role in Magritte's training of the signification of an image towards poetic meaning and the metaphysics of thought.[190] In lectures and texts Magritte reiterated his call for an evocative Symbolist-like indeterminacy in titling. 'The poetic title has nothing to teach us,' he stated, 'instead it should surprise and enchant us.'[191] In an interview with Jan Walravens he outlined a theory of titling modelled on the 'mysterious rapport' set in motion between the figures and **objects** in his paintings. Just as these motifs are suspended, relationally, in an uncertain, evocative syntax, so the title is made and received in another spiral of the same dislocated logic. These disjunctions give rise to a titular theory that while asserting the relative autonomy of both title and image, refusing in particular the 'illustrational' subordination of the image to the title caption, allows that they produce a collocation, or ensemble, that signifies as a function of their disparate associations:

The title maintains the same *rapport* with the painted forms as the forms maintain among themselves. The forms are assembled in an order that evokes mystery. The title is associated with the painted figure according to the same order. For example, the painting *Memory* 1948

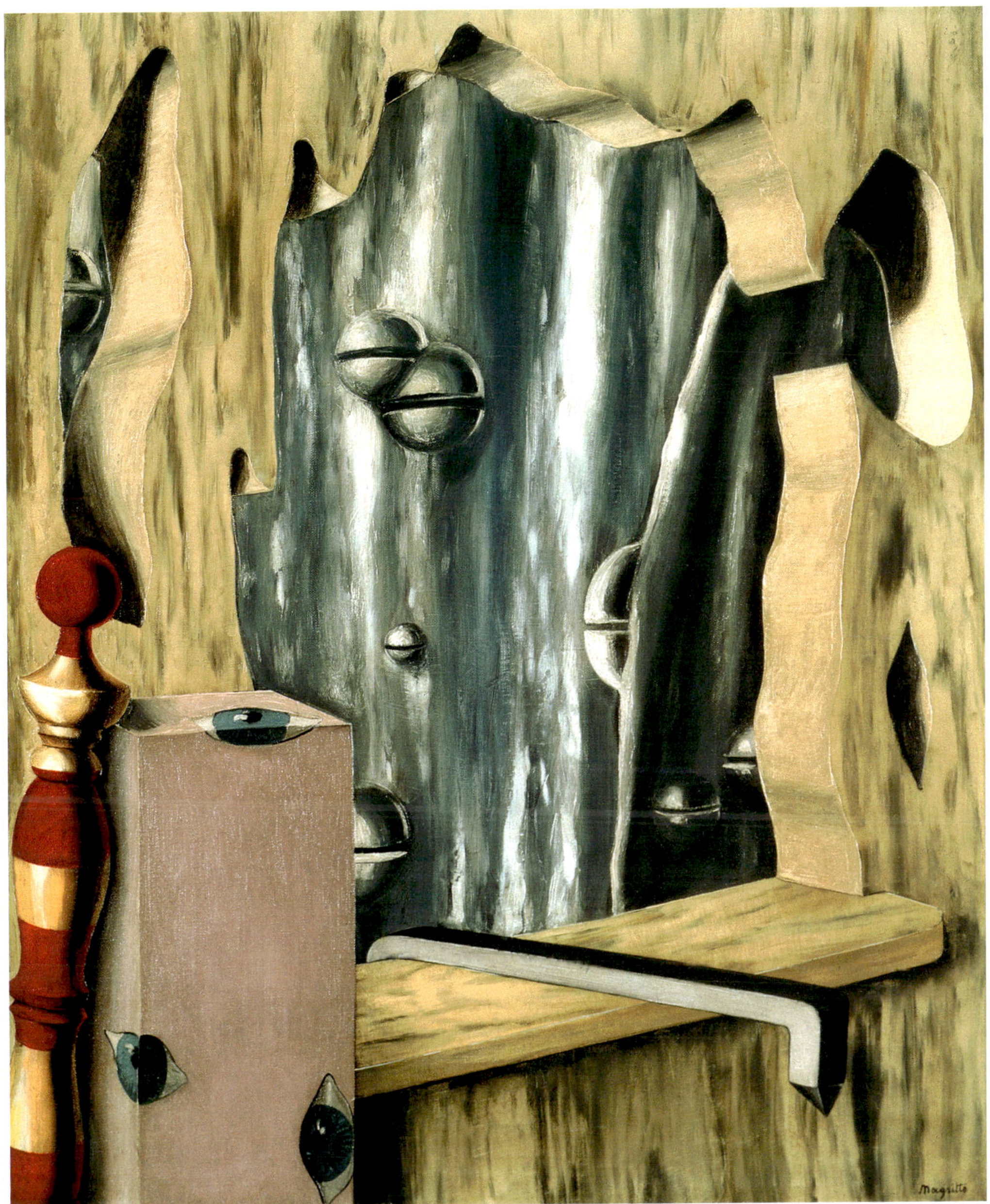

The Silvered Chasm
Le Gouffre argenté 1926, oil on canvas, 75 × 65 cm.
Museu Colecção Berardo, CR 87

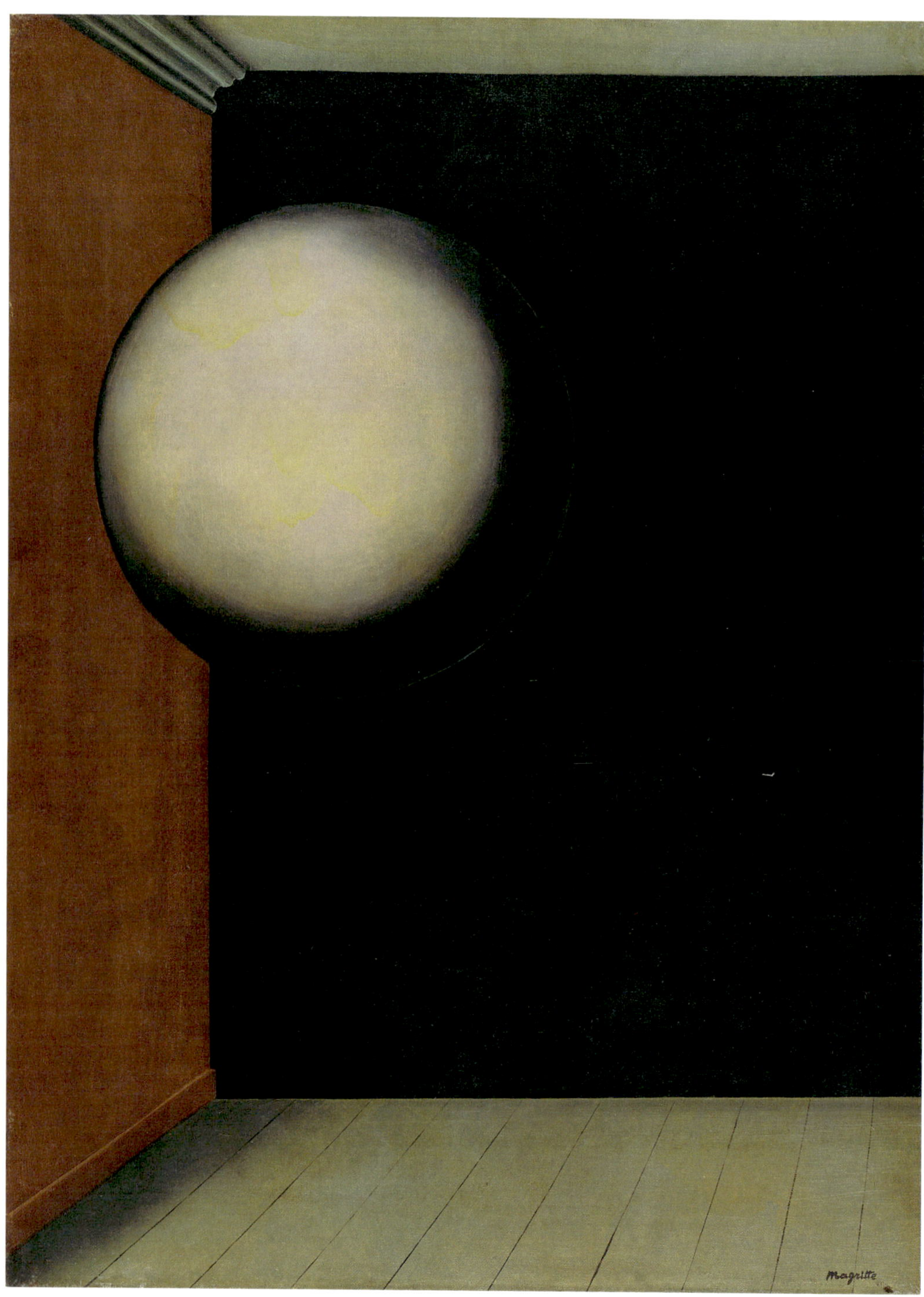

The Secret Life
La Vie secrète 1928, oil on canvas, 73 × 54 cm.
Kunsthaus Zurich, Vereinigung Zürcher
Kunstgesellschaft, CR 290

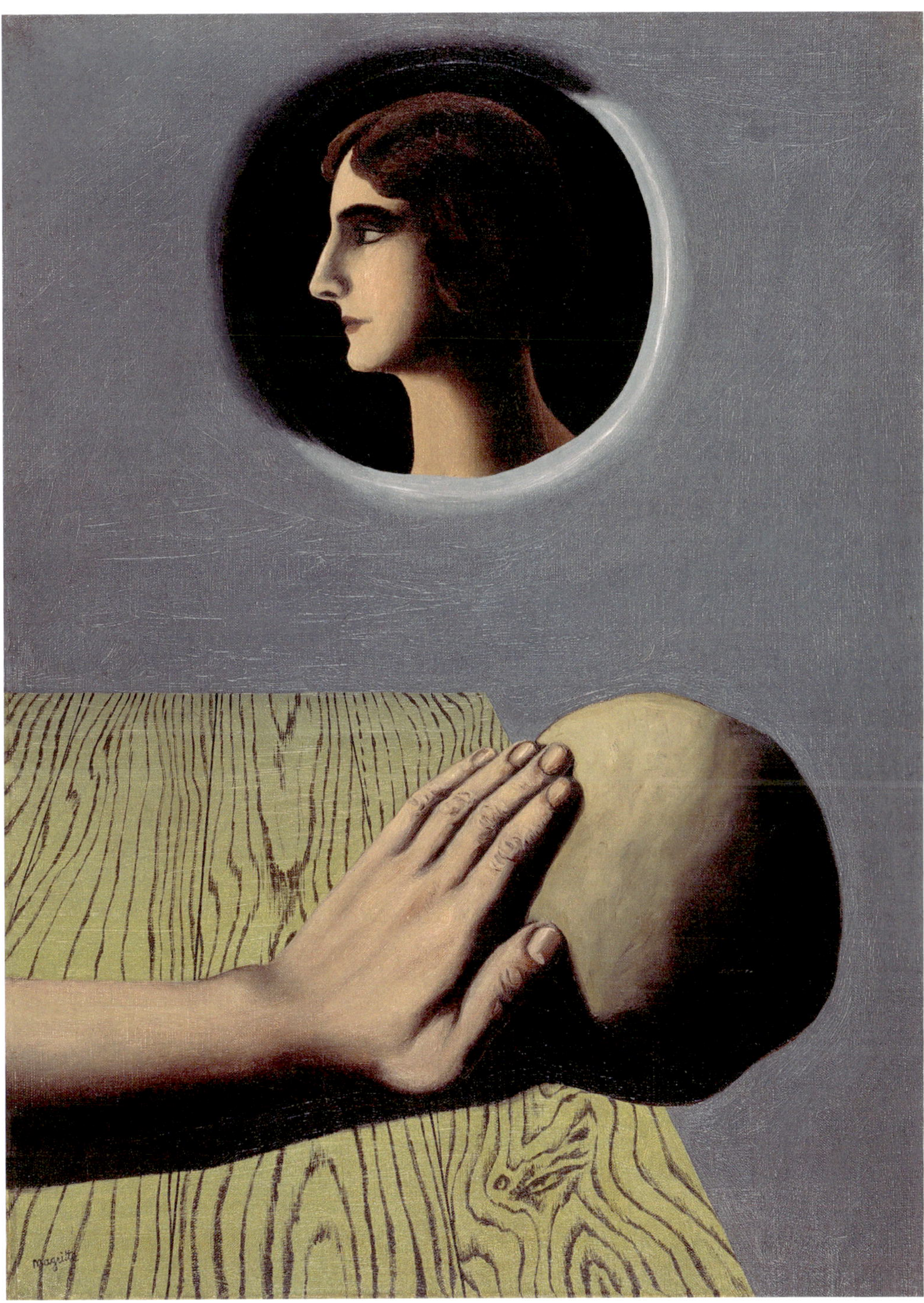

The Beneficial Promise
La Promesse salutaire 1927–8, oil on canvas,
73 × 54 cm. Isidore Ducasse Fine Arts, CR 198

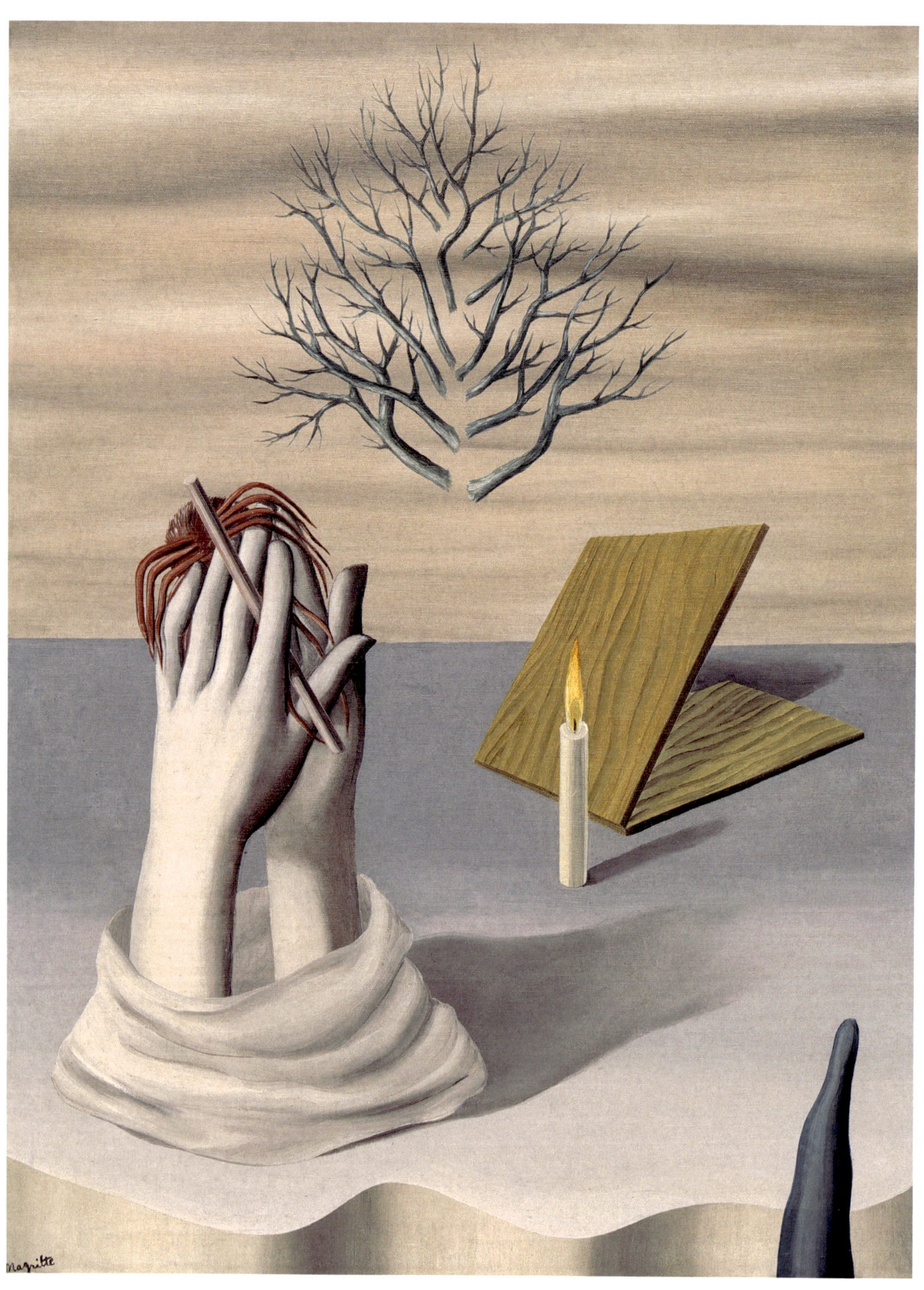

Dawn at Cayenne
L'Aube à Cayenne 1926, oil on canvas, 97 × 74 cm.
Isidore Ducasse Fine Arts, CR 118

shows a plaster figure on which a drop of blood is displayed. When I gave this title to the painting, I felt that the two went well together. One can speak of a painting and its title … The painting is not an illustration of the ideas that follow.[192]

During the later part of his career, Magritte, like **Francis Picabia** before him, solicited the effects of **chance** for his titles, paging through the Larousse and other dictionaries with the assistance of friends in search of suggestive words and phrases to append to his paintings.[193] It is clear, however, that Magritte, like **Martin Heidegger**, was aware that 'dictionaries have little to report about what words, spoken thoughtfully, say'.[194] He was also not averse to renaming his paintings after they had been produced and titled. Ronald Alley notes of *The Spirit of Geometry* c.1936 that 'Mme Magritte confirms (letter of 19 November 1976) that her husband did not like the original title "Maternity" and decided to change it'.[195] Other titles are more elaborate than meets the eye: his famous image *The Treachery of Images* 1929 was actually associated with four other names: *The Treason of Images, The Faithful Image, The Use of Speech, The Air and the Song.*[196]

The Treachery of Images occasioned one of the most sustained reflections on the economy of visual-textual and poetic signification, **Michel Foucault's** essay on Magritte, which shares its title with the artist's inscription. Magritte's representation of a pipe is staged with a deceptively simple logic that Foucault compares to the tradition of illustrative diagramming.[197] The digressive analogy which ensues concludes with a step-by-step itemisation of the plural and conflicting messages of the image. Magritte's gaming with the title of a work of art offers an explicit critique of the dependency of the classical order on 'the sovereign act of nomination'. As Laurie Edson notes: '[o]ne might say that it is the Name that organizes all Classical discourse.'[198] Threatening the name (the title) is also to threaten the passivity of the relation between words and images that was assumed in painting and sculpture until the late nineteenth century.

The Treachery of Images stands as both the terminus of, and antithesis to, the tradition of the descriptive title inherited by Modernism. The subversion of the denotative label by the insertion of a 'poetic' one introduces a semiotic layering in the reception of the image which insists on its status as a *representation*, and on **representation** as separate from reality. The image is now positioned as a sign. But what results is a compound sign joining visual and textual regimes through the inscription of the title within the bounds of the image. The countermanding of the image by the word is a statement against appearances and a bid for multiplicity in the reception and understanding of the image. This dissociation offers a preface to the wide range of dislocations that Magritte stages in his images: poetic **juxtapositions**, mislabelling, referential disjunctions, and the solicitation of text-assisted, dream-like states. (**JW**)

See also: **Meaning; Poetry;** *The Treachery of Images*

Harry Torczyner (1910–1998) Born in Antwerp, Torczyner was Magritte's New York-based lawyer. He met the artist in 1957, becoming one of his most important collectors and supporters in the post-War period. Torczyner played an instrumental role in organising the Magritte retrospective at the Museum of Modern Art in New York in 1965. In 1977 Torczyner published *Magritte: Ideas and Images*, a key source book of Magritte's writings. Over a period of ten years Torczyner and Magritte exchanged **letters** testifying to their close friendship. This illuminating correspondence was anthologised as *Letters Between Friends*, and published in English in 1994. (**DP**)

The Treachery of Images: '*Ceci n'est pas une pipe*' – 'This is not a pipe' – writes Magritte, below the image of what we must surely read as the epitome of a **pipe** – a pipe that floats in space against a featureless, creamy backdrop. At first glance we might assume some kind of provocation – certainly this is not a *real* pipe and the artist is either insulting our intelligence or, more likely, has something else in mind. This simple proposition, striking in the elegance and economy of its means, has attracted an inordinate amount of critical attention, not least of which is an extensive analysis by **Michel Foucault** published in 1968 that extended to an exchange of letters between critic and artist. Foucault's structuralist analysis, though controversial and not consistently convincing, served to substantially increase the

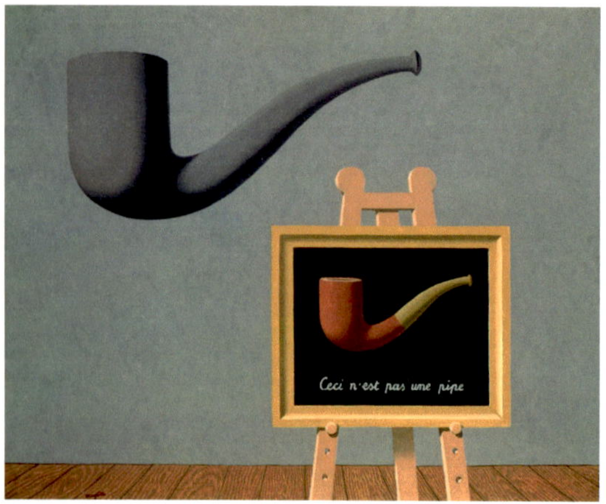

The Two Mysteries
Les Deux Mystères 1966, oil on canvas, 65 × 80 cm.
Private Collection, CR 1038

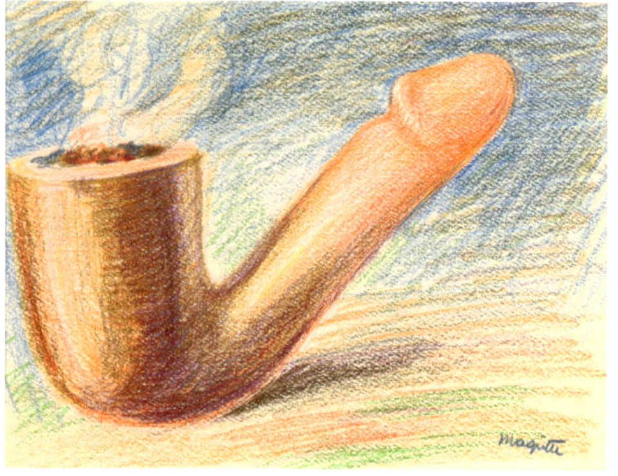

Untitled (Pipe-sex)
Sans titre (La Pipe-sexe) 1943, pencil on paper, 13.5 × 18 cm.
Private Collection

intellectual credibility of Magritte's work, requiring that his oeuvre be considered as a sustained critique of language and of representation.

As the linguist Ferdinand de Saussure made clear, in language there exists only an arbitrary relationship between the word and the thing it designates, whereas the broad cultural presumption is of some deep and intrinsic relationship between the two. In invoking the word, or the image of the thing, our mind flies directly to the designated **object**. It is this easy conflation of the two that constitutes one of the central targets of Magritte's critique. As James

Harkness puts it, Magritte's work forms part of the movement in modern art that aimed to separate painting from **language** by claiming the autonomy of the art object. Whereas the bulk of such work used abstraction as the means of its independence, Magritte instead 'uses literalism to undermine itself'.[199] Foucault never actually mentions the title *The Treachery of Images*, and his analysis bears largely on the later *The Two Mysteries* 1966, where the pipe with its paradoxical caption now appears framed on an artist's easel, like some pedantic classroom demonstration, while above it floats a larger, ghostly, *grisaille* replica.

Magritte's pipe of 1929 is surely rather too close to the glossy seduction of advertising to be taken seriously as an actual pipe – too close, too, to the ideal of the 'lost object' whose rediscovery would complete our lacking existence. Nor is this pipe lacking in an all-too-easy sexual symbolism – Freud's *The Interpretation of Dreams*, with which Magritte was familiar, states baldly that a pipe 'may represent the approximate shape of the male organ'.[200] Such a reading is confirmed by *The Philosopher's Lamp* 1936, perhaps a self-portrait of Magritte smoking a pipe, where the elongated, swollen nose plunges into the pipe bowl, while nearby a serpent-like lit candle stands erect. In *Freedom of Mind* 1948, a virtually naked woman – almost certainly his wife **Georgette** – standing by a stone balcony, cradles a pipe in her hand against her navel, lending a clearly erotic meaning to that incongruous object. Any remaining doubt about the sexual connotations of the series is removed by a 1943 drawing, *Untitled (Pipe-sex)*, in which the mouthpiece of the pipe is transformed into an erect penis, complete with fiery, smoking bowl, recalling that Freud also puts forward the idea that, in dreams, flying and floating are often associated with 'the remarkable phenomenon of erection', insofar as it involves 'an apparent suspension of the laws of gravity'.[201] This also demonstrates how in Magritte's world the apparently cool, dispassionate surface of our initial image conceals its diametric opposite.

Were we to heed Freud's warning that, sometimes, 'a cigar is just a cigar', we might also conclude that, sometimes at least, a pipe is 'just a pipe'. But if we return one final time to that swollen – 'engorged' – floating pipe of 1929, if 'This Is Not a Pipe', we can

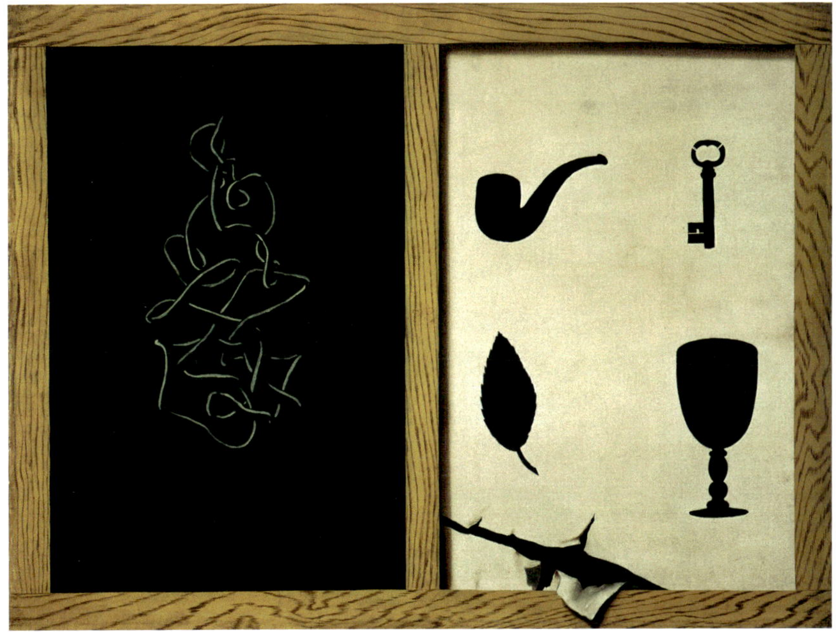

***The Alphabet of
Revelations***
*L'Alphabet des
révélations* 1929,
oil on canvas,
54 × 73 cm.
The Menil Collection,
Houston, CR 304

at least feel confident of one of its connotations. Magritte's image is therefore reducible neither to a linguistic analysis, nor to a demonstration on the nature of representation. However, it harbours an erotic sub-text that draws on the codes and techniques of advertising, pointing forward to the seductive fetishisation of the object typical of Pop Art and the Debordian 'spectacle' of the post-War era. (**NM**)

See also: **Chance; Eroticism; Meaning; *Objet trouvé*; Representation and Resemblance**

Trompe l'oeil: In painting trompe l'oeil – literally 'fooling the eye' – describes a technique of visual illusionism whereby the naturalistic image seemingly extends into three-dimensional space. Embracing the concepts of 'deception' and 'illusion', it constitutes a central pillar of Magritte's practice. From 1926 Magritte's paintings and **collages** demonstrate a fascination with the *faux bois* effect. It becomes clear that his primary concern is with perceptual effects. 'I always try to make sure that the actual painting isn't noticed,' he observed, 'that it is as little visible as possible.'[202] The inclusion of **curtains** to suggest

performance, or the style of schoolroom demonstrations, serves to further heighten the sense of theatrical artificiality – that what is on display here is **representation** itself.

With *The Alphabet of Revelations* 1929, Magritte presents a diptych in which a *faux bois* **frame** opens out onto an infinite void. In the left-hand frame, a tangle of metal hovers in the darkness, recalling children's puzzles in which twisted metal shapes have to be disentangled – but it is clear that here the puzzle is quite insoluble. The right-hand panel contains a bare canvas complete with painted shadows of an incongruous collection of familiar **objects**, suggesting another puzzle to be resolved. A trompe l'oeil tear in the canvas adds a note of melodrama and encourages our suspension of disbelief, enticing us to peer expectantly into the painted void. (**NM**)

See also: **Artifice; Ersatz; Metamorphosis; Pattern; Theatrical Display**

V

Vache Period: On 11 May 1948 Magritte opened his first solo exhibition in **Paris**. The infamous 'Vache' exhibition presented a group of quickly executed paintings and gouaches, uncharacteristically flamboyant and garishly aggressive in style and intent which stand apart from the other works in his oeuvre. The exhibition was intended as a kind of insult to Paris – Magritte's delayed response to his marginal position in relation to metropolitan **Surrealism** whilst living in the city from 1927 to 1930 – and to **André Breton** for his over-obfuscations of Surrealist ideas. By 1948 he had come to regard the French capital as 'a beautiful city without any raison d'être; aside from great vistas, it's a vacuum'.[203]

Magritte is known to have quickly created thirty-nine Vache works, of which twenty-five were exhibited. The subject matter is notable for being inspired by caricature and the popular imagination, in particular the comic imagery of Louis Forton's *Les Pieds Nickelés*, whilst other works deploy wilful pastiche and stylistic borrowings from Henri Matisse and **James Ensor**. Other works resemble crude reflections of his own work. *The Rainbow* 1948, for example, reads like a garish approximation of a text-image painting. **Louis Scutenaire and Irène Hamoir** were complicit in devising the acrimonious intent of the exhibition. As has been noted, the anarchic and liberated energy of the Vache work derives in part from Magritte's awareness that an exhibition staged at the inauspicious Galerie du Faubourg, located on Paris's Right Bank, would be ignored or at least critically derided. As Michel Draguet suggests, the relevance of the Vache work for contemporary artists rests in its 'radical negativity', its confounding of expectations, and its rejection of Modernism and its associations of creativity as progressive discourse.[204] (DP)

See also: **Parody and Pastiche; Renoir Period**

Geert Van Bruaene (1891–1964) Actor and gallerist. In December 1923 he opened the Cabinet Maldoror gallery and began his lifelong dealing in Magritte's work. He specialised in folk and avant-garde art, including Paul Klee, Wassily Kandinsky and László Moholy-Nagy, and was to own a number of galleries with flamboyant names. He also ran a number of bars, in 1944 founding La Fleur en Papier Doré, which became an important social hub for the luminaries of Belgian Surrealism. (DP)

Paul-Gustave Van Hecke (1887–1967) A key figure of Belgian modern art and one of the principal distributors of **Surrealism**. After the death of his father, a militant socialist, he worked in a soft furnishings factory before turning to the arts; his activities included being a journalist, critic, editor, curator, theatre and festival director, presenting himself primarily as a fashion designer. In 1916 he founded 'Maison de couture Norine' with his wife Honorine de Schryver, known as Norine (1887–1977). In 1920 he launched the journal *Sélection* with André de Ridder and opened a gallery of the same name, promoting Expressionism, alongside its partner gallery **Le Centaure**. Closed in 1922 for financial reasons, *Sélection* nonetheless continued to pursue its artistic campaign, publishing journals with investment from **E.L.T. Mesens**. It was through Mesens that Van Hecke met Magritte, who was commissioned in 1926 to produce advertising designs for *Norine*; in 1925 Magritte designed the **music score** cover for *Norine Blues* and in 1928 he painted Van Hecke's

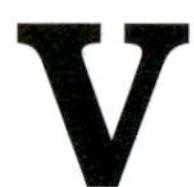

The Rainbow
L'Arc-en-ciel 1948, goauche on paper, 45.1 × 32.3 cm.
Private Collection, Switzerland, courtesy Simon Studer Art, Geneva, CR1275

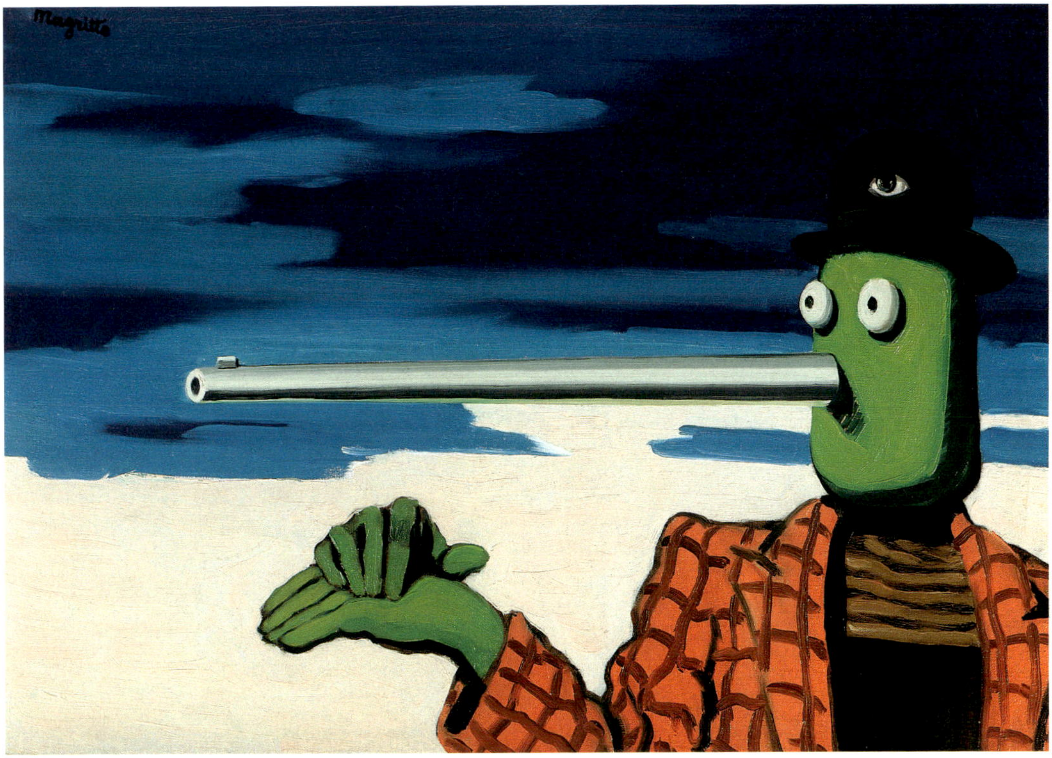

The Ellipsis
L'Ellipse 1948, oil on canvas, 50 × 73 cm. Royal Museums
of Fine Arts of Belgium, Brussels, CR 644

portrait. In 1927 Van Hecke founded the Galerie l'Époque. In 1928 he founded the quasi-Surrealist journal **Variétés** and in 1930 *L'Art vivant*. Hit by the economic crisis, Van Hecke's collection was liquidated by auction in May 1933. After the collapse, while the fashion house continued its activities, Van Hecke became chief editor of the Ghent journal *Vooruit* until 1938, and was later Director-General of Pathé Cinemas in Belgium. (**XC**)

Variétés: Edited by **Paul-Gustave Van Hecke**, *Variétés* never became, properly speaking, a Surrealist journal even though it regularly echoed the group's activities. Twenty-five were published between May 1928 and April 1930, with the issue of January 1929 carrying a number of Magritte illustrations. *Le Surréalisme en 1929*, published in June that year and devised by André Breton and Louis Aragon, constitutes an important document of the Surrealist movement. (**XC**)

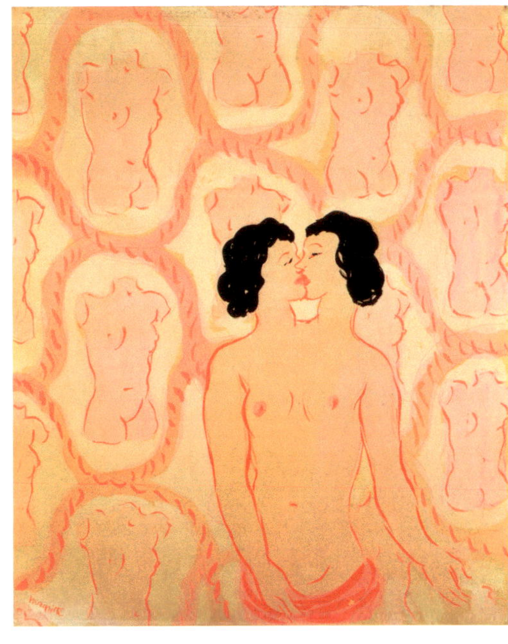

Lola de Valence
1948, gouache on paper, 46 × 37.6 cm.
René Magritte Museum, Brussels (Jette), CR 1269

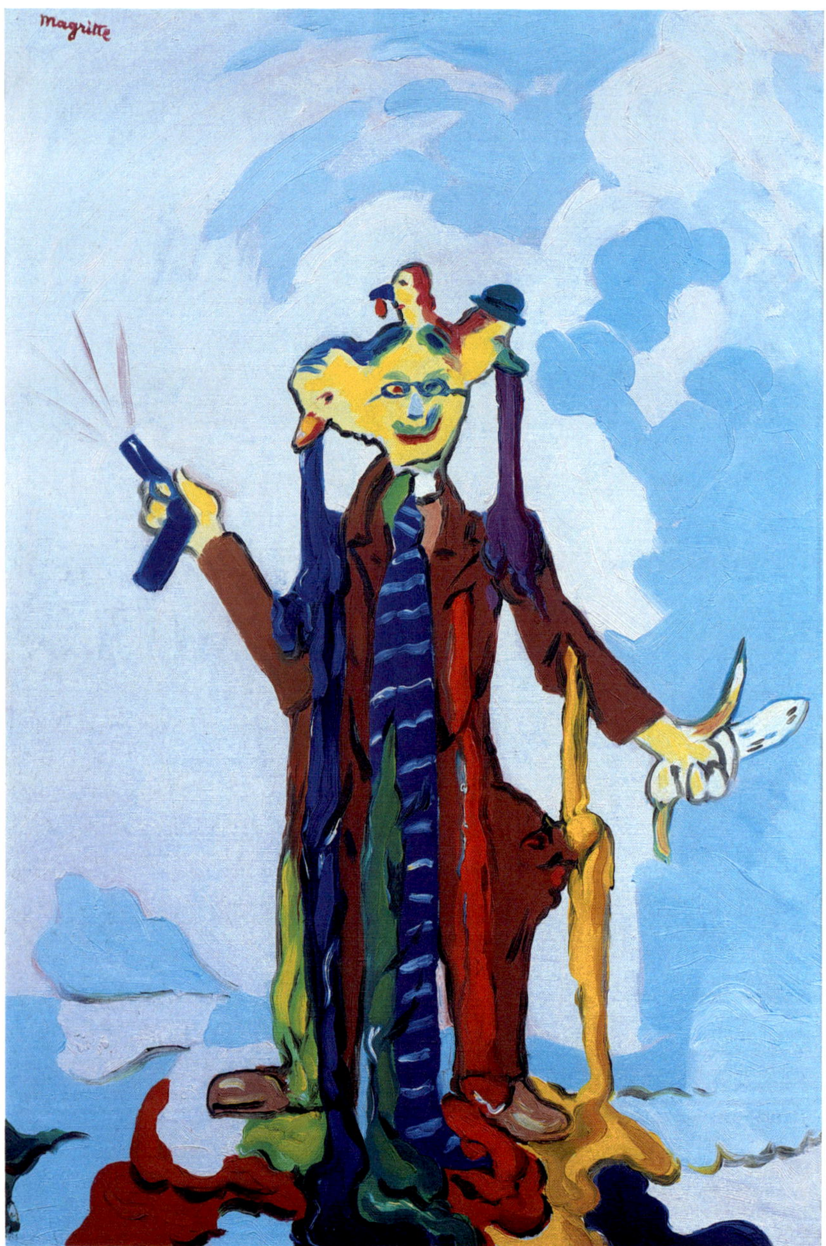

Pictorial Content
Le Contenu pictural 1948, oil on canvas, 73 × 50 cm.
Private Collection, CR 646

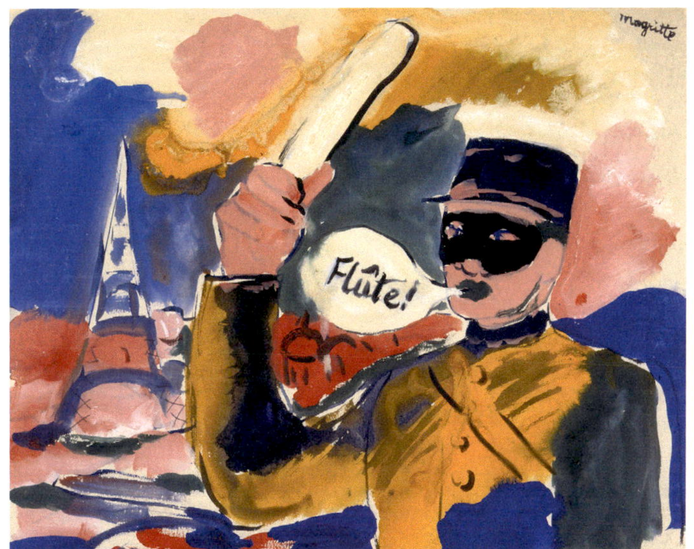

Drat it!
Flûte! 1948, gouache
on paper, 38 × 46 cm.
Collection Province de
Hainaut, Belgium, CR 1273

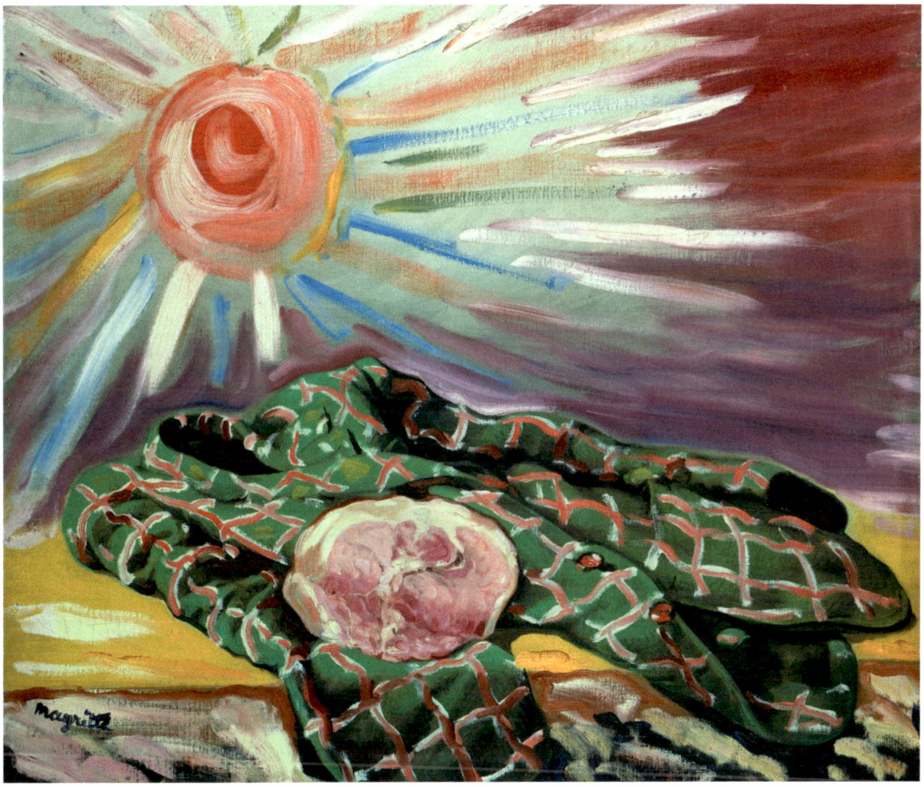

Seasickness
Le Mal de mer 1948, oil on canvas, 54 × 65 cm.
Private Collection, Brussels, CR 654

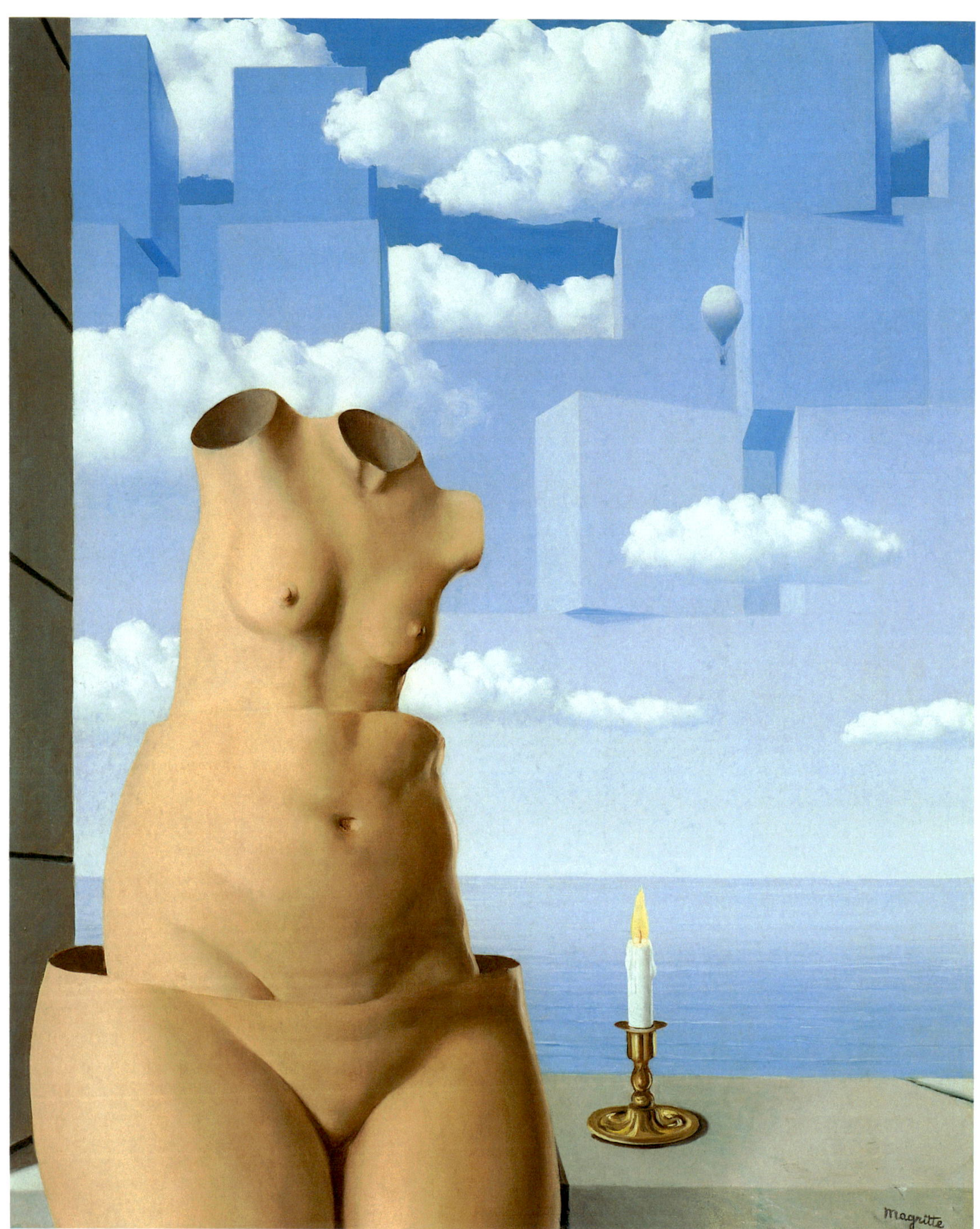

Megalomania
La Folie des grandeurs 1948, oil on canvas, 99.2 × 81.5 cm.
Hirshhorn Museum and Sculpture Garden, Smithsonian
Institution, Washington, DC. Gift of Joseph H. Hirshhorn,
1966, CR 672

Violence pervades a number of Magritte's images, though rarely overtly, as with the bloody corpse of *The Menaced Assassin* 1927. Violence is expressed for the most part in terms of dark, menacing spaces, in the fragmentation of bodies or of buildings, or in the creation of a threatening atmosphere. When violence erupts in these images it is often of a sexual nature, as with *The Titanic Days* 1928, in which a muscular, naked woman struggles with a clothed man, a scene that Magritte confirmed to **Marcel Lecomte** was one of attempted rape.[205] Magritte further observed that this was 'a more violent effort than hitherto, but I feel that the violence here is not merely external'.[206] This theme is developed in *The Rape* 1934 and its variations, in which a process of displacement is clearly at work. In this image the torso of a woman is displaced and the face eroticised, with the mouth transformed into genitalia. A similar process occurs in Luis Buñuel and **Salvador Dalí's** film *Un Chien andalou* 1929, in a scene where the underarm hair of the woman is transferred to the man's mouth, again suggesting a sexual metaphor, as with Meret Oppenheim's celebrated *Object (Fur Teacup)* of 1936. Magritte wrote of *The Rape* in terms of his procedure during the 1930s of seeking a 'solution' to a 'problem', though he gives no explanation beyond specifying the problem as 'woman', resolved in the shift of the torso to the face.[207] That the work should have provided the cover image of **André Breton's** *What is Surrealism?* 1934 suggests that it does, quite literally, embody surrealism's eroticised conception of 'woman'. (**NM**)

See also: **Elective Affinities; Eroticism; Female Form; Sigmund Freud; Psychoanalysis; Shock; World War II**

Visual Fracture: This idea of visual fracture can be seen in works representing a subject through the depiction of fragmented parts of its image across multiple canvases. *The Eternally Obvious* 1948, for example, presents a full-length nude figure across five framed canvases. Combined, they offer visual evidence of the corporeal form. Yet the individual elements can be rearranged, presenting the figure as if it were a series of movable objects disassociated from one another. The body's usual presentation as a continuous form is denied, the tightly cropped framed fragments emphasising the fundamental

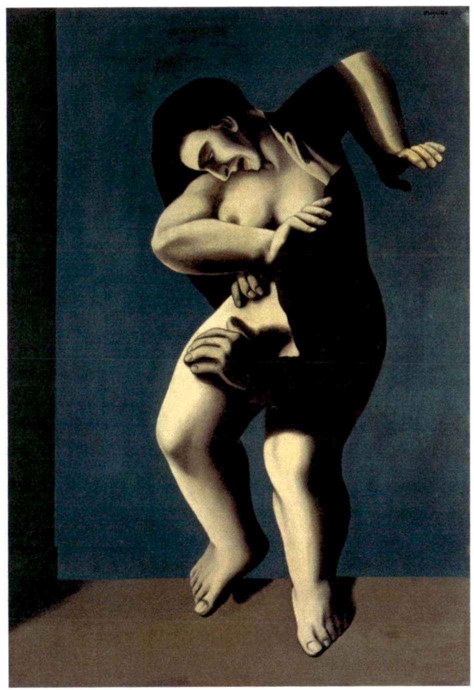

The Titanic Days
Les Jours gigantesques 1928, oil on canvas, 116 × 81 cm. Kunstsammlung Nordrhein-Westfalen, Düsseldorf, CR 247

artificiality of the image. Magritte created a number of such **object** works, perhaps the most celebrated being *Representation* 1937 – a canvas shaped to follow the outlined contours of the female pelvis – whose power is tied up with the cult of the Surrealist object, as well as with Surrealism's objectification of the female body in general. *Black Magic* 1942, an image first found by Magritte in 1934, presents a female nude morphing with the sky, combining visual implausibility with eroticism. Similarly the shattered nudes depicted in works such as *Megalomania* 1948 resemble Russian dolls, the figure with multiple layers of skin collapsing into itself. (**DP**)

See also: **Eroticism; Fetish; Frame**

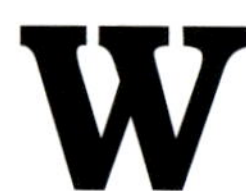

W

Wallpaper: In November 1921, shortly after completing his military service, Magritte began full-time employment as a designer at Peters-Lacroix, a manufacturer of wallpaper in Haren, at the north-eastern edge of Brussels. One of his work colleagues was the Belgian artist **Victor Servranckx**. In a letter to Pierre Flouquet he describes his meeting with the employer, writing 'armed with designs which I had feverishly composed and painted … I was received by a fellow with a long goatee beard who studied my drawings and seemed to like them … He spoke seriously about art – there are rules of harmony … all young artists think themselves geniuses'.[208] Magritte was required to create ornamental motifs. In a subsequent letter to Flouquet he writes 'although the designs I have to do are not modern, the work is nonetheless interesting … There's a special technique to be acquired for this job – small things one wouldn't suspect, rules to get to know which are well defined laws of harmony … since wallpaper is decorative the "two dimensions" must be respected.'[209] Swatch examples of Magritte-designed wallpaper are held in the collections of the Royal Museums of Fine Arts of Belgium and the Archives de la Ville de Bruxelles. **(DP)**

See also: **Artifice; Commercial Art; Pattern; Trompe l'oeil**

Jacques Wergifosse (1928–2006) Belgian poet. Wergifosse was sixteen years old when he first met Magritte and would become a longstanding friend and accomplice of the artist. Magritte wrote *Magic Lines*, an appreciation of Wergifosse's drawings which appeared in the printed review *Le Ciel bleu* in 1945. In turn, Wergifosse made a critical contribution to Magritte's conception of 'Sunlit Surrealism', including writing the introductory text for his 'Renoir' exhibition at the Société royale des Beaux-Arts, Verviers in 1947. The two remained in contact until at least 1958. **(DP)**

See also: **Book Illustration; Renoir Period**

Window, offers us a view from one space into another, while at the same time creating a barrier between the two spaces. Several of Magritte's paintings depict an interior room with a window at the back through which one can glimpse the exterior world – sky, sea, mountains or forest – suggesting a possibility of freedom, at once uplifting and (perhaps deliberately) banal.

In other paintings, there is a more complex and ambiguous interaction between interior and the exterior. The image of the world might be imprinted on the glass itself, an action that seems to have shattered it (*Evening Falls* 1964). In certain paintings the vertical panels of the opened window have sea, sky and **clouds** on them, but reveal only darkness beyond (*The Field Glass* 1963). Most famously, a canvas has been set on an easel before the window and the landscape on the canvas precisely matches up with the landscape seen through the window. Magritte

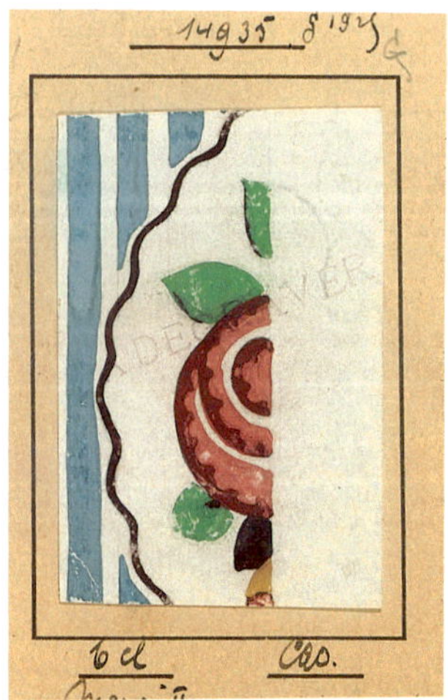

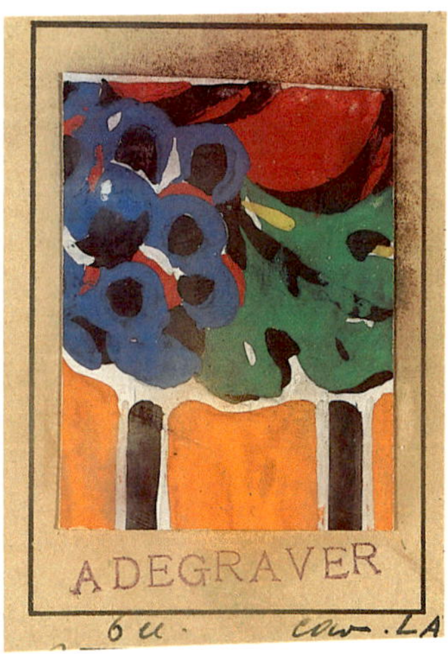

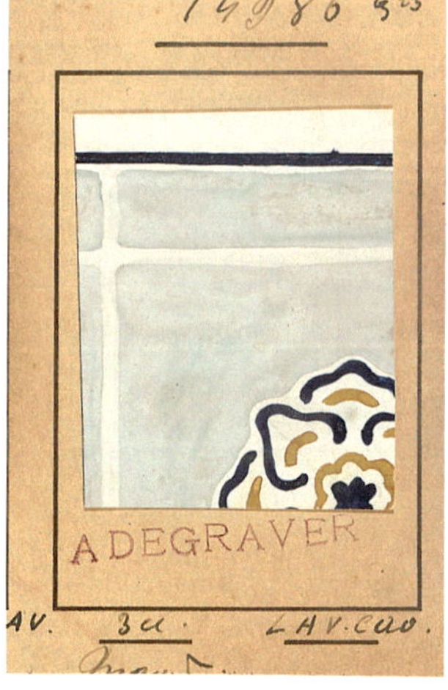

Wallpaper designs for the Peters-Lacroix factory, Haren, 1921–4, gouache on paper, various sizes, each approx. 9 × 6 cm.
Royal Museums of Fine Arts of Belgium, Brussels, CR x06

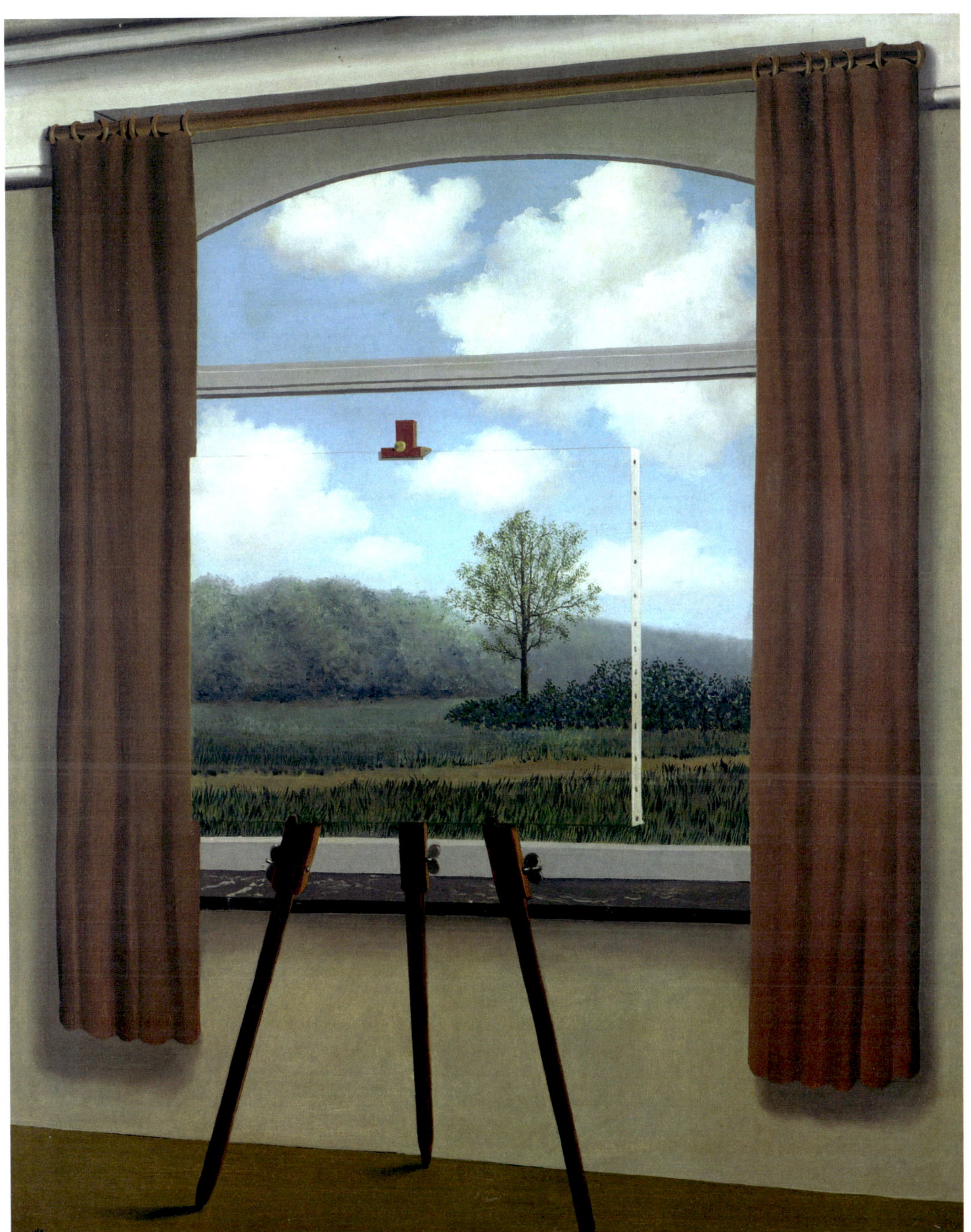

The Human Condition
La Condition humaine 1933, oil on canvas, 100 × 81 cm.
National Gallery of Art, Washington, DC. Gift of the
Collectors Committee, CR 351

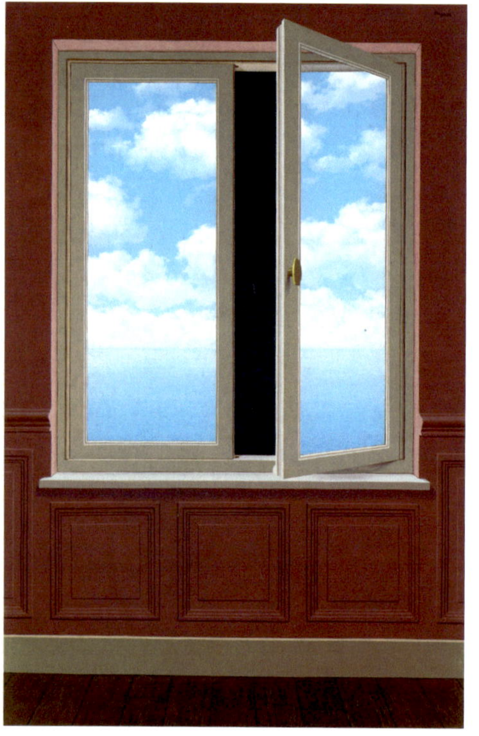

The Field-Glass
La Lunette d'approche 1963, oil on canvas, 175.5 × 116 cm.
The Menil Collection, Houston, CR 969

entitled this last image *The Human Condition*, stating that it was a response to the 'problem of the window'. The picture, said Magritte, was an analogy for 'how we see the world: we see it as being outside ourselves even though it is only a mental representation of it that we experience inside ourselves'.[210] Whether that interior image matches the exterior reality is something we can never be sure of. *The Human Condition* was painted in 1933 while the Magrittes were living in a ground-floor apartment at 135 Rue Esseghem in the Brussels suburb of Jette, and which is now the René Magritte Museum. The window in the painting closely resembles the actual front window of his house, which now looks out on to a row of houses on the other side of the narrow street. Some of these were in fact built after the time of the painting. In 1933, there would have been open fields on the other side of the street. In the guidebook to the museum the window is shown with a view of fields and trees montaged in, just as they are in the painting.[211] **(IW)**

See also: **Absence; Elective Affinities; Eye; Frame**

World War II: Too young to have been conscripted during World War I, Magritte completed his military service between 1920 and 1922, confirming a lifelong disdain for militarism.[212] Having escaped to Carcassonne from the Nazi invasion of 1940, the artist soon returned home; unlike many Surrealists in France, those in Belgium did not feel compelled to leave Europe during World War II. Back in Brussels, some necessarily modest and constrained activity remained possible, if only at some cost and risk. Magritte continued to contribute to publications and exhibitions, albeit with a lower profile than before the Occupation, and at the constant risk of denunciation from reactionary quarters. In particular, through the intermediary of **Marcel Mariën** who made regular journeys to Paris, Magritte contributed to publications by the Main à Plume Surrealist group, a coalition between younger artists and writers and a few established figures who had remained in France, including some no longer strictly in Surrealism's orbit.

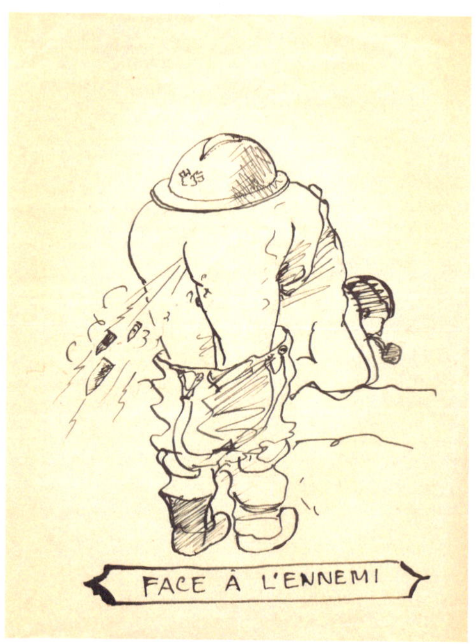

The Face of the Enemy
Face à l'ennemi, illustration on letter from René Magritte to Louis Scutenaire, 11 December 1939

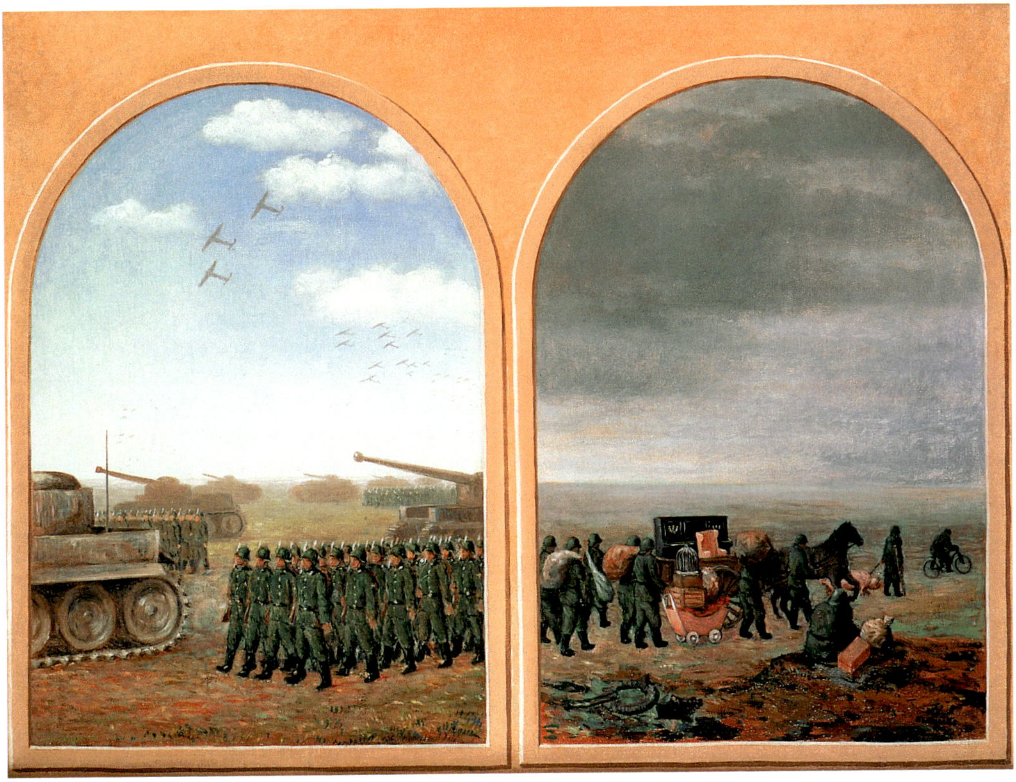

Applied Dialectics
La Dialectique appliquée 1944–5, oil on canvas, 60 × 80 cm.
Collection Leslee and David Rogath, CR 578

In common with prevailing Surrealist practice, Belgian Surrealists scrupulously avoided any direct reference to the conflict in their work, insisting that the imagination should never be shackled to circumstance. The closest Magritte came to this, perhaps, was the ominous airborne technology of *The Black Flag* 1937, a kind of premonition of the disasters to follow, and *Applied Dialectics* 1944–5. Magritte's primary act of resistance, then, was to depart from his signature style and devote 1943–47 to works featuring the **colours** and touches of popular Impressionist painters. The resulting works were seen almost universally as a hostile act of provocation, and ushered in an extended period during which the Surrealists gathered around Magritte in Brussels deliberately estranged themselves from **André Breton's** reformed Parisian group. (**KF**)

See also: **Renoir Period; Shock; Surrealism; Vache Period; Violence**

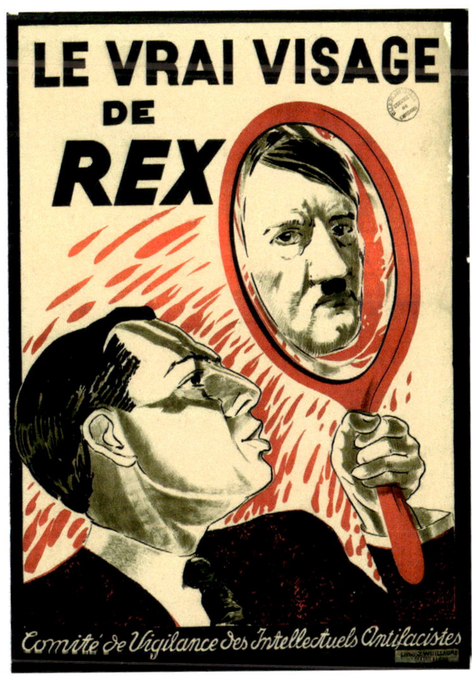

Le Vrai Visage de Rex
c.1937, anti-fascist poster depicting Léon Degrelle and Hitler, lithograph on paper, 80 × 57.3 cm. Archives de la Ville de Bruxelles

Z

Zwanzeur: In the Marolles district – one of the oldest neighbourhoods in Brussels – a dialect known as 'Brusseleer' is spoken. Formed from a mixture of Dutch and French, in Brusseleer 'zwanze' means farce, jest, a rebellious state of mind which produces the 'zwanzeur', or 'joker'. Sometimes bordering on self-ridicule, the 'zwanzeur' can also wilfully exaggerate or amplify the facts. It has been suggested that 'zwanze' amounts to an earthy form of resistance to the successive occupations which Belgium has endured during its history, notably during the Inquisition. If the relationships between Magritte and his collaborators sometimes displayed the mark of this spirit – see, for example, Magritte's correspondence with **Louis Scutenaire** or **Paul Colinet**, or the jokes in which the artist participated since his boyhood, such as displaying his neighbour's coffin in his lounge and inviting his friends over to observe their reactions, or leaving coins and banknotes on the stairs to Pablo Picasso's studio with **Marcel Mariën** – there has been a strong tendency since to consider all expressions of humour in modern and contemporary Belgian art as somehow 'Surrealist'. We should remind ourselves that Surrealist humour is often dark and laced with a moral dimension, far removed from the gesticulations of certain followers today who repeat well-worn processes for the purposes of commercial advertising or aesthetic ends. (**XC**)

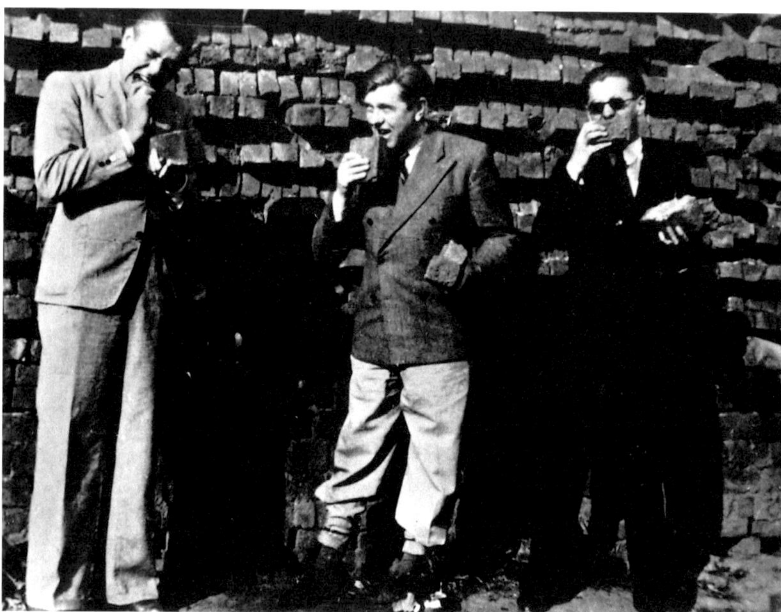

The Feast of Stones
Le Festin de pierres,
Paul and René Magritte,
Marcel Mariën, Brussels,
1942, photograph,
gelatin silver print,
40 × 29.5 cm,
Private Collection

Chronology

21 November 1898

Magritte born in Lessines, Hainaut province. His mother Régina Bertinchamps is a milliner, his father Léopold a merchant tailor and travelling businessman.

1910

Magritte begins attending a weekly painting class. Remembering his boyhood experiences, he later states: 'The art of painting seemed to me vaguely magical and the painter to be gifted with superior powers.'[213]

1912

24 February, suicide of Magritte's mother.

1913

René attends secondary school in Charleroi. He meets his future wife Georgette Berger at the annual fair.

1914

August, Germany invades and occupies Belgium. Magritte's family moves from Charleroi to Châtelet; René does not meet Georgette again until 1920.

1916

October, enters the Académie des Beaux-Arts in Brussels. The courses on which he enrols include 'Decorative Painting' and 'Ornamental Composition'.

1918

Earliest known commercial poster, advertising 'Pot au Feu Derbaix' stock cubes.

1919

April, contributes drawings to the review *Au Volant*, published by Victor and Pierre Bourgeois.
Begins sharing studio with Pierre Flouquet.
December, Victor Bourgeois and Aimé Declercq open the Centre d'Art in Brussels. Its inaugural exhibition includes posters designed by Magritte.

1920

Magritte and Pierre Flouquet present paintings at the Centre d'Art.

January, René meets Georgette again. In the same month he meets E.L.T. Mesens.
December, begins military service at the Beverlo Camp, near Leopoldsburg. He continues to paint and is stationed for a time with Pierre Bourgeois. He performs a final month of service during March 1922.

1921

November, begins full-time employment at Peters-Lacroix, wallpaper manufacturers, where he works for approximately two years.

1922

Meets Marcel Lecomte at beginning of year.
28 June, marries Georgette Berger in Saint-Josse, Brussels.

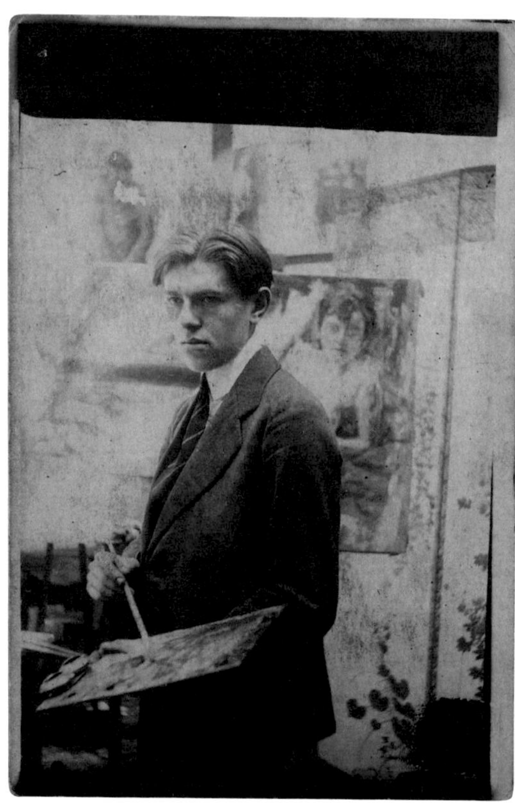

René Magritte in his studio, 1919

1923

April – May, presents work in Antwerp as part of an international group exhibition organised by the review *Ça ira*.
Artists include Willi Baumeister, Lyonel Feininger,
El Lissitzky, László Moholy-Nagy, Aleksander Rodchenko
and Victor Servranckx.

Magritte sees a reproduced image of Giorgio de Chirico's
The Song of Love 1914, a painting that proves critical in
his artistic development.

December, meets Camille Goemans.

1924

Creates commercial posters and designs for the couture
house Norine.

October, Magritte and E.L.T. Mesens contribute texts to
391, Francis Picabia's Dadaist periodical.

1925

Early in the year Magritte meets Paul Nougé.

Norine Blues, song composed by Paul Magritte with lyrics
by René and Georgette Magritte, is performed at a
Norine fashion show in Ostend. Magritte also designs
the cover of the sheet music score.

March, first and only edition of Dada review *Œsophage*,
edited by Magritte and E.L.T. Mesens.

Late in the year he creates his first Surrealist paintings and
earliest paper collage works.

1926

January, secures contract with Paul-Gustave Van Hecke,
whose Galerie Le Centaure agrees to purchase his
works. Magritte embarks on a prolific period producing
around 280 works over the next four years.

June – July, contributes to *Marie*, a review edited by E.L.T.
Mesens.

Summer, creates commercial design illustrations for the
autumn catalogue of S. Samuel et Cie, furriers, with
texts by Camille Goemans.

October, foundation of the Belgian Surrealist group.

1927

February, final issue of *Adieu à Marie* appears. Edited by
Paul Nougé, who becomes *de facto* leader of Surrealist
activity in Belgium.

April – May, first one-man exhibition, staged at Galerie
Le Centaure, Brussels. Sixty-one works are presented.

June, Magritte meets Louis Scutenaire.

Summer, Magritte again creates illustrations for the furrier

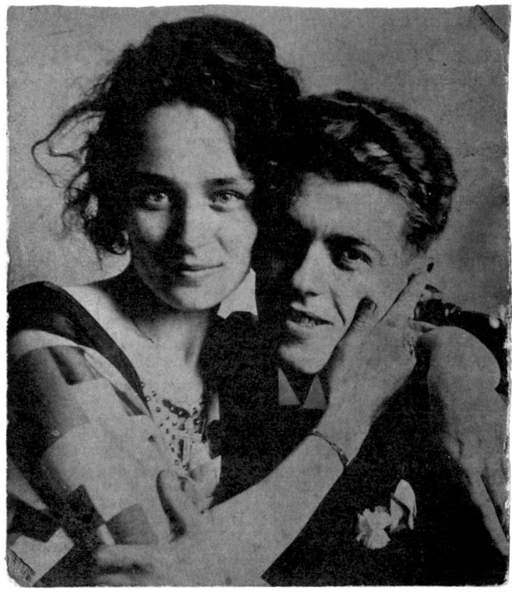

Georgette and René Magritte, 18 June 1922. Photograph, gelatin
silver print on paper, 7.6 × 6.9 cm. Private Collection

S. Samuel et Cie. Paul Nougé provides the accompanying captions.

Mid-September, Magritte and Georgette move to Paris.
Their address is 101 Avenue de Rosny, Le Perreux-
sur-Marne.

1928

January, one-man exhibition at the E.L.T. Mesens run
Galerie L'Époque, Brussels.

February, contributes to *Distances*, a monthly review
founded by Paul Nougé and Camille Goemans. Two
further issues appear in March and April.

April, excluded from the important Surrealist exhibition
at Galerie au Sacre du Printemps in Paris. However,
later in the year André Breton purchases works by
Magritte, marking the artist's belated acceptance by the
Parisian Surrealists.

24 August, Magritte's father dies in Brussels.

1929

February to March, series of five leaflets entitled *Le
Sens propre* published, each with a reproduction of a
Magritte painting accompanied by a poem by Camille
Goemans.

Spring, meets Salvador Dali.

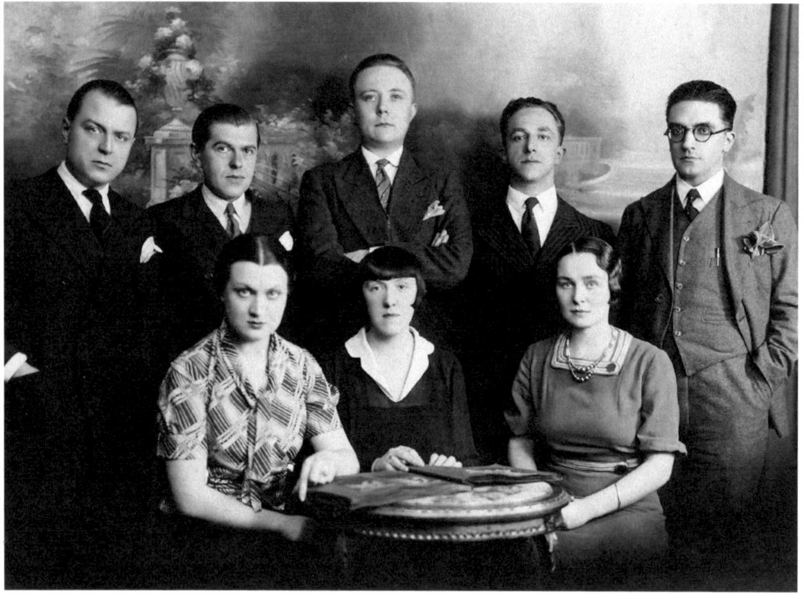

The Hunters' Gathering
Le Rendez-Vous de chasse, E.L.T. Mesens, René Magritte, Louis Scutenaire, André Breton, Paul Nougé, Irène Hamoir, Marthe Nougé, and Georgette Magritte, in the studio of Jos Rentmeesters, 1934

October, Galerie Goemans in Paris opens with group exhibition of Jean Arp, Salvador Dalí, Yves Tanguy and Magritte.

December, contributes to the final issue of the Parisian Surrealist journal *La Révolution surréaliste*. In the same month he falls out with André Breton, leading to Magritte's long estrangement from the Parisian Surrealists.

1930

April, personal and financial reasons force Camille Goemans to close his gallery.

July, the Magrittes leave Paris and move to 135 Rue Esseghem, Jette/Brussels, where they remain until 1954.

1931

In need of financial support, Magritte and his brother Paul establish Studio Dongo, a commercial design enterprise.

January, Magritte represented in *L'Art vivant en Belgique 1910–1930* at Galerie Georges Giroux, Brussels. Includes *The Annunciation* 1930, a painting lent by E.L.T. Mesens.

February, one-man exhibition at Salle Giso, Brussels.

April – May, exhibits for first time at the Palais des Beaux-Arts, Brussels.

1933

April, invited by André Breton to contribute to the periodical *Surrealism in the Service of the Revolution*, signaling Magritte's reconciliation with the Paris Surrealists. In June he is included in their group exhibition at the Galerie Pierre Colle, and in their exhibition at the Salon des Surindépendants, staged during October – November.

May – June, one-man exhibition at the Palais des Beaux-Arts, Brussels.

August, meets Paul Colinet.

1934

February, represented in *Le Nu dans l'art vivant*, exhibition at the Palais des Beaux-Arts, Brussels. Organised jointly by the L'Art vivant, a society formed to promote contemporary art, and the Société auxiliaire des Expositions du Palais des Beaux-Arts.

May – June, works presented in the *Minotaure* exhibition at the Palais des Beaux-Arts, Brussels.

July, publication of André Breton, *What is Surrealism?* with cover design by Magritte.

1935

August, the cover of the third issue of the *Bulletin international du surréalisme* features Magritte's *The Bungler* 1935.

September, Paul Éluard's poem 'René Magritte' published in *Cahiers d'art*, Paris.

1936

January, first one-man exhibition in the United States, at the Julien Levy Gallery, New York.

May, participates in *Exposition surréaliste d'objets*, at Galerie Charles Ratton in Paris, co-organised by André Breton.

June – July, fourteen works included in the *International Surrealist Exhibition*, London.

1937

February – March, spends five weeks at the London home of collector Edward James; works on three commissions.

July, meets Marcel Mariën.

December, *Trois peintres surréalistes: René Magritte, Man Ray, Yves Tanguy* at the Palais de Beaux-Arts, Brussels.

1938

January – February, participates in the *Exposition internationale du surréalisme* at the Galerie des Beaux-Arts, Paris, organised by André Breton and Paul Éluard.

April, E.L.T. Mesens and Roland Penrose take over the running of the London Gallery and devote inaugural exhibition to Magritte.

November, 'La Ligne de vie' lecture at the Koninklijk Museum voor Schone Kunsten, Antwerp. Constitutes the most revealing account Magritte gave of his artistic practice and ideas.

1939

May, one-man exhibition at the Palais des Beaux-Arts, Brussels.

Designs anti-fascism poster *Le Vrai Visage de Rex* for the Comité de Vigilance des Intellectuels anti-fascistes.

1940

February, first issue of *L'Invention collective*, Surrealist review. Magritte is a key contributor.

Autumn, creates first bottle works.

1941

January, exhibition at the Galerie Dietrich, Brussels.

1943

During the next four years Magritte enters his so-called 'Renoir Period', during which he adopts the painting style and palette of Impressionism.

August, the first monograph on Magritte is published, with text by Marcel Mariën.

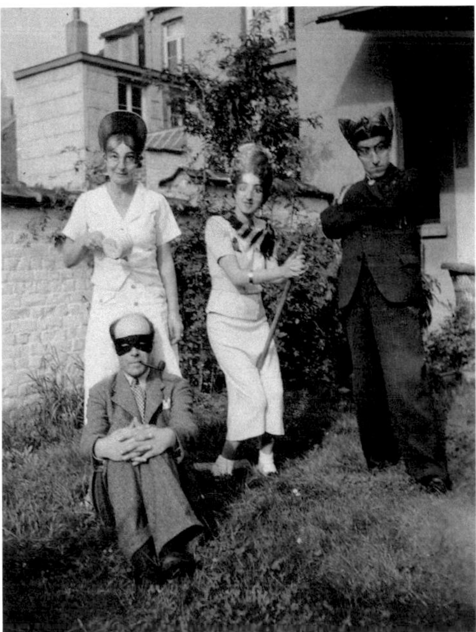

The Extraterrestrials III
Les Extra-Terrestres III, Paul Colinet, Georgette Magritte, Jacqueline Delcourt, and Maurice Singer, Rue Esseghem, Brussels, 1935. Photograph, gelatin silver print, 8.7 × 6.2 cm. Private Collection

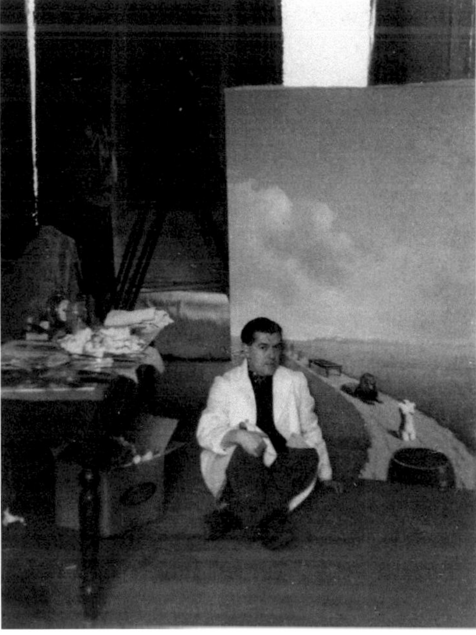

René Magritte and *Youth Illustrated*, at Edward James's house, 35 Wimpole Street, London, March 1937. Photograph, gelatin silver print, 13.7 × 9.3 cm. Private Collection

1944

January, Magritte's 'Renoir' works are presented at a one-man exhibition at Galerie Dietrich, Brussels.

Towards the end of the year meets the poet Jacques Wergifosse, who becomes a friend and collaborator.

1945

During the first half of the year produces illustrations for Comte de Lautréamont's *Les Chants de Maldoror*.

September, Communist newspaper *Le Drapeau rouge* announces Magritte's membership of the Belgian Communist Party.

1946

June, visits Paris, re-establishes contact with André Breton and Francis Picabia.

November, exhibition at Galerie Dietrich, Brussels.

1947

April, first one-man exhibition organised by Alexandre Iolas and presented at the Hugo Gallery, New York.

1948

January, exhibition at the Galerie Dietrich, Brussels. Marks the end of Magritte's Impressionist style of painting.

May, first one-man exhibition in Paris, exhibition of 'Vache' paintings.

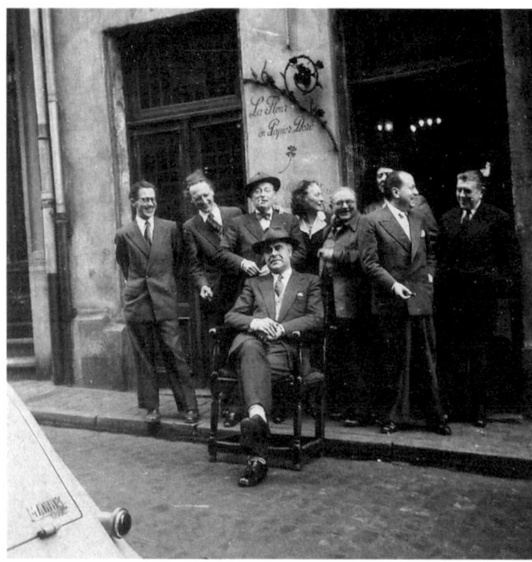

The Belgian Surrealist group, in front of the café La Fleur en Papier Doré, Brussels, March 1953. From left to right: Marcel Mariën, Albert Van Loock, Camille Goemans, Georgette Magritte, Geert Van Bruaene, Louis Scutenaire, E.L.T. Mesens, René Magritte and Paul Colinet sitting at centre. Photograph, gelatin silver print, 5.5 × 5.5 cm. Private Collection

1949

February – March, an exhibition of recent works presented at the Galerie Lou Cosyn, Brussels.

February and August, Alexandre Iolas visits Magritte in Brussels to discuss works to be shown at the Hugo Gallery, New York.

1950

September, exhibition at the Hugo Gallery, New York.

1952

August, first retrospective after the World War II staged at the Casino Communal in Knokke; organised by E.L.T. Mesens.

October, establishes *La Carte d'après nature*, a miniature review that appears intermittently up to April 1956.

1953

January – February, first exhibition in Italy at Galleria dell'Obelisco, Rome. Visited by Giorgio de Chirico.

March, exhibition at the Iolas Gallery, New York.

April, Gustave Nellens, proprietor of the Casino at Knokke commissions Magritte to decorate the Salle de Lustre with a panoramic mural.

1954

March, *Word vs Image*, an exhibition of twenty-one Magritte 'text-image' paintings is exhibited at the Sidney Janis Gallery, New York. The show brings much critical attention to Magritte's work.

May – June, first major retrospective staged at the Palais des Beaux-Arts, Brussels.

June – October, twenty-four works by Magritte are shown in the Belgian Pavilion at the Venice Biennale, its main theme being Surrealism.

1955

At the end of the year, the Magrittes move to a ground floor apartment at 404 Boulevard Lambermont.

1956

March, Magritte is commissioned to produce a mural for the Salle des Congrès of the new Palais des Beaux-Arts, Charleroi.

October, Magritte purchases super-8 cine camera and begins making Surrealist home movies featuring his wife and friends. He devises potential scenarios, some elucidated in sketches.

December, Alexandre Iolas becomes Magritte's sole representative and dealer.

1957

March, elected to the Libre Académie de Belgique.

March, exhibition at the Iolas Gallery, New York.

October, meets Harry Torczyner, a Belgian-born lawyer based in New York who becomes Magritte's legal adviser, collector of his work and close friend.

December, the Magrittes move to 97 Rue des Mimosas in Schaerbeek, their final residence.

1958

July, begins corresponding with André Bosmans.

Over the course of the year Magritte completes twenty-seven works, as well as some gouaches, making this one of his most prolific years since the late 1920s.

1959

March, exhibitions of Magritte's work open in New York at The Bodley Gallery and at Alexandre Iolas' Gallery.

Luc de Heusch directs the film *Magritte ou La Leçon des choses*.

1960

Magritte receives the 'Prix du couronnement de carrière' for painters from the Minister of Education.

February – March, Iolas continues to promote Magritte's work and organises an exhibition at the Galerie Rive Droite, Paris.

October, Suzi Gablik, a young artist and critic, spends eight months with the Magrittes. She prepares a study on the artist, which was published in 1970.

December, retrospective exhibitions in Houston and Dallas.

1961

May, first issue of *Rhétorique* published, the result of collaboration with André Bosmans.

Late September, two rival exhibitions open in London at the Obelisk and Grosvenor Galleries.

1962

June, retrospective opens at the Casino Communal in Knokke.

September – October, *The Vision of René Magritte* exhibition at the Walker Art Center, Minneapolis.

1964

May – June, retrospective at the Arkansas Art Center, Little Rock.

1965

A deterioration in Magritte's health forces him to interrupt his work.

December, major retrospective at the Museum of Modern Art, New York. The exhibition travels to the Rose Art Museum, Brandeis University, Waltham, Massachusetts; The Art Institute of Chicago; Pasadena Art Museum and the University Museum, Berkeley, California, where it closes on 1 November 1966.

December, monograph by Patrick Waldberg appears, with bibliography by André Blavier.

1966

April, the Magrittes are invited to Israel by its Ambassador to Belgium.

1967

January, exhibition at Iolas' Paris gallery.

August – September, major retrospective held at the Museum Boijmans Van Beuningen in Rotterdam, which travels to the Moderna Museet, Stockholm.

15 August, Magritte dies at home of pancreatic cancer at the age of 69. He is buried at Schaerbeek Cemetery.

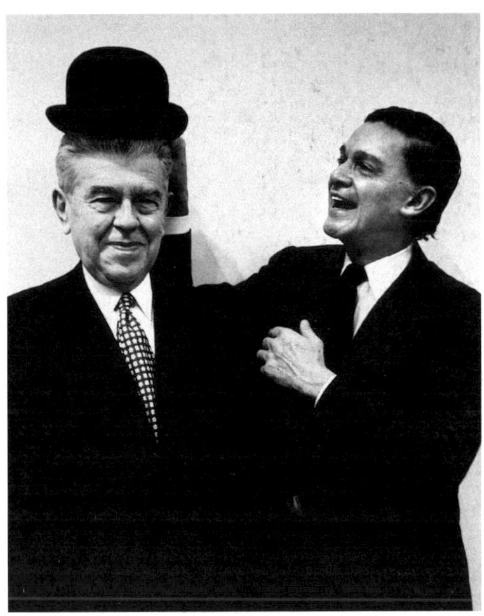

René Magritte and Alexandre Iolas, 16 December 1965. Photographed by Steve Shapiro for *Life* magazine

Select Bibliography

Catalogue Raisonné

David Sylvester, Sarah Whitfield (eds.), *René Magritte, Catalogue Raisonné*, 5 vols, London: Philip Wilson; Houston: The Menil Collection; Antwerp: Fonds Mercator, 1992–97.

Writings and Letters by Magritte

René Magritte, *Écrits complets*, André Blavier (ed.), Paris: Flammarion, 1979 (republished in 2001).

René Magritte, *Quatre-vingt-deux lettres de René Magritte à Mirabelle Dors et Maurice Rapin*, Paris, privately published, 1976.

René Magritte, *La Destination: lettres à Marcel Mariën (1937–1962)*, Marcel Mariën (ed.), Brussels: Les Lèvres Nues, 1977.

René Magritte, *Les Couleurs de la nuit*, Marcel Mariën (ed.), Brussels: Les Lèvres Nues, 1978.

René Magritte, *Lettres à André Bosmans (1958–1967)*, Francine Perceval (ed.), Brussels: Editions Seghers, 1990.

René Magritte, *Manifestes et autres écrits*, Marcel Mariën (ed.), Brussels: Les Lèvres Nues, 1972.

René Magritte, *Sous le manteau de Magritte* [letters to Colinet, James, Mesens, Éluard et al.], Marcel Mariën (ed.), Fleury-Mérogis: Éditions Fantomas, 1984.

René Magritte, Harry Torczyner, *Letters between Friends*, introduction by Sam Hunter, New York: Abrams, 1994.

Books on Magritte:

Patricia Allmer, *René Magritte: Beyond Painting*, Manchester and New York: Manchester University Press, 2009.

André Blavier, *Ceci n'est pas une pipe. Contribution furtive à l'étude d'un tableau de René Magritte*, Verviers: Temps Mêlés, 1973.

Richard Calvocoressi, *Magritte*, Oxford: Phaidon, 1979.

Jan Ceuleers, *René Magritte, 135 Rue Esseghem*, Jette-Brussels, Antwerp: Pandora, 1999.

Jacques Dopagne, *Magritte*, Paris: Hazan, 1997.

Michel Foucault, *Ceci n'est pas une pipe*, Montpellier: Fata Morgana, 1973. Published in English as *This Is Not a Pipe. With Illustrations and Letters by René Magritte*, James Harkness (trans. and ed.), Berkeley, Los Angeles and London: University of California Press, 1983.

Suzi Gablik, *Magritte*, London: Thames & Hudson, 1970.

Pere Gimferrer, *Magritte*, Barcelona: Poligrafa, 1986.

Siegfried Gohr, *Magritte*, Ghent and Amsterdam: Ludion, 2003.

Abraham M. Hammacher, *René Magritte*, London: Thames & Hudson; New York: Abrams, 1974.

Robert Hughes, *The Portable Magritte*, Antwerp: Ludion, 2009.

Ralf Konersmann, *René Magritte. Die Verbotene Reproduktion: Über die Sichtbarkeit des Denkens*, Frankfurt am Main: Fischer, 1991.

Marcel Mariën, *Apologies de Magritte*, Brussels: Didier Devillez, 1994.

Duane Michals, *A Visit with Magritte*, Providence, Rhode Island: Matrix, 1981.

Bernard Noël, *Magritte*, Paris: Flammarion, 1976.

Marcel Paquet, *Magritte ou l'éclipse de l'être*, Paris: La Différence, 1982.

Marcel Paquet, *René Magritte, 1898–1967. Der sichtbare Gedanke*, Cologne: Taschen, 1993.

René Passeron, *René Magritte*, Paris: Filipacchi, 1970.

José Pierre, *Magritte*, Paris: Somogy, 1984.

Alain Robbe-Grillet, *La Belle Captive*, Berkeley, Los Angeles and London: University of California Press, 1995.

Philippe Roberts-Jones, *Magritte poète visible*, Brussels: Laconti, 1972.

Patrick Roegiers (ed.), *Magritte and Photography*, London: Lund Humphries, 2005.

Georges Roque, *Ceci n'est pas un Magritte. Essai sur Magritte et la publicité*, Paris: Flammarion, 1983.

Ralf Schiebler, *Die Kunsttheorie René Magrittes*, Munich: Hanser, 1981.

Wieland Schmied, *René Magritte: Die Reize der Landschaft*, Munich: Piper, 1989.

Uwe M. Schneede, *René Magritte. Leben und Werk*, Cologne: DuMont, 1973.

Christoph Schreier, *René Magritte. Sprachbilder 1927–1930*, New York: Georg Olms, 1985.

Louis Scutenaire, *La Fidélité des images: René Magritte,*

Le Cinématographe et la photographie, Brussels: Lebeer Hossmann, 1976.

Louis Scutenaire, *René Magritte*, Brussels: Librairie Sélection, 1947 (written in 1942 and subsequently revised).

James Thrall Soby, *René Magritte*, New York: The Museum of Modern Art/Doubleday, 1965.

David Sylvester, *Magritte*, Houston: The Menil Collection, 1992 (revised edition, Brussels: Mercatorfonds, 2009).

Harry Torczyner (ed.), *Magritte: Ideas and Images*, Richard Miller (trans.), New York: Abrams, 1977.

Patrick Waldberg, *René Magritte*, Brussels: André de Rache, 1965.

Patrick Waldberg, *Magritte: Peintures*, Paris: La Différence, 1983.

Exhibition Catalogues

René Magritte et le Surréalisme en Belgique, Royal Museums of Fine Arts of Belgium, Brussels, 1982.

René Magritte, Fondation de l'Hermitage, Lausanne, 1987.

René Magritte, Kunsthalle der Hypo-Kulturstiftung, Munich, 1987–88.

René Magritte, National Museum of Modern Art, Tokyo, 1988.

Magritte – La période 'vache', Musée Cantini, Marseille, 1992.

Sarah Whitfield (ed.), *Magritte*, Hayward Gallery, South Bank Centre, London; The Metropolitan Museum of Art, New York; The Menil Collection, Houston; The Art Institute of Chicago, 1992–93.

Didier Ottinger (ed.), *Magritte*, Museum of Fine Arts, Montreal, 1996.

René Magritte: Die Kunst der Konversation, Kunstsammlung Nordhein-Westfalen, Düsseldorf, 1996–97.

Frederik Leen and Gisèle Ollinger-Zinque (eds.), *René Magritte 1898–1998*, Royal Museums of Fine Arts of Belgium, Brussels, 1998.

Magritte, Louisiana Museum of Art, Humlebaek, Denmark; San Francisco Museum of Modern Art; Scottish National Gallery of Modern Art, Edinburgh, 2000.

Daniel Abadie (ed.), *René Magritte*, Galerie Nationale du Jeu de Paume, Paris, 2003.

Patrick Roegiers (ed.), *Magritte et la photographie*, Palais des Beaux-Arts, Brussels, 2005.

René Magritte: The Key to Dreams, BA-CA Kunstforum, Vienna; Foundation Beyeler, Riehen/Basel, 2005.

Stephanie Barron and Michel Draguet (eds.), *Magritte and Contemporary Art: The Treachery of Images*, Los Angeles County Museum of Art, 2006.

Esther Schlicht and Max Hollein (eds.), *René Magritte 1948: La Période Vache*, Schirn Kunsthalle Frankfurt, 2008.

Michel Draguet (ed.), *Magritte tout et papier: Collages, dessins, gouaches*, Musée Maillol, Paris, 2006.

Notes

1 René Magritte, cited in Sarah Whitfield (ed.), *Magritte* (exh. cat.), London: South Bank Centre, 1992, p.141.

2 Ibid.

3 Jean Baudrillard, *Simulations*, Paul Foss, Paul Patton and Philip Beitchman (trans.), New York: Semiotext(e), 1983, p.9.

4 René Magritte, *Rhétorique*, no.9, 1963, cited in Harry Torczyner (ed.), *Magritte: Ideas and Images*, Richard Miller (trans.), New York: Abrams, 1977, p.65.

5 David Sylvester and Sarah Whitfield (eds.), *René Magritte: Catalogue Raisonné*, London: Philip Wilson; Houston: The Menil Collection; Antwerp: Fonds Mercator, 1992–97, vol.II, p.373.

6 Alain Robbe-Grillet, René Magritte and Ben Stoltzfus, *La Belle Captive: A Novel*, Berkeley, Los Angeles and London: University of California Press, 1995, p.201.

7 Paul Colinet, in Sylvester and Whitfield (eds.), *Catalogue Raisonné*, vol.II, p.244.

8 Interview with Jean Neyens, 1965/74, in André Blavier (ed.), *Écrits complets*, Paris: Flammarion, 2001, p.603.

9 René Magritte, 'La Ligne de vie I', in ibid. pp.103–30 (p.107).

10 René Magritte, 'Le Véritable Art de peindre', in ibid. pp.273–77 (p.273).

11 René Magritte, 'Interviews Quievreux', 1947, in ibid. p.250.

12 André Breton, 'Manifesto of Surrealism', in *Manifestoes of Surrealism*, Richard Seaver and Helen R. Lane (trans.), Ann Arbor: University of Michigan Press, 1972, p.26.

13 Suzi Gablik, *Magritte*, London: Thames & Hudson, 1985, p.70.

14 Patricia Allmer, *René Magritte: Beyond Painting*, Manchester and New York: Manchester University Press, 2009, p.120.

15 René Magritte, letter to Pierre Flouquet, November 1921, in Sylvester and Whitfield (eds.), *Catalogue Raisonné*, vol.I, p.29.

16 E.L.T. Mesens describing Magritte, interview with George Melly, 8 January 1969, Archives of the Royal Museums of Fine Arts of Belgium, Brussels.

17 René Magritte, statement reported by A. Gomez, May–June 1948, cited in Torczyner (ed.), *Magritte: Ideas and Images*, p.23.

18 Georges Bataille, Robert Lebel and Isabelle Waldberg (eds.), *Encyclopaedia Acephalica*, London: Atlas Press, 1995, p.51.

19 Foreword and story are reprinted in Fred Botting and Scott Wilson (eds.), *The Bataille Reader*, Oxford and Malden, Massachusetts: Blackwell, 1997, pp.223–36.

20 René Magritte, 'Interview Claude Vial', 1966, in Blavier (ed.), *Écrits complets*, p.642.

21 Gablik, *Magritte*, 1970, p.27.

22 'This is the Truth', in Blavier (ed.), *Écrits complets*, p.485.

23 *Lettres à André Bosmans 1958–1967*, Paris: Seghers-Isy Brachot, 1990.

24 See David Sylvester, *Magritte* (revised edition), Brussels: Mercatorfonds, 2009, p.265.

25 Cited in Whitfield (ed.), *Magritte*, 1992, cat.158.

26 David Sylvester, *Magritte*, London: Thames & Hudson, 1992, p.12.

27 Ibid. p.28.

28 Patrick Mauriès, *Cabinets of Curiosities*, London: Thames & Hudson, 2002, p.35.

29 Comte de Lautréamont, *Maldoror*, Cambridge: Exact Change, 1994, p.193.

30 Louis Scutenaire, *Avec Magritte*, cited in Sylvester and Whitfield (eds.), *Catalogue Raisonné*, vol.I, p.39.

31 René Magritte, 'La Ligne de vie', reproduced in Frederik Leen and Gisèle Ollinger-Zinque (eds.), *Magritte: 1898–1967* (exh. cat.), Royal Museums of Fine Arts of Belgium, Brussels, pub. Ghent: Ludion Press, 1998, p.44.

32 Max Ernst et al, *Max Ernst: œuvres, de 1919 à 1936*, Paris: Cahiers d'Art, 1937, p.42.

33 Mauriès, *Cabinets of Curiosities*, p.25.

34 René Magritte, interview with Paul Waldo Schwartz, 1969, in Blavier (ed.), *Écrits complets*, p.682.

35 René Magritte, response to questionnaire in *Le Savoir vivre*, 1946, in ibid. pp.229–30 (p.229).

36 The phrase is used by Magritte in his 'Esquisse autobiographique', in Blavier (ed.), *Écrits complets*,

pp.366–72 (p.367). Comprehensive details of Magritte's activities as a commercial artist can be found in Georges Roque, *Ceci n'est pas un Magritte: Essai sur Magritte et la publicité*, Paris: Flammarion, 1983.

37 Roque, *Ceci n'est pas un Magritte*, p.164.

38 See the notes to the dossier 'Magritte et le Parti Communiste', in Blavier (ed.), *Écrits complets*, pp.235–49 (p.236).

39 Patrick Waldberg, *René Magritte*, Brussels: André de Rache, 1965, p.208.

40 Ibid.

41 René Magritte, interview with Pierre Mazars, 1964, in Blavier (ed.), *Écrits complets*, p.599.

42 The story is reproduced and translated in Gablik, *Magritte*, 1970, pp.187–88.

43 René Magritte, commentary on *L'Empire des lumières* written for 1956 television programme, published in facsimile in *Peintres de l'imaginaire: symbolistes et surréalistes belges* (exh. cat.), Paris: Grand Palais, 1972, p.118.

44 René Magritte, letter to Alexandre Iolas, 12 November 1948, in Sylvester and Whitfield (eds.), *Catalogue Raisonné*, vol.II, p.154.

45 See Sigmund Freud, 'The Uncanny', in *The Standard Edition of the Complete Psychological Works of Sigmund Freud*, Vol.XVII, London: Vintage 2001, pp.219–52 (234–36). Freud himself draws extensively on Otto Rank's 1914 essay 'The Double'.

46 Interview with Pierre Descargues, 1961, in Blavier (ed.), *Écrits complets*, p.544. In 1953 Magritte made a similar comment in a letter, where he described the process of coming up with the final composition as 'frantic observation' for days on end until 'the idea of the form' of the subject matter appeared in the drawing (ibid. p.327).

47 René Magritte cited in Barron, 'The Problem(s) of René Magritte', in Barron and Draguet (eds.), *Magritte and Contemporary Art: The Treachery of Images* (exh. cat.), Los Angeles County Museum of Art, 2006, p.14.

48 René Magritte cited in Gablik, *Magritte*, 1985, p.72.

49 René Magritte, 'Les Mots et les images', *La Révolution surréaliste*, no.12, 15 December 1929, p.32.

50 René Magritte, 'L'homme au visage sans chemin', *Distances* no.1, February 1928, cited in Sylvester, *Magritte*, 2009, p.172.

51 Alain Robbe-Grillet, *Recollections of the Golden Triangle*, London: John Calder, 1984, p.53.

52 Comte de Lautréamont, *Maldoror*, p.193.

53 'Lifeline', Gablik, *Magritte*, 1970, p.185. Sylvester clarifies that the actual date must have been 1933 and not 1936.

54 Cited in Michel Remy, *Surrealism in Britain*, Aldershot and Brookfield, Vermont: Ashgate, 1999, p.149.

55 Edward James, letter to René Magritte, 35 Wimpole Street, London, 18 April 1937, Tate Library and Archive (author's translation).

56 Edward James, letter to Georgette Magritte, Waldorf Astoria Hotel, New York, 17 June 1940, Tate Library and Archive.

57 Edward James, letter to René Magritte, Beverly Hills, California, 15 November 1940, Tate Library and Archive.

58 'Hommage à James Ensor', *Le Drapeau Rouge*, nos.20–21, October 1945, in Torczyner (ed.), *Magritte: Ideas and Images*, p.67.

59 Magritte, letter to Patrick Waldberg, 1958, in ibid. p.67.

60 'La Ligne de vie I' (1938), in Blavier (ed.), *Écrits complets*, 2001, p.106.

61 'La Ligne de vie II', in ibid. p.142.

62 André Souris, 'Paul Nougé et ses complices', in Ferdinand Alquié (ed.), *Entretiens sur le surréalisme*, Paris and The Hague: Mouton, 1968, pp.452–53.

63 'Manifeste de l'amentalisme', 1946–47, in Blavier (ed.), *Écrits complets*, p.223.

64 'Manifeste de l'amentalisme', in ibid. pp.221–27.

65 Blavier (ed.), *Écrits complets*, p.212.

66 Ibid. p.208.

67 Interview with Guy Mertens, 'René Magritte, peintre de l'invisible, retour d'Israël', in *Pourquoi pas?*, Brussels, 26 May 1966; reprinted in ibid. p.636.

68 André Breton, excerpts from 'Anthology of Black Humour', in Franklin Rosemont (ed.), *What is Surrealism? Selected Writings*, New York: Pathfinder, 1978, p.189.

69 Interview with Jean Neyens, in Blavier (ed.), *Écrits complets*, p.602.

70 Sigmund Freud, 'Fetishism', 1927, in *The Pelican Freud Library*, vol.7, Harmondsworth and New York: Penguin Books, 1977, p.352.

71 Ibid. p.354.

72 See Alain Berenboom, 'Ceci n'est pas du cinéma', in Leen and Ollinger-Zinque (eds.), *Magritte: 1898–1967*, p.289.

73 René Magritte, 'L'Espace d'une pensée', in Blavier (ed.), *Écrits complets*, p.67.

74 'La Ligne de vie I', 1938, in ibid. p.111.

75 Gablik, *Magritte*, 1970, p.98.

76 René Magritte, in Sylvester and Whitfield (eds.), *Catalogue Raisonné*, vol.II, p.373, no.609.

77 Guy Debord and Gil Wolman, 'Methods of détournement', in Ken Knabb (ed. and trans.), *Situationist International Anthology*, Berkeley, California: Bureau of Public Secrets, 1981, p.10. The essay 'Mode d'emploi du détournement' was originally published by Marcel Mariën in *Les Lèvres Nues*, no.8, May 1956.

78 Daniel Filipacchi, cited in *Surrealism: Two Private Eyes* (exh. cat.), New York: Guggenheim Museum Publications, 1999, p.24.

79 Marcel Mariën, *Le Radeau de la Mémoire: Souvenirs Déterminés*, Brussels: Les Lèvres Nues, 1983, p.103.

80 Stewart Home, *Plagiarism: Art as Commodity and Strategies for its Negation*, London: Aporia Press, 1987, p.10.

81 René Magritte, letter to Michel Foucault, 23 May 1966, in Torczyner (ed.), *Magritte: Ideas and Images*, p.86.

82 René Magritte, interview on 22 August 1962, in Blavier (ed.), *Écrits complets*, p.572.

83 René Magritte, interview with Pierre Descargues, 1961, in ibid. p.544.

84 René Magritte, interview with Paul Waldo Schwartz, 1969, in ibid. p.684.

85 René Magritte, interview with Pierre Descargues, 1961, in ibid. p.544.

86 'L'Art bourgeois', in ibid. p.133.

87 On Magritte's study of the work of Martin Heidegger, which began in 1953, see ibid. pp.387–91.

88 There are three slightly different versions of the manuscript of Magritte's lecture 'La Ressemblance', 1959. The three manuscripts are reprinted in Blavier (ed.), *Écrits complets*, pp.493–96, 518–21 and 529–30.

89 On the relationship between Magritte and Iolas see Daniel Abadie, 'René Magritte et Alexandre Iolas, l'art de la conversation', in *Magritte* (exh. cat.), Galerie nationale du Jeu de Paume, Paris, 11 February – 9 July 2003, pp.267–73.

90 Magritte's emphasis. Letter from Magritte to Scutenaire, 18 February 1937, cited in Sylvester and Whitfield (eds.), *Catalogue Raisonné*, vol.II, p.52.

91 Blavier (ed.), *Écrits complets*, p.518.

92 René Magritte, quoted after Pierre Sterckx, 'Magrittes Bilder als "Dispositive",' in *René Magritte*, Kunstsammlung Nordrhein-Westfalen, Düsseldorf; Munich and New York: Prestel, p.57, note 9.

93 Walter Benjamin, 'Surrealism: The Last Snapshot of the European Intelligentsia', in *Selected Writings: Volume 2, 1927–1934*, Michael Jennings, Howard Eiland and Gary Smith (eds.), Cambridge, Massachusetts: Belknap, 1999, p.210.

94 René Magritte, postcard in *Rhétorique*, no.9, June 1963; Blavier (ed.), *Écrits complets*, p.585.

95 René Magritte, letter to Maurice Rapin, 20 June 1957; cited in Torczyner (ed.), *Magritte: Ideas and Images* (concise edition), Richard Miller (trans.), New York: Abrams, 1977, p.15.

96 Ibid.

97 'Staff notice circulated by Sabena in November 1966', cited in Sylvester and Whitfield (eds.), *Catalogue Raisonné*, vol.III, p.426.

98 Sylvester et al. note that 'In June 1959 Magritte's lawyer, Harry Torczyner, brought to his attention a record sleeve featuring *The Healer*' … 'Magritte reacted angrily to what he called this "Healer plagiarism" and for some weeks seriously considered bringing legal action against the record company.' Sylvester and Whitfield (eds.), *Catalogue Raisonné*, vol.II, p.236.

99 Cited from the catalogue of the exhibition *D'après*, Lugano, 1971, in Blavier (ed.), *Écrits complets*, p.644, note 2.

100 Ed Ruscha in Willoughby Sharpe, '… A Kind of Huh? An Interview with Edward Ruscha', in *Ruscha – Leave Any Information at the Signal*, Alexandra Schwartz (ed.), Cambridge, Massachusetts: MIT Press, 2002, p.65, mentioned by Lynn Zelevansky in 'An Interview with Ed Ruscha', Barron and Draguet (eds.), *Magritte and Contemporary Art: The Treachery of Images*, p.140.

101 In Sylvester and Whitfield (eds.), *Catalogue Raisonné*, vol.I, p.10.

102 Manfred Lurker, *Wörterbuch der Symbolik*, Stuttgart 1995, p.467.

103 René Magritte, ms., 13 November 1953, 'found among Mesen's papers', cited in Sylvester and Whitfield (eds.), *Catalogue Raisonné*, vol.III, p.220.

104 René Magritte, letter to M. Hornik, Spring 1959, in Blavier (ed.), *Écrits complets*, p.379; author's translation, Magritte's emphasis.

105 John C. Welchman, 'After the Wagnerian Bouillabaisse: Critical Theory and the Dada and Surrealist Word-Image', in Judi Freeman and John C. Welchman, *The Dada & Surrealist Word-Image* (exh. cat.), Los Angeles County Museum of Art, Cambridge, Massachusetts: MIT Press, 1989.

106 Miguel de Beistegui, *Thinking with Heidegger: Displacements*, Bloomington: Indiana University Press, 2003, p.182. The 2001 paperback edition of Heidegger's *Poetry, Language, Thought*, trans. Albert Hofstadter, in the HarperCollins 'Perennial Classics' series, has Magritte's *The Masterpiece or the Mysteries of the Horizon* 1955 on the cover.

107 Edward Sapir, *Language: An Introduction to the Study of Speech*, New York: Harcourt, Brace and Co., 1921, p.16.

108 Rosalind Krauss, *L'Amour fou: Photography & Surrealism*, London: Arts Council, 1986, p.5.

109 René Magritte, 'La Pensée et les Images' in *Magritte* (exh. cat.), Palais des Beaux-Arts, Brussels, 1954, in Blavier (ed.), *Écrits complets*, p.376.

110 René Magritte, undated letter to Paul Nougé, in Sylvester and Whitfield (eds.), *Catalogue Raisonné*, vol.I, pp.245–6.

111 Gilles Deleuze, *Francis Bacon: The Logic of Sensation*, London and New York: Continuum, 2002, p.21.

112 René Magritte, interview for *Life* magazine, 23 April 1966, cited in Blavier (ed.), *Écrits complets*, p.614.

113 Magritte in Blavier (ed.), *Écrits complets*, p.525. In 'La Ligne de vie I' (1938) Magritte writes: 'As far as the mystery, the enigma that my pictures presented, I would say that this was the best proof of my break with the entirety of the absurd mental practices that generally take the place of a genuine feeling of existence.' (p.109)

114 Ludwig Wittgenstein, *Tractatus Logico-Philosophicus*, David Pears and Brian McGuinness (trans.), London, Routledge and Kegan Paul, 1961, p.73 (6.44).

115 Interview with Jean Neyens, 1965, in Blavier (ed.), *Écrits complets*, p.604.

116 Interview with Suzi Gablik for *Studio*, London, March 1967, in Blavier (ed.), *Écrits complets*, p.646.

117 Paul Nougé, 'Reconnaissance d'Angèle Laval', in *Histoire de ne pas rire*, Brussels: Les Lèvres Nues, 1956, p.78.

118 Paul Nougé, 'Les Images défendues', in *Histoire de ne pas rire*, Lausanne: L'Age d'homme, 1980, pp.223–60, for example pages 239–41.

119 Ibid. p.239.

120 André Breton, *Nadja*, 1928, Richard Howard (trans.), New York: Grove Press, 1960, p.52.

121 'La Ressemblance', in Blavier (ed.), *Écrits complets*, pp.493–96 (p.493).

122 Roque, *Ceci n'est pas un Magritte: Essai sur Magritte et la publicité*, p.41.

123 René Magritte, cited in Leen and Ollinger-Zinque (eds.), *Magritte: 1898–1967*, p.16.

124 Richard Calvocoressi, *Magritte*, Oxford: Phaidon, 1979, p.10.

125 Ibid.

126 René Magritte and Paul Nougé, 'Colour–Colours, or an Experiment by Roland Penrose', Iqbal Singh (trans.), *London Bulletin*, no.17, 15 June 1939, pp.9–12.

127 René Magritte, in Sylvester and Whitfield (eds.), *Catalogue Raisonné*, vol.III, p.175.

128 René Magritte, letter to André Bosmans, 24 July 1961, cited in Torczyner (ed.), *Magritte: Ideas and Images*, p.154.

129 René Magritte, 'La Pensée et les Images', *Magritte* (exh. cat.), Brussels, May 1954, cited in ibid. p.72.

130 Blavier (ed.), *Écrits complets*, p.496.

131 Interview with Pierre du Bois, 1966, in ibid. p.652.

132 Ibid. p.519f.

133 Ibid. (English original), p.615.

134 *René Magritte: La Fidelité des images*, text by Louis Scutenaire; Brussels: Le Service de la Propagande Artistique du Ministère de la Culture française, 1978. For a thorough discussion of Magritte's photography, see Patrick Roegiers, *Magritte and Photography*, London: Lund Humphries, 2005.

135 Conversation with Louis Scutenaire and Irène Hamoir, 17 August 1978. The previous day, I had visited Georgette Magritte to view the photographs in her possession and found that she kept them in a cardboard shoebox, like any casual collection of personal photographs. Scutenaire and Hamoir owned copies of many of the same photographs, carefully mounted year by year and presented in a large album.

136 Christine de Naeyer, *Paul Nougé et la photographie*, Brussels: Didier Devillez, 1995, p.43.

137 First published in Paul Nougé, *Subversion des images*, Brussels: Les Lèvres Nues, 1968.

138 Duane Michals, *A Visit with Magritte*, Providence, Rhode Island: Matrix, 1981. Michals' visit was in 1965.

139 Sylvester and Whitfield (eds.), *Catalogue Raisonné*, vol.II, p.129.

140 René Magritte, 'Le Surréalisme en plein soleil', *Manifeste*, no.1, October 1946, in Blavier (ed.), *Écrits complets*, p.212.

141 René Magritte, unpublished notes written at the Sheraton-Gladstone Hotel, New York, 16 December 1965, cited in Torczyner (ed.), *Magritte: Ideas and Images*, p.56.

142 Ibid.

143 René Magritte, letter to E.L.T. Mesens, 5 November 1963, cited in Torczyner (ed.), ibid. p.56.

144 René Magritte, letter to Maurice Rapin, 20 June 1957; cited in Torczyner (ed.), *Magritte: Ideas and Images* (concise edition), p.15.

145 René Magritte, letter to Mirabelle Dors and Maurice Rapin, 7 March 1956, in ibid. p.13.

146 René Magritte, letter to to Edward James, 27 June 1937, in Sylvester and Whitfield (eds.), *Catalogue Raisonné*, vol.II, p.249.

147 Whitfield (ed.), *Magritte*, 1992, pp.4–5.

148 Interview with Otto Hahn, November 1964, cited in Sylvester and Whitfield (eds.), *Catalogue Raisonné*, vol.III., p.401.

149 René Magritte, 'Propos' (1969), in Blavier (ed.), *Écrits complets*, p.717.

150 *London Bulletin*, no.17, 15 June 1939, pp.9–12.

151 Magritte cited in Leen and Ollinger-Zinque (eds.), *Magritte: 1898–1967*, p.16.

152 Magritte, letter to Paul Éluard, 4 December 1941, in Sylvester and Whitfield (eds.), *Catalogue Raisonné*, vol.II, p.91.

153 Ibid., vol.II, p.154.

154 Specifically an illustration from Dr F.E. Bilz, *Das Neue Naturheilverfahren*, 1895, in ibid., vol.I, p.309.

155 Silvano Levy, 'Foucault on Magritte on Resemblance', *Modern Languages Review*, no.85, January 1990, p.51.

156 Magritte describing *Foolhardy* 1927 (CR 139), cited in Sylvester (ed.), *Magritte*, 1992, p.67.

157 Sylvester and Whitfield (eds.), *Catalogue Raisonné*, vol.I, p.296.

158 Magritte, catalogue of the Magritte exhibition, Galerie Rive Droite, Paris, 1960, cited in Torczyner (ed.), *Magritte: Ideas and Images* (concise edition), p.66.

159 Ibid. p.32.

160 Ibid. p.27.

161 Ibid. p.49.

162 Magritte, letter to Foucault, 23 May 1966, *Ceci n'est pas un Magritte*, p.57.

163 Sylvester and Whitfield (eds.), *Catalogue Raisonné*, vol.II, p.242.

164 Ibid., vol.III, p.355.

165 Breton, *Nadja*, 1960, p.39.

166 Ben Stoltzfus, 'Introduction', in Alain Robbe-Grillet, René Magritte and Ben Stoltzfus, *La Belle Captive: A Novel*, Berkeley, Los Angeles and London: University of California Press, 1995, p.2.

167 Remarks by Magritte reported by Jacques Miche, 13 January 1967, cited in Torczyner (ed.), *Magritte: Ideas and Images*, p.68.

168 Magritte, letter to Alexandre Iolas, 24 October 1952, in ibid. p.233.

169 Magritte, letter to Torczyner, 2 July 1963; cited in Torczyner (ed.), *Magritte: Ideas and Images* (concise edition), p.19.

170 See Sylvester and Whitfield (eds.), *Catalogue Raisonné*, vol.II, p.218; and Jack J. Spector, 'Magritte's *La lampe philosophique*: A Study of Word and Image in Surrealism', in *Dada/Surrealism*, no.7, 1977, pp.121–129.

171 In letters to Magritte, Alexandre Iolas, for example, referred to the bowler-hatted figure crossing a city bridge in *Pandora's Box* 1951 and to another such figure in *The Sirens' Song* 1952 as 'your portrait'. Sylvester et al note that 'there is no indication that Magritte regarded [them] as … self-portrait[s]'; Sylvester and Whitfield (eds.), *Catalogue Raisonné*, vol.III, pp.190, 198.

172 The photograph is reproduced as 'Fig.a' in ibid., vol.II, p.255.

173 The publicity photograph is reproduced as 'Fig.a', in ibid., vol.II, p.431.

174 Magritte, quoted in Louis Scutenaire, *Magritte*, 1943, in Torczyner (ed.), *Magritte: Ideas and Images* (concise edition), p.19.

175 Breton, *Nadja*, 1960, pp.159–60.

176 See, for example, chapter 2, 'Cabinets of Curiosities' in Allmer, *René Magritte: Beyond Painting*, pp.21–47. For more on the question of shop window displays and modern art, see John C. Welchman (ed.), *Sculpture and the Vitrine*, London: Henry Moore Institute/Ashgate, forthcoming 2011.

177 Sylvester and Whitfield (eds.), *Catalogue Raisonné*, vol.V, p.96.

178 'Art: Dali's Display', *Time*, 27 March 1939.

179 See Sylvester and Whitfield (eds.), *Catalogue Raisonné*, vol.II, p.347, which reproduces a photograph of the shop window.

180 Magritte, letter to Breton, 22 June 1934, cited in ibid., vol.II, p.30.

181 Ibid.

182 The work is reproduced and the label partially transcribed in ibid., vol.V, p.98.

183 Breton, 'Manifesto of Surrealism', in *Manifestoes of Surrealism*, Michigan: The University of Michigan Press, 2000, p.26.

184 Magritte, in Blavier (ed.), *Écrits complets*, p.329.

185 Magritte, 'Je pense à…', 1952, in ibid. p.327.

186 In Torczyner (ed.), *Magritte: Ideas and Images*, p.12.

187 André Breton, in *London Bulletin*, no.1, April 1938, p.6.

188 Such 'stage-set' compositions might also be related to Magritte's experience of designing stage-sets in October 1925 for a theatrical performance in Brussels by the Théâtre du Groupe Libre. See Marcel Mariën, *L'Activité Surréaliste en Belgique* 1979, Brussels: Lebeer Hossmann, p.131.

189 Jean Baudrillard, 'The Trompe-l'Oeil', in Norman Bryson (ed.), *Calligram: Essays in New Art History from France*, Cambridge: Cambridge University Press, 1988, p.57.

190 This entry is based on my discussion of Magritte in *Invisible Colors: A Visual History of Titles*, London and New York: Yale University Press, 1995, pp.242–45.

191 Magritte, 'Sur les titres', 1946, Blavier (ed.), *Écrits complets*, p.263.

192 Magritte, interview with Jan Walravens, November 1962, in ibid. pp.537–38; author's translation.

193 In 'This Is Not René Magritte', *Artforum*, vol.5, no.1, September 1966, p.33, Roger Shattuck, discussing Magritte's refutation of 'dictionary convention', notes, apropos the painting *The Soul of Bandits* 1960, that 'the page [with the entry 'violin'] in the 1950 Larousse … may have been at Magritte's elbow' as this work was produced.

194 Heidegger, 'The thing', in *Poetry, Language, Thought*, Albert Hofstadter (trans.), New York: HarperCollins, 2001, p.173.

195 Ronald Alley, *Catalogue of the Tate Gallery's Collection of Modern Art Other Than Works by British Artists*, London: Tate Gallery, 1981, p.464.

196 See Laurie Edson, 'Confronting the Signs: Words, Images, and the Reader-Spectator', *Dada-Surrealism*, no.13, 1984, pp.83–94.

197 Ibid. p.19.

198 Ibid. p.116.

199 James Harkness, 'Translator's Introduction', in Michel Foucault, *This Is Not a Pipe*, Berkeley, Los Angeles and London: University of California Press, 1983, p.9.

200 Sigmund Freud, *The Interpretation of Dreams*, Harmondsworth and New York: Penguin Books, 1976, p.157.

201 Ibid. p.518.

202 René Magritte, in Whitfield (ed.), *Magritte*, 1992, p.28.

203 Letter from René Magritte to Paul Nougé, 13 May 1948, cited in Torczyner (ed.), *Magritte: Ideas and Images*, p.60.

204 Michel Draguet, in *René Magritte: La Période Vache* (exh. cat.), Schirn Kunsthalle Frankfurt, p.138.

205 Letter from René Magritte to Marcel Lecomte, April 1928, cited in Whitfield (ed.), *Magritte*, cat. 36.

206 Sylvester and Whitfield (eds.), *Catalogue Raisonné*, vol.I, p.90.

207 René Magritte, 'La Ligne de vie', Blavier (ed.), *Écrits complets*, p.111.

208 Sylvester and Whitfield (eds.), *Catalogue Raisonné*, vol.I, p.30.

209 Ibid.

210 From the text 'La Ligne de vie', published in *L'Invention collective*, no.2, April 1940, translated as 'Lifeline' in Gablik, *Magritte*, 1970, p.184.

211 Jan Ceuleers, *René Magritte, 135 Rue Esseghem, Jette-Brussels*, Antwerp: Pandora, 1999, p.49.

212 See Roegiers, *Magritte and Photography*, pp.27–29.

213 Cited in Sylvester and Whitfield (eds.), *Catalogue Raisonné*, vol.I, p.6.

Acknowledgements

Magritte A to Z was produced to accompany *René Magritte: The Pleasure Principle*, an exhibition staged at Tate Liverpool from 24 June to 16 October 2011, and at the Albertina in Vienna from 9 November 2011 to 26 February 2012. During the realisation of the exhibition and publication we have been fortunate to have received the support of a number of individuals and institutions who generously loaned artworks to our exhibition. In particular, we would like to express our sincerest thanks to:

Danièle Hoslet, Archives of the City of Brussels;

Marc Quaghebeur, Laurence Pieropan and Jean Danhaive, Archives et Musée de la Littérature, Brussels;

Matthew Teitelbaum and Alison Beckett, Art Gallery of Ontario, Toronto;

James Cuno, Douglas Druick, Stephanie d'Alessandro and Suzanne McCullagh, The Art Institute of Chicago;

Ann Sumner and Chezzy Brownen, The Barber Institute of Fine Arts, The University of Birmingham;

Isabel Soares Alves, Berardo Collection, Lisbon;

Sjarel Ex, Museum Boijmans Van Beuningen, Rotterdam;

Isy, Isadora and Isy Gabriel Brachot, and Christine Duchiron-Brachot;

Lotte van Diggelen, Caldic Collectie, Rotterdam;

Xavier Canonne, Charleroi;

Roger Coisman, Brussels;

Gale and Ira Drukier, New York;

Daniel Filipacchi;

David and Michael Fleiss, and Rodica Sibleyras, Galerie 1900–2000, Paris;

Erika Költzsch, Galerie Haas AG, Zurich;

Till-Holger Borchert and Johan Coens, Groeninge-museum, Bruges;

Pierre-Olivier Rollin and Marie-France Desainte, Collection Province de Hainaut, Charleroi;

Hubertus Gaßner and Daniel Koep, Hamburger Kunsthalle;

Laura Bechter and Angelika Felder, Hauser & Wirth, Zurich;

Richard Koshalek, Kerry Brougher, Milena Kalinovska and Rebecca Withers, Hirshhorn Museum and Sculpture Garden, Smithsonian Institution, Washington, DC;

Sharon-Michi Kusunoki, The Edward James Trust, West Dean;

Jasper Johns;

Mr and Mrs Gilbert Kaplan, New York;

Paul Huvenne, Koninklijk Museum voor Schone Kunsten, Antwerp;

Christoph Becker and Karin Marti, Kunsthaus Zurich;

Marion Ackermann and Annette Kruszynski, Kunstsammlung Nordrhein-Westfalen, Düsseldorf;

Josef Helfenstein, Ebony McFarland and Judy Kwon, The Menil Collection, Houston;

Thomas P. Campbell and Gary Tinterow, The Metropolitan Museum of Art, New York;

Ariane Fradcourt and Odile Chopin, Ministère de la Communauté française, Brussels;

Coraly Aliboni, Musée des Beaux-Arts, Charleroi;

Claire Leblanc, Musée d'Ixelles, Brussels;

Guillermo Solana, Laura García Oliva, Lucia Cassol, Natalia Gastelut, Museo Thyssen-Bornemisza, Madrid;

Hartwig Fischer, Museum Folkwang, Essen;

Madeleine Grynsztejn and Jennifer Draffen, Museum of Contemporary Art, Chicago;

Peter C. Marzio†, Helga Aurisch, Gwendolyn Goffe and Maggie Williams, The Museum of Fine Arts, Houston;

Glenn D. Lowry, Ann Temkin, Ann Umland and Cora Rosevear, The Museum of Modern Art, New York;

Karola Kraus and Wolfgang Drechsler, Museum Moderner Kunst Stiftung Ludwig, Vienna;

Robert Hoozee and Moniek Nagels, Museum voor Schone Kunsten, Ghent;

Earl A. Powell III and Harry Cooper, National Gallery of Art Washington, DC;

Marc Mayer, Greg Spurgeon and Mathieu Pronovost, National Gallery of Canada, Ottawa;

Michael Houlihan and Oliver Fairclough, National Museums Wales;

E. John Bullard and Paul Tarver, New Orleans Museum of Art;

Sylvio Perlstein, Antwerp;

Carla Schulz-Hoffmann, Simone Kober and Bernhart Schwenk, Pinakothek der Moderne, Munich;

André Garitte, René Magritte Museum, Jette/Brussels;

Leslee and David Rogath;

Safflane Holdings Limited;

Neal Benezra and Gary Garrels, San Francisco Museum of Modern Art;
Simon Groom and Patrick Elliott, Scottish National Gallery of Modern Art, Edinburgh;
Udo Kittelmann and Dieter Scholz, Staatliche Museen Preußischer Kulturbesitz, Nationalgalerie, Berlin;
Sean Rainbird, Staatsgalerie Stuttgart;
Simon Studer and Sabine Colombier, Simon Studer Art, Geneva;
Peter van Beveren, Triton Foundation, The Netherlands, whose co-founder Willem Cordia sadly passed away during the development of our project;
Tani Arata and Koji Ariki, Utsunomiya Museum of Art, Japan;
Ronny, Jessy and Sofie Van de Velde, Ronny Van de Velde, Antwerp;
Josette Vanthournout and Andre Gordts;
and to those lenders who prefer to remain anonymous.

We would like to express special thanks to Michel Draguet, Virginie Devillez, Valérie Haerden, and Sophie Van Vliet of the Royal Museums of Fine Arts of Belgium, Brussels, whose advice and generous engagement with our project proved critical. Our foremost thanks, too, go to Charly Herscovici, President of the Magritte Foundation. His support and encouragement for our exhibition made a vital contribution.

At Tate Liverpool we are particularly grateful to the European Regional Development Fund for its commitment to and major support of this show. We would like to express thanks to Mr and Mrs Wilbur Ross, whose loan of important works and generosity enabled us to realise our exhibition to its full potential. We are also grateful for the support received from the Jacqueline Nonkels Fund [i], managed by the King Baudouin Foundation.

A number of individuals were generous to give support and share their expertise and we are especially grateful to those who took interest in the success of our exhibition. We would like to thank Abigail Asher from Guggenheim, Asher Associates Inc., and Olivier Camu, Andrea Fiuczynski, Ottavia Marchitelli, Wendy Battleson and Leah Sheehan at Christie's, who provided invaluable advice and lender liaison. Essential support was likewise provided by Anna McKnight, Helena Newman, Liz Koehn and Erika Batey at Sotheby's. We would like to thank Johnny Armbruster, Marie-Puck Broodthaers, Mia Vandekerckhove and Sarah Whitfield for their guidance and contribution, with thanks also to Avi Keitelman at Keitelman Gallery, Brussels. We were similarly grateful to receive guidance from Paolo Vedovi, Martin Desfossés and Clélie Debehault at Galerie Vedovi, Brussels.

Tate and the Albertina, Vienna are pleased to collaborate on this ambitious exhibition. At Tate we would like to express our thanks for the invaluable contribution of Wendy Lothian, who managed the complex transport arrangement with her customary professionalism and devotion. Likewise, we would like to thank Ken Simons and Barry Bentley for managing the installation of the exhibition. We would like to express our gratitude to Aida Strkljevic, Amy Higgitt, Ian Malone, Jemima Pyne, Rachel Skelton and Jennifer Martin for their contribution, with thanks also to our Development team for their fundraising efforts. At the Albertina our foremost thanks go to Gisela Fischer, who played a key role as lead curator, and to Margarete Heck and Barbara Buchbauer. Their skill and energy made a vital contribution to the realisation of our project.

We are enormously grateful to Patricia Allmer, Xavier Canonne, Krzysztof Fijalkowski, Neil Matheson, Ian Walker, and John Welchman for their research and insightful texts contained within this publication. Our thanks also go to Fiona Elliott and Matthew Barr for translating our texts. At Ludion we wish to thank Peter Ruyffelaere, Gunther De Wit and Sandra Darbé, with special thanks to Tony Waddingham for his unique design of the book, and tireless work.

The loan of artworks to this exhibition at Tate Liverpool has been made possible by the provision of insurance through the Government Indemnity Scheme. Tate Liverpool would like to thank the Department for Culture, Media and Sport and the Museums, Libraries and Archives Council for providing and arranging this indemnity.

Finally, the exhibition at the Albertina, Vienna has been sponsored generously by UNIQA. We are grateful for their support, and would further like to thank the Partners of the Albertina, SUPERFUND and SIGNA Holding GmbH.

Christoph Grunenberg
Director, Tate Liverpool

Klaus Albrecht Schröder
Director, Albertina, Vienna

Andrea Nixon
Executive Director,
Tate Liverpool

i. Jacqueline Nonkels was friends with members of the Surrealist movement in Belgium including René Magritte. In her will she created the Jacqueline Nonkels Fund, managed by the King Baudouin Foundation, which aims to raise awareness and publicise Belgian Surrealist heritage.

The European Regional Development Fund (ERDF) in the Northwest is pleased to support Tate Liverpool's *René Magritte: The Pleasure Principle* – the first major exhibition of the Belgian surrealist in the UK in ten years. This exceptional exhibition, which will shine a spotlight on Liverpool, and the Northwest as a whole, is enhancing the region's reputation as a 'go to' destination for culture.

England's Northwest already has a reputation as a vibrant, culturally dynamic region. This particular exhibition, which aims to focus on the less explored aspects of Magritte's life and artistic practice, enforces Tate Liverpool's reputation as one of the region's flagship cultural venues.

The exhibition will undoubtedly raise the international profile of the region's fantastic cultural life and demonstrates that we can deliver world-class visitor experiences year-on-year. As part of an ambitious programme of major exhibitions supported by ERDF at Tate Liverpool, it will bring even more visitors to enjoy the city.

ERDF is investing £31 million in the region's tourism and cultural sectors over the next five years, recognising the important role they play in establishing the Northwest as a great place to live, work and visit. In Merseyside, ERDF is also investing heavily in key transport and infrastructure projects that will make a real difference to the region's accessibility.

Over 40 per cent of ERDF's £75 million budget in the Northwest has been ring-fenced for Merseyside. *René Magritte: The Pleasure Principle* is one of a number of cultural projects being supported by ERDF this year, all of which aim to significantly enhance the profile of the region on a global stage.

David Malpass
Director of European Programme
European Regional Development Fund (ERDF)

Supported by

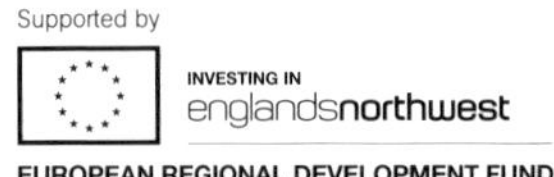

Sponsors and Donors

The Access to Volunteering Fund
The American Patrons of Tate
The Art Fund
Mr Tom Bloxham MBE
BT
British Embassy
Business in the Arts: North West
DLA Piper
Eleanor Rathbone Charitable Trust
European Regional Development Fund
European Union
The Guardian
The Henry Moore Foundation
Mr Yongsoo Huh
Jacqueline Nonkels Fund, managed by the
    King Baudouin Foundation
The Korea Foundation
Liverpool City Council
Liverpool Primary Care Trust
Liverpool Youth Service
Museums, Libraries and Archives Council
Northwest Regional Development Agency
North West Business Leadership Team
Mr and Mrs Wilbur Ross
Samsung
Stanley Thomas Johnson Foundation
Tate Liverpool Members
Tate Members
Unilever
Virgin Trains
Youth Opportunity Fund

Corporate Partners
David M Robinson (Jewellery) Ltd
DLA Piper
DWF
Hill Dickinson
Liverpool Hope University
Liverpool John Moores University
Unilever UK

Corporate Members
Andrew Collinge Ltd
Bruntwood
Cheetham Bell JWT
Deutsche Bank
Fraser Wealth Management
Grant Thornton
Individual Restaurant Company
KPMG
Lime Pictures
Royal Bank of Scotland

Patrons
Elkan Abrahamson
Diana Barbour
David Bell
Lady Beverley Bibby
Jo & Tom Bloxham MBE
Helen Burrell
Paul Carroll and Nathalie Bagnall
Jim Davies
Olwen McLaughlin
Barry Owen OBE
Sue and Ian Poole
Anthony Preston

First published 2011 by order of the Tate Trustees
by Tate Publishing, a division of Tate Enterprises Ltd,
Millbank, London SW1P 4RG
www.tate.org.uk/publishing

on the occasion of the exhibition
René Magritte: The Pleasure Principle

Tate Liverpool
24 June to 16 October 2011

Albertina, Vienna
9 November 2011 to 26 February 2012

A catalogue record for this book is available from the British Library
ISBN 978 1 84976 003 4

Distributed in the United States and Canada by ABRAMS, New York
Library of Congress Control Number: 2011929299

Originated by Ludion, Antwerp
Designed by Tony Waddingham
Colour separations and printing by DeckersSnoeck, Antwerp
Printed on sustainably sourced, certified paper

Front cover: René Magritte, *Time Transfixed* 1938,
The Art Institute of Chicago, Joseph Winterbotham Collection

Measurements of artworks are given in centimetres,
height before width.